THE INDIVIDUAL INVESTOR'S GUIDE TO COMPUTERIZED INVESTING®

AAii

AMERICAN
ASSOCIATION OF
INDIVIDUAL
INVESTORS®

The American Association of Individual Investors is an independent, not-for-profit corporation formed in 1978 for the purpose of assisting individuals in becoming effective managers of their own assets through programs of education, information, and research.

ISBN 1-883328-05-5
ISSN 1097-2862

Published by the American Association of Individual Investors, Chicago.

Data in this *Guide* were gathered from company releases. Factual material is not guaranteed but has been obtained from sources believed to be reliable.

PREFACE

Personal computers have become an indispensable tool for the individual investor competing in today's marketplace. One cannot help but be somewhat awed and even a little bit scared by the increased flow of financial information, coupled by the decreased response time the market takes to react to all of this data. Financial news is now generated and acted upon 24-hours a day, seven days a week.

Investors need to stay abreast and use timely and accurate information when making investment decisions, even if they are following a long-term buy-and-hold strategy. Fortunately, computers, software, and data networks continue to advance in features and capabilities, all the while becoming more affordable.

This Guide is designed to lead the individual investor through the key considerations in buying and upgrading computer hardware, and selecting systems for personal finance, portfolio management, fundamental stock screening, technical analysis and mutual fund screening. The top programs and services for each category are analyzed and rated. Comparison tables are provided for each category to enable you to select the appropriate application for your situation.

The Guide was the product of a team effort; Kenneth J. Michal, Associate Editor of *Computerized Investing*, Wayne A. Thorp, Assistant Financial Analyst, and Maria Crawford Scott, Editor of the *AAII Journal*, and I all authored one or more chapters of the Guide. Jean Henrich provided copy editing and proofreading services. Benjamin Talbot designed the book's cover. Anna M. Chan served as project editor of the book, directing the book into its final form.

John Bajkowski
Editor

TABLE OF CONTENTS

217 │CHAPTER 6: TECHNICAL ANALYSIS

309 | CHAPTER 7: MUTUAL FUND ANALYSIS

INTRODUCTION

How to Use This Guide

The personal computer holds great potential as a tool for assisting investors in their investment program. Our goal, throughout this Guide, is to help people realize this potential. This section presents information on how to use the book to find the information that is relevant and of interest to you. You may be tempted to skip past this introduction and dive right into the investment application reviews starting in Chapter 4. Feel free. This book is designed as a reference source; it is not meant to be read cover to cover. But if you want to get the most out of this book, you should read this introduction to understand how the book is organized and what it contains.

Book Organization

The book is organized into three main sections. Chapters 1, 2 and 3 provide an introductory examination of investing, investment software and information services, along with a discussion of the computer hardware required to make use of these programs. Chapters 4 through 7 provide descriptions of investment software and services along with reviews of the top products available on the market today. Each chapter focuses on a specific investment topic and concludes with a comparison grid so you can objectively rate the products feature-by-feature. Chapter 8 follows the same format as Chapters 4 through 7 but covers financial information services rather than investment applications. The appendix provides a comprehensive listing of investment-related Web sites. Finally, the book includes a complete index for quick reference.

The Guide contains a number of references to Internet Web sites complete with the uniform resource locator (URL). These URLs are used by your Internet browser to locate each site, like an address. URLs can be quite lengthy, resulting in inadvertent hyphenation due to page margins. Keep this in mind when entering the URL in your browser. If you receive an error when trying to reach a site, check to make sure that you have entered the URL correctly.

A Glance at the Contents

An Investment Overview

Chapter 1 serves as an introduction to investing, concentrating on basic elements in order to establish an investment plan and implement the computer as a tool. It covers fundamental principles of investing such as the trade-offs between optimizing return and minimizing risk and the importance of diversification. An investment plan cannot be established without an understanding of your individual investment profile. The chapter discusses risk tolerance, return needs, and time horizon to help determine what kind of investment plan will work for you.

Chapter 1 also discusses how to make investment decisions using active or passive stock selection strategies and technical and fundamental analysis. After determining a workable strategy that fits your profile you can initiate your financial plan. To complete your understanding of the different investment vehicles, bonds and mutual funds are explained in addition to market timing issues. The chapter continues with a discussion on tracking your investments and determining when and if to sell securities. The chapter concludes with a list of sources to direct you to more detailed information about investment techniques. This chapter is meant only as an overview to investing, so further research may prove essential depending on your initial expertise.

An Overview of Software and Information Services

Chapter 2 examines the software and information services market as it relates to investing. When dealing with computers, common sense dictates that you first find the software and data services that meet your needs, and then obtain the necessary hardware to operate these systems. This is good advice, but without knowledge of available software and its capabilities, it is difficult to make software decisions.

Chapter 2 takes the software market and breaks it into functional segments— from the accounting-oriented portfolio management programs to the more analytical programs, such as fundamental screening systems. Pointers are provided throughout these categories on what to look for when considering these applications and what operations each type of program does well and poorly. Developing a basic understanding of the different categories of investment software enables you to match a type of program with your specific needs. Chapter 2 also explores the area of financial information services, including the Internet. Read this to get a feel for the types of data and services available to investors, the different ways you can obtain this data, and the things to look out for when selecting an information service. Tips for selecting investment applications are provided to give you initial direction in the labyrinth of offerings. Once you determine the kind of program you need, you can skip ahead to the chapter devoted to that investment category and peruse the top products and their individual reviews.

Hardware Standards

Chapter 3 explores the hardware arena as it relates to the investment market. The chapter examines the current computer market, discusses the issue of upgrading or buying new, and looks at how the components fit together in a complete system. It details the equipment that has become the industry standard and what you need to run the current investment software. A glossary of computer equipment terms finishes off the chapter for those new to PC use.

The Examinations

Chapters 4 through 8 focus on the different types of investment software and financial information services. Chapters 4 through 7 begin with a general discussion of what a certain type of program can offer to enhance your proficiency as an investor. Application features are discussed, highlighting those that are considered standard and vital to the value of the applications. The second half of each chapter focuses on the products that are at the top in that investment arena. The reviews highlight the differences between the products and the standards discussed in the first half of the chapter. Each product includes a scorecard rating them against their peers. The scorecards rate five criteria:

Product/Service Name	
Performance	1
Usefulness	2
Documentation	3
Ease of Use	4
Value	5

These criteria are rated on a scale of one to five, five denoting the best score possible.

- *Performance* rates how well the program or service accomplishes its stated objectives.

- *Usefulness* rates whether the analysis performed is actually valuable and applicable to investment-making decisions.

- *Documentation* rates the quality of the printed materials, on-line help, and manufacturer support.

- *Ease of use* rates how simple the program is to install, learn, and operate.

- *Value* rates the cost of the program or service relative to the features provided.

The focus of Chapter 8 is financial information services—the on-line sources of data for your analysis. The chapter outlines the type of data to look for in portfolio tracking and fundamental, technical and mutual fund analysis. The emphasis is on your investment horizon and style when selecting a service. An introduction to Internet tools and features is provided to help you take advantage of this medium. Reviews of on-line services and Internet Web sites include ratings on the quality of portfolio tracking, fundamental stock analysis, technical analysis and mutual fund analysis. Ratings are also provided that measure the performance, ease of use and value of each service.

An appendix follows that includes a comprehensive list of investment Web sites. This guide provides you with the name and URL of the site along with its primary focus, the types of securities covered, and the services and information available. Each site is rated based on its content and thoroughness compared with other sites of similar focus and price structure.

Also scattered throughout the book are alerts meant to emphasize certain points. Tips are helpful points to consider in your selection process. Warnings are meant to alert you to a point of potential danger.

Chapter 1

AN OVERVIEW OF INVESTING

Setting up an Investment Plan

Fundamental Principles of Investing

Any successful plan must start with a base or foundation upon which to build. Developing a successful investment plan is no different. You may not need your computer for this section, but an understanding of the basics will mean that you can transform your computer from simply being a toy into an investment tool.

Risk and Return

Boiled down to its basics, investing is really about return and risk. The foundation of your investment portfolio rests on the investment principles of risk and return.

What is investment risk? Investment returns are never guaranteed and cannot be predicted with any amount of certainty. Instead, investors must make decisions using return expectations, which should be reasonable and mesh with reality. However, all investments are made with the possibility that your actual return won't meet your expectations. It is the uncertainty surrounding the actual outcome of your investment that creates risk; the greater the uncertainty, the greater the risk.

There are many sources of risk. These include:

- Business and industry risk—the uncertainty of an investment's ability to pay investors income, principal, and any other returns due to a significant fall-off in business (either firm-related or industry-wide) or bankruptcy. For instance, a stock's price may drop because earnings unexpectedly dropped due to an industry-wide slowdown.

- Inflation risk—the uncertainty over the future real (after-inflation) value of your investment. An investment that fails to keep pace with inflation will leave you with less purchasing power in the future than the original has today.

- Market risk—the risk that the general market or economic environment will cause the investment to lose value regardless of the particular security. For example, a stock may drop in value simply because the overall market has declined—this is stock market risk. A bond does not face stock market risk, but it does face its own kind of market risk: a drop in value due to a rise in interest rates. This is called interest rate risk.

- Liquidity risk—the risk of not being able to get out of the investment conveniently at a reasonable price. This can occur for a number of reasons. Volatile markets can cause liquidity problems if you must sell at a particular time—for instance, you may need to sell a stock at the very bottom of a bear market, forcing you to accept a considerable loss. Inactive markets can also cause liquidity problems—it may be difficult to sell your house, for example, if there are no buyers.

All investments confront these risks, but the degree of risk varies greatly. For instance, stocks face much less inflation risk than bonds, yet they face much greater liquidity risk.

Ironically, it is uncertainty that creates the potential for higher returns. Why? Because of the risk/return trade-off. Every investor wants the highest assured return possible, but different investors have varying degrees of uncertainty that they are willing to accept. In a competitive marketplace, this results in a trade-off: Low levels of uncertainty (low risk) are the most desirable and are therefore associated with low potential returns. High levels of uncertainty (high risk) are the most undesirable and are therefore associated with high potential returns.

Diversification

While potential returns should compensate you for risk, there are some risks that you will not be compensated for, and therefore they should be avoided. If you invest in a single security, your return will depend solely on that security; held by itself, the single security is highly risky. If you add nine other unrelated securities to that single security portfolio, the possible outcome changes—if that security flops, your entire return won't be as badly hurt. By diversifying your investments among 10 securities, you have substantially reduced the risk of the single security. However, that security's return will be the same whether held in isolation or in a portfolio. Diversification among securities that are unrelated substantially reduces your portfolio risk with little impact on potential returns. Diversification should occur at all levels of investing: You should be diversified among the major asset categories—stocks, fixed-income and money market investments—since these categories are affected by different market and economic factors; and you should be diversified within the major asset categories—for instance, among the various kinds of stocks (international or domestic) or fixed-income products.

Diversification is also important across market environments—the longer your holding period, the better. Time diversification helps reduce the risk that you may enter or leave a particular investment or category at an inopportune time in the economic cycle. It has much more of an impact on investments that have a high degree of volatility, such as stocks, where prices can fluctuate over the short term. Longer time periods smooth those fluctuations. Conversely, if you cannot remain invested in a volatile investment over relatively long time periods, those investments should be avoided. Time diversification is less important for relatively stable investments, such as certificates of deposit, money market funds and short-term bonds.

Your Investment Profile

A successful investment portfolio is one that is based on a balance between the risks you are willing to take and the returns you need to achieve your goals. An understanding of the various aspects of your investment profile allows you to assess that proper balance.

Risk Tolerance

The amount of risk you are willing to take on is an extremely important factor to consider before making an investment because of the severe consequences of taking on too much risk. Most investors who take on too much risk panic when confronted with losses they are unprepared for, and they frequently bail out, oftentimes sustaining substantial losses. This strategy—buying high and selling low—is guaranteed to produce an unhappy outcome. Properly assessing your tolerance for risk will prevent you from making panic decisions and abandoning your investment plan mid-stream at the worst possible time.

While many questionnaires seek to grade risk tolerance, the best approach is to simply examine the worst-case scenario—a loss over a one-year period—and ask yourself whether you could stick with your investment plan in the face of such a loss.

Keep in mind that it isn't necessary to eliminate a risky investment just because you have a low tolerance for risk—even a low-risk investor, for instance, can benefit by diversifying into riskier investments with part of their portfolio, while maintaining a low-risk profile. You should examine risk in the context of your total portfolio, rather than a single security or investment category.

Return Needs

Investors, of course, take on risk for the possibility of return. However, individuals differ greatly in their return needs. If you depend on your investment portfolio for part of your annual income, for example, you want returns that emphasize relatively higher annual payouts that tend to be consistent each year and protect principal. On the other hand, individuals who are saving for a future event—a child's education, a house, or retirement, for instance—want returns that tend to emphasize growth. Of course, many individuals may want a blending of the two—some current income, but also some growth.

Determining your return needs is important because you can't have all of everything—there is no investment that offers a high certain payout each year, protects your principal, and offers a high potential for future growth.

There are a number of trade-offs here, based on the risk/return trade-off. First, the price for principal protection is lower returns, usually in the form of lower annual income. There is also a trade-off between income and growth: The more certain the annual payment, the less risky the investment, and therefore the lower the potential return in the form of growth.

Time Horizon

Your time horizon will also affect your investment plan. Time diversification—remaining invested through various market cycles—is most critical for volatile investments such as stocks, where prices fluctuate greatly over the short term, but are considerably smoothed over longer time periods.

If your time horizon is short, you cannot effectively be diversified across different market environments. Longer time horizons allow you to take on greater risks—with a greater return potential—because some of that risk can be reduced through time diversification.

How should time horizon be measured? Your time horizon starts whenever your investment portfolio is implemented and ends when you will need to take the money out of your investment portfolio. If you are investing to save for a specific event, such as tuition payments or the purchase of a house, your time horizon is fairly easily measured—it ends when you need the cash.

If you are investing to accumulate a sum for periodic withdrawals, such as during retirement, your time horizon is more difficult to quantify as you approach the time when withdrawals begin. For instance, when you retire, you may need to take out only part of your investment portfolio as income each year. Your time horizon will be a blend—partly short-term and partly intermediate- or longer-term.

What constitutes short-, intermediate-, and long-term horizons? To diversify over various economic cycles, you must be invested through one complete economic cycle at the very least. In general, the economic cycle lasts about five years, which can be considered a long-term horizon.

What about short- and intermediate-term horizons? Since these horizons are less than five years, stocks shouldn't be considered. In addition, the sooner you need the investment, the greater the need for principal protection and ease of selling. The time horizon effectively limits you to fixed-income securities:

- If you need the money within a year or two, you are limited to the shorter end of the fixed-income spectrum—money market funds, very short-term bonds and short-term certificates of deposit.

- An intermediate-term outlook—two to five years—allows you a little more room to earn higher returns using intermediate-term (less than five years) bonds and intermediate-term certificates of deposit.

Your Investment Plan

A successful investment plan matches the investment characteristics of the various asset categories to your personal risk and return needs. You can get a rough idea of the risk/return trade-offs in a portfolio by using the approach illustrated in Table 1: Portfolio Risk and Return: A Rough Guide. First, calculate the percentage (weighting) of the total portfolio that is invested in each of the broad asset categories; then multiply the weightings for each category by estimates for growth, yield, total return (growth plus yield) and the worst one-year possible loss; lastly, add up these results.

How do you estimate return and potential loss? The potential growth, yield and total return figures in Table 1 on page 11 are estimates based on long-term historical results for each of the asset categories; significant year-to-year variation, however, can be expected. The downside risk figures are the worst bear market declines for each category; the downside risk for the total portfolio assumes that all asset categories would decline simultaneously—a very conservative assumption.

Of course, there are several possible portfolio combinations. While the approach in Table 1 provides a simplified method for analyzing a portfolio, computer software programs offer more sophisticated approaches as well as long-term historical data that can help you tailor a portfolio to fit your needs. These programs also can help you monitor and maintain your portfolio once you have developed your investment plan. Chapter 4 provides an overview of portfolio management programs. Successful stock investing is not a matter of picking stocks willy-nilly, but rather involves an overall style or strategy. This refers to the techniques used to select individual stocks and combine them to form stock portfolios. In addition, there are broad timing decisions concerning when to enter or exit the stock market.

Table 1
Portfolio Risk and Return: A Rough Guide*

Asset Category	Portfolio Weight (%)	Potential Capital Growth (%)	Current Yield (%)	Total Return (%)	Downside Risk Potential (%)
Money Market Funds	10	0	5	5	0
Bonds	20	0	8	8	(10)
Growth & Income	30	5	4	9	(20)
Growth	20	7	3	10	(30)
Aggressive Growth	10	11	1	12	(40)
International	10	11	1	12	(40)
Portfolio**:		**5**	**4**	**9**	**(22)**

*Potential growth and current yield are long-term average estimates based on historical relationships among mutual fund categories; significant year-to-year variation can be expected. The downside risk figures are estimates of annual decline during severe bear market conditions; the downside risk for the portfolio is based on the conservative assumption that all asset categories would decline simultaneously.
**Portfolio weight multiplied by return or risk. For example, Downside Risk Potential for the portfolio is: $(20\% \times -10) + (30\% \times -20) + (20\% \times -30) + (10\% \times -40) + (10\% \times -40) = -22\%$

Making Investment Decisions

Most stock selection strategies can be classified as active or passive; timing strategies tend to be either buy-and-hold or market timing.

Passive Investing

Passive investing means that no active investment decisions need to be made. This consists of simply buying and holding "the market," and it would provide a market rate of return, less any management and transaction costs, which can be held to a minimum. In practice, passive investing consists of buying and holding stocks that track an index, most commonly the Standard & Poor's 500. But other market segments, such as small-cap stock indexes and international stock indexes, should also be considered to develop a diversified portfolio.

This no-style approach is the benchmark against which any other approach should be measured. An active approach is more expensive, whether it involves your own time and expenses (if you are selecting stocks yourself), or incurs a management fee charged by a mutual fund adviser or private investment adviser. In addition, stocks are usually bought and sold more frequently in an active approach, incurring both transaction costs and taxes on gains.

The index fund approach offers several advantages. It is difficult to outperform the overall stock market without added risk—even if it is possible to beat the market, it is difficult for investors to pick, in advance, an approach that will do so. Costs must be kept to a minimum, and active management can skew a portfolio toward a particular market segment, producing returns that differ from expectations. An index fund that tracks a broad-based index is, by definition, truly diversified. And it is always fully invested in the market.

Active Investing

For any active approach to be useful, it must produce a return above the market rate of return plus the higher costs associated with active management, without increasing the risk. This higher return represents the value of that approach.

Many investors, of course, feel that it is possible to "beat the market" and use active approaches to add value. Active stock selection approaches can be divided by methodology:

- technical analysis or

- fundamental analysis.

Technical Analysis

Technical analysis is an approach that tries to predict the future price of a stock or the future direction of the stock market based on past price and volume changes. Charts and graphs of stock prices and volume on a periodic basis (daily, weekly, monthly, etc.) are closely examined to detect developing patterns. The underlying assumption is that stock prices and the stock market follow discernible patterns, and if the beginning of a pattern can be identified, the balance of the pattern can be predicted well enough to yield returns above the market. The computer is well-suited for technical analysis, which involves manipulating large data series and extensive use of charts and graphs. Chapter 6 (starting on page 217) examines technical analysis programs.

Fundamental Analysis

Fundamental analysis, in contrast, is primarily concerned with the underlying fundamental worth of a firm and its potential for growth. To assess this, fundamental investors focus on data from individual firms' financial statements—their income statements, cash flow statements and balance sheets. Since absolute numbers are difficult to analyze on their own, ratios—one financial figure relative to another—are used to put the numbers into perspective; ratios allow investors to compare financial data among firms, and to judge a firm's financial data relative to historical levels and industry norms.

Fundamental analysis can be divided into many camps, but two of the most popular are:

- growth investing and

- value investing.

Growth investors look for companies with rapid and expanding growth and whose stock prices will grow accordingly with the company's success. Value investors look for companies whose current stock price looks cheap relative to some measure of the firm's real current value, and whose stock price will rise once the market recognizes the firm's real worth.

In addition, some fundamental investors use a top-down approach, which analyzes industries and firms in the context of the overall economic cycle. All camps, however, use valuation formulas in an attempt to put a value on the firm, for comparison with the current price. Fundamental analysis computer programs can provide investors with a variety of valuation methods, as well as extensive databases that include the current and historical financial statement data of numerous firms; these programs are examined in Chapter 5 starting on page 137.

Entering the Bond World

Active bond selection tends to focus on credit quality and maturity, both of which directly affect yields—higher yields among fixed-income securities are associated with higher credit risks and/or longer maturities. Credit quality is determined by the issuer of the bond, with the high-quality, low default-risk sector consisting of U.S. government bonds, high-grade corporate bonds and high-grade municipals. U.S. government bonds offer the most protection against default, but diversification among high-grade corporate and municipal issuers can substantially reduce this risk.

The biggest risk facing bond investors, however, is interest rate risk, and this is directly affected by maturity. Interest rate risk is the risk that a bond's price will drop when interest rates rise, and rise when rates fall. The prices of longer-term bonds are much more volatile than shorter-term bonds when an interest rate change occurs.

Some bond investors use a top-down approach that analyzes the economy and attempts to forecast the likely direction of interest rates; they then invest in the sector of the bond market that will benefit most from or be least hurt by the expected interest rate move. Other bond investors attempt to find bonds that are, in their opinion, mispriced by the market—for instance, an investor may feel that an issuer has less credit risk and therefore its bonds represent hidden value that will go up in price once the market recognizes the issuer's higher credit quality. Computer programs do not tend to focus on bond analysis, but financial information services do provide up-to-date information on bond prices and yields; Chapter 8 provides a description of financial information services

Using Mutual Funds

You don't have to rely on yourself to make active security selections. Instead, you can hire an adviser to make the security selection decisions for you by investing in a mutual fund.

A mutual fund pools investors' money to invest in a portfolio of securities that is managed by an investment adviser. Mutual funds are able to attract some of the best investment talent as portfolio managers at relatively low cost because of the economies of scale provided by the large pool of assets. Brokerage expenses can also be held down. Most mutual funds are also able to provide investors with access to a diversified group of securities that normally only a large portfolio can provide.

Mutual funds can be found in every asset category, including such diverse areas as smaller-firm stocks, international stocks, international bonds and emerging markets. There are also index funds—passively managed mutual funds that track an index, allowing investors to keep transaction costs and advisory fees to a bare minimum. In addition, there are 'asset allocation' funds that invest in all major asset categories. The low minimum investments required by many mutual funds means that investors have the flexibility to build their entire portfolio out of mutual funds, or to use mutual funds as a supplement to individual security selection. The sheer number of mutual funds to choose among, along with the wide variety of types and features offered, makes mutual funds ideally suited to analysis by computer. Many mutual fund screening programs are available to help you in your selection process, and these are covered in Chapter 7 starting on page 309.

Timing Transactions

Along with choosing among strategies, your investment decisions also involve how often and when you will buy and sell securities. There are two basic approaches to the timing question:

- market timing or

- buy-and-hold.

Market Timing

A market timing approach involves an attempt to leave the market entirely during downturns and reinvest when the market begins to head back up. Although it is often associated with technical analysis, certain fundamental investors sometimes attempt to time the market—for instance, if they feel the market is overvalued on a fundamental basis. A bond market timing approach attempts to forecast the direction of interest rates and invest accordingly.

If investors could actually enter and leave the market at the right time, it would lead to much higher returns. However, there is no satisfactory evidence that market upturns and downturns, or the direction of interest rates, can be predicted with enough precision to offset the increased transaction costs, not to mention the adverse tax consequences. And if you guess incorrectly, your actual return could be substantially different than expected. In addition, a market-timing approach does not allow time diversification to work in your favor—being invested across different market environments. In general, the longer your holding period, the better.

Buy-and-Hold

Buy-and-hold simply means that the portion of your portfolio committed to stocks is fully invested in the stock market at all times. In other words, while you may buy and sell individual stocks, or change to a different mutual fund, your stock portfolio remains invested in the stock market. A buy-and-hold approach to bonds simply commits a portion of the portfolio to bonds without attempting to forecast the direction of interest rates.

Tracking Your Investments

All investors want to know: How are my investments doing? There are several ways to answer this question.

Examining Your Portfolio's Return

First, there is your overall portfolio. Calculating the return of your total portfolio isn't that difficult and many portfolio management computer programs (see Chapter 4: Portfolio Management on page 75) will perform the calculations for you. But is it really necessary to measure the performance of your portfolio as a whole? Measuring the performance of your total portfolio is useful primarily for one reason—to see if the long-term terminal value that you hoped to achieve with your investment strategy is still realistic.

In general, you should be examining the return on your portfolio to make sure it is within the target range you expected, based on your investment mix. If it isn't, you may need to make some adjustments in your future projections—for instance, you may have to increase your savings rate, you may have to take on more risk to achieve the target that you set, or you may simply have to adjust your target value downward, settling for less in the future. This needn't be done frequently—certainly not more than once a year, since you are examining a long-term strategy.

Measuring the Separate Elements of Your Portfolio

Measuring the performance of the various investments that make up your portfolio, on the other hand, should be done much more frequently—either quarterly or semiannually. The purpose of this monitoring is to see how well the professional expertise you have hired (or are performing yourself) is doing.

For instance, you should examine the performance of each mutual fund against its peers (funds with similar objectives) and an appropriate index (an index that covers investments similar to those the fund is investing in) over the same time period. The index and peer-average returns provide benchmarks that allow you to better judge the manager's performance. For example, if your fund is up 10% for the quarter and the benchmark index is up 12%, your portfolio manager hasn't really added any value to your investment. On the other hand, if your fund is down 10% while the index is down 15%, your manager has added considerable value—he or she has limited the loss.

You do not need to make your own calculations to measure the performance of your mutual fund holdings; there are many publications that provide information on mutual fund performance and that also provide appropriate benchmarks for comparison. (See AAII Publications on page 19 and Mutual Fund Publications on page 20.) The mutual fund programs covered in Chapter 7 can help you assess the performance of your own funds.

If you are investing in stocks or bonds on your own, measure your individual stock or bond portfolio performance against an appropriate index or similarly managed mutual fund as a test of your own investment decision-making ability. The portfolio management programs covered in Chapter 4 can assist you in this process.

To Sell or Not to Sell

What do you do with this performance information? For mutual funds, if the performance figures are good relative to the benchmarks—no problem. If the figures are unsatisfactory, you have to decide if you want to sell the fund and look elsewhere. Keep in mind that if you sell, you need to find a suitable replacement—

one that you feel will do better in the future. And you would not select a fund based on only a short-term track record. Similarly, you should not dump a fund simply because performance has been sub-par in the short term. While you should examine performance quarterly, don't be overly jumpy if results are poor. Instead, use the opportunity to take a closer look and try to determine why the performance is off; see if you still have confidence in the manager's ability over the long term.

If you are managing your own stock portfolio, you probably won't want to fire yourself even if performance is off. But you may want to consider revising your overall stock selection strategy. Consider the evaluation of the individual stock performance within your stock portfolio. That process should be an ongoing function of your stock selection strategy, not part of your overall portfolio maintenance program.

Monitoring and Rebalancing Your Portfolio

In addition to performance measurement, you also need to review the overall composition of your portfolio and make adjustments when necessary. There are three primary reasons for making adjustments:

- There are changes in your investor profile that may necessitate an overhaul of your allocation strategy.

- There have been a number of successful investments in the portfolio, and they have become so overweighted that your current investment mix no longer reflects your original plan.

- There are particular investments within the portfolio that are not performing as well as expected, and they may need to be dropped.

When making adjustments to your portfolio, for whatever reason, there are several important considerations to keep in mind:

- Try to avoid tax liabilities.

For example, if you need to rebalance your portfolio—for instance, stocks have become overweighted or your profile has changed and you want to de-emphasize stocks—use new money generated from salary, income, and capital gains distributions, or from one-time sources such as poorly performing investments, property sales, and inheritances. Investments should be sold because of poor performance, not to rebalance your portfolio.

- When you are making a major transition from one major investment category to another, do so gradually so that the effects of the market at one point in time don't dramatically affect your portfolio value.

For example, if you are moving to a heavier commitment in stocks, don't accomplish this by investing one large lump sum; instead, divide the lump sum into equal parts and invest it periodically (monthly or quarterly) over a long time period of one or two years; this is known as dollar cost averaging.

- A decision to sell an investment can be complicated by tax considerations and the need to find a suitable replacement. Make sure you focus on future return and not on the past.

Learning More About Investing

Investment Textbooks
Listed in order of difficulty, from beginning-level to more advanced.

- Hirt, Geoffrey A. and Stanley Block; "Fundamentals of Investment Management," sixth edition; Richard D. Irwin/McGraw-Hill, Homewood, Ill., 1999. A very understandable and well-written book for the novice. Numerous examples and excellent references for sources of investment information.

- Gitman, Lawrence J. and Michael D. Joehnk, "Fundamentals of Investing," seventh edition, Addison-Wesley, Reading, Mass., 1999. Understandable and well-written, with a focus on portfolios and strategies for implementing investment goals in light of risk/return trade-offs.

- Reilly, Frank K. and Keith C. Brown; "Investment Analysis and Portfolio Management," fifth edition; The Dryden Press, Fort Worth, Texas, 1997. An advanced text book covering in-depth examinations of portfolio management and investment analysis.

Two Classics

- Graham, Benjamin; "The Intelligent Investor," fourth edition; HarperCollins, New York, 1986. A version of Security Analysis (below), written for the individual investor (vs. the professional).

- Cottle, Sidney, Roger F. Murray, and Frank E. Block; "Graham and Dodd's Security Analysis," fifth edition; McGraw-Hill Inc., New York, 1988. One of the most important books for the security analyst. Discusses the behavior of the securities markets, balance sheet analysis, interpretation of financial data, specific standards for bond investment, techniques of selecting stocks for investment, projections of earnings and dividends, methods for valuing growth stocks, and stock-option warrants. This is an update of the classic Security Analysis: Principles and Techniques by Benjamin Graham, David Dodd, and Sidney Cottle, which introduced the valuation approach to security analysis.

AAII Publications

AAII publications are available by sending a letter stating the name of the publication and a check to the American Association of Individual Investors, 625 North Michigan Avenue, Chicago, Illinois 60611, or you can charge your order with Visa or MasterCard by calling (312) 280-0170 or (800) 428-2244 or by fax (312) 280-9883 or sending an E-mail to members@aaii.com or visiting our Web site at www.aaii.com.

- *The Individual Investor's Guide to Low-Load Mutual Funds*; this annual publication is free to AAII members and is mailed in March of every year. It covers over 900 low-load mutual funds and includes 10 years of data as well as risk and return performance measures. The price is $24.95 for non-members; additional copies are available to members for $19.

- *Quarterly Low-Load Mutual Fund Update*; this publication is mailed at the beginning of each quarter (January, April, July and October). It covers over 900 low-load mutual funds and provides a summary of fund performance by quarter over the last year and over the most recent three- and five-year periods. A computerized version is also available as a menu-driven program on diskette and includes the printed newsletter. The non- member price is $30 for the newsletter and $50 for the computerized version. The member price is $24 a year for the newsletter and $39 a year for the computerized version.

AAII Investor Library: The following five books are $68 for non-members and $54 for members.

- *Investing Basics and Beyond*; this booklet leads you step-by-step through the process of developing a personal investment profile while taking into consideration lifestyle and age. The focus is on portfolio development and maintenance. The book is $15 for non-members and $12 for members.

- *Stock Investing Strategies*; this booklet teaches you the basics of fundamental stock analysis without miring you in intricate details. Using a simple worksheet, various valuation methods are described and illustrated. Appendixes show you how to perform stock screening on a computerized database using each method to develop a list of stocks. The book is $20 for non-members and $16 for members.

- *Portfolio Building*; this booklet explains how to apply the essential concepts of portfolio building to real-world situations. Topics include: asset allocation, measuring your portfolio performance, portfolio tuning and maintenance, and keeping your portfolio in balance. The book is $15 for non-members and $12 for members.

- *Retirement Planning*; this booklet will help you develop a retirement strategy by looking at the options available for accumulating retirement assets and how to manage those assets during and after retirement. A worksheet and tables are provided to help determine a personal savings plan, followed by coverage of employer-sponsored defined-contribution plans such as 401(k)s and how to invest retirement assets from an asset allocation point of view. Also explained are the different types of IRAs and their features. The book is $15.00 for non-members and $12.00 for members.

- *Stock Market Winners*; this booklet focuses on proven stock-picking strategies from well-known investors such as: Warren Buffett, Peter Lynch, Philip Fisher, David Dreman, Benjamin Graham, William O'Neil ... and others. Included is information on how to use your computer to develop stock screens based on these investor techniques and how to create and implement your own stock-picking strategy. The book is $20 for non-members and $16 for members.

Mutual Fund Publications

- *Morningstar Mutual Funds*, Morningstar Inc., 225 W. Wacker Dr., Chicago, Ill. 60606; (800) 735-0700; www.morningstar.com. Published every other week, this service provides full-page reports on 1,700 mutual funds. Each fund page is revised roughly three times a year. This is the mutual fund version of the Value Line stock reports.

- *Morningstar Mutual Fund 500*, Morningstar Inc., 225 W. Wacker Dr., Chicago, Ill. 60606; (800) 735-0700; www.morningstar.com. Published annually, this reference book provides data on 500 mutual funds that Morningstar has identified to be of "exceptional merit."

- *The Value Line Mutual Fund Survey*, 220 East 42nd St., 6th Floor, New York, N.Y. 10017; (800) 634-3583; www.valueline.com. Published every two weeks, this rivals Morningstar Mutual Funds. It provides full-page analyses on 1,500 mutual funds, with each fund revised roughly three times a year.

- *The Handbook for No-Load Fund Investors*, The No-Load Fund Investor, Inc., P.O. Box 318, Irvington-on-Hudson, N.Y. 10533; (800) 535-8760; www.sheldonjacobs.com. This annual publication provides an explanation of how to invest in mutual funds, as well as a directory of no-load and closed-end funds. Tables are used to compare and evaluate mutual fund performance.

Chapter 2

OVERVIEW OF INVESTMENT SOFTWARE & INFORMATION SERVICES

Your computer can be an effective tool to help you with your investments. However, determining what level of functionality you need can prove to be the most difficult part in making that tool an efficient one. Before you can select a computer system, you must focus on what you want your system to accomplish. This issue becomes even more complex when you factor in all the investment software and on-line and Internet services from which you can choose.

Each chapter in this guide emphasizes analyzing your own needs—a process that is vital to software selection no matter what type of program you're considering. When analyzing your investment needs, examine the tasks you are performing now and consider those in the future to help you determine what kind of program is best suited for you.

What Is Investment Software?

Investment software generally fall into the following categories: portfolio management, fundamental stock analysis, technical analysis and mutual fund analysis. A chapter is devoted to each of these categories, outlining standard features of computer programs within each field, identifying items to seek out when selecting programs, and reviewing top programs on the market today.

Remember that the computer can help you manipulate the data you already have, allow you to study more securities more efficiently, and help establish discipline within your investment regime, but it will not pick the investments for you. Only through an understanding of the computer and the programs you use can you enhance your investing strategies.

Categories of Investment Software

Portfolio Management Applications

By far the most common type of software investors use is portfolio management programs. It is easy to see why this category is so popular. Portfolio management is the process of maintaining records on your investments and analyzing the various characteristics of a portfolio, such as performance, allocation of assets and diversification. Keeping track of your securities, their cost basis, their current value and their performance can be a time-consuming and tedious process. A computer can automate the process, giving you time to concentrate on your overall investment strategy and security analysis, not to mention your golf game.

Portfolio management systems should be specifically written to help you monitor your investment portfolio; however, some of these applications may not provide the information you need to evaluate your performance accurately. Sometimes, portfolio management is part of a larger financial planning application that can also keep track of your checkbook and help plan for long-term financial goals. Other portfolio management applications are simply bookkeeping systems whose benefits may be limited. With a good program, however, there are many benefits. Once you have entered the data initially needed to begin using these programs, you may later realize substantial time savings as the program performs calculations and maintains a necessary record of portfolio activity.

The accurate determination of portfolio performance requires dealing with transactions as they occur, even if at irregularly-spaced intervals. Moreover, withdrawals must be accounted for properly to determine portfolio returns.

Internal rate of return (IRR) is the appropriate value-weighted measure of portfolio return. This is the rate of return that fully accounts for cash withdrawals and deposits over the life of the portfolio. This measure can be compared to market returns to determine whether you are earning a sufficient return.

Portfolio management applications should be able to deal with the reinvestment of dividends or other income and be able to account for the changes in returns. They should also be capable of handling not only all of your current investments but also any investment vehicle you might consider in the future.

Most portfolio management applications will prepare tax Schedules B and D, which list interest and dividend income and capital gains and losses. If the program does not actually prepare a report suitable for use with tax filing, it should be able to group information for you to use on a printed return, or with another program. Another feature that is very useful, especially for investors with large portfolios or for active traders, is the integration to an on-line database to obtain current price information for portfolio updating. A new class of Web-based portfolio management systems are naturally tied in to automatic updates, but most software-based systems can also be updated automatically. When used in conjunction with information on the market itself, such as the Standard & Poor's 500 stock index, this can provide the basis for making fundamental portfolio allocation decisions. Some portfolio management programs can connect to a discount broker to record your transactions, thereby saving even more time. Portfolio management programs are evaluated in Chapter 4 on page 75.

Fundamental Screening

Most (but not all) of the commercially available fundamental investment systems are designed to screen data rather than judge a security's worth on the basis of fundamental valuation principles. There are now a number of applications on the market that will screen a data set of 1,500 to 15,000 companies on any number of fundamental variables, with the majority of these applications available through the Internet.

As an illustration of the screening process, consider an investor who is interested in smaller market-value companies with low price-to-book ratios, yet showing strong price momentum. The investor could decide to screen a database for companies with a market value between $50 and $500 million. In addition, the investor might look for those stocks in this group whose price-to-book ratios are low, below 1.5. Furthermore, the investor may wish to closely examine only those companies with price increases over last six months that have outpaced 75% of all firms. The screening program could go through the database rapidly and select the companies that meet these criteria. Of course, once the stocks are selected, the investor must further evaluate the individual companies before making any investment. There are many important judgment factors that the computer cannot analyze. However, many of the reviewed fundamental screening systems provide a rich database suitable for fundamental valuation.

A fundamental screening system should give you access to a large database and the flexibility to create different criteria for screening—you should not just be locked into preset criteria. The program should allow transfer of data to other applications, such as a spreadsheet program. Without this latter capability you cannot perform further analysis essential for effective security selection.

In comparing stock screening services, critical factors include:

- the universe of stocks supported by the database,

- the depth of stock information,

- the flexibility of screening software,

- the frequency of updates,

- the method of distributing the information,

- the computer systems it works on, and

- price.

These factors are discussed in great depth in Chapter 5 on page 137, which also includes an evaluation of fundamental stock screening systems.

Mutual Fund Analysis and Screening

Similar to fundamental screening systems for stocks, there are many applications that allow the screening of mutual funds. At a minimum these applications should be able to rank funds by the highest return figures in a specific investment category. At the other end of the spectrum are systems that can display your current asset allocation and compare the individual assets held by each fund. The high-end systems will cover more funds and give more specific data on each fund.

Using a mutual fund screening application enables you to quickly compare broad classes of mutual funds and view how your holdings performed within their category. Most systems can rank relative performance, and some allow for the specific screening of data numbers. Like stock screening systems, an investor can specify data elements and minimum or maximum numbers for each criteria. One example is to look for aggressive growth funds with total returns greater than 20% for the last three years and a beta less than 1.00.

With the assistance of mutual fund screening system, investors can save time selecting and managing their funds. Some of these services use CD-ROMs, but more and more systems require on-line connections to sort through funds. Read Chapter 7 on page 309 for an examination of mutual fund analysis and screening applications.

Technical Analysis and Screening

The term technical analysis covers a variety of techniques that study relationships between a security's past price and volume movements and patterns to forecast security and market price direction. This analysis is generally best interpreted with the use of charts, and in many cases the analysis is entirely graphical.

Technical analysis is well suited for computers because it involves the manipulation of a large amount of data. One example is to compute a moving average price over time. This is just an average over several time periods—days, weeks or whatever time period the analyst feels is appropriate. The interval remains constant, but the beginning and ending points move through time and reflect new information and market conditions. The analyst is not concerned with the reason prices move but simply with the pattern of movements. If the daily price crosses over the moving average line and closes above it, that behavior is regarded as a sign of strength and perhaps signals a buy recommendation.

Because the essence of technical analysis is price trends, it is essential that these programs provide access to price and volume information. If a program accesses an on-line database, it should capture the data directly. This saves time and money since you don't have to work through the multiple layers of command menus.

There are a number of programs and data services available that will not only compute the price and/or volume graphs that you want, but they also can log on to an information service, automatically obtain the latest information and update the graphs with that information. Many programs come with or have optional downloading programs that help you manage your data.

More powerful technical analysis programs allow you to test strategies to see how they would have performed in the past. Some programs will even go one step further and actually adjust the rules you are testing to see what would have worked best for you. To save time, programs can scan a large database of stocks to see which securities, industries or indexes meet your buy or sell criteria. Most of the technical screening programs rely on the user to build a historical database. With the rising popularity of flat-fee databases and CD-ROM distribution, constructing such a database is now much more feasible. Chapter 6 on page 217 delves into technical analysis programs.

What Is a Financial Information Service?

From the very earliest days of financial markets, the gathering and processing of information has been crucial and the stock exchanges have always used state-of-the-art communications networks. Most of this communication has involved transmitting the latest price quotes to investors, and this remains the focus today. Nevertheless, investors now can also obtain detailed and comprehensive information on securities. This includes current and historical financial and market data to aid in their analyses.

Financial information services and on-line databases provide historical financial, market and economic information, as well as current stock market prices and financial news. Some services also provide the ability to conduct transactions on-line. Information is delivered via phone lines, networks, FM radio, satellite or cable TV.

Similar to software programs, financial information services vary greatly in scope and purpose. In selecting a service, you need to focus on how it provides data, what information is provided, which systems and programs can use the data and the pricing structure. In doing this, you may notice that some are strictly raw data providers while others are complete systems that include both software and data.

Information services may be broadly based networks such as America Online and CompuServe, which provide information on a variety of topics extending far beyond the investment field. In contrast, other systems may limit themselves to providing information on a specific type of asset or data, such as futures, options or historical pricing. All of the major on-line services have moved toward offering flat rate access for around $20 per month.

The impact of the Internet in the area of investment is tremendous. The Internet broke many barriers to financial data providers. The Internet offers instant access to a wide range of individuals, many of whom are investors. It is also far easier and cheaper for companies to provide data over the Internet. The combination of a large potential audience coupled with relatively easy and inexpensive Internet Web site development has resulted in an explosion of affordable data services for the individual investor. Financial services and popular Internet Web sites are evaluated in Chapter 8 on page 361, while the appendix (page 421) provides a comprehensive listing of investment-oriented Web sites.

Tips for Selecting Investment Software

With the information in this guidebook you should be able to narrow down your search to a reasonable number of products that merit further investigation. Here are a few things you should do and consider before making your final choice.

Simple Networking

Talk to other users; find out what they are using and what they think about your final candidates. There are three good avenues to seek other investors' opinions:

- computerized investing groups

    There are groups that meet on a regular basis to discuss and present approaches to a computerized investment program. These computer special interest groups (SIGs) are a valuable resource that can be used to get opinions on the pros and cons of various systems when you get to the point of picking a package.

- Internet World Wide Web sites or Newsgroups

    If there is no group in your area, or if you are just looking for further contacts on the subject, Internet World Wide Web sites or Newsgroups provide a way to exchange ideas and programs through your computer.

- dial-up financial information services

Many of the financial information services, such as CompuServe, America Online and Prodigy have forums that focus on computer-assisted investing. The AAII Web site (www.aaii.com) offers articles from *Computerized Investing* and message areas devoted to discussions on the topic.

Check Your Budget

Is the price within your budget? Do not make the mistake of thinking that the higher the price, the better the program. There are excellent products in every price range.

Does the program use a cost-effective data service? If you plan on using a data service to save time from data entry, you may quickly find out that the initial program cost was just a small part of the overall cost of operating the system. Programs vary in data service support. Before you commit to a product, find out how much it will cost to obtain electronic data. Also, services price data access in different ways—flat charge for unlimited access, per minute connect time charges, extra charges for certain data or a charge per character of information downloaded. Generating comparable costs from different services can take some time, but try to estimate your data needs and do some comparison price shopping.

Data Compatibility

Make sure that the program can export its data if needed. This will allow you to share data among programs and allow you to continue to use the data you have collected should you want to switch programs in a few years.

Do Your Research

Contact software vendors to request the most recent program information. Investment programs make up a narrow niche and are not readily available in software stores. You will generally need to deal with the vendors directly. Get a demo of the programs you are interested in, even if there is a small fee. Many vendors now offer downloadable demos at their Web sites, often for free. Without testing a program, you will not know whether you can or even want to learn how to use the package. And even more importantly, the demo will help to ensure that the program actually does what you want it to do. Web sites often offer a free trial period, so take advantage of this offer and try out the services before subscribing.

Look at the support policies of the company. Does it offer telephone support, and if so, when is it available? Some vendors charge for providing help. Some may operate a Web site that you can connect to, not only to solve problems but also to provide operating tips and program updates. Some vendors produce product newsletters that can be a valuable resource for getting the most out of the product.

Before you make your purchase check on the company's return policy. Some software vendors offer full refunds but provide a time limit; others charge a restocking fee or do not refund the postage and handling; others do not provide any refund.

It is best to purchase mail-order items with a credit card so that if you have problems either receiving the product or getting it to work, you have some recourse or even bargaining power. The Fair Credit Billing Act gives you some power to withhold payment on items purchased if you have made a good faith effort to return an item or have given the seller a reasonable opportunity to correct any problems. With a check you have little recourse to get your money back once it has been cashed.

Conclusion

Personal computers are excellent tools for the investor. What the computer should allow you to do is spend your time evaluating the results of your research, rather than on repetitive tasks. The computer can process a lot of information rapidly. It can do numerous iterations that test sensitivity to changes in your fundamental assumptions, and it can display that information in an easily understandable format with graphics.

You should keep in mind, though, that you are relying on the financial expertise of the authors of any software package or service you are using, so carefully check the documentation they provide. If the manual does not explain what the program does and why it does it, you should view the product with some skepticism. The program should tell you more than simply what to do. The advice of the computer is no more relevant than the advice of a human being—after all, it was a human who told the computer what to do in the first place. Remember that almost all investment analysis software is based on observation of past market trends and relationships and some grounding in the theory of valuation. If the past is not a guide to the future, then using a computer will make you no better an investor than you were before. If you do not understand basic valuation principles, you cannot be an effective investor, with or without a computer.

Perhaps the best strategy is to view your computer as a tool, a little more sophisticated than your pencil and tablet of scratch paper, but still a tool. With a basic understanding of financial markets, investment analysis techniques and your personal financial objectives, you can use this tool to become a better investor. With an understanding of the past performance of different investments and of your own needs, you can formulate reasonable financial goals. The computer can then be a valuable aid in reaching those goals.

Chapter 3

WHAT EQUIPMENT DO YOU NEED?

The Year in Review

As we enter a new millenium, computerized investors have at their fingertips the most powerful tools ever seen on the consumer market. Processor speeds are reaching ever-faster speeds, hard drives are becoming bigger and bigger—every facet of computing is evolving at an ever-increasing rate. As for the past year, manufacturers have seemingly taken a breather from the frenetic pace they had set over the past two years. Value has become the key selling product. Technologies that have entered the market over the past couple of years—DVD, SuperDisks, etc.—have become standard equipment on many new systems, manufacturers have focused their energies this past year on building faster and more powerful systems at attractive price points. Processors such as AMD's (Advanced Micro Devices) Athlon chip boast speeds of 650 megahertz—with 700 megahertz chips scheduled to be available by the end of 1999.

The year 1999 also saw the re-emergence of Apple Computer as a force to still be reckoned with. The iMac has become a top seller in the market with over two million units sold. Apple's market share has been propelled to roughly 11% (up from 5%–6% a year prior). While there has been much hype surrounding the introduction of the iMac and iBook, there has not been much for the computerized investor to cheer about in terms of Mac software. Macintosh-compatible investment software remains scarce, with the majority being personal finance programs such as Quicken or Microsoft Money.

As always, computer companies are constantly jockeying for position and market share. Companies compete on two distinct planes—power and value. On one hand you have companies scrambling to be called the fastest, while on the other hand you have those touting themselves as providing the most bang for your buck. When new technologies enter the market and gain acceptance, older ones invariably are marked down in price as companies try to clear their inventories. Such was the case with Pentium II systems when the Pentium III was released in February 1999. Through this process, consumers can benefit in one of two ways—they are given technology that is more advanced, or they can purchase the former top-of-the-line equipment at a fraction of its original cost.

The goal of this guide is to expose you to the world of computerized investing—both in terms of computer hardware and investment software. The process of purchasing a new computer can be a daunting task. Issues abound, such as how much system you need to perform desired tasks and how to slow the inevitable process of obsolescence. In order to make the right purchase decision, you need to be aware of these issues through education and research. The following should provide some insight into the process.

Before You Shop

What to Consider

Some common complaints among computer buyers are that they either didn't get a system that met their computing needs or spent too much on extras they will never use. These problems often arise from the fact that they did not sit down beforehand and analyze what they will be doing with the computer. Ideally, you will identify what it is you want to do and purchase a system accordingly. If you are looking for a system with which to surf the Internet, a high-end system with all the bells and whistles would probably be a waste of money. Likewise, if you wish to perform technical analysis or run other system-intensive software, an "Internet-in-a-box" system would be ill-advised.

Keep in mind that a computer is simply a platform. By itself, it cannot perform any functions—it is the software that tells the computer what to do and, in doing so, performs the functions we want. Just as a computer cannot function without software, software cannot perform without the proper computer. It is vitally important that you purchase a computer that supports the software you plan to use.

Intended Uses

An important factor to consider when purchasing a new computer is the current and future intended uses of the system. Depending on what you want to do with the system, especially in terms of computer-assisted investment analysis, you will require one with certain capabilities.

In the realm of investment analysis, technical analysis is probably the most system-intensive. This type of analysis relies on the manipulation and graphical display of a great deal of data—typically daily data over several years. In order to perform such tasks, a computer requires a processor that can quickly perform the calculations. Furthermore, a high-quality monitor and possibly a color printer are necessary to examine and print charts and graphs. If you are looking to store a large amount of historical data for many companies—typical of fundamental screening and analysis programs—a large hard drive would be useful. For day-to-day downloading of data or for Internet-based research, a high-speed modem is a necessity. In contrast, most portfolio management programs require more simple processing requirements and, likewise, less advanced computers.

While shopping for a new computer system, you need to be forward thinking—where will computing be in the future and what may your computing needs be down the road? While the computer hardware is advancing in leaps and bounds, software that fully utilizes the functionality of today's high-end systems is slow in coming. Much of the software on the market today was written for use with technology from several years ago. As you decide which system you are going to purchase, be mindful of both your current and potential future needs.

Cost

For most consumers, the underlying factor that drives any big-ticket purchase is their budget. Unless money is no object, you should have an idea of how much you are willing to spend on a new system. To reiterate, knowing what you want to do with the computer will allow you to gauge how much system you need. In addition, knowing how much you can afford allows you to place priorities on various options if your budget is tight. For example, you may wish to forgo a larger hard drive and, instead, load up on memory.

If money is not a major concern, then the best rule of thumb to follow is to purchase as much computer as you can afford. With more and more powerful systems entering the market in a constant stream, obsolescence is a legitimate concern. By spending more on a new system—thus buying a more technologically advanced system—chances are it will become obsolete more slowly. While you may save yourself some money at the start by purchasing a lesser system, you will probably find yourself having to make upgrades earlier on or replacing the system altogether sooner than you would had you purchased a top-of-the-line system to begin with.

Tip→	Purchase as much computer as you can afford to prevent your system from becoming obsolete too quickly.

The Vendor

Once you have decided on the system that you want, you need to decide where you will buy it. When deciding upon a computer vendor, you should consider their reputation for reliability, service, and support. Computers and their components are delicate pieces of machinery and, like any other piece of equipment, are bound to fail from time to time. When something does go wrong, the vendor's ability to promptly diagnose and rectify the problem will go a long way toward making your computer-buying experience an enjoyable one.

Tip→	When deciding upon a computer vendor, you should consider their reputation for reliability, service, and support.

The Ins and Outs of Computers

When you think of a computer, you may think of a singular item. However, a computer consists of various components—the processor, hard drive, disk drives, video and sound cards, etc. Each component requires a certain amount of understanding to make sure you create an overall system that is right for you. The major components are discussed below.

Processors: From Athlon to P-III

In the overall scheme of things, the processor is one of the smallest pieces of a computer system. However without it, the computer is rendered useless. The processor is the brain of the computer. The faster the processor, the faster the computer is able to execute operations and perform calculations. Chip (processor) manufacturers are continually battling each other for the title of fastest processor. Consequently, faster and more powerful processors enter the market every several months. In fact, Moore's Law—credited to the co-founder of Intel, states that processor speeds double every 18 months. It is perhaps disheartening to know that if you were buy a new system today, in less than two years there will probably be systems available that are twice as fast. In fact, the rate at which chip technology is advancing is almost wholly responsible for computer obsolescence.

The most significant developments in the chip market this past year were the introduction of Intel's Pentium III and AMD's Athlon (K-7) processors. These chips, part of the next generation of microprocessors, offer enhanced performance—especially in terms of multi-media and Internet usage at higher clock speeds.

Today the vast majority of PCs on the market contain chips from one of three manufacturers—AMD, Cyrix, and Intel. As of June 1999, Intel processors could be found in over 59% of new computers purchased. While Intel has been the undisputed king of processors for several years, it has been facing ever-mounting competition from AMD and, to a lessor extent, Cyrix over the past few years. At the time this section was written, AMD ruled supreme over PC chips with its 650MHz (megahertz) Athlon processor. Intel ranks a close second with its 600MHz Pentium III chip. In head-to-head tests, the Athlon and Pentium III are all but even in their performance although the Athlon is priced some 15% lower than the Pentium III. AMD promises a 700MHz model by the end of 1999; rest assured that Intel will not let itself be outdone by the competition.

While the Athlon and Pentium III represent the high-end processor market, competition is just as keen in the value market. Here AMD, Intel, and Cyrix vie for market share with the K6-2 or -3, Celeron, and M II, respectively. These chips do not offer the processing power of their high-end cousins. However, they offer enough power for all but the most power-hungry users, at only a fraction of the cost.

In Macintosh systems, chances are you'll find either a PowerPC G3 (G3 for short) or PowerPC G4 processor from Motorola. The G3 is found in the low-cost iMac and iBook, while the G4 is found in the high-end PowerMac. In head-to-head comparisons, the G3 and G4 rival and often outperform equivalent Pentium processors. One drawback is that it is not available in speeds above 500MHz.

Data Storage Media

As today's programs become more sophisticated, their needs grow in terms of the amount of hard disk space required for installation and in terms of the amount of memory they require for proper operation. To ensure that your computer will be able to meet the demands of today's and tomorrow's software, make sure it has an adequate amount of data storage media. Data storage media can be broken down into several types: temporary and permanent, internal, external, and re-movable.

Memory

In computers, temporary memory is just that—temporary. In other words, data is lost when the computer is turned off. In personal computers, RAM (random access memory), is the form of temporary data storage. The amount of RAM a system has impacts several aspects of computing, specifically what kind and how many programs can be used on a system at the same time.

The more applications you run simultaneously, the larger the files you deal with: and the more complex your operating system, the more RAM you will need. Even with a top-of-the-line processor, a lack of memory can hinder your system's performance. The graphical operating systems available today—Mac OS, Windows 9x, and Windows NT—all benefit from additional memory. Windows 3.1—which is no longer produced by Microsoft—can operate with only 4M (megabytes) of RAM. However, its "sweet spot"—the optimum amount of memory for peak performance—is 12M. In order to run Microsoft Word or Excel for Windows 9x, for example, you will require a system with at least 8M of RAM. Most systems ship today with at least 64M of RAM, which is the bare minimum you should buy. With memory prices continually falling in price—$1–$2 per megabyte—you may want to consider purchasing a system with 128M or more. This will probably cost you less than $170 and will be money well spent. When prioritizing various components of a new computer, you would be better served by forgoing a larger hard drive or more powerful processor in favor of more memory.

Tip→	When prioritizing various components of a new computer, you would be better served by forgoing a larger hard drive or more powerful processor in favor of more memory.

There may come a time when you wish to add additional memory to your computer. Two things will impact your ability to do so—the number of slots the computer has as well as the maximum amount of memory the system can handle. If the system has empty slots, you can simply add new memory components. However, if they are all full, you will have to remove existing memory components in order to add ones of larger increments. As an example, if all the sockets are filled with 16M dual in-line memory modules (DIMMs) you would have to remove them in order to increase the amount of RAM. In contrast, a system with only one 32M or 64M DIMM makes it easier to add more memory. Most new systems built today can be expanded up 384, 512, or even 768 megabytes of RAM.

Hard Drives

Temporary memory, as we have shown, is an important element of a computer. Inevitably, however, the need will arise where you will want to save data so that you can use it at a later time. This is where permanent storage comes into play. With permanent storage, the data is retained once the computer is shut off. The primary type of permanent storage found in personal computers is the hard drive. When discussing hard drives, there are three important issues—compatibility, speed, and capacity.

The Many Flavors of IDE and SCSI

Before you can decide what size hard drive you want, you should first select the drive interface—the method it uses to communicate with the computer itself. The two basic choices are IDE (integrated drive electronics) and SCSI (small computer systems interface), although there are several variations of both as well. One of the key differences between the two models and their variations is the transfer rate—the rate at which data is transferred to and from the hard disk. IDE is, for most users, the drive of choice. IDE drives are slower than SCSI drives, but offer speeds that are more than adequate for most users. In addition, they tend to cost less than SCSI drives.

When looking at non-SCSI drives, you will probably run across acronyms such as IDE, EIDE, and ATA. The main thing you need to know is that they all have basically the same technology—the nomenclature simply has to do with the rate at which data is transferred (read off or written to the drive).

SCSI drives offer the best performance and have traditionally been found in Macintosh and high-end Windows NT systems, although as a cost-cutting measure they are no longer standard on Macintosh systems. In addition, they are preferred when selecting an external drive. In recent years, however, SCSI drives have found their way into the mainstream market as well. With SCSI drives, you have a multitude of models from which to choose—Ultra SCSI, Wide SCSI, and Ultra-wide, as well as SCSI-2 and SCSI-3 drives. Here again the technology is basically the same—the main difference being burst-rate, or maximum transfer rate (for more on transfer rates, see below). SCSI drives are also generally only available for higher-capacity drives—above 10G (gigabytes).

As is usually the case, you will pay more for the higher performance and flexibility you receive with a SCSI drive. Unlike IDE or ATA drives which can be installed and used without extra hardware, SCSI drives require a controller card that allows it to interface with the computer. If your system does not have a SCSI controller, you could spend anywhere from $100 to perhaps several hundred dollars. As an example, an 18G Ultra2 Wide SCSI drive costs over $1,100 while an EIDE drive of the same capacity costs around $250.

Transfer Rate

When reading the specifications for a hard drive, you will probably run across several transfer rates—internal, burst, and sustained. The internal transfer rate of a hard drive measures the speed at which data can move between the drive head and the drive platter. A drive's burst-transfer rate refers to the maximum data transfer rate the drive can achieve for short periods of time. New IDE or Ultra ATA drives have burst-transfer rates of 33Mbps, 44Mbps, or even 66Mbps (megabytes per second). SCSI drives have burst-transfer rates of up to 80Mbps. The transfer rate with which you should be most concerned is the minimum sustained rate—which tells you how quickly data can move to and from the platter. For most desktop applications, a sustained rate of 3.5Mbps should serve you just fine.

Rotational Speed

The rotational speed of a hard disk is how fast the interior "platter" spins. Typically, the faster the drive spins, the better its performance. Rotational speeds tend to range from 4,000rpm to 5,400rpm (revolutions per minute) while high-end drives spin at speeds of 7,200rpm to 10,000rpm.

Density

The density of a drive has to do with how closely "packed" the data is on the platter. The higher the density (the more tightly packed the data is), the more data that can be stored on the drive. Drives with higher densities, all things being equal, should have a higher transfer rate as well. This is because more data is passing under the drive head with each revolution of the drive platter. Therefore, it is also possible for a drive with a slower rotation speed to still have a higher transfer rate.

Capacity

Earlier we spoke of how Moore's Law states that clock speeds for processors are doubling every 18 months. This is impressive until you realize that hard drive capacities are doubling every *12* months. At this rate, consumers can expect 100G drives to be available by 2001.

The matter of greatest practical importance when choosing a hard drive is its size. Today's graphical systems and many of the applications on the market can demand a great deal of available disk space. When selecting a drive, keep in mind the types of software programs you will be using. You want to make sure you have enough free disk space so that you do not have to delete files or programs to make room on your hard drive.

As you look at new computers, you should purchase one with a hard drive that has a capacity between 10G and 14G. While this may seem like a tremendous amount of storage space, keep in kind that if you are going to be using any type of real-time or historical data service, you will want to have the capacity to store this data. Outside of a computerized investing context, if you want to do any type of graphical design work or will be dealing with multi-media files, you will need sizable amounts of free hard disk space. Having this amount of storage will give the flexibility of installing numerous programs and saving a great deal of data without having to delete programs or files. A 13G ATA/EIDE drive costs around $160 and a 13G Ultra Wide SCSI drive will cost slightly over $200 (SCSI-2 and SCSI-3 drives usually have capacities above 18G).

Tip→ When shopping for a new computer system, you should choose one with a hard drive capacity of at least 10G (gigabytes).

41

Floppy Drives

While not as glamorous as a processor or a SCSI drive, a floppy drive is still a necessity—make sure your system has one. Beyond providing short-term storage, backups and file transfer, floppy drives are invaluable in the event of a major system crash. Using your floppy drive, you are able to boot, or start, the system. iMac, iBooks, and Powerbooks do not ship with a floppy drive, so be prepared to spend about $100 to purchase a floppy drive that connects to the USB Port on these systems.

Introduced within the last couple of years, "SuperDisk" drives (formerly referred to as LS-120 drives) from Imation are being offered up as a replacement for the typical floppy drive. This drive can read both traditional 3.5" floppies with up to 1.44M of storage space, as well as "SuperDisks" which can hold 120M of data. The advantages with SuperDisks is that, beyond having comparable storage capacity as other removable media such as Zip disks, which can store up to 250M, you can still read or write 3.5" floppy disks—a feature other removable storage media do not offer. Some of the major computer retailers provide Super-Disk drives as an upgrade option for desktops for around $100. More likely, however, you will find SuperDisk drives as an option on laptop systems. The drives themselves cost around $150 and the 120M disks cost about $15 apiece. Sony, the originator of the standard 3.5" floppy, has also entered the fray with its HiFD, which can store up to 200M on a proprietary disk, while still being able to read standard 3.5" floppies.

CD-ROM, CD-R, CD-RW, and DVD

CD-ROM (compact disc read-only memory) drives allow you to read data from compact discs as well as play ordinary music CDs. Compared to floppy drives, CD-ROM drives have data transfer rates that are much higher. However, they cannot match the transfer speeds of hard drives. As is the case with hard drives, the speed at which the CD spins translates into how fast graphics and video are read from the CD and displayed on the system. With slower drives, you may experience pauses in the video from time to time as the data is being transferred. CD-ROM drives range in speed from eight- to 52-speed and can either be internal or external. An internal 40-speed CD-ROM drive costs an average of $60. One last item of mention is the way you insert CDs into the drive. Most internal drives allow you to place a disc in a drawer that slides in and out of the drive with the press of a button. With external drives, there may be a tray system where you place the disc into a tray or case, and then manually insert into the drive. Ideally, you want an internal CD-ROM drive with a drawer system, since they tend to be easier to use.

CD-Rs (recordable compact disks) allow you to save data on CDs—something you are unable to do with a regular CD-ROM drive. CDs offer a tremendous amount of storage capacity—up to 650M—compared to other types of removable storage media. Furthermore, CDs are relatively cheap (less than $2 per disk). While CD-Rs do offer the advantage of being able to write to the CD, once it has been cut or written, the disc cannot be used again. Another drawback is that CD-R drives both read and write at speeds much slower than those of regular CD-ROM discs. The fastest a CD-R drive can write at is eight-speed. While most cannot read at speeds of more than 8x, some CD-R drives can read at speeds of up to 24x. An internal 6x/8x (writes at six-speed and reads at eight-speed) CD-R drive costs just about $220.

The shortcomings of not being able to re-record CD-Rs was solved with the introduction of CD-RW (re-writable compact disc) drives. CD-RW discs can be reused hundreds of times and can be read in any standard multi-session drive. Again, however, the read and write at speeds are well below those of regular CD-ROM drives and the discs cost more—around $10 per disc. There has been some price convergence between CD-R and CD-RW drives over the past year—the average cost for an internal 6x/24x CD-RW drive is around $200. Lastly, CD-RW drives can handle CDs, CD-Rs, and CD-RWs.

DVD or DVD-ROM, which stands for digital versatile disc, is making its way into the computing mainstream. Although there are a number of movie titles being released for DVD, software development has been almost nil, with the exception of some titles in the gaming area and reference area (such as encyclopedias). The hope is, with the release of Windows 98 and its better support for the DVD file system and built-in drivers and decoders, the number of software applications available for DVD will increase.

First-generation DVD drives were limited in their ability to play CD-R discs. Today's DVD drives can read all types of CDs—standard music CDs, CD-Rs, and CD-RWs. Make sure your DVD drive delivers 4.8x DVD performance or better. While this speed may seem slow when compared to a standard CD-ROM drive, remember that 1x DVD throughput is 1,250Kbps and a CD is only 150Kbps (kilobytes per second).

Beyond the physical drive, you will also need a decoder to view the video contained on a DVD disc. There are two types of decoders—software and hardware. Hardware decoding is less CPU-intensive and is recommended for systems with processors less than a Pentium II—a problem you will not experience if you purchase a brand new, top-of-the-line system. Depending on the type of graphics card your system has—again dependent on its age—you may also need a hardware decoder.

Brand new systems should have the processing power to support software decoding, although it still places a considerable burden on the CPU which, in turn, could reduce video quality. Computer retailers typically offer DVD upgrades with either software or hardware decoding for under $100.

In addition, there are recordable DVDs (DVD-RAM), which allow users to write data to discs just like CD-Rs and CD-RWs. These drives are also able to read all CD formats. The main attraction DVD-RAM has is its capacity—5.2G for double-sided cartridges or 2.6G for single-sided. This means that for one double-sided cartridge, you are given the storage capacity of over five 1G Jaz cartridges, eight 650M CDs, or over 3,600 standard 3.5" floppies.

Expect to pay about a $100 premium for a DVD drive over a traditional CD-ROM drive. A rival standard has also recently arisen—DVD+RW (DVD plus rewritable). While the writing technique is similar to that of DVD-RAM, current DVD drives cannot read DVD+RW discs. The same is true for DVD+RW drives, which can read all CD formats except DVD-RAM. It still remains to be seen which standard will ultimately win out, but it seems safe to say that writable DVD is here to stay.

Additional Removable Storage Options

Removable disk drives approximate the speed of slow hard drives and allow you to store, access, and even execute programs directly from them. These drives have uses as short-, medium-, and long-term storage, as well as transferring and transporting data from one system to another. Removable drives can also be either internal or external. Unless you plan on using the drive with multiple computers, you should go with an internal drive. Otherwise, you would probably require a parallel port or SCSI version.

To save yourself a great deal of torment, it is highly suggested that you establish an effective backup system for your computer. While breakdowns of computer *equipment* are infrequent, crashes caused by ill-behaving software can wreak havoc on your system. Abnormal program terminations, a.k.a. "program bombs," can corrupt system files and render your system inoperable. Without frequent and up-to-date backups, you could spend hours attempting to rebuild your systems. Don't wait until it is too late to implement a backup system.

Warning→	Without frequent and up-to-date backups, you could spend hours attempting to rebuild your systems. Don't wait until it is too late to implement a backup system.

Tape Drives

As the size of hard drives continue to grow, and the amount of data stored on them, tape backup drives are becoming a more desirable method of storage. Since the speed at which data is retrieved is considerably slower than that of a floppy disk, backup tape drives are generally used for more long-term storage of files. The three main types on the market today for consumer use are QIC (quarter-inch cartridge), DAT (digital audio tape) and its DDS (digital data standard) standard, and 8mm helical-scan.

Zip/Jaz Drives

The industry leaders in removable storage are Iomega's Zip and Jaz drives. Internal Zip drives offer data transfer rates slightly below that of a hard drive, while external parallel port drives operate at much slower speeds. Zip drives offer both 100M of storage and 250M. Zip 100 drives typically cost around $100 and are available in both internal and external models. Most computer manufacturers offer Zip 100s as an additional option. Zip 250 drives are also available as both internal and external and cost around $170. Six-packs of 250M disks and 100M disks cost $100 and $80, respectively.

The Jaz drive offers 1G or 2G of storage capacity per disk, but it is becoming increasingly difficult to find new 1G drives. The 2G drives currently cost $350 with a three-pack of 2G disks costing $300.

Tip→	If you are looking for a removable drive, the Iomega Zip or Jaz drive should fit most storage needs. For basic backup needs, an internal Zip drive, with 100M or 250M of storage space per disk and a reasonable price tag, is a good choice.

Monitors: Size Matters

While the computer itself performs the analysis and tasks you want, the monitor is important in that it displays the finished product. When shopping for your new computer system, make sure the quote you receive includes the monitor, as not all companies include this cost in their computer prices. As you are comparing prices for your new system, don't attempt to save money by skimping on the monitor. While other aspects of a computer, such as the amount of memory, can be upgraded or expanded by simply adding more, a monitor can only be upgraded by buying a whole new one. The increased viewing area and clarity of a better monitor will be well worth the money (not to mention the fact that your eyes will thank you).

When looking at monitors, there are basically four critical factors to consider:

Warning→	When you see a quote for a new computer system, make sure a monitor is included. Some companies quote computer prices without including a monitor.

- Size

- Resolution

- Refresh rate

- Dot Pitch

The size of the monitor determines how much "real estate" you have for displaying data. Typical monitor sizes for personal computers range from 15" to 19". Monitors that are 21" and larger are generally reserved for desktop publishing and computer-aided design (CAD) applications. Most new computers today come with a 17" monitor standard, otherwise a 15" monitor is typically provided. Upgrading from a 15" to a 17" monitor is usually less than $250 and will provide you with over 30% more viewing area. You can find 19" monitors for under $500—the price of a high-quality 17" monitor. The extra cost will be more than recovered in reduced eye discomfort over several years of ownership. If you do decide on a larger monitor, keep in mind the desktop space you will need for it. A monitor is typically as deep as the diagonal length of the screen. If you are short on desk space, you may opt for a short-depth monitor, or a flat panel display. However, be aware that these will cost extra over a standard monitor.

Tip→	As a rule, purchase the largest monitor you can afford, since you will be viewing it as often as you use your computer.

A monitor's resolution is the number of pixels in both the horizontal and vertical directions and determines the relative size of the objects on the desktop. A higher resolution means objects will appear more clearly on the screen. When running at high resolutions, such as 1024 by 768 or higher, the need for a larger monitor becomes more apparent. At such resolutions on a 14" monitor, for example, the objects become so small that viewing becomes difficult.

Keep in mind that the signal for the monitor comes from the video card. The type of video card in the computer will limit the display modes you can use on the monitor. Therefore, make sure the video card can support the best modes offered by the monitor.

> **Warning→** Even if you have the money for a larger monitor, make sure you have the desktop space for it as well. Typically a monitor is as deep as the diagonal length of the screen.

The refresh rate of a monitor refers to the number of times the screen is redrawn each second. The higher the refresh rate, the less the screen flickers or strobes. Reducing the flickering of the screen lessons the strain on the eyes. For the best viewing, look for a monitor with a refresh rate of at least 75Hz (hertz). For larger displays such as 19" or 21" monitors, a refresh rate of 85MHz is recommended.

Dot pitch has to do with the distance between the phosphors in the monitor and only applies to CRT (cathode ray tubes) monitors, not LCD displays. As a rule, the smaller the pitch, the clearer the images that appear on the screen. The largest you should go is a 0.28mm diagonal dot pitch, while a dot pitch of 0.25mm or smaller offers a clearer display.

In conclusion, a new monitor should be at least 17", support a high refresh rate (at least 75Hz), and have a dot pitch no larger than 0.28mm. Purchased separately, such a monitor currently costs around $350.

Sound and Video

> **Warning→** Before spending money on a new monitor, make sure your video card can support the best display modes offered by the monitor.

With the advancements that have been made in PC audio and video the past few years, you have the potential of turning your computer into a home entertainment system. Even if this isn't your goal, you shouldn't skimp when it comes to quality audio and video for your new system. If you purchase a system with a DVD player, you will want to get a surround sound speaker system to enjoy the Dolby surround associated with DVD movies. Be aware that many of today's more advanced investment software packages offer multimedia tutorials that integrate sound and video into them.

The most popular sound cards today are those that offer Wavetable sound. For the fullest sound possible, make sure the sound card you purchase offers 64-voice Wavetable sound. Cards offering 64-voice sound cost $50 and up.

> **Tip→** For the fullest sound possible, make sure the sound card you purchase offers 64-voice Wavetable sound.

With the advent of MMX technology, 3-D has arrived with the PC. Most of the video boards that ship with today's computers offer both 2-D and 3-D graphics. Even if you aren't planning on doing any gaming with your PC, the extra cost is negligible. For quality 2-D and 3-D graphics, you should select a video board with at least 4M of video RAM. Video RAM of 8M will benefit those people with monitors with high refresh rates and resolutions as well as those looking for optimal 3-D performance. Cards such as these cost between $100 and $200.

> **Tip→** For quality 2-D and 3-D graphics, you should select a video board with at least 4M of video RAM.

The latest audio option to enter the market is "3D" audio. Most new systems have sound cards that support 3D audio. 3D audio provides enhanced audio with depth and realism—an added bonus for games and movies. To complement these new audio cards, systems are sold with surround sound speaker systems that best broadcast the enhanced audio.

At this point there is no overriding standard—in fact there are several from which to choose. While a technical discussion of these standards is beyond the scope of this chapter, be aware that such options are available when selecting a new computer system.

Printers

Printers, while technically not part of the computer itself, are a vital part of any computer system. You will find this out when you want to print out text, a Web page, or a chart. Printers, just like computers, come in many different kinds with numerous options and issues to consider. Some of these include:

- Resolution

- Printer Language

- Memory

- Cartridge/Toner Life

- Performance Requirements

The standard for resolution today is 600x600 dpi (dots per inch), but higher and lower resolutions are also available. If possible, you should avoid printers with lower resolutions. Furthermore, you don't need high resolutions such as 1,200 dpi unless you plan to print high-quality graphics, i.e. photographs. Keep in mind that many inkjets have different resolutions for color and black and white (monochrome).

Printer languages have become less important since Windows has largely taken over the desktop, but they are items that you still need to be aware of. If you plan on printing only on your own printer and use only Windows programs, any printer language will do as long as you have a Windows or Windows 95 driver, as appropriate. A driver is software that allows the printer and your software to interact. If you need to print from DOS programs, avoid Windows GDI printers, or at least make sure they can use a widely used language, such as PCL. If you think you will be sharing files with others and need to maintain the formatting exactly, PostScript is still the language of choice.

The amount of memory in a printer can make a difference in speed and print quality. Some color laser printers, for example, keep their base price down by including just enough memory for 300-dpi printing. If you want a higher resolution, you'll need more memory. Make sure you'll have enough memory for the kinds of documents that you plan to print. When you compare printer prices from different sources, make sure the printers have the same amount of memory.

Take a look at both the price of an ink or toner cartridge for any given printer and the number of pages it will print. An inexpensive cartridge that prints relatively few pages may actually be much more costly than a more expensive cartridge that prints more pages. Higher-capacity cartridges also mean you won't have to change them as often, which can be particularly important depending on how much printing you plan on doing. If you are using a color inkjet printer, look for a model that uses separate black/white and color cartridges.

Make sure you get a printer whose performance matches your needs. In general, laser printers are faster than inkjets, though the fastest inkjets are as fast as many personal lasers. The rated speeds for printers refer to the time it takes to print a page once the actual printing begins, rather than actual print times that include processing time for each image.

Another performance issue to consider is that a printer can affect the performance of your computer, depending on whether the printer itself does the rasterizing—the work of turning printer commands into an image—or whether it relies on your computer to do the work. Most laser and solid-ink printers, as well as some inkjets, have a processor and enough memory so the printer itself can rasterize the image. This lets the computer hand the print job over to the printer for processing, and lets you get back to work while the print job finishes. Most ink-jets and some laser do all the work at the host computer, sending only the final image to the printer. This makes for a less expensive printer, because the printer doesn't need a processor or much memory, but it ties up the host computer during printing.

Having covered some of the issues to consider when looking for a printer, we can now examine the types of printers. Printers for use with personal computers fall into two main technology groups:

- Inkjet

- Laser

Inkjet printers offer both black and white or color printing. They work by squirting liquid ink through a nozzle that forms the image of text or graphics on the page. They are fairly cheap, fast, quiet, and achieve respectable resolution—at least business-letter quality. Color printing is usually an additional option, at additional cost. This feature can be useful for distinguishing between data on printed graphs with multiple lines or bars—often a concern when printing reports from investment software and information from the World Wide Web. Having the added flexibility of printing in color typically warrants the increased cost. A good-quality color inkjet printer will cost $100 and up, offering good print quality, speed, and color at a reasonable price.

Laser printers should support either PCL levels 1-6 (Printer Control Language) and/or Postscript levels 1, 2 or 3. These are printer control standards that affect the quality of the printed output. They represent two separate schemes for transmitting character descriptions to the printer. Postscript, developed by Adobe, is the standard within the desktop publishing industry. The fonts and graphics supported by PCL are usually adequate for normal business use.

Laser printers work by bonding powdered toner ink to high-quality paper under high-heat conditions. Laser printers are fast, increasingly cheap to manufacture, and produce the best output of the two technologies. Personal laser printers do not usually support color, although this technology is becoming more accessible all the time. Black and white laser printers cost, on average, $150 and up while color personal laser printers start at around $1,300.

Tip→	If you are seeking good print quality, speed, and color for a reasonable price, a color inkjet printer provides the best mix for your new system.

Modems: The Key to the Internet

A modem (modulator/demodulator) allows communications between computers over POTS (plain old telephone lines) and is generally used to access commercial on-line services, Internet service providers (ISPs), or the Internet.

Today's modems are capable of using advanced error correction and data compression to achieve much higher data transfer rates than their basic connection speeds allow. A 28.8Kbps (kilobits per second) modem may allow data transfer at 115.2Kbps when correctly configured and accessing another equivalent, compatible modem.

Most new computers ship with 56.6Kbps modems. These modems allow you to download data at 56Kbps but will only allow you to upload data at 33.6Kbps. In reality, due to FCC regulations, the modems are capable of up to 53Kbps. Furthermore, when line conditions are taken into account, the average rate you will currently achieve is up to 46.6Kbps.

On February 6, 1998, the International Telecommunication Union, the governing body of world telecommunications, agreed on a standard for 56K modems: V.90. In doing so, it ended a struggle between two competing, non-compatible standards: K56flex from Rockwell International/Lucent Technologies and x2 from 3Com. In the past, Internet service providers had to provide modem pools and servers to cater to both of these technologies. With a universal standard, they can devote resources to a single standard, benefiting the consumer. A V.90 56Kbps data modem can run from $30 to just under $200 and offer a variety of bells and whistles.

Warning→	No matter what type of modem you purchase, make sure the Internet service provider or on-line service you subscribe to is compatible with your modem.

No matter what type of modem you end up purchasing, make sure that the Internet service provider or on-line service you subscribe to is compatible with your modem.

Alternatives to modems, which tend to offer much greater connection speeds, are also available depending on your geographic location. These include ADSL (asymmetric digital subscriber lines), cable modem, and satellite. ADSL service is offered by phone companies, although not in all areas. It uses standard phone lines and offers theoretical download rates of 128Kbps to 8Mbps. Most services offer download speeds of up to 1.5Mbps. ADSL service costs between $50 and $250 per month, with an additional $100 to $300 for equipment and installation.

As is the case with all of these methods, ISP (Internet service provider) fees are extra. ADSL has been plagued by the lack of an industry standard—the same problem the 56Kbps modem industry had until 1998. However, the adoption of the G.Lite standard should allow ADSL to gain wider acceptance.

Cable modems offer an "always on" Internet connection with speeds ranging from 3Mbps to 4Mbps. Cable modem service, unlike ADSL, usually does not allow you to select your own ISP—which means you are locked into one service and fee structure. Monthly fees range from $40 to $50 per month. Setup costs vary by region—$100–$300.

Depending on your geographic location, your only high-speed Internet option may be satellite. Hughes Electronics DirecPC provides download speeds of up to 400Kbps. The service, however, does have several drawbacks. First, you still need a phone connection in order to upload, or send, data. This means you may have to install a second phone line. Furthermore, beyond the $200 cost for equipment, you are levied *hourly* usage fees—$30 for 25 hours, $50 for 100 hours, or $130 for 200 hours. Lastly, the 24" dish you install outside must have a clear view of the southern sky.

Operating Systems

The primary operating systems supported today on IBM-compatible personal computers are DOS, Windows 3.x (3.1 and 3.11), Windows 9x (95 or 98), and Windows NT. At this point in time, a new computer system should have Windows 98 or Windows NT 4.0 pre-installed.

Apple Computer has the proprietary rights to the Mac OS (operating system) and no Apple computer is shipped without the Mac OS. The latest version of the Mac OS is system 8.5 and should be found on all new Macintosh systems.

At this point in time Windows 9x is the operating system of choice for the individual investor. Windows NT 4.0, which offers a more stable platform, suffers from a lack of software and hardware support found with Windows 9x. For portable computer users, Windows 9x also has the best built-in support as well. PCMCIA (standard credit card-sized plug-in adapters such as modems) and battery conservation features built into portable systems require special control drivers that are native to the Windows 9x operating system. These drivers can be added to Windows 3.x systems but often lead to restricted memory access. Third-party software often must be used with Windows NT systems to take advantage of items such as PCMCIA cards.

Windows 2000, which is marked for release late in 1999, should become the standard operating system for high-end compatible PCs. Windows 2000 promises the stability of Windows NT with the hardware plug and play support of Windows 98.

Desktops vs. Laptops

After deciding whether or not you will purchase a new computer, inevitably the question of whether to go with a desktop or laptop system will arise. While both have their merits, their functionality (and usefulness to you) depends in large part on the intended uses of the computer.

As you analyze your computing needs and any of these concerns come to mind, perhaps a laptop will serve your needs better than a desktop:

- Do you work while travelling?

- Will you need to move the computer from room to room or location to location?

- Do you have space (desktop) constraints?

However, if your concerns tend to lie in any of these directions, a desktop may be the preferred choice:

- Will you be working at one location?

- Do you plan to upgrade in the future?

- Do you have budget constraints?

- Do you prefer a larger display?

- Are you interested in the best performance and the latest features?

When dealing with desktop and laptop systems, be aware that you face differing upgrade possibilities. Desktop systems tend to be easier to upgrade and repair, largely because there are a number of "generic" components available that can be installed with relative ease and without compatibility issues. Laptops, on the other hand, are more delicate creatures and offer less upgrade possibilities. In addition, they are more difficult and expensive to upgrade and repair. If you wish to upgrade a laptop, oftentimes you need to go directly to the manufacturer to obtain component parts to ensure they function properly with the system.

Lastly, there is a sizable price difference between laptops and desktops. Given two relatively identical systems in terms of computing power, the desktop system will cost several hundred dollars less than the laptop as the following table shows.

	Dell Inspiron 7500 Notebook	**Dell Dimension**
Processor	400MHz Pentium III	600MHz Pentium III
Memory	128M RAM	128M RAM
Display	15"	17" (16.0" viewable area)
DVD-ROM	24x max	40x max
Hard Drive	6.x DVD w/software decoding	6.x DVD w/hardware decoding
Modem	56K	56K
Cost	$3,364	$1,873

To Upgrade or Buy a New System?

If you currently own a computer, after examining your computing needs the next logical question would be whether your current system can support what you want to do. As an example, let's take a look at an average system from four years ago: Pentium 75 processor, 16M of memory, and a 15" monitor. On a system such as this, many of the components can either be replaced or enhanced to boost the system's overall performance. If this cannot be done, the next step would be to decide whether it is worth the time, money, and effort to upgrade your system, or whether you should simply purchase an entirely new system.

If you decide that upgrading the system is a viable option, here are some of the ways you can enhance the components, along with current prices. As an aside, it is also a good idea to contact the computer manufacturer before you upgrade to make sure you are using appropriate components.

 Warning→ Before you attempt to upgrade your system, contact the manufacturer to make sure you are using the correct components.

Faster Processor

The first element to look at when upgrading a computer is the processor. The processor dictates how quickly information is processed. If your existing system is not built around at least a Pentium-class or equivalent processor, you would probably be best served to purchase a whole new system. While there are potential upgrades that could be made, the time, cost, and potential headaches are not worth the end result—a sub-standard system (at best).

If you have an older Pentium processor, you may be able to squeeze a little more life from the existing system by upgrading the CPU. Upgrade modules are available that allow you to upgrade a 75MHz Pentium to an MMX-enhanced processor running at 233MHz for around $100 or a 333MHz for around $180.

Be aware that, of all upgrades, upgrading the CPU can be the trickiest. If you aren't comfortable performing that kind of surgery on your system, leave it to an expert, or leave it alone!

More Memory

Computer memory, or RAM (random access memory), comes in two main types: SIMMs (single in-line memory modules) and DIMMs (dual in-line memory modules). SIMMs tend to be found in older systems, while DIMMs are found in newer ones. DIMMs cannot be installed in the place of SIMMs and vice versa. The slot configuration of your motherboard will dictate the combinations of DIMMs or SIMMs you will need to install to achieve the required amount. On average, an 8M EDO (extended data out) SIMM, which is faster than conventional SIMMs, will cost around $25. A 32M DIMM costs around $75. The bare minimum amount of memory you need to run most Windows software today is 16M. Considering how inexpensive memory has become, you may want to consider installing 64M of memory. Furthermore, depending on how long you plan on keeping your existing system, it may be worthwhile to upgrade to 128M of memory. Adding additional memory will benefit those users running Windows applications.

Bigger Hard Drive

Those who are constantly deleting files or programs in order to make room for new ones should consider a new hard drive. In addition, if you are planning on performing fundamental screening or technical analysis, you may need a larger hard drive to accommodate the large amounts of data these types of analysis require. If your system currently has an IDE drive (integrated drive electronics), you can either add a second drive or replace the existing one. For systems with older ESDI drive systems, finding a replacement will be much harder. If you think you will be purchasing a new system in the near future, it would probably be best to purchase an IDE drive. Furthermore, you may wish to limit yourself to spending no more than $200. In today's market, this will still get you a drive with a capacity of 2.5G to 17G. If your system uses SCSI (small drive computer systems interface), which is what most old Macs use, you may wish to go with a relatively inexpensive, low-capacity drive. Otherwise, if you want, buy a top-of-the line, high-capacity SCSI drive that you can transfer to a new system down the road.

Faster Video

In order to display data more rapidly on your monitor you can add a faster video card to your system. Before you purchase a new video card, however, be sure that your monitor will support the best settings of the new card in order to get the best performance. For a graphics acceleration card with 16M of video RAM that will support 3-D graphics, the cost will be $100 and higher.

Larger Monitor

By replacing your existing monitor with a larger one, you are able to see more data at a higher resolution. However, this is only the case if the video card in your system will support the best settings of the monitor. Before you spend the money on a new monitor, make sure it will be supported by your existing video card. The benefits of a larger viewing area will become apparent when working with spreadsheet-like views of company information. The average cost for a 17" monitor is $300.

Multimedia Capability

More and more, today's software is being shipped on CD-ROM disks and it implements sound into the program. In order to enjoy the full experience of these programs, look into purchasing a multimedia kit comprised of a sound card, CD-ROM, and speakers. A multimedia kit consisting of a 16x CD-ROM drive, sound card, and speakers costs an average of $100.

Modem

If you happen to still be using a 14.4Kbps modem, an upgrade to a 56.6Kbps modem will enhance your Internet experience. If you have a 28.8Kbps modem, the decision is yours. While there will be some improvement in speed, it will not double the speed that you connect at. An internal 56.6Kbps modem will cost you around $70.

The Results

Let's get back to the example of an average system from four years ago. Taking this system and performing a variety of component upgrades, replacements, and additions, we arrive at a system approaching a Pentium/333 with 64M of memory, a 17G hard drive, enhanced video performance, multimedia capabilities, and a 17" monitor, all for around $1,100 (assuming all the components can be installed on your own).

The Pitfalls to Upgrading

Looking at the resulting system after performing the various upgrades, you are still faced with the reality that you have a system equal to a low-end modern day system. You may be extending the useful life of the system for another year or two, but at the end of that time period you will still have to commit to purchasing a new system.

Be aware that there are hidden costs involved in upgrading a computer. First of all, depending on how comfortable you are with opening up the system and adding or removing components, you may have to have the upgrades installed by a professional. Be prepared to pay a healthy sum to have this work done by someone else. In addition, if you use components from a variety of different vendors, you run the risk of having conflicts arise that may render one or all of the systems inoperable.

Tip→	Before performing any upgrade of your system, analyze the costs associated with upgrading (both monetary and non-monetary) and compare those costs with the price of purchasing a new system.

Lastly, before you think that the only thing your outdated computer is good for is an over-sized paperweight, be aware that it can be a tax write-off by donating it to a qualifying organization such as many schools and charities.

Your Purchasing Plan

At this point, you are on the home stretch. You have answered the difficult questions of whether you need to upgrade or buy a new system, you have decided on the components you want with your new system, and you have chosen between either a desktop or laptop system. While the light at the end of the tunnel may be visible, you have one important decision left; one that could make or break your entire purchase: Where do you buy your new system?

Where to Buy

In today's marketplace, you basically have two choices of where to buy a computer—directly through a mail-order vendor or from a local retail store. While many systems, such as Dell and Gateway, are only available from mail-order sources, several large and reliable manufacturers, such as IBM and Compaq, make computers that are available at retail outlets. In addition, there are a large number of computer "superstores" that market a wide variety of personal computers. These stores offer convenience as well as discounted prices. They carry a wide range of software and hardware, although you should not expect to find many of the specialized investment software packages there.

Mail Order

Most mail-order sources are reliable, but as is the case with any retailer, you must consider the possibility that not everything will work right out of the box. Companies like Dell and Gateway 2000 have a good reputation for delivering what they promise when they promise it. One major trade-off with purchasing from a mail-order company is the lack of face-to-face assistance offered by retailers should something go wrong. You do, however, typically have free telephone support. In addition, most mail-order companies offer one year of free on-site service as part of any warranty. These two options should cover the majority of problems, at least for the first year. After that, should something go wrong, chances are you will have to ship the computer back to the manufacturer for any repairs. Here you will have to pay for the shipping and insurance costs.

> **Tip→** One major trade-off with purchasing from a mail-order company is the lack of face-to-face assistance offered by retailers should something go wrong.

For those looking for repair service coverage for a longer period of time, many larger mail-order companies have signed third-party agreements to provide continuing maintenance. However, these contracts can be quite expensive and are not worth the additional cost for periods beyond three years. Another line of defense is the "buyer protection plans" offered by most credit card companies. In case you are not satisfied with your new computer, you can look to the credit card company as a personal advocate.

A typical mail-order source will charge 20% to 25% less than the manufacturer's suggested retail price. Direct mail vendors such as Dell will offer equipment that may cost 5% or 10% less than a comparable machine sold through other sources. Remember, though, to figure in shipping and handling charges and any applicable sales tax.

Mail-order manufacturers generally build their systems to buyer specifications. As a result, you are more apt to find the exact system you are looking for through a mail-order company. In addition, due to inventory practices, these companies also tend to be able to bring new technologies to consumers in a more timely manner than retail companies since it takes less time to sell out inventories of older technologies. On the flip-side, however, these same practices may also mean that you may have to wait for a popular technology to be restocked.

Retail

Buying from a retail store doesn't necessarily mean you will be paying full price. Many retailers offer discounts on hardware or package deals with a system purchase, which provides savings to the consumer. On the other hand, once you have purchased the system, it may be difficult to get a retailer to offer free consultation and technical support.

When you walk into a retail store, you are typically confronted with several computers of various configurations. While it may be possible to find a system that offers almost everything you are looking for, be prepared for the possibility that you will have to alter your wants to fit the systems available. When you do decide on a system, find out how long it has been on the shelf so you can get an idea of how new the components are.

Cross-Company Considerations

There are several areas you need to consider whether you purchase from a retailer or mail-order company. Those include:

- Reliability

- Service and technical support

- Return policies

When you purchase a new computer, you want it to work right out the box. Some companies have a better reputation than others when it comes to delivering products that work the first time. You want to make sure the company you choose has a reputation of delivering working products, not ones that are DOA!

In the event that something goes wrong, you want a company with a technical support staff that can properly diagnose and solve your problems. Before that, however, you want to be able to get through to a real person on the telephone. You can test this for yourself by calling a company's technical support number and timing how long you are on hold (provided the line is not busy) before you reach a technician.

If are unsatisfied with your purchase, some companies will give you a full refund, less shipping and handling for mail-order companies. Some retail companies also charge a restocking fee when taking a system back. Find out how much it will cost you should you return the computer.

The best way to find out about the reliability of a computer is either through your own research or through word-of-mouth. Talk with friends or co-workers who have purchased a computer recently and ask them about their experience. Attend a meeting of a local computer special interest group if there is one in your area. Magazines such as PC Magazine or PC World conduct regular surveys that could give you an idea of a particular company's performance. You can also try the Better Business Bureau or your state's Department of Consumer Affairs for further details.

Tip→	You can test a company's technical support by calling the technical support number and timing how long you are on hold (provided the line is not busy) before you reach a technician.

Warranties: Hedging Your Bets

After spending thousands of dollars on a new PC, you don't want to turn around and spend more money if the hard drive is wiped out by a virus or the modem stops working. Most mail-order companies offer on-site service for the first year of a warranty, oftentimes at no additional cost. If you are not comfortable with replacing computer components and waiting for a replacement part to arrive (you may need to return the defective part before you receive the replacement), you may opt for an extended on-site service agreement. While this will cost you extra, the peace of mind it gives you may well be worth it. When considering the length of any computer service agreement, however, it is probably not worth the money to purchase one that lasts for more than three years. Especially in this era of rapidly-changing technology, in three years you will probably be considering purchasing a whole new system, anyway.

If you are new to the computer game, do not try to save money by going with a scaled-down warranty. Ideally, a service agreement will cover parts and labor for at least two years, free on-site service for the first year, and a free 24-hours-a-day, seven-days a week toll-free technical support line.

Tip→	When considering the length of any computer service agreement, it is probably not worth the money to purchase one that lasts for more than three years.

Surge Protectors

A small and relatively inexpensive piece of equipment many people overlook is a surge protector. Costing from $100 and up, they can keep you from having to re-place a $2,000+ system. Many surge protectors offer insurance as well, often as much as $25,000 or $50,000. If your computer is damaged by a power surge or lightning strike while it is plugged into such a surge protector, you are entitled to compensation from the manufacturer.

Tip→	A surge protector is a small and relatively inexpensive piece of equip-ment that can offer insurance against damage caused by power surges.

Putting It All Together: The Final Specifications

To reiterate, individual computing needs are just that and will vary from person to person. The type of system you buy depends largely on what you need and what you can afford. Buy the best system you can, since computer technology is changing so rapidly. Consider also the current and future intended uses of the system. Be concerned about the vendor's reputation for reliability, service, and support.

A typical new IBM-compatible desktop system should include the following:

- Pentium III 600+MHz processor or equivalent

- 128M of memory

- 10G–14G hard drive

- 3.5" floppy drive & Zip disk or equivalent removable storage medium

- 6x–8x DVD-ROM drive

- Wavetable sound card capable of 64 voices

- 56.6Kbps internal modem

- 17" monitor

- color inkjet printer

- As of September 1999, a system such as this costs around $1,952 from a mail-order source (excluding taxes and shipping charges).

A typical Macintosh system, roughly comparable to the IBM-compatible system should include:

- 450MHz PowerPC G4 processor

- 128M RAM

- 20G hard drive

- Zip disk

- DVD-ROM drive

- Built-in sound

- 56Kbps internal modem with software

- 17" monitor

- color inkjet printer

As of September 1999, a system such as this, purchased directly from Apple, would cost around $3,000 (excluding tax and shipping charges).

In Closing...

Given the rapid changes in technology, the only thing certain is that what is top-of-the-line this year will be relegated to mid-line by the next. Some readers and users have voiced their concern that the systems discussed here are too advanced

for their needs. Our goal has been to recommend systems that will provide sufficient computing power for the next few years and, perhaps, beyond. The ultimate
decision, however, is yours to make. Good luck!

Glossary of Equipment Terms

ADSL

Short for asymmetric digital subscriber line, a technology that allows more data to be sent over existing copper telephone lines (POTS, plain old telephone lines). ADSL supports data rates of from 1.5 to 9 Mbps when receiving data (known as the downstream rate) and from 16 to 640 Kbps when sending data (known as the upstream rate).

Athlon

AMD's seventh-generation 650MHz microprocessor for x86 systems introduced in 1999.

ATA (Advanced Technology Attachment)

Method of interface between a computer's motherboard and hard drive. ATA is the "official" name that the American National Standards Institute (ANSI) uses for IDE (Integrated Drive Electronics). (See IDE)

Bandwidth

The amount of data that can be transmitted in a fixed amount of time.

Baud

A measure of the speed of data transmission. Baud was the prevalent measure for data transmission speed and was confused with bps (bits per second). Bps is a more accurate expression to describe data transmission speed. (See Kbps)

BIOS (basic input/output system)

Built-in software that determines what a computer can do without accessing programs from a disk. On PCs, the BIOS contains all the code required to control the keyboard, display screen, disk drives, and serial communications.

Byte

A unit of computer storage made up of eight binary digits (bits). A byte has the storage capability of a single character, such as a letter, number, or typographic for example "f," "3," or "?").

Cable modem

A modem that operates over cable TV lines. Because the coaxial cable used by cable TV provides much greater bandwidth than telephone lines, a cable modem can be used to achieve extremely fast access to the World Wide Web.

CD-ROM (Compact Disc-Read Only Memory)
A compact disc format used to hold large amounts of data—up to 650M.

CD-R (CD-Recordable)
A recordable CD-ROM technology used to create CD-ROM and audio CDs. The drive allows the disc to be written once.

CD-RW (CD-ReWritable)
A rewritable CD-ROM technology that can be used to write to CD-R discs and read CD-ROMs. A CD-RW disc can be reused multiple times.

CPU (Central processing unit)
The part of a computer that controls all the other parts. The "brain" of a computer. (See processor and microprocessor)

CRT (cathode ray tube)
The technology used in most televisions and computer display screens. A CRT works by moving an electron beam back and forth across the back of the screen. Each time the beam makes a pass across the screen, it lights up phosphor dots on the inside of the glass tube, thereby illuminating the active portions of the screen. By drawing many such lines from the top to the bottom of the screen, it creates an entire screenful of images.

Clock speed
Also called clock rate, the speed at which a microprocessor executes instructions. An internal clock regulates the rate at which instructions are executed and coordinates various computer components. Measured in megahertz (Mhz).

DAT (Digital Audio Tape)
A type of magnetic tape that uses a helical scan read/write head to record data. DAT cartridges hold between 2G to 24G of data.

Data transfer rate
The speed at which data can be transmitted from one device to another. Data rates are often measured in megabits (Mbps--million bits) or megabytes (Mbps--million bytes) per second.

DDS (Digital Data Storage)
The industry standard for digital audio tape (DAT) formats. (See DAT)

Density
Refers to how tightly information is packed together on a storage medium (tape or disk). A higher density means that data are closer together, so the medium can hold more information.

DIMM (double in-line memory module)
A double SIMM—a module that holds RAM chips on a circuit board with pins to connect it to the motherboard or the memory board. (See SIMM)

Disk drive
A very fast input/output device that reads and writes data onto a disk.

Diskette
A small portable magnetic disk used for data storage. These are sometimes called "floppy disks" or "floppies." Floppies are 3.5" (in size and 5.25" on older computers), with several densities and formats.

DOS (Disk Operating System)
The name of the operating system first used in IBM's personal computers. PC-DOS or MS-DOS operates by line-oriented commands and is non-graphical.

Dot pitch
Dot pitch specifications for a monitor controls the sharpness of the image. Desktop monitors usually come with a 0.28mm or lower dot pitch.

DPI (dots per inch)
Refers to the resolution of images. The more dots per inch, the higher the resolution.

DRAM (Dynamic Random Access Memory)
A type of memory used to store information on a computer.

Driver
Software that allows the printer and your software program to interact.

DVD (Digital Video or Digital Versatile Disc)
The newer video CD and high-capacity CD-ROM technology. The disc is similar to a CD-ROM, but it can be recorded on both sides. A double-sided cartridge holds 5.2G, equal to eight CD-ROMs.

DVD-RAM
Rewritable compact discs developed by the DVD Consortium that provides much greater data storage than today's CD-RW systems.

DVD+RW
A new standard for rewritable DVD that is in competition with the DVD-RAM standard. The two standards are incompatible. DVD+RW disks have a slightly higher capacity—3G per side, versus 2.6G per side for DVD-RAM disks.

EIDE (Enhanced Integrated Drive Electronics)
A standard mass storage device interface. It supports data rates of between 4Mbps and 16.6Mbps, about three to four times faster than the old IDE standard.

G.Lite
Single consumer-oriented global standard for high-speed data access over phone lines.

GDI (Graphical Device Interface)
A Windows standard for representing graphical objects and transmitting them to output devices, such as monitors and printers.

Gigabyte (Gig or GB or G)
A measure of memory capacity. Equal to 1,024 megabytes.

Hard disk (HD)
Part of a magnetic storage device unit that is a computer's primary storage medium. This unit includes a hard disk drive (HDD). Most hard disks are not portable, but permanently sealed in the drive. There are also removable hard disks available, e.g., Jaz drives.

Hard disk drive (Hard drive or HDD)
The hard disk drive controls the positioning, reading, and writing of the hard disk. The hard disk drive (often shortened to "hard drive") and the hard disk (see above) are not the same thing, but they are packaged as a unit and often referred to as one.

Hardware
The physical devices that make up a computer system, e.g., disks, CPU, modems.

Helical scan
A tape recording method that increases storage capacity by running tracks diagonally from top to bottom.

Hertz
The frequency of electrical vibrations (cycles) per second. Abbreviated "Hz," one hertz is equal to one cycle per second.

HiFD (High Floppy Disk)
A high-density floppy disk developed by Sony that can hold 200M of data and support data transfer rates of up to 3.6MBps. HiFD disk drives can read and write old 1.44M floppy disks in addition to the new high-density disks.

IDE (Integrated Drive Electronics)
IDE is a standard electronic interface used between a computer motherboard's data paths and the computer's disk storage devices.

Inkjet printer
A printer that propels droplets of ink directly onto paper to create either characters or images.

Jaz drive
A removable disk drive developed by Iomega for storing a large amount of data. Jaz disks between 1G and 2G of data.

K56flex (56 Kbps downstream)
K56flex is a modem and transmission technology from the Rockwell Corporation and Lucent Technologies for sending data to your computer on ordinary phone lines at a speed of 56 Kbps (thousand bits per second).

Kbps (thousands of bits or kilobits per second)
A measure of data transfer speed, more specifically, a measure of bandwidth (the amount of information that can flow in a given time) on a data transmission medium such as coaxial cable.

Kilobyte (Kb or Kbyte or K)
Approximately a thousand bytes. A measure of disk storage.

Laptop
A small portable computer, also called a notebook computer.

Laser printer
A printer that works by bonding powdered toner ink to high-quality paper under high-heat conditions.

LCD (liquid crystal display)
A type of display used in digital watches and many portable computers. LCD displays use two sheets of polarizing material with a liquid crystal solution between them. An electric current passed through the liquid causes the crystals to align, either allowing light to pass through or blocking the light.

Mac OS
Operating system for Apple Macintosh-based computers. The latest version of the Mac OS is system 8.1.

Megabyte (MB or M)
A measure of computer processor storage and real and virtual memory, a megabyte is about one million bytes, exactly 1,024K.

Megahertz (MHz)
A megahertz (MHz or sometimes Mhz) is a million cycles of electromagnetic currency alternation per second and is used as a unit of measure for the "clock speed" of computer microprocessors.

Memory
Internal working storage areas in the computer. Usually refers to physical memory, or the collection of RAM chips that temporarily holds data that may be needed immediately. It should be distinguished from storage, or the physical medium that holds the larger data amounts that won't fit into RAM. Storage devices include hard disks, floppy disks, and CD-ROMs. (See RAM)

Microprocessor
A single chip that holds a CPU. The hardware that is activated when the computer is turned on. The microprocessor performs logic operations that include adding, subtracting, and retrieving numbers from one area to another based on a set of given instructions.

MMX (MultiMedia EXtensions)
A set of instructions built into Intel CPU chips for enhanced audio, video, graphics and modem operations. MMX is found in Pentium MMX, Pentium II, and Pentium III chips, but not in Pentiums or Pentium Pros.

Modem (modulator/demodulator)
A modem converts computer digital signals to analog signals for transmitting data over telephone lines.

Moore's Law
Principle coined by Intel's co-founder that states that processor speeds double every 18 months.

Motherboard
The main circuit board in a computer that contains sockets for connecting additional boards. In a personal computer, the motherboard contains the CPU, mass storage interfaces, keyboard controller and supporting chips.

Mouse
The device that a computer user employs to control the movements of the cursor on the display screen.

MS-DOS (Microsoft Disk Operating System)
The Microsoft-marketed version of DOS, the first widely-installed operating system in personal computers. (See DOS)

Operating system
Software that runs other computer programs. Responsible for basic tasks such as data management and input/output control. (See DOS, MS-DOS, and Mac OS)

PCL (printer control language)
The page description language (PDL) developed by Hewlett Packard and used in many of their laser and ink-jet printers.

PCMCIA (Personal Computer Memory Card International Association)
PCMCIA is an organization consisting of some 500 companies that has developed a standard for small, credit card-sized devices, called PC Cards or PCMCIA cards. These 16-bit devices are typically found in notebook computers and are used to add memory, or to attach modems and disk drives.

Pentium
Intel's 32-bit microprocessor that was introduced in 1993 to succeed the 486 processor. Variations of the Pentium now include the Celeron, Pentium Pro, Pentium MMX, Pentium II, and Pentium III.

Pitch
The spacing between the phosphers that make up an image on a computer monitor. Measured in millimeters, the smaller the space, the finer an image can be.

Pixel
A single unit on a display screen. The higher the pixel resolution (the more rows and columns of pixels), the clearer the information displayed.

PostScript
A page description language (PDL) developed by Adobe. PostScript commands are in ASCII text that are translated into the printer's machine language by a PostScript interpreter built into the printer. There are three basic versions of PostScript. Level 2 supports color printing and Level 3 supports fonts and better graphic handling.

PowerPC G3 (G3)
Motorola's microprocessor usually found in Macintosh's iMac and iBook, available at speeds of up to 333MHz.

PowerPC G4 (G4)
Motorola's microprocessor usually found in Macintosh's PowerMac, available at speeds of up to 500MHz.

Processor
A computer's logic circuitry that processes basic instructions that run a computer. (See microprocessor and CPU)

QIC (Quarter-Inch Cartridge)
A standard magnetic tape drive used for backup. QIC tapes come in full-size (also called data-cartridge) and minicartridges.

RAM (random-access memory)
A type of temporary computer memory that is comprised of a group of memory chips. The "random" in RAM means that the contents of each byte can be directly accessed without regard to the bytes before or after it. Data stored in RAM is lost when the computer is turned off.

Refresh rate
The rate at which the images on your monitor are redrawn. Higher refresh rates reduce flickering on your screen; the rate should be at least 75Hz.

Resolution

Refers to how sharp or clear an image is. On screen, resolution refers to the number of pixels that make up the image.

ROM (read-only memory)

ROM is computer memory that is built into your computer. ROM cannot be removed and can only be read, not written to. For example, ROM is responsible for the program that "boots" your computer each time it is turned on. Unlike RAM, ROM data is not lost when the computer is turned off.

SCSI (Small Computer System Interface)

SCSI, pronounced SKUH-zee, is a parallel standard interface to attach peripheral hardware to the computer such as disk drives, tape drives, CD-ROM drives, printers, and scanners. Variations of SCSI include: SCSI-2, SCSI-3, Ultra-SCSI, and Wide-SCSI.

SIMM (single in-line memory module)

A SIMM is a small circuit board that can hold a group of memory chips that connect to the computer motherboard. SIMMs have evolved into DIMM (dual inline) packages. Opposing SIMM pins are on the same circuit path, while DIMM pins are isolated on each side, providing double the circuit paths. (See DIMM)

Software

Software is a general term for the programs used to operate computers and related devices; anything electronically stored. (The term hardware refers to the physical aspects of computers, such as the display devices.)

Sound card

An expansion circuit board that enables the computer to output sound through speakers connected to the board, to record sound input from a microphone connected to the computer, and manipulate sound stored on a disc.

SuperDisk

A floppy disk drive from Imation Corporation (www.imation.com), that uses the LS-120 technology and supports high-density diskettes. SuperDisk diskettes hold 120M, and SuperDisk drives have the capability to read and write standard 1.44MB floppies as well.

Surge protector

A device that helps guard communication lines and the power supply from unexpected electrical surges.

Tape Drive
A data storage device similar to a tape recorder in that it reads data from and writes data onto a tape. Tape drives are usually used for long-term storage or backups.

Ultra ATA
An enhanced version of the IDE interface that transfers data at up to 66Mbps. (See IDE)

V.90
International Telecommunications Union (ITU) standard for 56Kbps (thousands of bits per second) modulation.

Video card (video adaptor)
A circuit board that is plugged into a personal computer to provide display capabilities. The display capabilities of a computer depend on the compatibility of the logical circuitry (provided in the video card) and the display monitor.

Wavetable
A type of sound generator often built in a sound card. A wavetable contains digitalized samples of real instrument sounds or effect (FX) sounds.

Windows NT
The Microsoft Windows operating system with advanced capability, designed for users who need faster performance and a system that's a little more fail-safe than Windows 95.

Windows 98
Microsoft's Windows latest operating system for personal computers. Windows 98 features the active desktop, which integrates Microsoft's Internet Explorer browser with the operating system itself.

x2
U.S. Robotics proprietary protocol for sending data to and from your computer on ordinary phone lines at a speed of 56Kbps (thousands of bits per second).

Zip drive
A 3.5" removable floppy disk drive from Iomega for storing a large amount of data. Zip disks can hold up to 250M of data.

PORTFOLIO
MANAGEMENT

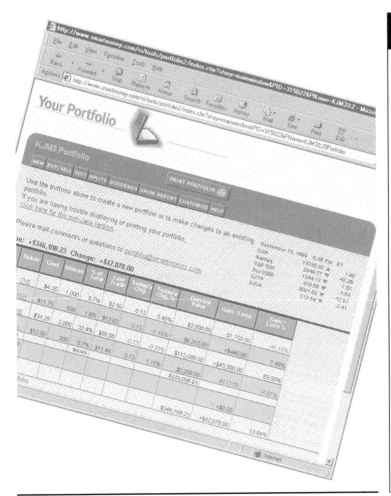

No matter what techniques you use to select your investments, you must have a system in place to track your holdings. This process of portfolio management should extend beyond a simple accounting of a security's purchase and sale price and provide a feedback system for tracking the performance of the security, its interaction with other securities in your portfolio, the allocation of assets within your portfolio, and the overall performance of your portfolio. Here we examine portfolio management systems designed to help you accomplish these tasks.

This chapter covers software-based portfolio management systems separately from their on-line counterparts. However, we also test the top on-line portfolio manager, the MSN MoneyCentral Investor portfolio module, alongside the software packages. This on-line module is just like a software program in that it is downloaded, installed on your system, and menu-driven. Technically termed an applet, this dynamic module uses Microsoft ActiveX technology and runs within your browser software. The MSN MoneyCentral Investor portfolio module is included in the disk-based comparison grid and is subject to the same criteria as the software. This allows you to compare the functionality and flexibility available with the MSN MoneyCentral Investor module against the more powerful software applications.

On-line portfolio managers are improving, but not capable of handling the full range of accounting reports needed for items such as filling out tax reports. The majority of on-line portfolio managers are still designed to be assistants to software programs—keeping individuals up-to-date on their portfolios and notifying them of any current market events that might affect them via E-mail or other Web capabilities.

On-line portfolio managers are best compared head-to-head—in an apples-to-apples fashion. The MSN MoneyCentral Investor site is also featured in this Web-specific section of the chapter, where the discussion focuses more on the on-line capabilities and characteristics of such tools, like E-mail alerts and links to newswire services. This sub-section of Chapter 4: Portfolio Management can be found starting on page 107. A brief review of each site—a total of eight in all—will be followed by separate on-line portfolio manager-specific comparison grids.

The Program Checklist

When shopping for a portfolio management program, it is best to develop a checklist of features to consider when comparing programs. These features include:

- costs,

- systems,

- securities/assets handled,

- transactions handled,

- reporting strength and flexibility,

- data updates, and

- ease of use.

Cost

When the issue of cost comes into question, shoppers should look beyond the retail price tag. The time spent learning how to use a program, configuring it to your data source, and entering in all of your pertinent trading histories and individual security information should be considered part of your overall cost. These three issues alone far outweigh the importance of the retail price of a program in the long run. Therefore, take your time in selecting a portfolio management application. Make sure your final choice meets your individual needs. If you simply go out and buy the program with the most number of features, you may find it still sitting on a shelf collecting dust two years from now because it was too difficult to use and really did not meet your needs in the first place. At the same time, you do not want to buy too simple a program and be forced to switch to another one after a few years.

Warning→	Take your time when selecting a portfolio management application by looking beyond the price tag and focus on how the program fits your individual portfolio management needs.

Consider the above cost issues before investing your money and, more importantly, possibly wasting your time. When analyzing your situation, consider not only your current needs, but any possible future needs as well.

Few areas of analysis warrant program testing and review more than portfolio management. If a demo of the program you are interested in is available, be sure to get it and "test drive" the program. Often the cost of the demo can be applied toward the purchase price. Most of the program vendors discussed in this chapter offer free demos downloadable at their Web sites; they are noted in the comparison grid with an asterisk.

> **Tip→** If a demo of the program you are interested in is available, be sure to get it and "test drive" the program.

Systems

Although there are still two programs that run under DOS (The Investor's Accountant and Portfolio Analyzer, both from Hamilton Software), the shift toward the Windows platform is almost complete. The word from the Hamilton Software camp at the time of this writing is that Windows-based versions of both programs are in the works, but still in the early stages of development.

Macintosh users will be happy to know that their lone ally in the portfolio management software business, Intuit, has finally come out with a new version of Quicken that can run on the Mac. This is after a one-year hiatus from producing any Mac-based portfolio management software. Quicken 2000 hit shelves in the fall of 1999 and is available for Windows and Mac. With the absence of StreetSmart and WealthBuilder—due to the fact that they were not ready for the year 2000—the Mac user essentially has only one software choice with Quicken 2000.

The Web-based tools are platform independent, meaning that the service is accessible to all computers with an Internet connection and a modern browser. It is an open alternative to all users—Windows and Mac advocates alike.

Editor's Note: *Each of the applications discussed in this chapter are certified Y2K/Year 2000 compliant.*

Securities/Assets Handled

When looking at the scope of securities accommodated by any prospective program, consider not only the types of securities or assets that you currently hold, but also those securities you might want to purchase in the future. All programs cover the basic security classes—stocks, bonds, mutual funds, and cash. Some programs specialize in one area, such as mutual funds. However, while a program in question may cover one area well, it might be difficult to track other types of securities should the scope of your investment holdings expand.

> **Tip→** When looking at the securities accommodated by a program, consider not only the types of securities or assets that you currently hold, but also those securities you might want to purchase in the future.

If your portfolio includes unusual securities or assets, such as derivatives, pay close attention to whether or not the program handles them. The comparison grid at the end of this chapter also covers other features that relate to security and asset coverage—take note that transaction types, security lot assignments, reports, and even data services can affect how you track, organize, and analyze your portfolio.

> **Warning→** If your portfolio includes unusual securities or assets, pay close attention to whether or not the program you are interested in handles them.

Any solid portfolio management program should also allow you to measure the diversification of your holdings. These programs can sort your portfolio into various categories in order to measure diversification. Some programs even measure the diversification within a particular asset class. For example, you may want to examine the sector or industry breakdown of your stock portfolio or the state-by-state make-up of a municipal bond portfolio.

Transactions Handled

The transactions supported by the program are closely related to the types of securities that the program is designed to handle. Make sure that any potential program includes all the relevant transactions you might require as well.

> **Tip→** Make sure that any potential program includes all the relevant transactions you might require.

All the programs compared here handle the basic, fundamental transactions such as buy/sell, cash dividends, and interest income. However, the ability to handle purchases on margin, short sales, and the reinvestment of dividends are key areas where the programs vary in their coverage.

Related to the issue of transactions is the ability to specify security lot assignments to any given transaction. This is an important feature, especially to those interested in tax liability issues and tracking performance. (A lot is the total number of units involved in a trade on a securities exchange. For example, in a stock transaction, a round lot includes 100 shares.) If you reinvest dividends from your mutual funds and stocks, you will find yourself tracking numerous lots over a long period of time. Any good portfolio management package will automatically match buy and sell lots for different accounting strategies for the purpose of reducing one's tax exposure. These strategies include: first-in-first-out (FIFO),

FIGURE 4.0
*Transaction
codes featured
in Captool
Individual
Investor for
Windows.*

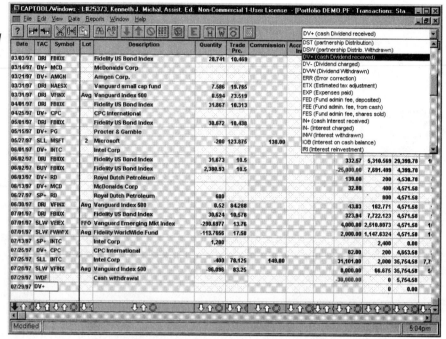

average cost, or specific lot. Finding an application that handles all three lot assignment methods can be a key factor when deciding between programs. Security lot assignments are detailed in the comparison grid immediately below the transactions section.

> Tip→   Finding an application that handles all three security lot assignment methods is key when deciding on a program.

Reports

Reports allow you to analyze your portfolio and investments. The 17 applications in this chapter vary widely in the types of reports they provide as well as in the strength and flexibility these reports offer. Again, check to see if the programs that you are considering have the types of reports you want, but also look at other reports offered that you do not currently use in your analysis. They might enhance the overall evaluation of your portfolio. While you want to be sure that a program provides enough flexibility and functionality to complete your current task list, consider possible future needs with regard to securities and transactions handled along with reporting capabilities. Doing so now will save you time and effort down the road.

> **Tip→**
>
> Check to see if the programs that you are considering have the types of reports you want, but also look at other reports that might enhance the overall evaluation of your portfolio.

Current Holdings

The current holdings report exhibits the composition of your portfolio. It is a basic report that indicates which securities are in the portfolio, their original cost, current value, gain or loss, and perhaps some security statistics such as dividend yield, price-earnings ratio, or beta.

Holdings by Lots

The holdings by lot report breaks down the composition of the current holdings report into finer increments, indicating each purchase at a specific date and price. This provides a clear, detailed history of your transactions.

Cash Portfolio Status

Cash portfolio status reports the cash balance tied to the holdings within a portfolio. This report is helpful in determining the portfolio's security purchasing power.

Tax Schedules

Tax schedules pertain to the Schedule B and Schedule D reports. Designed for computing interest and dividends received from a portfolio, Schedule B reports allow you to estimate tax liabilities (or credit) before year-end statements arrive. Tax Schedule D reports compute long- and short-term capital gains and group assets that will yield capital gains with tax liabilities. If you are going to rely on your portfolio management program to produce these schedules, make sure that adjustments can be made should tax laws change regarding factors such as short- or long-term holding periods in the future.

> **Warning→**
>
> If you are going to rely on your portfolio management program to produce your tax schedules, make sure that adjustments can be made should tax laws change.

FIGURE 4.1
A Tax Schedule D report for computing capital gains found in the Financial Navigator program.

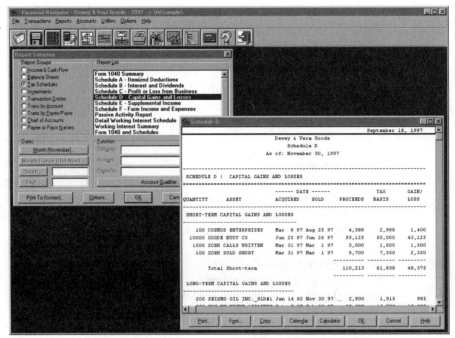

Projected Cash Flow

The projected cash flow report serves as a forecast of the expected portfolio cash income from dividends, interest, and bond maturities. This report is useful for estimating retirement income and allows you to structure asset holdings based on future needs.

The issue of flexibility comes into play with the options of customized reports and batch processing capabilities. Customization choices range from those that are content-related, such as time period, to those that are cosmetics-related, like column and row headings. Batch, or group, processing simply involves completing multiple print jobs of different types of reports at one time.

Performance Reports

The section of the grid entitled performance reports depicts the various ways a program summarizes how well your investment holdings have fared. A basic part of the portfolio management process is to determine and analyze performance and, therefore, this section should be studied carefully. The number of performance reports offered helps some programs stand out from their competitors. The level of performance reports available is discussed in the brief summary of each program that follows.

Tip→ **Be sure to carefully study what performance reports each program offers as it may help some programs stand out from their competitors.**

A program that provides reports for securities, industries, and asset classes will not only give you the performance of each segment, but also will provide portfolio allocation analysis. Some programs allow for an examination among various asset classes—such as domestic or foreign equities, bonds or cash—while others provide industry breakdowns.

It is important to find a program that has the ability to produce reports covering not only a single portfolio but also multiple portfolios. You will want a program that addresses the diversified aspects of all your holdings for all your portfolios, rather than one that can only concentrate on a single portfolio.

Tip→ **Be on the lookout for a program that has the ability to produce reports for multiple portfolios.**

All of the programs in this chapter provide a return for the current holding period, which examines gain or loss from the time the security is purchased. Most programs now also offer returns for designated periods—called "between period returns" in the comparison grid. Programs that feature the ability to designate time periods allow you to monitor security performance during a known market environment, as well as to examine all your securities over the same time period. To designate time periods, a program must be able to store snapshots of your portfolio holdings and values at specific points of time and not just the current positions and prices.

Value-Weighted Internal Rate of Return vs. Time-Weighted Rate of Return

Portfolio return reports paint the clearest picture of how well your investment holdings have performed. Value-weighted (or dollar-weighted) internal rate of return (IRR) and time-weighted rate of return are both calculated by portfolio management software. But which one is right for your analysis?

For the individual investor looking to gauge the true performance of a personal portfolio, the internal rate of return is desired. In this instance, it will provide the performance measurement of your overall portfolio. The internal rate of return is considered both a value-weighted and time-weighted calculation because it considers the time when inflows and outflows are made to the portfolio, the amount of these flows, and the combined impact upon the rate of return.

Tip→	For the individual investor, the internal rate of return is desired for gauging actual overall portfolio performance.

The time-weighted return is most often used to analyze the performance of investment decisions made by a portfolio or money manager. The time-weighted calculation ignores the impact of any cash added to or removed from the portfolio because the manager most often does not have control over such events. However, an individual does have control over any inflows or outflows of money and, therefore, needs to consider their impact upon the actual performance of the portfolio. Look for applications that offer both returns, but be sure to check for the value-weighted internal rate of return.

Warning→	The time-weighted calculation ignores the impact of any cash added to or removed from the portfolio. However, an individual does have control over inflows or outflows of money and, therefore, needs to consider their impact on return calculations.

Tip→	Look for applications that offer both time-weighted and value-weighted returns, but be sure to check for the value-weighted internal rate of return.

When a program provides tax-adjusted returns, this simply means that it generates pretax and aftertax returns. These programs automatically calculate the tax liabilities of your transactions and report their impact on the rate of return of the securities and portfolios. Look for programs that allow you to customize the tax rates to your situation and vary the rates over time to reflect changing personal situations and tax laws.

Programs that follow AIMR standards adhere to the accounting standards established by the Association of Investment Management and Research. These include: calculating a total time-weighted rate of return, providing year-by-year rates of return, and allowing for consideration of portfolio management costs. The standards encompass both methodology and presentation formats and are geared toward defining how money managers should report this performance to current and prospective clients.

FIGURE 4.2
A value-weighted internal rate of return report developed for multiple portfolios from The Investor's Accountant.

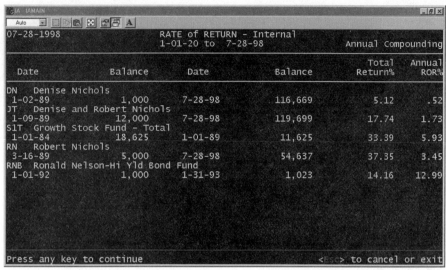

FIGURE 4.3
The Captool Individual Investor features this complete performance report, which provides both value-weighted IRRs and time-weighted returns.

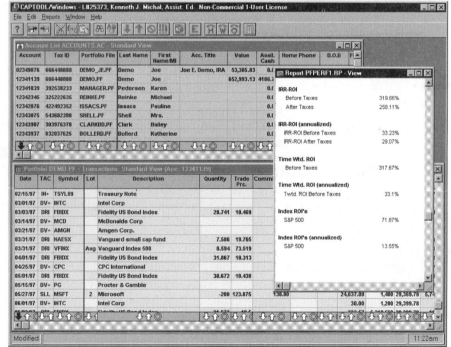

Useful reports are a key consideration in selecting a program. If a demo of the program you are considering is not available, request that the company send you printouts of the available reports using a sample portfolio.

Tip→	If a demo of the program you are considering is not available, request that the company send you printouts of the available reports using a sample portfolio.

Data Support

It is common for portfolio management programs to offer a direct connection to an on-line service for price updates. The comparison grid indicates the information services supported by each program. Along with data services, the grid also shows the various formats supported for exporting and importing information. Note that in most cases this refers only to the transfer of security price information.

Ease of Use

The great intangible aspect involved in selecting a portfolio management program centers around how easy the program is to use. In general, there is a trade-off between a simple, easy-to-use interface and a strong set of portfolio management and analytical features. The more advanced programs seem to bring along an extensive interface with their highly evolved skill levels.

When considering how easy the program is to learn, also consider how easy and quick it is going to be to perform your normal maintenance tasks, such as entry of purchases and sales and the reinvestment of dividends. While a deep and well organized menu structure may help you quickly learn how to use a system, needlessly having to go through several menu choices to input a dividend payment will quickly grow tiresome. When falling in love with a program's extensive coverage and functionality, remember that a longer learning curve will most likely be involved.

Warning→	When considering how easy the program is to learn, also consider how easy and quick it is going to be to perform your normal maintenance tasks.

As mentioned earlier, no area of analysis warrants getting a demo more than portfolio management. You can check out the program's interface and consider how easy it is to maneuver around in the program before committing to it. Few demo versions come with instructions, so browse the vendor's Web site for any help files and try E-mailing questions to the vendor's technical support staff to measure their responsiveness.

Tip→	No area of analysis warrants getting a demo more than portfolio management. Few demo versions come with instructions, so browse the vendor's Web site and E-mail questions to the vendor's technical support staff.

The Standouts

The standout software programs in the area of portfolio management include: Captool Individual Investor, Financial Navigator, The Investor's Accountant, and a new program, Reeally! from Mantic Software. With its migration to Windows, Captool has a stranglehold on the number-one ranking for overall portfolio management functionality and value. This group of top-notch programs is now dominated by Windows applications; whereas in the past, DOS was king. The choice for the Mac user remains Intuit's Quicken software. Unfortunately, when compared to the non-Mac portfolio management programs, Quicken 2000 for the Mac falls short of their standards.

Reviews

Capital Gainz	
Performance	3
Usefulness	3
Documentation	2
Ease of Use	4
Value	3

Capital Gainz 6.0
by Alley Cat Software, Inc.
$69—Windows
(919) 542-6117
www.alleycatsw.com

Capital Gainz is a general-purpose portfolio management application. The program is geared toward the average investor and is rather easy to use. It covers basic securities and assets and provides for a solid amount of transactions.

All of the major holdings reports are present along with tax Schedules B and D. Performance reports include those for security and industry and for multiple portfolios, which can be developed between peri-

FIGURE 4.4
A purchase report from Capital Gainz, adding shares of the Fidelity Select Brokerage & Investment mutual fund to a portfolio.

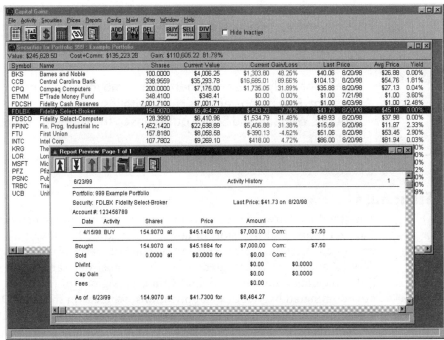

ods. However, reports can neither be customized nor run in batches. Capital Gainz generates a time-weighted rate of return. It supports the most number of data services of all the programs in this chapter.

Captool Individual Investor	
Performance	5
Usefulness	5
Documentation	4
Ease of Use	3
Value	5

Captool Individual Investor 1.1
by Captools Co.
$249—Windows
(800) 826-8082
www.captools.com

Captool Individual Investor for Windows has continued the standard of excellence set by its DOS predecessor. This portfolio management dynamo remains the best choice for the individual investor looking to monitor and evaluate portfolio holdings. The Captool stable of programs also offers an even more advanced program set for the professional investor.

FIGURE 4.5
Account and transaction ledgers found in Captool Individual Investor for Windows.

The lead horse in this stable, Captool Individual Investor, is priced at $249. It is still at version 1.1, but the program receives continual mini-updates, with over 30 releases this year alone. Captool Global Investor, a version designed to include foreign-denominated securities in a common portfolio, has a price tag of $499. Two expanded versions of Captool—Professional Investor Level 1 and Level 2— are also available, with Level 1 costing $999 and a $1,999 price tag on the Level 2 program. Professional Investor provides investment advisors who handle a large number of accounts with the ability to maintain records to meet compliance requirements, conduct portfolio rebalancing, and generate client-specific statements and reports. Level 1 is designed and licensed for a single user, while Level 2 can be licensed for up to three users at a single site, like a network for example.

With its transformation to Windows, Captool did not skip a beat in overall coverage of securities and transactions. Report capabilities are still top-notch and performance measures are most extensive. And, when it comes to user-defined features, there is not much more a user could want. It is the same exact program as the old DOS model, now running under a Windows interface. The new interface has improved, but some of the old trappings still remain—one example: the traditional three-character transaction codes found in past versions of the program are still present in the new one.

Captool remains a powerhouse application that sheds none of its complexity in moving to a Windows platform. It is not just one of those general-purpose recordkeeping/personal finance applications. Of all the programs included here, Captool remains the cream of the crop.

FIGURE 4.6
*Captool
Individual
Investor
portfolio
valuation
chart.*

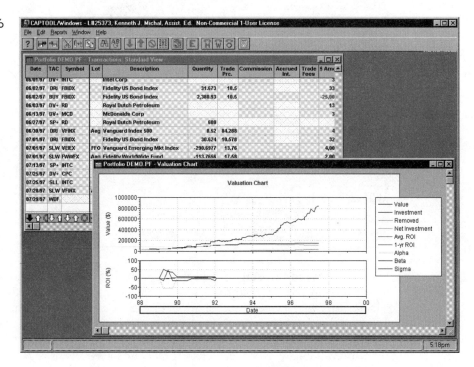

If you attempted to use the old DOS version of Captool in the past and gave up on it, you might want to give this new version a spin around the block, free demo downloads are available from Captools at their Web site (www.captools.com). However, the program is not for the meek; only a dedicated individual with time to learn the system and how it operates will come close to utilizing the power of this application. Take heed: This is a skilled tool that requires a skilled user.

Financial Navigator	
Performance	4
Usefulness	5
Documentation	5
Ease of Use	4
Value	4

Financial Navigator 7.0
by Financial Navigator International
$349.00—Windows
(800) 468-3636
www.finnav.com

The recently updated Financial Navigator is an advanced portfolio manager with some unique capabilities that extend beyond the scope of its peers. The program provides financial management for users with complex financial situations, such as marketable securities investments, real estate ownership, trusts, non-profits, and estates. The program also assists small business owners with Schedule C filings for business profits/losses. The program handles six different tax schedules in all. Financial Navigator can also handle multiple businesses and cash flow planning as well as executive stock options.

FIGURE 4.7
An executive stock option report generated by Financial Navigator.

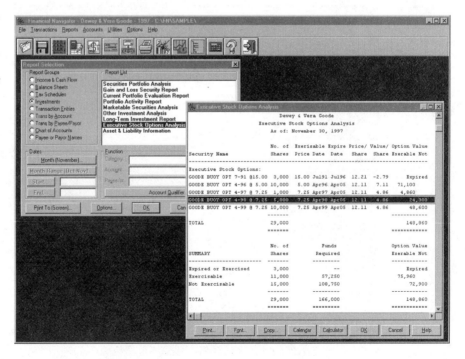

Financial Navigator carries a complete package of securities and transactions. Performance is measured through reports for securities and assets and through single and multiple portfolio reports. Reports can be generated for the holding period of the asset only but the program does offer over 100 different reports that can be customized and run in batches.

Financial Navigator is one of the better software packages, and it has continually been updated. The program was one of the first to move to the Windows platform, which set it apart from other portfolio managers in the past. This most recent update may have been prompted by the competition's move to the Windows world.

However, some glaring weaknesses of the program still have not been addressed. For example, Financial Navigator does not allow for tax-adjusted returns and it only allows average cost basis for mutual funds and the most common method, specific lot, for use when selling lots. These examples are clear misses.

FIGURE 4.8
Unrealized gains and losses activity provided by the Financial Navigator program.

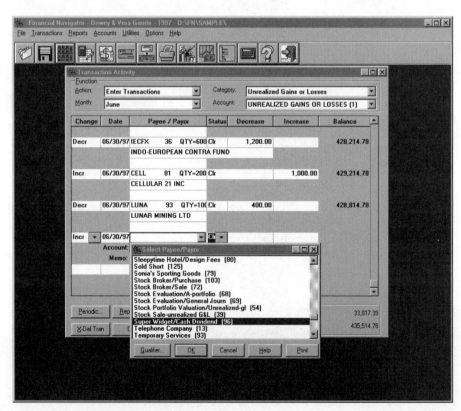

Nevertheless, Financial Navigator still ranks near the upper echelon of programs. It is possibly the most advanced multi-dimensional portfolio management and personal finance program on the market today. Yet, it is suitable for the individual investor looking to get more from a program than the prototypical personal finance program can provide. For example, if you are a Quicken user and you feel as though you need more from your program, you might want to give Financial Navigator a try for detailed portfolio tracking and performance monitoring, as well as addressing your core personal finance objectives.

The Investor's Accountant	
Performance	4
Usefulness	4
Documentation	3
Ease of Use	2
Value	4

The Investor's Accountant 6.0
by Hamilton Software, Inc.
$395.00—DOS
(800) 733-9607
www.hamiltonsoftware.com

This package from the Hamilton Software library is a comprehensive system that incorporates the functions of portfolio management with various investment analysis measures.

The Investor's Accountant handles a formidable range of transactions. The program covers all the basic holding reports but includes only performance reports for your portfolios and individual securities. The reports can

FIGURE 4.9
The main menu screen of The Investor's Accountant.

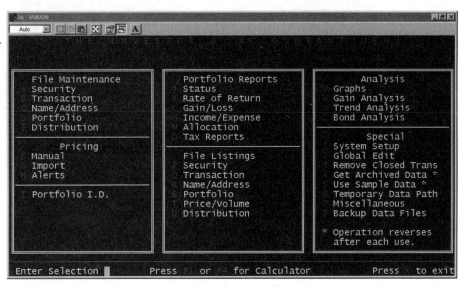

measure performance between any two points in time and can also estimate tax liability. The Investor's Accountant can generate before-tax or aftertax internal rate of return and time-weighted rate of return reports. The reports cannot, however, be run in batches and they are not customizable.

Extra functions for The Investor's Accountant include alerts for prices, dividends, expirations, and percentage gain or loss. The Investor's Accountant also follows security performance and market trends through graphics analysis, including moving averages and price-volume. These added features, coupled with the solid portfolio analysis provided by this DOS veteran, rank The Investor's Accountant among the top programs. With Captool's move to Windows, The Investor's Accountant becomes the top choice for the DOS fan and is among the upper class of applications in its field. The program is best suited for the advanced user who is familiar with DOS-based applications and favors their functionality. A Windows version is currently in development—look for a beta version to be issued in the coming year.

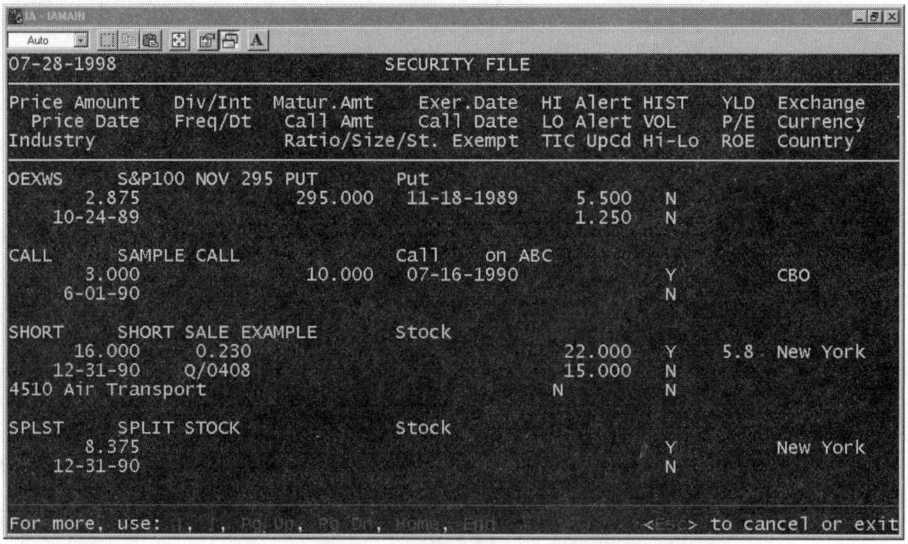

FIGURE 4.10
A security file, taken from The Investor's Accountant, detailing the activity within a portfolio.

Money 2000	
Performance	3
Usefulness	4
Documentation	3
Ease of Use	5
Value	4

Money 2000
by Microsoft, Inc.
$34.95(Basic)–$64.95(Deluxe)—Windows
(800) 426-9400
www.microsoft.com/money

In early September of 1999, software giant Microsoft released the newest version of their popular Windows software program Money 2000. Money 2000 is one of two personal finance programs included in this chapter—Quicken being the other—that are geared toward assisting investors with the full range of money management activities. Money 2000 provides portfolio tracking measures and handles basic personal finance tasks as well.

Money and Quicken software have always shared a similar look and feel. Another similarity, is that Money 2000, like Quicken, comes in two different models—the basic version, designed to assist in the overall managing of one's investments, and the deluxe package, now referred to as Money 2000 Deluxe. Money 2000 Deluxe includes Money 2000 as well as several additional financial planning modules, including Lifetime Planner and several other new add-on tools.

One Money 2000 Deluxe exclusive used to be a free six-month subscription to the Microsoft MoneyCentral Investor Web site, which normally costs $9.95 a month. With Microsoft just announcing that all services on the site are free, this great offer has lost its luster. This is a free service to all and the Money perk is nothing but fluff. From the MSN MoneyCentral Investor site, users can track portfolios, generate stock charts, receive stock quotes and news, and perform stock and mutual fund screening using the site's Investment Finder tool. The MSN MoneyCentral Investor Web site is reviewed later in this section on page 105 and again in the On-Line Portfolio Managers section on page 119.

Although the special offer to the MSN MoneyCentral Investor site is all hype, there are some new tools that add great value to the Money 2000 Deluxe package. They include: the Life Event Modeler, which performs "what if" calculations to determine the impact of certain financial events on one's holdings; Purchase Wizard, which evaluates different ways to get money for financing big-ticket purchases; and Portfolio Review, which offers a detailed analysis of your investments. Two additional new features, seen before on Quicken, are discussed immediately following.

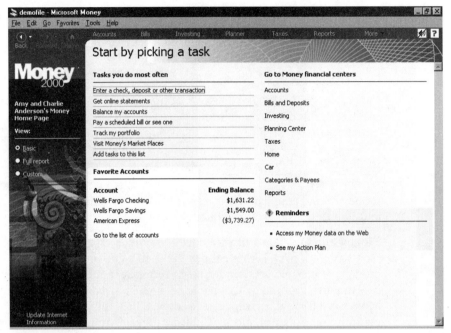

FIGURE 4.11
Money 2000's
Money Home
serves as the
program's
control center.

It appears as though Microsoft is always one step behind Intuit in the race for putting out the most popular, most user-friendly personal finance software. A perfect example of this is the newest feature available on Money 2000 Deluxe, Money Web Express. Money Web Express allows Money users to access their Money program anytime, anywhere via the Microsoft MSN MoneyCentral Investor Web site. With Money Web Express you can check account balances and enter transactions when you are or the road or away from your desktop PC. This same functionality was first introduced by Intuit last year with their Quicken Deluxe 99 program.

Another new feature, long-since present on Quicken software, is complete integration with a new Microsoft tax preparation software package called Tax-Saver—which is to be released for this coming tax season. For many years and many different versions of Quicken, a similar relationship existed between Quicken and Intuit's TurboTax program and Web site. Perhaps the Microsoft Money team wanted to wait and see how these ideas took off first. But whatever the reason or case may be, it seems like this "monkey-see-monkey-do" relationship between the two software companies will always be present.

Not much has changed in the Money 2000 program and user interface. The interface is clean and organized and still offers a look resembling a Web site home page. When attempting to log onto the MSN MoneyCentral Investor Web site, many users will question if they have left the confines of the Money software program—they look that much alike.

Money 2000 handles an extensive amount of securities, offers complete transaction coverage, and all three primary security lot assignment methods are present. The basic holdings reports are present, including holdings by lots. Schedules B and D tax reporting are also available. Performance report options are somewhat lacking however: security and asset class performance reports are for single portfolios only. Yet the return reports can be created for user-specified time periods.

New this year on Money 2000 is a value-weighted internal rate of return—the better of the two return calculation choices for individual investors. Return reports cannot, however, be adjusted for taxes.

FIGURE 4.12
A portfolio review report from Money 2000 includes risk profile and accounts summary sections.

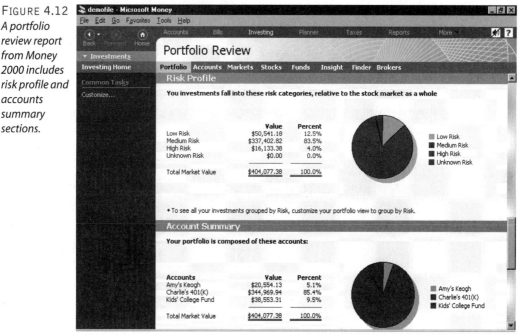

Money 2000—like Quicken 2000 (page 100)—is a portfolio manager and, at the same time, offers assistance with various personal finance issues. Reviewing the new Money on its merits as a pure portfolio monitoring and evaluation tool has it rating overall much better than past versions. However, compared to other power-house applications in the field, Money 2000 is average at best.

Previous users of the program will receive a rebate of $10.00 (Money users) or $20.00 (Money Deluxe users) from Microsoft after purchasing the new version of Money.

NAIC Personal Record Keeper	
Performance	3
Usefulness	4
Documentation	3
Ease of Use	4
Value	3

NAIC Personal Record Keeper 2.5
by NAIC/Quant IX Software
$99.00—Windows
(248) 583-6242
www.quantixsoftware.com

NAIC Personal Record Keeper is one of the more basic portfolio management tools on the market today. The name fits the product in that it is best suited for basic recordkeeping and some performance analysis. The program has recently been updated and some significant functions have been added.

FIGURE 4.13
A sale of 100 shares of Briggs & Stratton is recorded using the FIFO method in NAIC Personal Record Keeper.

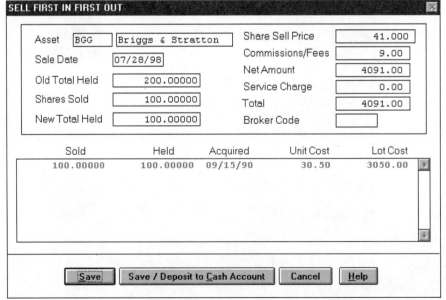

Developed by Quant IX Software and marketed by the National Association of Investors Corporation (NAIC), Personal Record Keeper handles the complete roster of securities and a fair range of transactions, including any purchases made by investment clubs. The program tracks an unlimited number of portfolios, with each portfolio tracking an unlimited number of securities. Cost basis is calculated using each of the three assignment methods. The program covers all of the main reports and various performance reports, as well as Schedules B and D tax reports. Reports can be generated between periods and run in batches, however, they cannot be customized. An approximate time-weighted return can be calculated for the portfolio, but cannot be adjusted for taxes. Personal Record Keeper follows the AIMR accounting presentation standards.

Portfolio Analyzer	
Performance	3
Usefulness	3
Documentation	3
Ease of Use	2
Value	2

Portfolio Analyzer 6.0
by Hamilton Software, Inc.
$99.00—DOS
(800) 733-9607
www.hamiltonsoftware.com

In the Hamilton Software stable, Portfolio Analyzer serves as the younger sibling of The Investor's Accountant. For a DOS program, it is fairly easy to use.

As an elementary portfolio manager, Portfolio Analyzer features similar security and transaction coverage as that of its larger family member. The major differences come into play with the reports and the versatility of those reports. Security allocation, single and multiple portfolio, and value-weighted return reports are the performance reports that can be produced by Portfolio Analyzer. The Investor's Accountant provides both a value-weighted rate of return and a time-weighted one. With Portfolio Analyzer, performance can be measured only for the time period the security is held whereas The Investor's Accountant measures performance for the holding period as well as a user-specified period.

Portfolio Analyzer is another general-purpose portfolio manager, on the same playing field with applications such as Personal Record Keeper. It might not be as intuitive as a Windows program, but for the individual who prefers DOS it is a good choice. A Windows version is currently in development—look for a beta testing stage sometime soon.

FIGURE 4.14
The scaled down functionality of Portfolio Analyzer can be seen in this main menu.

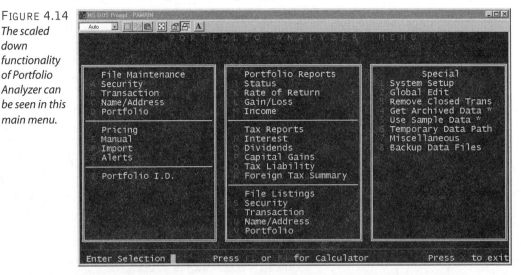

Quicken 2000	
Performance	3
Usefulness	4
Documentation	4
Ease of Use	5
Value	4

Quicken 2000
by Intuit Inc.
$39.95(Basic)–$59.95(Deluxe)—Macintosh, Windows
(800) 446-8848
www.quicken2000.com

The borrow/steal relationship between Microsoft Money and Quicken works both ways as we saw last year with Intuit borrowing the home page idea used in Microsoft's Money 98 program. This new Web page-look gave Quicken 99 a fresh interface that the program desperately needed and is still found in the newest Quicken—Quicken 2000. It is no longer called the Quicken Home Page, but the "My Finances" screen in the Windows program and "Quicken Insights" in the Mac version.

Two primary versions of Quicken remain—Quicken Basic 2000 and Quicken Deluxe 2000. Deluxe includes all that the basic version offers, as well as several additional analysis modules. And as is the case each fall season with the expanded Quicken program, a couple of new features and tools have been added to the mix—just enough to warrant another program upgrade.

FIGURE 4.15

The new "Quicken Insights" screen, taken from the new Quicken Deluxe 2000 for the Macintosh.

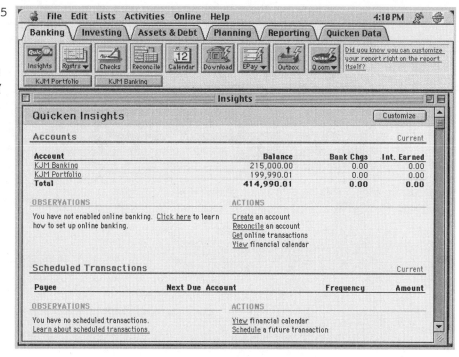

Quicken 2000 (like Microsoft Money 2000 on page 95) is both a portfolio management program and a personal finance application. It prints checks, categorizes all spending, and contains functions for on-line banking and bill payments, as well as tracking bank and credit card accounts.

As a pure portfolio monitoring and evaluation tool, the new Quicken is still rather basic in its coverage—only tracking the normal security types—but has stepped up its functionality in several core portfolio analysis areas. For example, the complete array of transactions is available, including short/cover and the receiving and delivery of securities. Another new feature is the availability of the three primary security lot assignment methods, as well as a couple others, such as LIFO and maximum gain. Quicken 2000 report options have also been beefed up with the addition of a projected cash flow report to go along with security and asset class performance reports now for multiple portfolios. These reports can still be customized and generated between periods. Schedules B and D tax reporting are also available.

With Quicken 2000, Intuit—like Microsoft with Money 2000—has also transformed their calculated return into a value-weighted internal rate of return—the desired return of the individual investor. Also new for 2000 is the capability to calculate your returns after taxes.

FIGURE 4.16
Drop-down menus, including this one for transactions, are found throughout Quicken 2000.

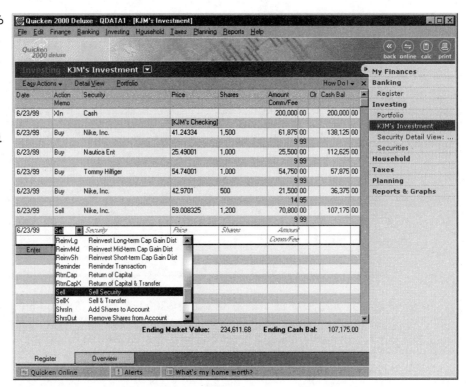

With the release of Quicken Deluxe 99 last season, a significant amount of special enhancements were added to the program—especially features that allowed the program to go with you via a Web-based line of communication. New features included a WebEntry module for entering financial information into your Quicken program via the Web and a QuickEntry program that lets you enter transactions into your register without having to open Quicken. Also new were several Internet-linked tools that can be utilized right inside the Quicken interface—the program launches a browser and goes out to the Web for you without leaving the cozy confines of Quicken. Also, Intuit's TurboTax program got its own site, WebTurboTax, which is now where most of the tax preparation and planning take place. On-line tax preparation functionality via WebTurboTax is available for both versions of Quicken. But the ability to import Quicken data into the TurboTax program is only found on Quicken Deluxe 2000.

Quicken Deluxe 2000 also has its share of new interactive Internet-linked features including access to security news, interactive multiple security charting, and a Stock Evaluator module that helps users analyze stocks using various proven techniques. Also available with the new Quicken Deluxe 2000 is an employee stock option tracking utility, access to downloadable home and car values, and portfolio rebalancing assistance. Quicken Deluxe 2000 also features six different step-by-step Life Event Planners, including one for retirement, college, and new home purchase.

Quicken 2000 is a decent portfolio manager for tracking investments and, at the same time, offers assistance in keeping up with various personal finance issues. Quicken 2000 is available for Windows and Mac. Quicken is a very popular software program, due to its ease-of-use and versatility, not to mention all of its mini-program-like add-on modules. Its multi-dimensional nature makes it an attractive application both as a portfolio manager and as a personal finance program. However, the Quicken program is average at best in the arena of portfolio management.

Previous users of the program will receive a rebate of $10.00 (Quicken users) or $20.00 (Quicken Deluxe users) after purchasing the new Quicken.

Reeally!	
Performance	4
Usefulness	4
Documentation	2
Ease of Use	3
Value	4

Reeally! 1.239
by Mantic Software Corp.
$150.00(Standard)–$525(Pro)—Windows
(800) 730-2919
www.manticsoft.com

A promising rookie has joined the roster of portfolio management programs reviewed. Reeally! from Mantic Software offers some quality features that help place it among the top new programs in today's field. Reeally! comes in two versions, a Standard and a Pro version. The Standard program is for portfolios consisting of only stocks and mutual funds and costs $150. The Pro version is the more practical of the two, supporting portfolios with a wide variety of assets. It is priced at $525.

FIGURE 4.17
A mutual fund portfolio transaction ledger from Reeally! features an open positions function.

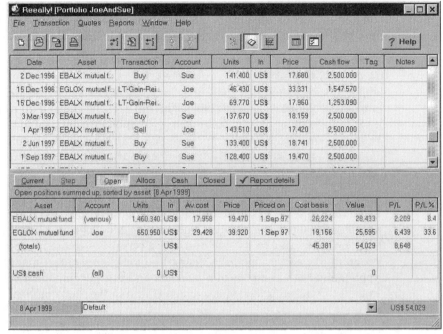

Reeally! Pro offers solid support of security choices including bonds, options and futures. However, the two programs have several limitations when it comes to basic security identification. Reeally! does not provide CUSIP listing functions nor does it allow for SIC industry code classifications.

Transactions handled is quite solid, with Reeally! offering the complete array of options including short/cover, margin, and receive/deliver. Two of the three main security lot methods—FIFO and specific lot—are available and Reeally! boasts a user-defined function called "transaction tagging" that allows users to implement any lot scheme desired.

The strongest set of features found in the Reeally! program are the program's reports and returns, encompassing basic holding reports, performance returns, and graphical performance charts.

All the standard holding reports are present and Reeally! features a rather unique return calculation for performance. It incorporates both the AIMR-standardized rules for time-weighted returns and similar formula operations found in the IRR value-weighted return. The returns module also provides detailed charting capabilities. Users can graph, compare, and print performance measures for an entire portfolio or any one of three different filtered subsets—which can be viewed side-by-side. This type of comparison is done via the same tagging method mentioned above. Reeally! features five different return graphs in all. An in-depth discussion of the various returns calculated and graphs generated by Reeally! is provided in the program's Help system.

Two clear misses found in the report module's capabilities are the inability to adjust returns for taxes and the lack of a projected cash flow report. Another negative is that the reports cannot be customized.

Reeally! is a very good portfolio management program that is quite strong on functionality, but a little lacking when it comes to basic tracking features—such as security identification—that are vital elements needed by the average user. Having said all that, Reeally! is still a solid application that breathes new life into the portfolio management software arena.

MSN MoneyCentral Investor	
Performance	3
Usefulness	3
Documentation	2
Ease of Use	5
Value	3

MSN MoneyCentral Investor
by Microsoft, Inc.
Free—any PC with Internet access
800/426-9400
moneycentral.msn.com/investor

The Microsoft MSN MoneyCentral Investor site is an on-line portfolio management tool included in this software comparison because it is the best candidate for matching up against the software programs.

Until not too long ago, this site used to be fee-based. A subscription costing $9.95 a month gave users full access to the site and all its trappings.

The MSN MoneyCentral Investor site, one of a few sites considered as a "one-stop" multi-dimensional investment center, is now free to all registered users. Formerly known to our readers as the fee-based Microsoft Investor Web site, the site was recently redesigned and renamed. Looking at the comparison grids, it is clear that the MSN MoneyCentral Investor portfolio manager's capabilities are general purpose in nature. However, the site does move well beyond the standard tracking procedures of its on-line manager contemporaries and into the evaluation side of portfolio management.

MSN MoneyCentral Investor's portfolio application handles an above-average range of securities, including options, and offers ticker identification for securities. The different transactions handled is a very respectable list that includes buy/sell, short/cover, stock and cash dividends, the reinvestment of dividends, and splits. In terms of holdings reports, the MSN MoneyCentral Investor site can

FIGURE 4.18
The on-line portfolio tracking module found on the Microsoft MSN MoneyCentral Investor Web site.

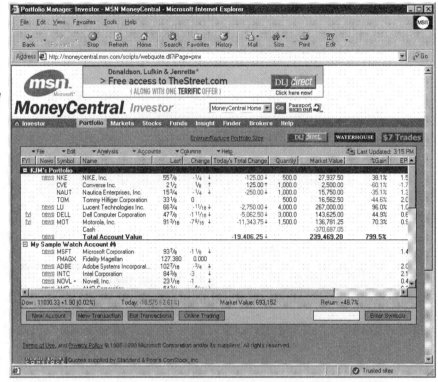

generate not only a current holdings report, but the more fine-tuned holdings by lots report as well. The portfolio module also tracks a cash balance. The roster of available performance reports is also quite impressive. For example, the site can generate security, industry, and asset class performance reports between user-specified periods and can even create performance reports for more than one portfolio.

The MSN MoneyCentral Investor site can track up to 50 mini-portfolios containing up to 5,000 total securities. Portfolios can be updated at any time manually by the user or automatically when you are in the module. The frequency of these automatic updates is based upon a time frame selected by the user, which can be as short as a minute. The site no longer offers E-mail alerts, which is a glaring negative, but does offer a daily E-mail delivered either as a mid-day update or as an end-of-day complete market wrap-up.

The Microsoft MSN MoneyCentral Investor site is a multi-dimensional power-house site geared toward detailed analysis by the individual investor, providing not only a portfolio tracking module but also extensive screening tools. In addition, access to broad news archives, consensus earnings estimates and analyst recommendations, company reports, and expanded company fundamentals is also provided. This on-line portfolio manager is a solid application—one that is sufficient for the portfolio tracking purposes of average investors. It is a product that can clearly stand on its own in the portfolio management software arena.

On-Line Portfolio Managers

An on-line portfolio manager allows registered users to track one or nore portfolios from a Web site or on-line service. Updates to portfolios, links to news stories and news headlines, and access to other analysis modules are also provided at these sites. Some on-line portfolio management applications are just part of a larger, more comprehensive Web site that charge users a monthly fee to access the site's tools, although the trend is now toward dropping these fees. Most often, the basic portfolio tracking functions are provided free of charge to registered users.

These on-line monitoring tools, however, will in no way offer you the same capabilities as the top portfolio management software programs. Rather, they are best seen as tools for keeping you abreast of what is happening with your portfolio and notifying you of current events that might affect your investment holdings.

An on-line manager is like a personal assistant, helping to monitor the activity of your portfolio. On-line portfolio managers do not profess to do what software can do. They can track a portfolio quite effectively, but they do not generate reports or calculate returns to the degree that software does. They are, however, clearly heading in that direction.

Warning→ On-line managers can track a portfolio quite effectively, but they do not generate reports or calculate returns to the degree that software does.

On-line systems can, however, perform some services that software programs do not have the capability to offer, which can greatly enhance your overall evaluation of any portfolio. They can provide timely and vital information unavailable through software in ways not compatible with the typical software interface. This is due directly to the Internet—specifically, the wealth of investment data available and the opportunities for providing timely information via E-mail. For these reasons, an on-line portfolio manager can be a truly valuable complement to any portfolio tracking software program.

> **Tip→** On-line portfolio systems complement software programs by offering a wealth of investment data via the Internet and timely E-mail updates.

Nevertheless, these on-line portfolio systems are not for everyone. The sophisticated investor, trading everything from equities to derivatives, will not be able to monitor all his holdings. The majority of the applications discussed here are geared toward the type of monitoring done by the typical individual investor, whose holdings are comprised primarily of stocks and mutual funds.

> **Warning→** The majority of the on-line applications discussed here are geared toward the type of monitoring done by the typical individual investor, whose holdings are comprised primarily of stocks and mutual funds.

The On-Line Portfolio Manager Checklist

Just like shopping for a portfolio management software program, it is a good idea to first develop a checklist of specific features to consider when comparing on-line applications. These features include:

- frequency of updates,

- links to brokerages,

- links to newswire services,

- E-mail alerts,

- access to additional analysis tools,

- number of portfolios that can be tracked,

- number of securities that can be tracked per portfolio, and

- types of securities handled.

Frequency of Updates

Perhaps the most important elements of the checklist are the frequency of the updates and whether a portfolio is updated automatically or by the user. News, additional tools, and overall activity reporting are of great benefit, but the tracking, the maintenance, and the updating of holdings are the key basic functions desired by all investors.

Tip→	One of the most important elements of the checklist is the frequency of the portfolio updates and if the updates are done automatically or by the user.

Some investors are so accustomed to updating their holdings on their own that they would rather do it themselves. Others might welcome a site that takes the task off their hands. In most cases, portfolios are updated automatically every couple of minutes or so while the user is at the site. In some instances however, portfolios need to be refreshed manually by the user—either by logging onto the site and then having the site update the portfolio or by going to a specific link on the site and clicking a button.

Links to Brokerages

There are four unique features available only with on-line portfolio management systems. The first is a direct download function of one's on-line discount brokerage accounts. This direct download function works like a link to your brokerage account. When a change is made to your account holdings, say you purchase 1,000 shares of a new stock, you simply log into your on-line portfolio manager and download the change directly into your on-line portfolio—free of the need for you to record it yourself manually.

Tip→	A feature available only with on-line portfolio managers is direct account downloading from your on-line discount broker.

The roster of on-line discount brokerage firms who provide this functionality to their customers includes Charles Schwab, E*Trade, and Fidelity. However, the list of sites that have such account downloading partnerships is a short one. MSN MoneyCentral Investor and Quicken.com are the only sites to currently offer the capability.

Look for this rare capability feature to become more commonplace among on-line portfolio tracking sites in the very near future.

Links to Newswire Services

Another unique feature found only with on-line portfolio managers is direct links to newswire stories and news headlines on the companies you currently track in your portfolios. These news stories are often located right on the portfolio's current holdings ledger.

> **Tip→** Another feature only available with on-line portfolio managers is direct links to newswire services.

Newswire services range from the standard set (Business Wire, PR Newswire) that can be found almost anywhere on the Web to a more upper tier of limited-access newswires and news resources (Wall Street Journal Interactive, MSNBC, and perhaps Reuters). In most instances, links are provided to complete news articles, while other times they are merely news headlines.

This is a basic feature, offered by all the sites reviewed here. The depth and breadth of coverage is what can set some sites apart from others, not to mention access to any subscription-based market news stories like those from Wall Street Journal Interactive or TheStreet.com.

E-Mail Alerts

The third, and most significant feature that helps differentiate an on-line portfolio manager from a software program is E-mail capabilities. An E-mail alert is a notification that something has happened with your portfolio or that something will affect your portfolio in some way. They can warn you of danger (a stock falling below a price target) or merely notify you of general activity (a stock split). The alert could convey something as simple as a dividend being declared for one of the stocks that you own. Or maybe you own shares in a certain sector fund and that sector has just hit on a new technological discovery—with E-mail alerts, you are notified of such an event.

> **Tip→** The most significant feature differentiating on-line managers from software is E-mail capabilities.

E-mail alerts are not junk mail and they do not clog up your inbox with unnecessary messages. E-mail alerts are set up in a user profile and they only notify you of events happening to the securities you are tracking, either in your primary portfolios or your "watchlists" (more on this on page 113).

FIGURE 4.19
*An E-mail alert
from the
INVESTools site
is sent to your
inbox
notifying you
that Nike, Inc.,
has hit a price
target.*

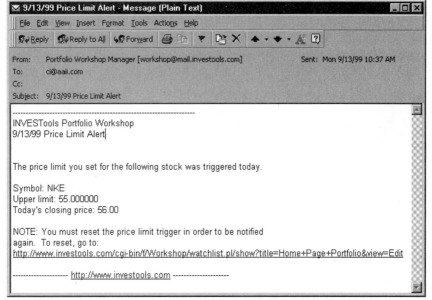

Tip→ A profile is set up so that the user is simply notified of events affecting their portfolio holdings.

E-mail alert-enabled portfolio managers have somewhat become the standard. Four out of eight on-line managers listed here offer some type of E-mail alert. Currently, all E-mail alert functionality is conducted in a delayed basis—the E-mail alert arrives in your inbox approximately 15 minutes after the event has taken place. To illustrate this, think about the above example—a stock hitting a price target. Once the stock hits the price limit, the E-mail alert is triggered, created, and 15 minutes later it is sent off to your E-mail box.

Timeliness is no doubt a factor here, and perhaps some would question if any real investment decisions can be made when such alerts warn you 15 minutes after the fact. Nevertheless, knowledge is power! And you might not learn of such events until maybe a day or two later—when it is *really* too late. Looking at E-mail alerts this way, their value becomes much clearer.

Warning→ E-mail alerts are currently sent on a delayed basis—15 to 20 minutes after an event has taken place.

Access to Additional Analysis Tools

The fourth and final unique feature available only with on-line portfolio management systems is access to an abundance of additional tools for further research and analysis. The degree of quality of these additional tools helps to add great value to the overall site.

Tip→	Access to additional analysis tools is the final unique feature available only with on-line portfolio management tools.

FIGURE 4.20
The stock screening module featured on the new MSN MoneyCentral Investor site showing the results of a growth screen.

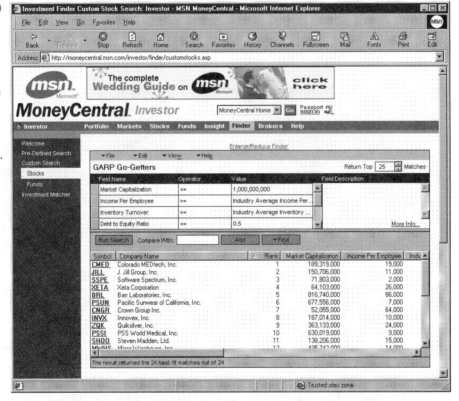

The most popular tools include stock and mutual find screening modules, interactive technical charting applications, and financial planning assistance. With screening modules, be sure to check out the depth of data and number of data fields available for screening—two key factors that help differentiate the tools. In terms of charting, the availability of technical indicators and user-defined time frames are just some of the things to look for. Other nice features to look for include access to fundamental data, earnings estimates, company and fund reports, market statistics, and any financial calculators.

Tip→	Two key factors that best differentiate these additional analysis tools for screening are the depth of data and the number of data fields available.

Access to such tools is quite variable, and they are offered in some capacity by all the sites reviewed here. The depth of data and the degree of functionality of the modules is what can set some sites apart from others.

Tip→	When reviewing additional charting modules found at an on-line tracking site, look for technical indicators and the ability to set user-defined time frames.

Number of Portfolios

The number of portfolios that can be tracked at these sites also varies and might prove to be an initial criteria that quickly narrows your choices. The number ranges from a single portfolio to an unlimited number of portfolios. Two sites allow its registered users to set up an infinite number of portfolios.

Most, if not all, of these on-line portfolio tracking systems will allow you to track a portfolio of stocks or mutual funds that you do not own but would like to keep an eye on. Referred to as a "watchlist" or "watch" portfolio, the data entry is done differently for this type of portfolio. Also, the monitoring measures are set up a little differently for watchlists, so that you can judge whether these securities would make good investments.

Warning→	The number of portfolios that can be tracked at on-line portfolio management sites is quite variable.

Number of Securities per Portfolio

When it comes to the number of investments or securities that can be tracked within a single portfolio, the totals get quite out of hand. The lowest total number of securities for one portfolio is 10. The maximum number of securities that can be tracked by the majority of these sites is between 100 and 200 unique investments per portfolio.

Tip→	Be sure to check on the number of securities that can be tracked per portfolio—a total that is also quite variable.

Even the number that can be tracked by the MSN Moneycentral Investor site and Quicken.com is a staggering 5,000 securities spread out over 50 portfolios. These are totals that most investors will not even come close to reaching, but it may be nice to know the capacity is there.

Types of Securities Handled

The last item on our on-line portfolio manager shopping list is the types of securities that can be tracked by the module. This element is listed last because it is the simplest factor to determine whether or not an on-line portfolio manager is right for you. As mentioned earlier, these on-line tools are not for everyone—especially the sophisticated individual investor.

If you own investments beyond stocks, funds, and bonds, these tools might not provide the capabilities your portfolio requires. Of the eight offerings discussed here, only three services track investment instruments other than stocks, mutual funds, and bonds. Most will cover the major indexes. The specific coverage of securities is noted for each Web site in the descriptions that follow. Each of the sites allow you to get quotes on any stock or mutual fund included in their particular database.

Warning→	If you are a sophisticated investor with holdings other than stocks, funds, and bonds, these on-line tracking tools might not be of much value to you.

The Standouts

The sites that stand out from all other on-line portfolio managers are the MSN Moneycentral Investor and, to a lesser degree, SmartMoney and Quicken.com. Between the trio, the MSN MoneyCentral Investor site gets the nod as the overall best because of its capabilities, update frequency, and additional investment analysis tools—not to mention the fact that it is completely free. Again, MSN MoneyCentral Investor is the only site that has portfolio tracking capabilities closely rivaling those of some of the general-purpose portfolio management software programs.

Reviews

CBS MarketWatch	
Performance	2
Usefulness	2
Documentation	3
Ease of Use	5
Value	2

CBS MarketWatch

by MarketWatch.com, Inc.
Free—any PC with Internet access
(415) 733-0500
cbs.marketwatch.com

CBS MarketWatch, quite possibly the best investment-related Web site for company and market news, provides an on-line portfolio manager to its registered users free of charge.

On the MarketWatch site, it states that the site can handle an unlimited number of portfolios, but it asks that users limit those portfolios to 200 securities per portfolio—consisting of stocks, mutual funds, options,

FIGURE 4.21
A value view taken from the CBS MarketWatch site provides dollar value change and percentage change.

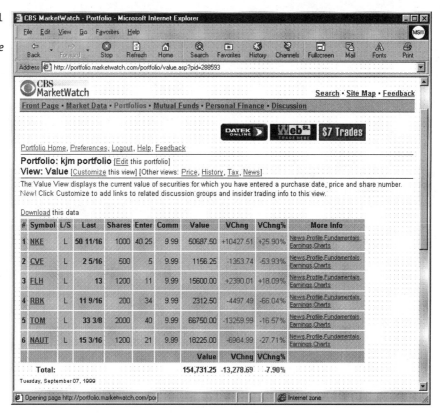

and futures. Portfolios can be updated manually or there is an option to have them updated automatically every five minutes. News services include AP, CBS MarketWatch, Reuters, and UPI. Subsidiary BigCharts.com provides all interactive charting capabilities.

The MarketWatch on-line portfolio manager interface is completely customizable. It can display up to 15 columns of data and information. Also, 14 different types of news stories and reports can be linked to any one of the four main portfolio views.

The MarketWatch site offers a basic tracking tool that is clearly grounded in the news-side of portfolio monitoring. Standard options are present here, but little extras can be found.

INVESTools	
Performance	3
Usefulness	3
Documentation	2
Ease of Use	4
Value	3

INVESTools
by INVESTools, Inc.
Free–$9.95/mo.—any PC with Internet access
(800) 567-2683
www.investools.com

The primarily fee-based INVESTools Web site is rather interesting site in that it offers two different portfolio managers with two different price structures.

A single portfolio consisting of 10 securities can be tracked for free at the site. Under the site's Portfolio Workshop area, which operates as a premium service, a single portfolio of 100 securities can be monitored for $9.95 a month. Two types of securities can be tracked at the INVESTools site—stocks and mutual funds. E-mail alerts, available only with a subscription, are triggered for the securities you hold when news travels over the wires (primarily supplied by Comtex) and when price levels are breached. The subscription-based Workshop also provides user-defined stock screening capabilities using Market Guide's stock database, access to Zacks Investment Research, and advanced technical charting. The first month is free for this subscription.

Those who sign up for the free service gain access to historical and intraday charts, nine pre-defined stock screens, and news headlines. E-mail alert functions are not available to free users. There is currently no mutual fund screening module at this site.

FIGURE 4.22
The INVESTools portfolio manager features four different views, including one for fundamentals.

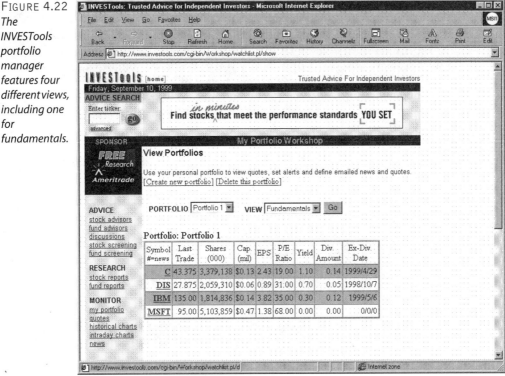

This is a well-organized site for portfolio tracking and evaluation. Additional research and analysis tools are very strong, however, portfolio reports are almost non-existent. INVESTools is a respectable site, yet the monthly fee keeps it from being the best value.

Morningstar.com	
Performance	3
Usefulness	4
Documentation	2
Ease of Use	4
Value	3

Morningstar.com
by Morningstar, Inc.
Free–$9.95/ mo.—any PC with Internet access
(800) 507-9622
www.morningstar.com

Screening software developer and leading source for mutual fund data, Morningstar, Inc., supports a free on-line portfolio tracker at the newly redesigned Web site—accessible via either the www.morningstar.com or www.morningstar.net URLs. There is also a premium service available for $9.95 a month.

The site, now to be referred to as Morningstar.com, has capabilities to track 10 portfolios, each holding 50 securities per portfolio. Stocks and mutual funds are the only securities handled. The on-line manager can also keep a cash balance. Newswire services include Dow Jones and Reuters. E-mail alerts, sent to premium service subscribers only, notify you of events as complex as a heavy volume price movement and as simple as the change of a ticker symbol. Morningstar's on-line portfolio manager works in conjunction with two of the most popular general-purpose portfolio management software programs—Microsoft Money and Quicken.

FIGURE 4.23
The Snapshot portfolio page on new Morningstar.com site provides an asset allocation pie chart.

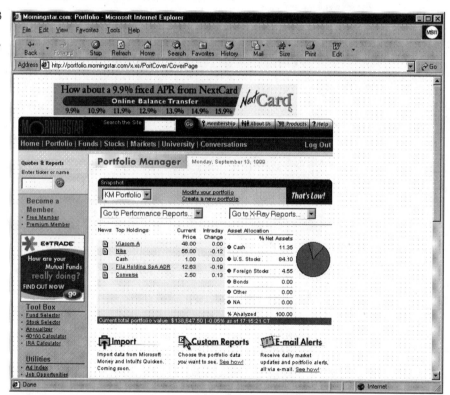

Morningstar.com's portfolio interface can be set to five different views, including performance, intraday, and fundamental views. A portfolio snapshot provides an asset allocation pie chart. Morningstar.com features a unique way to examine your portfolios, called X-Rays. These X-Rays are slightly different from standard views in that they can break down your portfolio and present your holdings in different formats. Three different free X-Rays can be displayed, including Asset

Class, Stock Stats, and Fees & Expenses. Stock Sector and World Regions X-Rays are two of the four additional X-Rays available with a premium service subscription.

Morningstar.com offers a solid list of report capabilities including performance reports for securities, industries, and asset classes and against a benchmark comparison. The reports can also be generated to include multiple portfolios.

This is another quality site for portfolio tracking and evaluation. Additional analysis tools are available for free and via the premium service subscription—with the subscription-based screening tools being some of the best on the Web. Advanced Morningstar quicktake stock and fund reports, available with premium service, are also top-notch.

MSN MoneyCentral Investor	
Performance	4
Usefulness	5
Documentation	2
Ease of Use	5
Value	5

MSN MoneyCentral Investor
by Microsoft, Inc.
Free—any PC with Internet access
(800) 426-9400
moneycentral.msn.com/investor

The Microsoft MSN MoneyCentral Investor site has undergone many updates and remains one of the most powerful investment tools on the Web. This site is currently free to all registered users and offers on-line portfolio tracking capabilities as part of its package of services.

The on-line portfolio manager allows you to track one portfolio that can include up to 50 accounts—which are essentially 50 mini-portfolios—tracking up to 5,000 securities total. MSN MoneyCentral Investor also allows you to track a "watch account" portfolio. For more information on securities and transactions handled and performance reports offered, please see the discussion of this site in the previous section starting on page 105.

MSN MoneyCentral Investor offers news stories and headlines from Business Wire, the cable channel MSNBC, PR Newswire, and Reuters. The site also provides a market summary report—updated several times throughout the trading day—from the Wall Street Journal Interactive edition. The site no longer offers E-mail alerts, but does offer a daily E-mail delivered either as a mid-day update or as an end-of-day complete market wrap-up.

MSN MoneyCentral Investor provides unique tracking opportunities for DLJdirect, E*Trade, Fidelity Investments, Schwab, and Waterhouse Securities on-line brokerage customers. Account holders at any of the above five firms can down-

FIGURE 4.24
Drop-down menus are available for selecting security types and transactions within the MSN MoneyCentral Investor site transaction window.

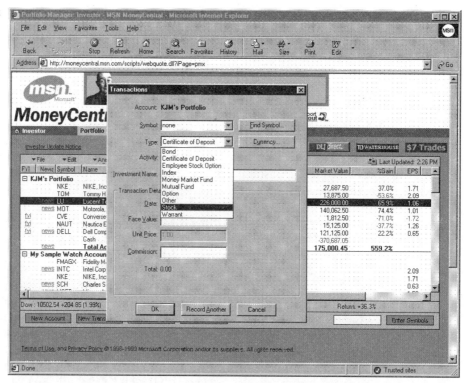

load account information directly from their brokerage account into a portfolio established on MSN MoneyCentral Investor—one of only two sites reviewed here to currently offer such an option to its users (Quicken.com being the other).

The Microsoft MSN MoneyCentral Investor site is a multi-dimensional power-house site, providing not only a portfolio tracking module but also extensive screening tools. Other features of note include: access to an abundance of news coverage, consensus earnings estimates and analyst recommendations, company reports, and expanded company fundamentals. The MSN MoneyCentral Investor on-line portfolio manager is by far the most complete module of the eight sites discussed in this section. For a look at how the MSN MoneyCentral Investor site stacks up against software-based portfolio management programs, take a look at its review in the previous section on page 105.

FIGURE 4.25
*MSN
MoneyCentral
Investor
generates a
multi-portfolio
YTD
performance
report,
displayed here
as a bar chart.*

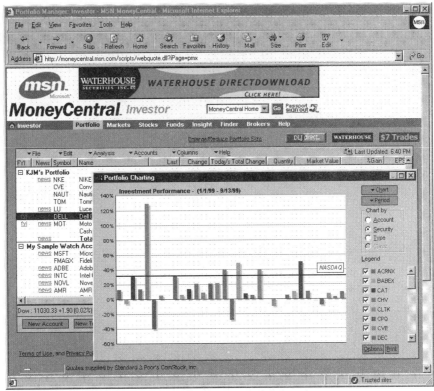

Quicken.com	
Performance	4
Usefulness	4
Documentation	2
Ease of Use	5
Value	4

Quicken.com
by Intuit Inc.
Free—any PC with Internet access
(800) 446-8848
www.quicken.com

The popular portfolio management software program Quicken now has its own Web site where users can track their personal portfolios via an on-line portfolio module. In addition to a standard HTML-based portfolio tracker, a dynamic ActiveX portfolio tool (see page 76) is also available at the Quicken.com site.

Quicken.com currently offers the same tracking options as the Microsoft MSN MoneyCentral Investor Web site—50 portfolios with 100 securities per portfolio. Portfolios can consist of stocks, mutual funds, and bonds and can be updated

FIGURE 4.26
A personalized Quicken.com home page features a user's portfolios in a fully-customizable mini-portfolio module.

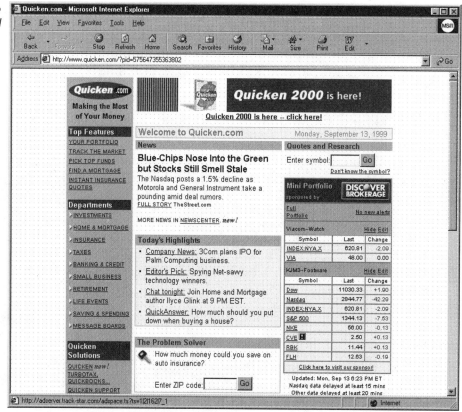

manually by the user or automatically as often as every minute. The ActiveX portfolio module allows portfolios to be updated manually or automatically every minute. Also like the MSN MoneyCentral Investor site, Quicken.com offers the unique capability to download account information directly from an on-line brokerage account—currently the site can only provide this service to Waterhouse Securities customers. News services include Dow Jones and PR Newswire. A new market update report from TheStreet.com is posted on Quicken.com every hour of the trading day. The two on-line portfolio manager interfaces are completely customizable. The standard interface, for example, can display up to 20 columns of data and information. A special customizable mini-portfolio also appears on a personalized, user-specific home page of the Quicken.com site.

Alerts are available at this site, however, they lack the E-mail characteristics one would normally prefer with their alerts. The alerts offered on Quicken.com are simply icons in the form of yellow exclamation marks, which appear next to the corresponding tickers. A summary of current alerts can also be accessed from a link at the top of the on-line portfolio module. News, dividend announcements, and splits trigger these alerts.

Before MSN MoneyCentral Investor became a free site, Quicken.com was the best free resource on the Web. Things have indeed changed and it will be interesting to see what Intuit does in the coming year in response to Microsoft's move. Nevertheless, the Quicken.com site remains one of the better free havens for the individual investor to monitor their investment holdings.

SmartMoney.com	
Performance	4
Usefulness	4
Documentation	3
Ease of Use	5
Value	4

SmartMoney.com
by SmartMoney Magazine
Free—any PC with Internet access
www.smartmoney.com

SmartMoney magazine's Web site hosts a free on-line portfolio manager. The site offers both a standard on-line portfolio manager and a Java-enhanced tracking tool. Registered users can enter up to 20 portfolios and can easily switch back and forth between the two modules and not lose any data or have to double-enter their holdings.

The 20 portfolios can hold a maximum of 30 securities—comprised of any mix of stocks, mutual funds, or options. The portfolios can also track a cash balance. Free E-mail alerts are sent to your desktop regarding news stories and splits. Newswire services include SmartMoney magazine and Dow Jones. Security and asset class performance reports can be generated—even cost basis can be checked via the average cost method.

A solid mutual fund screening tool is another Java-based module available at the site, in addition to charting capabilities and financial planning assistance.

The SmartMoney.com Web site is clearly one of the better sites for tracking a portfolio. This technology-driven site ranks among the top sites regardless of a free or fee-based nature.

FIGURE 4.27
The sleek, Java-enhanced on-line portfolio manager found on the SmartMoney.com site keeps you up-to-date on your holdings and the markets.

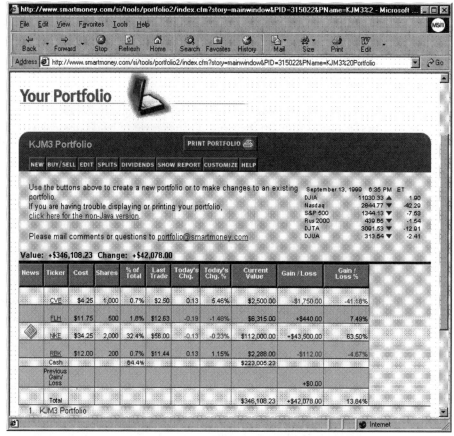

	Thomson Investors Network	
Performance	3	
Usefulness	4	
Documentation	3	
Ease of Use	5	
Value	3	

Thomson Investors Network
by Thomson Financial Services, Inc.
Free–$34.95/yr.—any PC with Internet access
(301) 545-4999
www.thomsoninvest.net

Thomson Investors Network, a primarily fee-based Web site, also supports an on-line portfolio management tool. The site charges $34.95 for a one-year subscription. However, the newly-updated portfolio manager can be accessed without a subscription. The free portfolio manager allows users to track a single portfolio consisting of 10 securities. The free portfolio tracker also provides total percent gain and total dollar return as well as total cost basis.

FIGURE 4.28
The Thomson Investors Network on-line portfolio manager has a linked quote and news LiveTicker module.

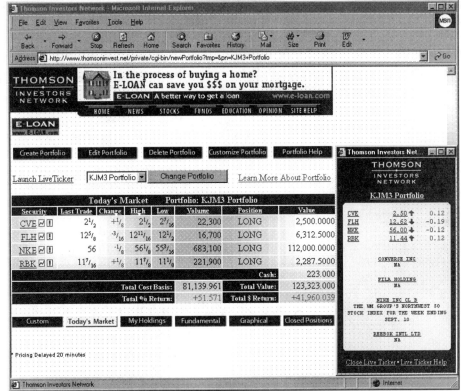

With a subscription, Thomson Investors Network's on-line portfolio manager can track up to 25 portfolios with 25 securities—either stocks or mutual funds—per portfolio. Portfolios are updated each time the user logs onto the site. Flashes, or E-mail alerts, are sent to your desktop when any changes occur to your portfolio such as a stock hitting a price target or a change in a stock's rating. These "flashes" are available to users with a subscription as well as those using the free access.

Thomson's on-line portfolio manager can generate security performance reports and create those reports for user-specified time periods. Thomson Investors Network also has solid stock and mutual fund screening and charting modules.

Thomson Investors Network remains one of the better investment Web sites, and the free portfolio tracking capabilities on the site are quite solid. However, the current monthly fee is far too high and shows that the operators are somewhat out of touch with their competition. Now that Thomson has revamped the tracking tool, an overhaul of its price structure, which is definitely overdue, should be next.

Yahoo! Finance	
Performance	2
Usefulness	3
Documentation	2
Ease of Use	4
Value	2

Yahoo! Finance
by Yahoo! Inc.
Free—any PC with Internet access
(408) 731-3300
quote.yahoo.com

The Yahoo! Finance site has undergone yet another significant change recently—adding a Java-based portfolio module to its on-line portfolio management section. The Java applet looks like a juiced-up spreadsheet and has drop-down menus for switching portfolios and changing views. Four views are provided in all, including one called DayWatch, which supplies current data for last trade, volume, average volume, and the day's trading range. Each view includes a More Info column that provides links for each of the securities in your portfolios. These links include charts, quotes, news, SEC-filings, profiles, research reports, insider trading data, and messages from the Yahoo! Finance message boards.

Yahoo! Finance, a popular site for market and economic news and statistics, is a completely free site and offers all of its portfolio tracking for free to registered users.

Like CBS MarketWatch, The Yahoo! Finance site allows you to monitor as many portfolios as you wish, each holding up to 200 securities per portfolio. Portfolios can be comprised of stocks, mutual funds, or indexes and need to be updated manually. The Yahoo! Finance site includes a reminder feature that acts as an alert, minus the E-mail element. These reminders focus on price limits. Once a price limit is reached, an up or down arrow will appear for that security within the column labeled "last trade" in the holdings table. Newswire services include Reuters and TheStreet.com company headlines.

Yahoo! Finance is yet another free site that offers the individual investor portfolio tracking capabilities—albeit, modest capabilities—in a user-friendly inteface. However, the site offers many news links, several quality analysis modules, and the aforementioned unlimited portfolio storage.

FIGURE 4.29
The new Java-based on-line portfolio tracking tool for the Yahoo! Finance site offers four views including a DayWatch display.

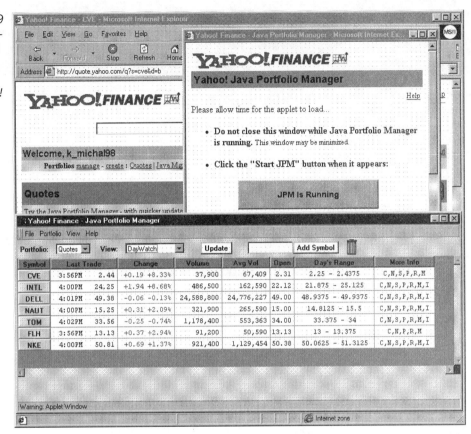

Portfolio Management: Disk-Based Services		Capital Gainz 6.0	Captool Individual Investor 1.1
Company		AlleyCat Software, Inc.	Captools Co.
Telephone		(919) 542-6117	(800) 826-8082
Web Site		www.alleycatsw.com	www.captools.com
E-mail Address		dlcohen@alleycatsw.com	sales@captools.com
Price (AAII Member Discount)		$69.00 (10%)	$249.00 (20%)
Demo Available (Cost, *=cost via Internet)		✖ (free*)	✖ (free*)
Platform (DOS, Mac, Windows, Internet)		Windows	Windows
Maximum Portfolios/Securities per Portfolio		999/unlimited	unlimited/unlimited
Maximum Securities/Transactions per Security		unlimited/unlimited	unlimited/unlimited
Securities/ Assets Handled	Cash/Stocks/Mutual Funds	✖	✖
	Bonds (Fixed/Variable/Zero/PIK)	✖ (fixed/variable/zero)	✖
	Annuities		✖
	Options/Futures/Warrants		✖
	Real Estate/Partnerships		✖
	User-Defined		✖
Security Classification	Identification (Name/Ticker/CUSIP)	✖	✖
	Account Number/Management Firm	✖	✖ (account number)
	Asset Class (Pre-Defined/User-Defined)	✖	✖
	Industry (SIC Codes/User-Defined)	✖ (user-defined)	✖
Transactions Handled	Deposit/Withdrawal; Buy/Sell	✖ (buy/sell)	✖
	Short/Cover	✖	✖
	Margin	✖	✖
	Receive/Deliver Security		✖
	Return of Capital		✖
	Dividends (Cash/Stock/Splits/Reinvest)	✖	✖
	Interest Income	✖	✖
	Bond With Discount/Premium	✖	✖
	Treatment of Fees/Commissions	✖	✖
Security Lot Assignments (Avg.Cost/FIFO/Specific Lot)		✖	✖
Reports	Current Holdings	✖	✖
	Holdings by Lots	✖	✖
	Cash Portfolio Status	✖	✖
	Tax Schedules (Interest/Div/Cap Gains)	✖	✖
	Projected Cash Flow		✖
	Customized Reports; Batch Reporting		✖
Performance Reports	Security/Industry/Asset	✖ (security/industry)	✖
	Portfolio (Single/Multiple)	✖	✖
	Holding Period/Between Period Returns	✖	✖
	Value-Weighted IRR/Time-Weighted Ret.	✖ (time-weighted)	✖
	Tax-Adjusted Returns		✖
	Benchmark Comparison		✖
	Follows AIMR Standards		✖
Data Support	Data Services Supported	AOL, CompuServe, Prodigy, Internet, MetaStock, Reuters, TC2000	AOL, CompuServe, Prodigy, Internet, DJN/R, Dial/Data
	Import Formats Supported	comma-delimited	ASCII, quote-comma-delimited
	Export Formats Supported	comma-delimited	ASCII, quote-comma-delimited

Portfolio Management: Disk-Based Services		Financial Navigator 7.0	The Investor's Accountant 6.0
Company		Financial Navigator International	Hamilton Software, Inc.
Telephone		(800) 468-3636	(800) 733-9607
Web Site		www.finnav.com	www.hamiltonsoftware.com
E-mail Address		sales@finnav.com	info@hamiltonsoftware.com
Price (AAII Member Discount)		$349.00 (10%)	$395.00 (25%)
Demo Available (Cost, *=cost via Internet)		✖ (free*)	✖ ($5.00)
Platform (DOS, Mac, Windows, Internet)		Windows	
Maximum Portfolios/Securities per Portfolio		unlimited/unlimited	unlimited/32,766
Maximum Securities/Transactions per Security		unlimited/unlimited	32,766/unlimited
Securities/ Assets Handled	Cash/Stocks/Mutual Funds	✖	✖
	Bonds (Fixed/Variable/Zero/PIK)	✖ (fixed/variable/zero)	✖
	Annuities	✖	✖
	Options/Futures/Warrants	✖	✖
	Real Estate/Partnerships	✖	✖ (real estate)
	User-Defined	✖	✖
Security Classification	Identification (Name/Ticker/CUSIP)	✖	✖
	Account Number/Management Firm	✖	
	Asset Class (Pre-Defined/User-Defined)	✖	✖
	Industry (SIC Codes/User-Defined)	✖ (user-defined)	✖ (user-defined)
Transactions Handled	Deposit/Withdrawal; Buy/Sell	✖	✖
	Short/Cover	✖	✖
	Margin	✖	✖
	Receive/Deliver Security	✖	
	Return of Capital	✖	✖
	Dividends (Cash/Stock/Splits/Reinvest)	✖	✖
	Interest Income	✖	✖
	Bond With Discount/Premium	✖	✖
	Treatment of Fees/Commissions	✖	✖
Security Lot Assignments (Avg.Cost/FIFO/Specific Lot)		✖ (average cost/specific lot)	✖
Reports	Current Holdings	✖	✖
	Holdings by Lots	✖	✖
	Cash Portfolio Status	✖	✖
	Tax Schedules (Interest/Div/Cap Gains)	✖	✖
	Projected Cash Flow	✖	✖
	Customized Reports; Batch Reporting	✖	
Performance Reports	Security/Industry/Asset	✖ (security/asset)	✖ (security)
	Portfolio (Single/Multiple)	✖	✖
	Holding Period/Between Period Returns	✖ (holding period)	✖
	Value-Weighted IRR/Time-Weighted Ret	✖ (value weighted IRR)	✖
	Tax-Adjusted Returns		✖
	Benchmark Comparison		
	Follows AIMR Standards		✖
Data Support	Data Services Supported	IDC, Internet	AOL, CompuServe, Prodigy, Telescan
	Import Formats Supported		ASCII, CSV, tab-delimited
	Export Formats Supported	ASCII, clipboard	ASCII, CSV, quote-delimited

Portfolio Management: Disk-Based Services		Money 2000 Deluxe	NAIC Personal Record Keeper 2.5
Company		Microsoft, Inc.	NAIC/Quant IX Software
Telephone		(800) 426-9400	(248) 583-6242
Web Site		www.microsoft.com/money	www.quantixsoftware.com
E-mail Address			info@quantixsoftware.com
Price (AAII Member Discount)		$34.95 Basic; $64.95 Fin'l Suite	$99.00
Demo Available (Cost, *=cost via Internet)			✖ (free*)
Platform (DOS, Mac, Windows, Internet)		Windows	Windows
Maximum Portfolios/Securities per Portfolio		unlimited/unlimited	unlimited/unlimited
Maximum Securities/Transactions per Security		unlimited/unlimited	unlimited/unlimited
Securities/ Assets Handled	Cash/Stocks/Mutual Funds	✖	✖
	Bonds (Fixed/Variable/Zero/PIK)	✖ (fixed/variable/zero)	✖
	Annuities	✖	✖
	Options/Futures/Warrants	✖ (warrants)	✖
	Real Estate/Partnerships	✖	✖
	User-Defined	✖	✖
Security Classification	Identification (Name/Ticker/CUSIP)	✖ (name/ticker)	✖
	Account Number/Management Firm	✖	✖
	Asset Class (Pre-Defined/User-Defined)	✖ (pre-defined)	✖ (pre-defined)
	Industry (SIC Codes/User-Defined)	✖ (SIC codes)	✖ (SIC codes)
Transactions Handled	Deposit/Withdrawal; Buy/Sell	✖	✖
	Short/Cover	✖	
	Margin	✖	✖
	Receive/Deliver Security	✖	
	Return of Capital	✖	✖
	Dividends (Cash/Stock/Splits/Reinvest)	✖	✖
	Interest Income	✖	✖
	Bond With Discount/Premium	✖	✖
	Treatment of Fees/Commissions	✖	✖
Security Lot Assignments (Avg.Cost/FIFO/Specific Lot)		✖	✖
Reports	Current Holdings	✖	✖
	Holdings by Lots	✖	✖
	Cash Portfolio Status	✖	✖
	Tax Schedules (Interest/Div/Cap Gains)	✖	✖
	Projected Cash Flow		✖
	Customized Reports; Batch Reporting	customized reports	batch reporting
Performance Reports	Security/Industry/Asset	✖ (security/asset)	✖
	Portfolio (Single/Multiple)	✖ (single)	✖
	Holding Period/Between Period Returns	✖	✖
	Value-Weighted IRR/Time-Weighted Ret.	✖ (value-weighted IRR)	✖ (time-weighted)
	Tax-Adjusted Returns		
	Benchmark Comparison		✖
	Follows AIMR Standards		✖
Data Support	Data Services Supported	Any Internet service provider	CompuServe, Prodigy, Internet
	Import Formats Supported	Money, OFX, Quicken	ASCII, CSV
	Export Formats Supported	Excel, OFX, Quicken	ASCII, Excel, DIF, WK1, WRI

Portfolio Management: Disk-Based Services		Portfolio Analyzer 6.0	Quicken Deluxe 2000
Company		Hamilton Software, Inc.	Intuit Inc.
Telephone		(800) 733-9607	(800) 446-8848
Web Site		www.hamiltonsoftware.com	www.quicken.com
E-mail Address		info@hamiltonsoftware.com	
Price (AAII Member Discount)		$99.00	$29.95 Basic; $59.95 Deluxe
Demo Available (Cost, *=cost via Internet)		✖ ($5.00)	
Platform (DOS, Mac, Windows, Internet)			Mac/Windows
Maximum Portfolios/Securities per Portfolio		unlimited/32,766	512/1000+
Maximum Securities/Transactions per Security		32,766/unlimited	1000+/unlimited
Securities/ Assets Handled	Cash/Stocks/Mutual Funds	✖	✖
	Bonds (Fixed/Variable/Zero/PIK)	✖	✖ (fixed/variable/zero)
	Annuities	✖	✖
	Options/Futures/Warrants	✖	
	Real Estate/Partnerships	✖ (real estate)	
	User-Defined	✖	
Security Classification	Identification (Name/Ticker/CUSIP)	✖	✖ (name/ticker)
	Account Number/Management Firm		✖
	Asset Class (Pre-Defined/User-Defined)	✖	✖
	Industry (SIC Codes/User-Defined)		
Transactions Handled	Deposit/Withdrawal; Buy/Sell	✖	✖
	Short/Cover	✖	✖
	Margin	✖	✖
	Receive/Deliver Security		✖
	Return of Capital	✖	✖
	Dividends (Cash/Stock/Splits/Reinvest)	✖	✖
	Interest Income	✖	✖
	Bond With Discount/Premium	✖	✖
	Treatment of Fees/Commissions	✖	✖
Security Lot Assignments (Avg.Cost/FIFO/Specific Lot)		✖	✖
Reports	Current Holdings	✖	✖
	Holdings by Lots	✖	✖
	Cash Portfolio Status	✖	✖
	Tax Schedules (Interest/Div/Cap Gains)	✖	✖
	Projected Cash Flow	✖	✖
	Customized Reports; Batch Reporting		customized reports
Performance Reports	Security/Industry/Asset	✖ (security)	✖ (security/asset)
	Portfolio (Single/Multiple)	✖	✖
	Holding Period/Between Period Returns	✖ (holding period)	✖
	Value-Weighted IRR/Time-Weighted Ret.	✖ (value-weighted IRR)	✖ (value-weighted IRR)
	Tax-Adjusted Returns	✖	✖
	Benchmark Comparison		✖
	Follows AIMR Standards		✖
Data Support	Data Services Supported	AOL, CompuServe, Prodigy, Telescan	Any Internet service provider
	Import Formats Supported	ASCII, CSV, tab-delimited	CSV, Money, Quicken
	Export Formats Supported	ASCII, CSV	ASCII, tab-delimited, Lotus, Quicken

Portfolio Management: Disk-Based Services		Reeally! 1.239	MSN MoneyCentral Investor
Company		Mantic Software Corp.	Microsoft, Inc.
Telephone		(800) 730-2919	(800) 426-9400
Web Site		www.manticsoft.com	moneycentral.msn.com/investor
E-mail Address		mantic@manticsoft.com	webmaster@msn.com
Price (AAII Member Discount)		$150 Standard; $525 Pro	free with Internet access
Demo Available (Cost, *=cost via Internet)		✖ (free*)	
Platform (DOS, Mac, Windows, Internet)		Windows	Internet
Maximum Portfolios/Securities per Portfolio		unlimited/unlimited	50/100
Maximum Securities/Transactions per Security		unlimited/unlimited	5,000/NA
Securities/ Assets Handled	Cash/Stocks/Mutual Funds	✖	✖
	Bonds (Fixed/Variable/Zero/PIK)	✖ (fixed/variable/zero)	✖
	Annuities	✖	
	Options/Futures/Warrants	✖ (options/futures)	✖ (options)
	Real Estate/Partnerships	✖	
	User-Defined	✖	✖
Security Classification	Identification (Name/Ticker/CUSIP)	✖ (name/ticker)	✖ (ticker)
	Account Number/Management Firm	✖	
	Asset Class (Pre-Defined/User-Defined)	✖	
	Industry (SIC Codes/User-Defined)	✖ (user-defined)	
Transactions Handled	Deposit/Withdrawal; Buy/Sell	✖	✖ (buy/sell)
	Short/Cover	✖	✖
	Margin	✖	
	Receive/Deliver Security	✖	✖
	Return of Capital	✖	✖
	Dividends (Cash/Stock/Splits/Reinvest)	✖	✖ (stock/split/reinvest)
	Interest Income	✖	✖
	Bond With Discount/Premium	✖	
	Treatment of Fees/Commissions	✖	✖
Security Lot Assignments (Avg.Cost/FIFO/Specific Lot)		✖ (FIFO/specific lot)	
Reports	Current Holdings	✖	✖
	Holdings by Lots	✖	✖
	Cash Portfolio Status	✖	✖
	Tax Schedules (Interest/Div/Cap Gains)	✖	
	Projected Cash Flow		
	Customized Reports; Batch Reporting	batch reporting	customized reports
Performance Reports	Security/Industry/Asset	✖	✖
	Portfolio (Single/Multiple)	✖	✖
	Holding Period/Between Period Returns	✖	✖
	Value-Weighted IRR/Time-Weighted Ret.	✖	
	Tax-Adjusted Returns		
	Benchmark Comparison	✖	
	Follows AIMR Standards	✖	
Data Support	Data Services Supported	Internet	NA
	Import Formats Supported	ASCII, Quicken	Money, OFX, Quicken, Yahoo!
	Export Formats Supported	ASCII	Money, Tab-delimited, TXT

Porfolio Management: Internet-Based Services		CBS MarketWatch	INVESTools
Company		MarketWatch.com, Inc.	INVESTools, Inc.
Telephone		(415) 733-0500	(800) 567-2683
Web Site		cbs.marketwatch.com	www.investools.com
E-mail Address			service@investools.com
Subscription Price (AAII Member Discount)		free w/ Internet access	free-$9.95/mo.
On-line Portfolio Module Works in Conjunction with			
Software (Software Titles)			
Automatic Portfolio Updates (Frequency of Updates)		✖ (every 5 minutes)	
Brokerage Services—Links			
Newswire Services—Links		✖ (AP, Business Wire, CBS Market-Watch, PR Newswire, Reuters, UPI)	✖ (Comtex)
E-mail Alerts	Alerts (News/Price Targets/Div/Splits)		✖ (news/price targets)
	Free/Subscription-based		subscription
	Delayed Alerts/Real-time Alerts		delayed
Additional Analysis Tools	Stock/Mutual Fund Screening	✖ (stock screening)	✖
	Interactive Charting	✖	✖
	Financial Planning	✖	
Maximum Portfolios/Securities per Portfolio		unlimited/200	1/10 or 1/100
Maximum Securities/Transactions per Security		unlimited/NA	100/NA
Securities/ Assets Handled	Cash/Stocks/Mutual Funds	✖ (stocks/mutual funds)	✖ (stocks/mutual funds)
	Bonds (Fixed/Variable/Zero/PIK)		
	Annuities		
	Options/Futures/Warrants	✖ (options/futures)	
	Real Estate/Partnerships		
	User-Defined		
Security Classification	Identification (Name/Ticker/CUSIP)	✖ (name/ticker)	✖ (name/ticker)
	Account Number/Management Firm		
	Asset Class (Pre-Defined/User-Defined)		
	Industry (SIC Codes/User-Defined)		
Transactions Handled	Deposit/Withdrawal; Buy/Sell	✖ (buy/sell)	✖ (buy/sell)
	Short/Cover	✖	
	Margin		
	Receive/Deliver Security		
	Dividends (Cash/Stock/Splits/Reinvest)		
	Interest Income		
	Treatment of Fees/Commissions		
Security Lot Assignments (Avg.Cost/FIFO/Specific Lot)			
Reports	Current Holdings (Total/By Lots)	✖ (total)	✖ (total)
	Cash Portfolio Status		
	Tax Schedules (Interest/Div/Cap Gains)	✖ (capital gains)	
	Customized Reports		
Performance Reports	Security/Industry/Asset	✖ (security)	
	Portfolio (Single/Multiple)	✖ (single)	
	Holding Period/Between Period Returns	✖ (holding period)	
	Benchmark Comparison		

Porfolio Management: Internet-Based Services		Morningstar.com	MSN MoneyCentral Investor
Company		Morningstar, Inc.	Microsoft, Inc.
Telephone		(800) 507-9622	(800) 426-9400
Web Site		www.morningstar.com	moneycentral.msn.com/investor
E-mail Address		joe@morningstar.com	
Subscription Price (AAII Member Discount)		free-$9.95/mo.	free with Internet access
On-line Portfolio Module Works in Conjunction with Software (Software Titles)		✖ (Money, Quicken)	✖ (Money)
Automatic Portfolio Updates (Frequency of Updates)			✖ (every minute)
Brokerage Services—Links			✖ (DLJdirect, E*Trade, Fidelity, Schwab, Waterhouse)
Newswire Services—Links		✖ (Business Wire, Dow Jones, PR Newswire, Reuters)	✖ (Business Wire, MSNBC, PR Newswire, Reuters, Wall Street Journal Interactive)
E-mail Alerts	Alerts (News/Price Targets/Div/Splits)	✖	
	Free/Subscription-based	subscription	
	Delayed Alerts/Real-time Alerts	delayed	
Additional Analysis Tools	Stock/Mutual Fund Screening	✖	✖
	Interactive Charting	✖	✖
	Financial Planning	✖	✖
Maximum Portfolios/Securities per Portfolio		10/50	50/100
Maximum Securities/Transactions per Security		500/NA	5,000/NA
Securities/ Assets Handled	Cash/Stocks/Mutual Funds	✖	✖
	Bonds (Fixed/Variable/Zero/PIK)		✖
	Annuities		
	Options/Futures/Warrants		✖ (options)
	Real Estate/Partnerships		
	User-Defined		✖
Security Classification	Identification (Name/Ticker/CUSIP)	✖ (name, ticker)	✖ (ticker)
	Account Number/Management Firm	✖ (management firm)	
	Asset Class (Pre-Defined/User-Defined)	✖	
	Industry (SIC Codes/User-Defined)	✖	
Transactions Handled	Deposit/Withdrawal; Buy/Sell	✖ (buy/sell)	✖
	Short/Cover	✖	✖
	Margin		
	Receive/Deliver Security		✖
	Dividends (Cash/Stock/Splits/Reinvest)	✖	✖ (stock/split/reinvest)
	Interest Income		✖
	Treatment of Fees/Commissions		✖
Security Lot Assignments (Avg.Cost/FIFO/Specific Lot)			
Reports	Current Holdings (Total/By Lots)	✖ (total)	✖
	Cash Portfolio Status	✖	✖
	Tax Schedules (Interest/Div/Cap Gains)		
	Customized Reports		✖
Performance Reports	Security/Industry/Asset	✖	✖
	Portfolio (Single/Multiple)	✖	✖
	Holding Period/Between Period Returns	✖ (holding period)	✖
	Benchmark Comparison	✖	

Porfolio Management: Internet-Based Services		Quicken.com	SmartMoney.com
Company		Intuit Inc.	SmartMoney Magazine
Telephone		(800) 446-8848	
Web Site		www.quicken.com	www.smartmoney.com
E-mail Address			support@smartmoney.com
Subscription Price (AAII Member Discount)		free w/ Internet access	free w/ Internet access
On-line Portfolio Module Works in Conjunction with Software (Software Titles)		✖ (Quicken)	
Automatic Portfolio Updates (Frequency of Updates)		✖ (every minute)	
Brokerage Services—Links		✖ (Waterhouse)	
Newswire Services—Links		✖ (Dow Jones, PR Newswire, TheStreet.com)	✖ (SmartMoney, Dow Jones, Business Wire, PR Newswire)
E-mail Alerts	Alerts (News/Price Targets/Div/Splits)		✖ (news/splits)
	Free/Subscription-based		free
	Delayed Alerts/Real-time Alerts		delayed alerts
Additional Analysis Tools	Stock/Mutual Fund Screening	✖	✖ (mutual fund screening)
	Interactive Charting	✖	✖
	Financial Planning	✖	✖
Maximum Portfolios/Securities per Portfolio		50/100	20/30
Maximum Securities/Transactions per Security		5,000/NA	600/NA
Securities/ Assets Handled	Cash/Stocks/Mutual Funds	✖	✖
	Bonds (Fixed/Variable/Zero/PIK)	✖	
	Annuities		
	Options/Futures/Warrants		✖ (options)
	Real Estate/Partnerships		
	User-Defined		
Security Classification	Identification (Name/Ticker/CUSIP)	✖ (name, ticker)	✖ (name/ticker)
	Account Number/Management Firm		
	Asset Class (Pre-Defined/User-Defined)		
	Industry (SIC Codes/User-Defined)		
Transactions Handled	Deposit/Withdrawal; Buy/Sell	✖ (buy/sell)	✖ (buy/sell)
	Short/Cover		
	Margin		
	Receive/Deliver Security		
	Dividends (Cash/Stock/Splits/Reinvest)		✖ (stock/reinvest/splits)
	Interest Income		
	Treatment of Fees/Commissions		✖
Security Lot Assignments (Avg.Cost/FIFO/Specific Lot)			✖ (average cost)
Reports	Current Holdings (Total/By Lots)	✖	✖ (total)
	Cash Portfolio Status		✖
	Tax Schedules (Interest/Div/Cap Gains)		
	Customized Reports	✖	
Performance Reports	Security/Industry/Asset	✖ (security)	✖ (security/asset)
	Portfolio (Single/Multiple)	✖	✖ (single)
	Holding Period/Between Period Returns	✖ (holding period)	✖ (holding period)
	Benchmark Comparison		

135

Porfolio Management: Internet-Based Services		Thomson Investors Network	Yahoo! Finance
Company		Thomson Financial Services, Inc.	Yahoo! Inc.
Telephone		(301) 545-4999	(408) 731-3300
Web Site		www.thomsoninvest.net	quote.yahoo.com
E-mail Address		custserv@thomsoninvest.net	finance-admin@yahoo-inc.com
Subscription Price (AAII Member Discount)		free–$34.95/yr.	free
On-line Portfolio Module Works in Conjunction with			
Software (Software Titles)			
Automatic Portfolio Updates (Frequency of Updates)			
Brokerage Services—Links			
Newswire Services—Links		✖ (AP, Business Wire, Comtex, PR Newswire, Reuters)	✖ (AP, Business Wire, PR Newswire, Reuters, Standard & Poor's, TheStreet.com)
E-mail Alerts	Alerts (News/Price Targets/Div/Splits)	✖	
	Free/Subscription-based	free	
	Delayed Alerts/Real-time Alerts	delayed	
Additional Analysis Tools	Stock/Mutual Fund Screening	✖	✖ (stock screening)
	Interactive Charting	✖	✖
	Financial Planning	✖	✖
Maximum Portfolios/Securities per Portfolio		1/10 or 25/25	unlimited/200
Maximum Securities/Transactions per Security		625/NA	unlimited/NA
Securities/ Assets Handled	Cash/Stocks/Mutual Funds	✖ (stocks/mutual funds)	✖
	Bonds (Fixed/Variable/Zero/PIK)		✖ (fixed/variable)
	Annuities		
	Options/Futures/Warrants		
	Real Estate/Partnerships		
	User-Defined		
Security Classification	Identification (Name/Ticker/CUSIP)	✖	✖ (name, ticker)
	Account Number/Management Firm		
	Asset Class (Pre-Defined/User-Defined)		
	Industry (SIC Codes/User-Defined)		
Transactions Handled	Deposit/Withdrawal; Buy/Sell	✖ (buy/sell)	✖ (buy/sell)
	Short/Cover		
	Margin		
	Receive/Deliver Security		
	Dividends (Cash/Stock/Splits/Reinvest)	✖ (stock/reinvest)	
	Interest Income		
	Treatment of Fees/Commissions	✖	
Security Lot Assignments (Avg.Cost/FIFO/Specific Lot)			
Reports	Current Holdings (Total/By Lots)	✖ (total)	✖ (total)
	Cash Portfolio Status		✖
	Tax Schedules (Interest/Div/Cap Gains)	✖ (dividends)	
	Customized Reports		
Performance Reports	Security/Industry/Asset	✖ (security)	✖ (security)
	Portfolio (Single/Multiple)	✖ (single)	✖
	Holding Period/Between Period Returns	✖	✖ (holding period)
	Benchmark Comparison	✖	✖

Chapter 5

FUNDAMENTAL
STOCK ANALYSIS

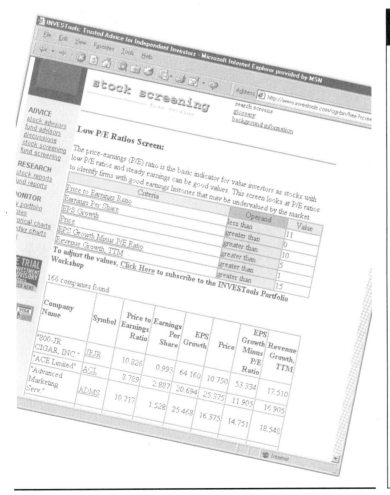

Investors are constantly bombarded with stock tips and investing ideas—magazines, Web sites and airwaves are crowded with gurus trying to identify the next Microsoft. Eager brokers are calling about the latest hot stock—even friends and relatives exchange ideas over a beer at the barbecue. While some of these picks may actually perform well, investors are faced with a hodgepodge of ideas to examine for soundness and whether they fit into their overall portfolio design. With over 9,000 U.S.-listed stocks available for purchase, it is not surprising that many investors are turning toward computer programs to help locate and analyze stocks in a more organized and systematic way.

This chapter discusses programs geared toward fundamental stock analysis, which examines the underlying performance of a company to form long-term expectations of future company and stock price performance. This expectation is formed by analyzing the following ingredients for a company:

- financial statements

- product mix

- management

- competitive position

- industry prospects

- underlying economic trends

In contrast, technical analysis relies only on examining historical price and volume patterns to predict future price performance. Technical analysis software is covered in Chapter 6 starting on page 217.

Types of Analysis

Software for fundamental analysis is usually divided into two primary categories—screening and valuation. Screening refers to the act of searching through a large universe of stocks to locate a few that might hold promise and warrant further analysis. Valuation, on the other hand, refers to examining one company in detail and applying a series of models to determine if the current price can be considered fair.

Computers are well suited for fundamental screening because the screening process involves the manipulation of quantitative company and industry statistics.

On the other hand, because so much of valuation rests on your personal forecasts for the economy, a company's industry, and the company itself, computers are crude tools for fundamental valuation. The few valuation programs on the market are little more than spreadsheet templates whose main benefit is providing a consistent framework to analyze stocks.

Warning→	Because so much of valuation rests on your personal forecasts for the economy, a company's industry, and the company itself, computers are crude tools for fundamental valuation.

Fundamental Stock Screening

It is with screening that the computer becomes a valuable tool for the fundamental investor. Computer screening is the process of applying a filter that includes one or more quantitative parameters (criteria) against a large group of stocks in order to cull out a small set of stocks that share some common characteristics. It allows you to focus your attention on a smaller but more promising group of stocks. For example, you can concentrate on a segment of the market such as stocks with low price-earnings ratios, or small-capitalization companies that may be neglected by the marketplace.

Unlike the conglomeration of stock ideas that may come your way, stock screening programs allow you to focus on stocks appropriate to your risk tolerance and performance objectives. Aggressive investors can use these programs to seek out companies with expanding earnings and price momentum. More conservative investors looking for income generation may seek out companies with above average dividend yields that seem safe relative to earnings. Even if you wish to rely on outside tips for investing ideas, the company and industry data in the stock screening programs can provide an initial impression of a company and its prospects or confirm an idea that was, at first, suspect.

Creating Stock Screens

It is important to understand the screening process and carefully define your investment objectives before selecting a stock screening system. Screening is a multi-stage process:

1. You must first clearly define the objective of your screen.

2. Next, you must construct primary criteria that identify the stocks that match your screening objective.

3. Then you need to construct a set of secondary criteria that helps to ensure that the companies passing the primary screen did so because they truly meet your objectives and not out of coincidence.

4. And last, you must keep in mind that even the best screen represents only a starting point for in-depth analysis.

This process can be best illustrated through an example of the screening process.

Defining a Clear Objective

For example, a young couple usually has little wealth and a long time horizon. They are seeking to accumulate wealth, do not need income from their investments and are willing to accept greater risk for the prospect of greater returns. They might choose to focus their investments on smaller, growth-oriented companies. On the other hand, a retired couple typically has a shorter time horizon and may be more concerned with preserving their accumulated wealth and obtaining additional income from their portfolio to supplement their pension. Therefore, they might choose a value approach that seeks out larger, more stable growth stocks with above-average dividend yields and lower price volatility.

Tip→	The objective should reflect your return objectives, risk tolerance and investment philosophy.

Establishing Primary Screening Criteria

The primary screening criteria should flow naturally from your objective, and should attempt to filter only those companies that meet your objective. If you are a growth investor, the results of the screen should provide you with a list of companies that match the growth stage of your life cycle (like young, growing firms rather than mature cyclical firms).

It is often helpful to examine the approach of successful investors whose investment philosophy and approach match your own as a source for establishing screening criteria. For our screening example, we will use the approach of Ralph Wanger, the well-known lead portfolio manager of the Acorn mutual fund. Ralph Wanger seeks out smaller, inexpensive and obscure niche companies and details his approach in the book, "A Zebra in Lion Country: Ralph Wanger's Investment Survival Guide."

Wanger develops a strategy to avoid a haphazard collection of stocks selling at high premiums to low or nonexistent earnings. He feels that successful investors develop a philosophy that dictates the type of stocks they wish to own and then stick to their catechism. Computerized screening systems are good at applying a consistent set of criteria and providing an automatic system of discipline.

Small-Cap Stocks

Ralph Wanger prefers to invest in smaller-capitalization stocks (small-caps), which he defines as companies below $1 billion in market capitalization (share price times number of shares outstanding).

Smaller companies typically have only one or two lines of business, making them easier to understand than larger firms with many lines of business. The further you stray from stocks you really understand, the greater the chance that you are gambling, not investing.

Smaller companies have more room to grow. No company can sustain a high growth rate forever, and eventually a firm's size starts to weigh it down. Larger companies cannot sustain the high growth rates that are possible with a smaller firm.

Ralph Wanger also argues that managers of smaller companies are generally better at responding to changes. They often have large ownership positions and an aggressive spirit. There are fewer layers of management, so decisions are made more quickly.

You need to select a screening program that covers small-capitalization stocks if you want to follow a selection strategy similar to Mr. Wanger's. We will use AAII's Stock Investor Professional to illustrate the screening process. Our first screen looks for companies with a market capitalization of less than or equal to $1 billion (see Figure 5.0 on page 142). This filter cuts the program's 9,184-company universe down to 7,608 stocks. Wanger's small-cap definition is not as restrictive as most academic studies, but roughly follows the standards used by other small-cap managers.

Wanger chooses to avoid extremely small companies, termed micro-caps, because he feels that they can be too risky—"one misstep and they [micro-caps] are out." Therefore, $100 million is specified as a lower market capitalization limit for our screen, cutting the list down to 2,841.

Ralph Wanger also prefers established companies with proven management over start-ups, near venture capital stocks and initial public offerings (IPOs). Screening programs do not typically indicate when a company went public. Five years of financial statements doesn't necessarily confirm that the company went public

FIGURE 5.0
Screening filter excluding companies with a market capitalization above $1 billion displayed in Stock Investor Professional.

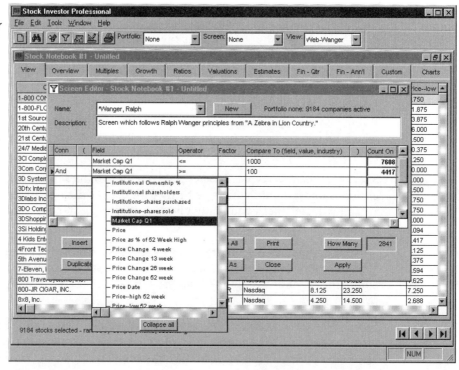

five years ago as most companies are in operation for years before becoming an IPO. The majority of financial data services will make an effort to fill in the historical financial statements of a firm once they start tracking the company. If your screening program provides historical price data, a screen requiring a stock price for a certain number of years identifies how long the company has been publicly traded. We require a stock price five years ago for our screen. Remember you can adjust this requirement to be more or less conservative. Specifying that a company had a share price five years ago cuts the number of passing companies down to 1,625.

Keep in mind that in working with screening programs, you must develop a feel for how to turn ideas and concepts into quantitative screening filters.

Tip→	In working with screening programs, you must develop a feel for how to turn ideas and concepts into quantitative screening filters.

Niche Players

Ralph Wanger seeks out companies with a dominant market position. These firms often have a special niche, which makes it difficult for other firms to compete with them. It may be a geographical niche as in the case of a strong regional bank, a technological niche supported by patents, or it could just simply be a strong marketing presence that makes it costly for new competitors to gain market share.

Wanger suggests that it is best to stick with only the leaders in the industry. Avoid the weak "me too" companies. It is better to own the best company in a marginal industry than the third runner-up in a major industry.

To try to find these firms, you must establish screening criteria that captures companies with a dominant market position. Since screening is only a preliminary process, a careful examination of the passing companies and their industries will reveal whether a company truly is the industry market leader. Profit margins can often pinpoint companies with a competitive advantage. However, profit margins are typically very industry-specific. Companies in competitive industries selling commodity items at a brisk pace usually have low profit margins and make their profits by producing and selling their goods cheaply and quickly. Other industries are characterized by the production of specialized items that take a long time to produce and carry a higher profit. Vast differences may exist within an industry. For example, within the retail industry a supermarket will have lower profit margins and higher turnover than a jewelry store. Therefore, a simple screen for high profit margins will not be very useful because it will be dominated by companies in industries known to have traditionally high margins. Some screening programs allow you to specify screening filters that compare a firm's variable against the norm for the industry. If your screening program does not offer this, then you will have to perform separate screens for separate industries or simply ignore the filter temporarily and perform a screen by hand on the companies that passed all the other filters.

Stock Investor allows its users to compare a company variable to an industry median or average, so we require a profit margin that is higher than the median for its industry. The median is the mid-point value for a series of numbers. And as a guard against companies with just a strong one-time showing, we also screen for firms with current profit margins greater than or equal to their profit margins a few years ago. This cuts the number of passing companies down to 561.

As with all preliminary screening criteria, you should closely examine the stocks passing the profit margin segment of the overall screen to determine whether the companies actually have a strong industry position that will continue to hold true over the long run. (Keep this in mind as you work your way toward a shorter list of passing companies.)

Tip→	Wanger looks for the leaders in the industry. It is better to own the best company in a marginal industry than the third runner-up in a major industry.

Types of Screening Criteria

Figure 5.1 is typical of the screening editor found in better software-based screening programs and highlights the type of filters you should be able to create with a program. The first three lines of the screen compare a data field found in the program against a user-entered number: for example, market capitalization less than or equal to $1,000 million. This is the most basic type of filter found in all programs. Some programs extend this capability by allowing users to specify both upper and lower limits for a data field within one filter line.

FIGURE 5.1
An illustration of the editor used to establish and test the screening criteria.

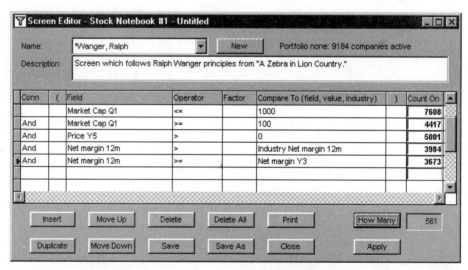

The next level of complexity compares one data item against another data item in the program—a very important option found in most software screening programs, but rare with on-line systems. An example of this is found in the final filter line that compares the current net (profit) margin against the net (profit) margin in year three. This screening option allows you to construct screens that are more flexible and need less direct updating over time.

The most complex screening criteria is one that compares a company field against some overall variable stored directly in the program. This option could report the average of a field for all firms or even the specific industry average for a company. For example, you may want to construct a screen that filters out companies with a price-earnings ratio higher than the average price-earnings ratio for all companies. The fourth screening line in Figure 5.1 compares net margin for the company against the median net margin for its industry.

Growth at a Reasonable Price

When determining if an investment represents an attractive purchase, it is important to separate the company from the stock. While Ralph Wanger seeks out sound companies, he will only consider them for purchase if they are available at an attractive price.

The price-earnings ratio is one of the most basic measures of value for investors. The price-earnings ratio, or multiple, is computed by dividing a stock's price by its most recent 12 months' earnings per share. The price-earnings ratio is followed so closely because it embodies the market's expectations of future company performance through the price component of the ratio and relates the expectation to historical company performance as measured by earnings per share.

Many studies point to the profitability of investing in out-of-favor stocks. Value investors seek out firms with low price-earnings ratios with the belief that the market may have overreacted to negative news or is not correctly discounting their future earnings potential. A simple screen for low price-earnings ratios, however, can be misleading as a guide to undervalued stocks. Typically, firms with high growth potential trade with correspondingly high price-earnings ratios, while those with low price-earnings ratios are expected to have low growth or greater risk of achieving future earnings.

The key is to buy growth at a reasonable price. The share price should be cheap relative to indicators of growth prospects for items such as earnings, sales or cash flow, or relative to the asset value of the firm.

Tip→ The key is to buy growth at a reasonable price. The share price should be cheap relative to indicators of growth prospects for items such as earnings, sales or cash flow, or relative to the asset value of the firm.

145

However, low price-earnings stocks often become even lower price-earnings stocks, while growth stocks with high price-earnings ratios can become average price-earnings stocks with any bad news.

The ratio of price-earnings to earnings growth (PEG) is a common valuation tool that equates the assumptions built into the price-earnings ratio to the actual earnings growth rate of the firms. Firms with price-earnings ratios equal to their growth rate (a ratio of 1.0) are considered fairly valued.

When the price-earnings ratio is above the growth rate (a ratio above 1.0) the stock is considered overvalued, while a price-earnings ratio below the company's growth rate (a ratio less than 1.0) may point to an undervalued stock.

Adding a filter that looks for companies with a price-earnings-to-growth ratio below one leaves us with 246 companies. Note that the price-earnings-to-growth filter does not relieve you from a careful examination of the earnings prospects for companies that pass the screen. Its strength lies in equating growth to valuation levels.

Tip→ When the price-earnings ratio is above the growth rate the stock may be considered overvalued, while a price-earnings ratio below the company's growth rate may point to an undervalued stock.

Conditioning Screens

Even with a clear objective and a well-built primary screen, you can expect a number of companies to slip past your filter that do not embody the type of company you are seeking. A high dividend yield screen will probably contain some companies ready to cut their dividend.

A well-designed screen should make use of conditioning or secondary screens that help to ensure that the passing companies meet the screen's ultimate objective. Conditioning screens differ from primary screening criteria in that when used alone to filter companies they do not locate companies that meet your objective.

Ralph Wanger prefers to avoid marginal, underfunded companies of any size. He feels that financial strength makes corporate growth sustainable. Wanger looks for companies with low debt, adequate working capital and conservative accounting.

Prudent use of debt allows companies to expand and increase return on shareholder equity. However, the balance sheet should be examined to see if the company has too much debt or to see if debt is rising to dangerous levels.

Appropriate debt levels vary from industry to industry, so it is best to screen against industry norms. For example, utilities typically can safely carry higher levels of debt as opposed to highly cyclical firms.

Warning→	The balance sheet should be examined to see if the company has too much debt or to see if debt is rising to dangerous levels relative to its industry.

When we screen out firms with higher levels of total liabilities to total assets than their industry median, the number of passing companies reduces from 246 to 142. The ratio of total liabilities to total assets is more encompassing than simply looking at long-term debt to equity. This is especially true for the smaller-cap firms within the Wanger screen. Small-cap firms cannot typically float long-term debt and must rely more on short-term financing.

Additional secondary screens can include an examination of the balance sheet to compare the levels of liabilities over time, a study of the relationship of inventories and receivables to sales and a review of the notes accompanying the financial statements to consider factors such as the size of the pension liabilities. If inventories, for example, are increasing faster than sales, it may point to a shift in the buying habits of customers to products of competitors.

Traditional screens for working capital look at ratios such as the quick and current ratios, which compare short-term assets to short-term liabilities. However, these measures are very static and not as useful as measures that test the company's ability to meet current and future obligations.

Tip→	A well-designed screen should make use of conditioning or secondary screens that help to ensure that the passing companies meet the screen's ultimate objective.

A screen for positive cash flow over the last 12 months and each of the last three fiscal years tests both working capital and confirms the quality of earnings. Earnings can be influenced by many management assumptions trickling through the accounting statements. Cash flow is less influenced by these types of varying assumptions, making it more comparable across a wide range of companies. This filter reduces the list of passing companies to 132.

Management

Good management is critical for the long-term success of a company. Wanger tries to get a sense of the ability and honesty of the people running the firm. Management must be shareholder-oriented with the management owning a large chunk of the firm.

For our next screen, we look for companies with inside ownership of at least 20% of the outstanding shares. This filter eliminates another 17 companies, leaving 115.

Most stock screening programs rely on SEC filings made by beneficial owners to calculate the number of insiders. Since any shareholder who owns 5% of the outstanding shares is classified as an insider under the system, precautions must be taken when interpreting the results. A useful secondary screen includes careful reading of the proxy statement and 10-K filings to confirm that managers are owners with a significant interest.

Neglected Stocks

A filter excluding companies with excessive institutional ownership is a final screen for the Ralph Wanger example, since Wanger's goal is to stand out from the herd and purchase quality neglected stocks at reasonable prices.

The smaller the analyst interest when the stock is researched and purchased, the better the chance that you are buying a mispriced stock. Once discovered by Wall Street, the earnings multiple that investors are willing to pay for the company's earnings may increase, leading to a handsome profit.

Many measures of institutional interest exist. The percentage of outstanding shares held by institutions indicates who may take hold of the reins, along with the potential stock correction, if the herd heads for the exit door all at once. This figure may be skewed by large holdings by a few institutions such as an endowment fund—many investors also look at the number of institutions holding the stock or the number of analysts providing estimates for recommendations as proxies for institutional interest.

A screen excluding companies with institutional ownership above the database median leaves us with eight companies.

Figure 5.2 displays all of the screening criteria. The column labeled "Count On" keeps track of the number of companies passing each filter independently. This shows how restrictive each individual criterion was in the screen. For example, it shows that the PE to EPS growth ratio was the most restrictive screening element, allowing only 1,704 companies to pass.

Coming up with a final screen is often a trial and error process, so it is desirable to find a program that gives you feedback on the restrictiveness of each filter in order to make appropriate adjustments.

FIGURE 5.2
Complete list of screening criteria used in the filter to capture Ralph Wanger's investment style.

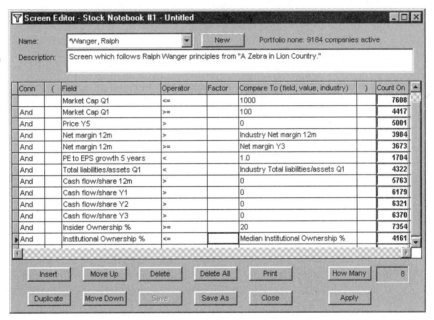

Tip→

Coming up with a final screen is often a trial and error process, so it is desirable to find a program that gives you feedback on the restrictiveness of each filter in order to make appropriate adjustments.

Screening as a First Step

Screening is the first step in the stock selection process. Selection of the final candidates requires careful analysis of the stocks passing the filter. First you must understand the company's products, industry position and financial statements. The sources of company profit and growth must be well understood. You must also consider the negatives that might impact the prospects of the company. You would then only invest if the market price does not fully reflect the company's position and its prospects. Screening programs help to push the odds in your favor. Screens help to impose a discipline to the selection process and highlight companies worthy of in-depth analysis.

Comparing Screening Services

When comparing stock screening services, you should consider the following critical factors:

- the universe of stocks supported by the database

- depth of stock information

- flexibility of screening software

- frequency of updates

- distribution methods

- computer systems supported

- price

Information on these areas is detailed in the following pages and in the two comparison grids at the end of this chapter. The comparison grid starting on page 199 lists information about subscription and distribution requirements, options and prices; program features; and basic database content. The comparison grid starting on page 209 details the financial statement elements provided from the income statement, balance sheet, and cash flow statement.

Company Universe

Screening dictates that the search process start with a broad universe of companies. Better screening programs cover a wide range of companies. Some offer substantial coverage that includes Nasdaq National Market companies and even Nasdaq Small Cap companies. This is one of the easiest ways to gather data about smaller firms. Information on the number of companies tracked and the exchanges is provided in the comparison grid.

When contemplating a data vendor, consider the types of companies you are trying to find. If your focus is only on larger, more established firms, then Value Line Investment Survey's pool of 1,700 companies may suffice. However, if you are seeking smaller, less-followed firms, look for a service that covers a wider range of stocks.

Depth of Company Information

Screening services vary in the depth of information provided. Some services, such as INVESTools, provide fewer data items for each company and instead depend on summary statistics such as growth rates and rankings when providing background data. Other services, such as Stock Investor and MSN MoneyCentral Investor, provide both summary statistics and the raw data behind these numbers.

In considering a data service, look not only at the number of variables but also specifically at which statistics are provided. Investment Survey allows you to screen for companies based on Value Line's proprietary rankings and projected growth rates, which may be more important for some investors than the completeness of the database. Telescan's TIP@Wallstreet system and the Wall Street City Web site are the services that extensively combine both fundamental and technical factors for screening.

Tip→	In considering a data service, look not only at the number of variables but also specifically at which statistics are provided.

When performing fundamental screening, the information generally falls into the following categories:

- multiples

- historical growth rates

- estimates and recommendations

- financial ratios

- financial statement data

- industry comparisons

- price and share data

- company information

Multiples

Multiples are the core variables of many fundamental screens. They relate the current stock price to a tangible company item such as earnings per share or book value per share. Multiples provide an indication of how the market values the company's future prospects. Companies with brighter futures typically trade with higher multiples. Value investors expect the market to overreact to news and push the multiples too high, producing an overvalued company, or too low, indicating an undervalued company.

Look for a broad range of multiples covering items such as earnings, book value, cash flow, and dividends. Historical ratios help indicate normal trading ranges and provide a base from which to compare current multiples. Therefore, historical average multiples are a key element when choosing a service.

FIGURE 5.3
Multiples displayed in Morningstar's Principia Plus for Stocks.

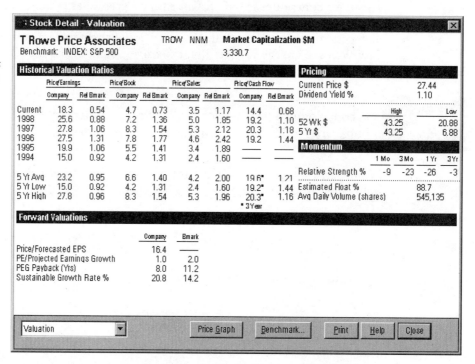

| Tip→ | Look for a broad range of multiples covering items such as earnings, book value, cash flow, and dividends for a wide range of time periods. |

Historical Growth Rates

Growth rates paint a picture of past company performance and provide an easy way to compare companies. Investors seek out quickly growing firms with the hope that growth will continue to drive the stock price up. Five-year growth rates are normally presented for sales, earnings, and dividends. The more powerful programs either have a wider range of growth rates for various time periods or allow you to calculate growth rates for a user-designated company item over a selected period.

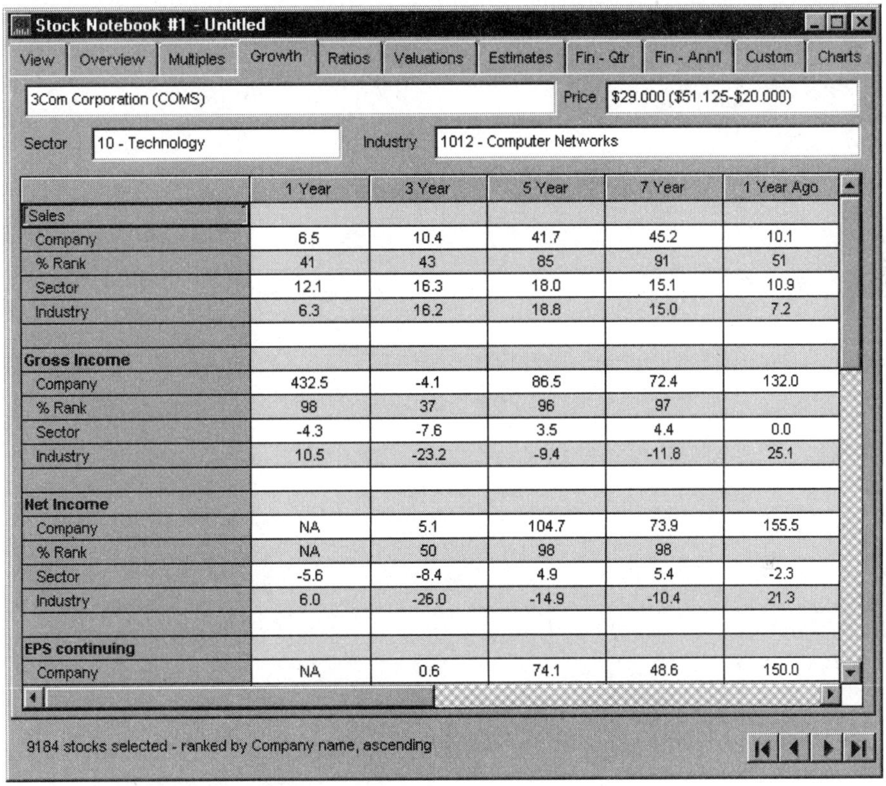

FIGURE 5.4
Partial display of growth rates shown in AAII's Stock Investor Professional.

Stock Notebook #1 - Untitled

| View | Overview | Multiples | Growth | Ratios | Valuations | Estimates | Fin - Qtr | Fin - Ann'l | Custom | Charts |

3Com Corporation (COMS)   Price $29.000 ($51.125-$20.000)

Sector 10 - Technology   Industry 1012 - Computer Networks

	1 Year	3 Year	5 Year	7 Year	1 Year Ago
Sales					
Company	6.5	10.4	41.7	45.2	10.1
% Rank	41	43	85	91	51
Sector	12.1	16.3	18.0	15.1	10.9
Industry	6.3	16.2	18.8	15.0	7.2
Gross Income					
Company	432.5	-4.1	86.5	72.4	132.0
% Rank	98	37	96	97	
Sector	-4.3	-7.6	3.5	4.4	0.0
Industry	10.5	-23.2	-9.4	-11.8	25.1
Net Income					
Company	NA	5.1	104.7	73.9	155.5
% Rank	NA	50	98	98	
Sector	-5.6	-8.4	4.9	5.4	-2.3
Industry	6.0	-26.0	-14.9	-10.4	21.3
EPS continuing					
Company	NA	0.6	74.1	48.6	150.0

9184 stocks selected - ranked by Company name, ascending

Estimates and Recommendations

The market is driven by expectations. A growing number of screening services are presenting consensus earnings estimates and buy/hold/sell recommendations. Consensus estimates are calculated by polling thousands of analysts for earnings estimates of the companies they cover (see Figure 5.5). Services also poll analysts to report their ratings on the overall attractiveness of stocks as an attempt to derive uniform consensus recommendations.

| Tip→ | Changes to recommendations and earnings estimates may be as important to study as the actual figures themselves. Look for an indication of recent revisions or surprises. |

FIGURE 5.5
*Thompson
Investors
Network
provides
consensus
estimates and
analyst
recommenda-
tions.*

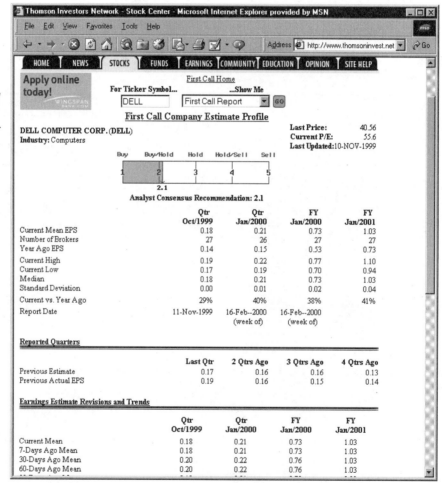

Some of the larger stock reporting services such as Standard and Poor's and Value Line calculate and report their own estimates and recommendations. Value Line Investment Survey makes extensive use of its publisher's proprietary figures (see Figure 5.6). These estimates and recommendations allow investors to directly gauge the expectations built into the stock price.

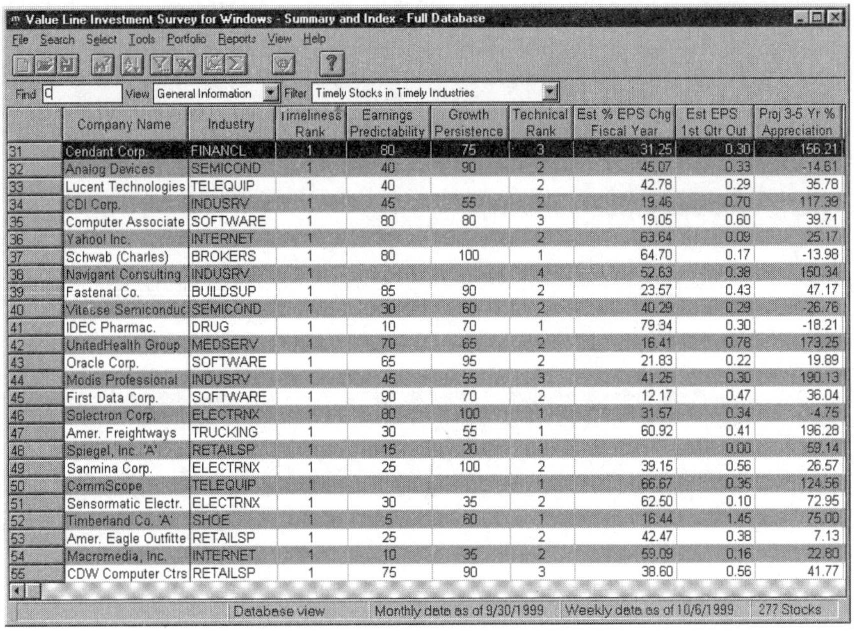

FIGURE 5.6
*Value Line
provides
proprietary
estimates and
ratings.*

	Company Name	Industry	Timeliness Rank	Earnings Predictability	Growth Persistence	Technical Rank	Est % EPS Chg Fiscal Year	Est EPS 1st Qtr Out	Proj 3-5 Yr % Appreciation
31	Cendant Corp.	FINANCL	1	80	75	3	31.25	0.30	156.21
32	Analog Devices	SEMICOND	1	40	90	2	45.07	0.33	-14.61
33	Lucent Technologies	TELEQUIP	1	40		2	42.78	0.29	35.78
34	CDI Corp.	INDUSRV	1	45	55	2	19.46	0.70	117.39
35	Computer Associate	SOFTWARE	1	80	80	3	19.05	0.60	39.71
36	Yahoo! Inc.	INTERNET	1			2	63.64	0.09	25.17
37	Schwab (Charles)	BROKERS	1	80	100	1	64.70	0.17	-13.98
38	Navigant Consulting	INDUSRV	1			4	52.63	0.38	150.34
39	Fastenal Co.	BUILDSUP	1	85	90	2	23.57	0.43	47.17
40	Vitesse Semiconduc	SEMICOND	1	30	60	2	40.29	0.29	-26.76
41	IDEC Pharmac.	DRUG	1	10	70	1	79.34	0.30	-18.21
42	UnitedHealth Group	MEDSERV	1	70	65	2	16.41	0.78	173.25
43	Oracle Corp.	SOFTWARE	1	65	95	2	21.83	0.22	19.89
44	Modis Professional	INDUSRV	1	45	55	3	41.25	0.30	190.13
45	First Data Corp.	SOFTWARE	1	90	70	2	12.17	0.47	36.04
46	Solectron Corp.	ELECTRNX	1	80	100	1	31.57	0.34	-4.75
47	Amer. Freightways	TRUCKING	1	30	55	1	60.92	0.41	196.28
48	Spiegel, Inc 'A'	RETAILSP	1	15	20	1		0.00	59.14
49	Sanmina Corp.	ELECTRNX	1	25	100	2	39.15	0.56	26.57
50	CommScope	TELEQUIP	1			1	66.67	0.35	124.56
51	Sensormatic Electr.	ELECTRNX	1	30	35	2	62.50	0.10	72.95
52	Timberland Co. 'A'	SHOE	1	5	60	1	16.44	1.45	75.00
53	Amer. Eagle Outfitte	RETAILSP	1	25		2	42.47	0.38	7.13
54	Macromedia, Inc.	INTERNET	1	10	35	2	59.09	0.16	22.80
55	CDW Computer Ctrs	RETAILSP	1	75	90	3	38.60	0.56	41.77

Database view   Monthly data as of 9/30/1999   Weekly data as of 10/6/1999   277 Stocks

Financial Ratios

Ratios help you summarize financial statement data into a format that can be easily manipulated to compare year-to-year changes for a company or to compare one company against another.

Leverage ratios examine the company's use of debt in its financial structure. Effective use of debt can enhance shareholder profitability at the risk of saddling the company with an interest payment that must be made in good times and bad. Companies that were once stars, such as Boston Market, have gone bankrupt in part due to excess use of debt. Common leverage ratios include debt to equity, liabilities as a percentage of assets, and long-term debt as a percentage of capital.

Liquidity ratios try to gauge a firm's ability to meet its short-term obligations. While liquidity measures are of greater interest to creditors than equity investors, you may want to glance at these ratios if you are looking for high-yielding stocks. Typical liquidity ratios include the quick ratio and current ratio.

Profitability ratios benchmark company performance and help highlight trends when examined over time—as well as indicate strong and weak performance when compared to other firms. Common profitability ratios include return on assets (ROA), return on equity (ROE), gross margins, operating profit margins, and net profit margins.

Asset management ratios examine how well the company is using its capital and resources in the course of its business. Inventory turnover and asset turnover ratios are two common asset management measures. These ratios are very industry-specific and cannot be used effectively without taking industry norms into account (see Figure 5.7).

Industry Comparisons

Industry comparisons are useful in identifying standout firms. Multiples, growth rates and ratios give you an added measure of information when analyzed in the context of industry norms. Industry multiples may highlight out-of-favor sectors ready for a rebound.

FIGURE 5.7
America Online offers a variety of ratios for the company and its industry on its Ratio Comparisons report.

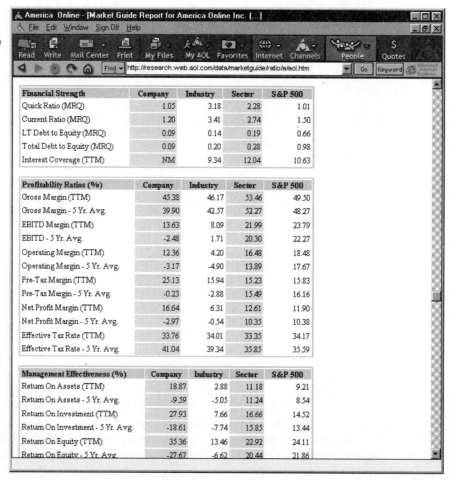

Financial Strength	Company	Industry	Sector	S&P 500
Quick Ratio (MRQ)	1.05	3.18	2.28	1.01
Current Ratio (MRQ)	1.20	3.41	2.74	1.50
LT Debt to Equity (MRQ)	0.09	0.14	0.19	0.66
Total Debt to Equity (MRQ)	0.09	0.20	0.28	0.98
Interest Coverage (TTM)	NM	9.34	12.04	10.63

Profitability Ratios (%)	Company	Industry	Sector	S&P 500
Gross Margin (TTM)	45.38	46.17	53.46	49.50
Gross Margin - 5 Yr. Avg.	39.90	42.57	52.27	48.27
EBITD Margin (TTM)	13.63	8.09	21.99	23.79
EBITD - 5 Yr. Avg.	-2.48	1.71	20.30	22.27
Operating Margin (TTM)	12.36	4.20	16.48	18.48
Operating Margin - 5 Yr. Avg.	-3.17	-4.90	13.89	17.67
Pre-Tax Margin (TTM)	25.13	15.94	15.23	15.83
Pre-Tax Margin - 5 Yr. Avg.	-0.23	-2.88	15.49	16.16
Net Profit Margin (TTM)	16.64	6.31	12.61	11.90
Net Profit Margin - 5 Yr. Avg.	-2.97	-0.54	10.35	10.38
Effective Tax Rate (TTM)	33.76	34.01	33.35	34.17
Effective Tax Rate - 5 Yr. Avg.	41.04	39.34	35.85	35.59

Management Effectiveness (%)	Company	Industry	Sector	S&P 500
Return On Assets (TTM)	18.87	2.88	11.18	9.21
Return On Assets - 5 Yr. Avg.	-9.59	-5.05	11.24	8.54
Return On Investment (TTM)	27.93	7.66	16.66	14.52
Return On Investment - 5 Yr. Avg.	-18.61	-7.74	15.85	13.44
Return On Equity (TTM)	35.36	13.46	22.92	24.11
Return On Equity - 5 Yr. Avg.	-27.67	-6.62	20.44	21.86

However, most ratios vary widely among industries and cannot be examined outside an industry context (see Figure 5.7). Look for programs that provide industry statistics or at least allow you to screen for companies in a similar industry and then analyze those firms as a group. Some programs even allow you to screen for companies outperforming industry norms.

Financial Statement Data

The raw data serves as the basis for the calculation of ratios, growth rates, and multiples. Financial statement data is useful for analyzing a single firm, but is difficult to use directly in screening and ranking. Nevertheless, the better products include enough information from the income statement, balance sheet, and cash flow statement to judge whether the ratios and growth rates properly reflect the company's prospects. Some products offer practically no raw data, while others provide a rich history (see Figure 5.8). The second comparison grid beginning on page 209 details the financial statement information provided by the programs. By examining the year-by-year earnings of a firm you can gain a feel for performance consistency and earnings trends (which growth rates often mask).

Price and Share Data

The price and share data describe various market-related aspects of the company's common stock. The extent and detail of historical price data as well as volume data is listed in the comparison grid. Other measures such as beta, relative strength, market capitalization and holdings by insiders and institutions are also noted. If you focus on price momentum, look for enough price data to examine price movement or summary statistics such as relative strength. Those looking for neglected stocks are typically attracted to measures like institutional holdings and market capitalization.

Company Information

Company information consists of basic data such as the firm's address and phone number, so you can request financial statements or speak to the investor relations department for clarification. Basic company descriptions are also common. The inclusion of expanded descriptions, which also cover recent operating results, is the latest trend (see Figure 5.10).

Distribution Methods

The fundamental screening services basically use two different types of data access and distribution techniques—you must either acquire the complete database and store it on your computer for screening or dial up to another computer to perform the screen and view the results.

FIGURE 5.8
*Section of the
financial
statements
from
Quicken.com.*

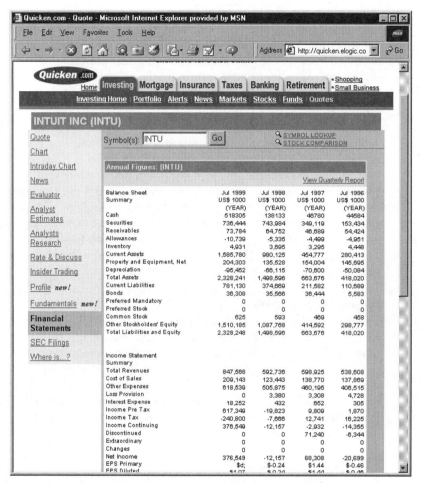

Tip→	By examining the year-by-year earnings of a firm you can gain a feel for performance consistency and earnings trends (which growth rates often mask).

AAII's Stock Investor is an example of a system that ships the complete database to your system, while Telescan's ProSearch on TIP@Wallstreet performs the screening on-line. The advantage of having the complete database on your computer is that you can perform as many screens as you want, wherever you are, whenever you want, and typically with much more flexible software. When the

FIGURE 5.9
*MSN
MoneyCentral
Investor allows
users to export
price and
volume data
from its
charting
module.*

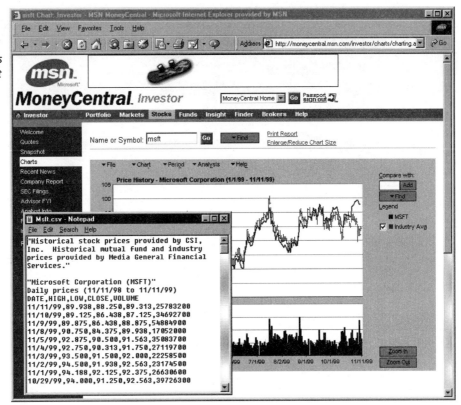

screening is performed on-line the data tends to be fresher, with updated price-related ratios (on a daily or weekly basis). With on-line programs you do not need to devote a great deal of hard disk space to the data, but screening tends to be more cumbersome and less powerful. The pure on-line vendors always require a phone call to perform a screen.

You have some choices as far as the delivery method is concerned. Current options for the individual investor include floppy disks, CD-ROM and modem. Some services rely on a combination of both disk and on-line distribution techniques. For example, Value Line uses floppies and CDs to distribute the program and the complete data set, but allows subscribers to receive weekly data updates on-line.

FIGURE 5.10
*Morning-
star.com
provides
detailed
analysis for a
wide range of
companies.*

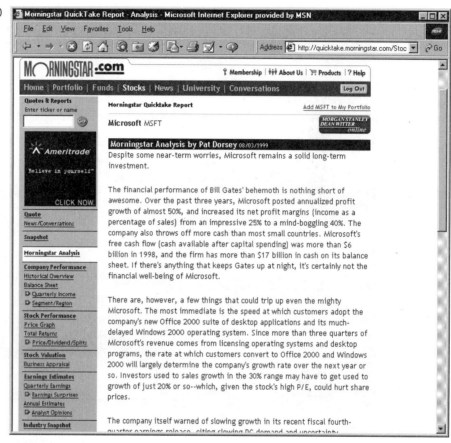

Screening Features

The next feature to consider when selecting a screening service is the flexibility
of the screening software. Screening services that distribute a complete database
and allow you to manipulate the data tend to offer more flexibility than strictly
dial-up services. The comparison grid on pages 199 through 208 includes several
categories that describe the screening features provided by the services.

The core feature of any screening program is its set of screening capabilities. The
program should provide access to all data items for screening. When designing
screening criteria, the program should allow you to screen against a constant
value or another field. Some programs even allow you to compare a value against
industry norms. Programs like Value Line's Investment Survey and AAII's Stock

Investor provide database statistics such as average, median, high and low values for each field to help you construct reasonable screening criteria. The program should also keep track of the number of companies passing each filter. Please note that most Web-based screening tools do not allow you to save a set of screening criteria for use in a later session. This will force you to reconstruct the entire screen every time you wish to apply the screen.

Tip→	The core feature of any screening program is its set of screening capabilities.

FIGURE 5.11
*MSN
MoneyCentral
Investor
provides
flexible
screening
capabilities.*

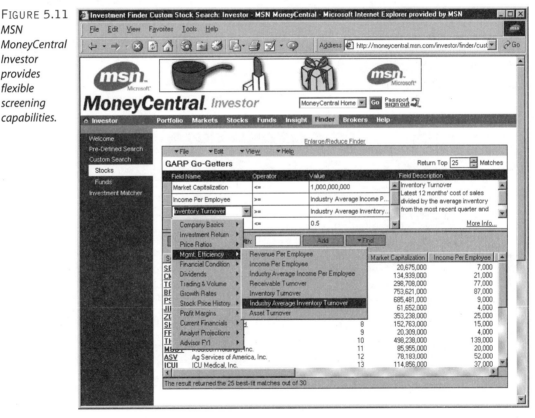

Warning→	Most Web-based screening tools do not allow you to save a set of screening criteria for use in a later session. This will force you to reconstruct the entire screen every time you wish to apply the screen.

Custom Variables

Most of the disk-based programs allow user-defined variables for analysis, so you can evaluate companies according to your own formulas. With these custom variables you can elect to create ratios omitted by the program developers or even enter valuation models that attempt to determine a fair market price. Once a user-defined variable is created, the current crop of programs allows you to screen with that variable and export the information.

FIGURE 5.12
Module within Value Line Investment Survey for Windows used to create and edit custom field.

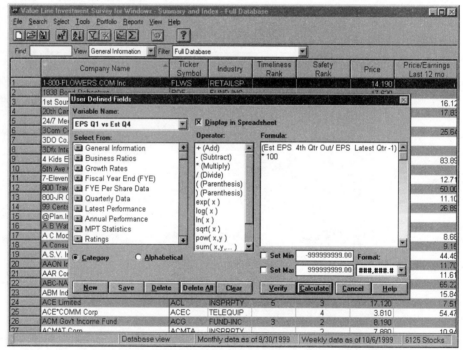

Reporting Capabilities

A single company report will typically detail all of the information provided by the database for a company. Tabular reports allow you to compare specific data items for a group of companies. Less common, but still useful, is an industry report that lists the statistics for a particular industry. A few of the programs display and print basic charts, conveying price information in efficient formats.

FIGURE 5.13
Range of reports available in Stock Investor Professional.

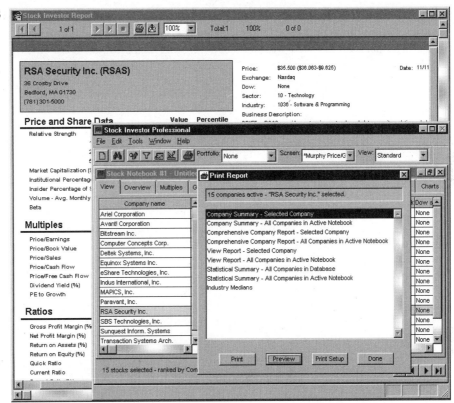

Exporting Data

Look for programs that allow you to export the data for use in a spreadsheet template or fundamental valuation program. Some programs limit the export to a few fields at a time while others are quite flexible. To some degree the importance of exporting depends upon the overall strength of the software. It seems that exporting is less vital when the software program offers a rich database and flexible user-defined field calculation, useful statistics, portfolio tracking, powerful screening and insightful reports.

Ease of Use

Typically, the more feature-rich the program is, the more difficult it is to learn how to operate the system. These systems are generally written for sophisticated audiences. However, ease of use does vary among the programs. The individual program reviews that follow this discussion deal with this issue.

Frequency of Data Updates

On-line services typically update their database on a daily or weekly basis. If the complete database resides on your computer, then you must select a delivery schedule, which will help you determine the annual cost. Options range from weekly updates to annual updates.

You should think about several issues to help you decide what frequency of data updates you require.

- First, how much money do you plan to invest in the stocks that you select as a result of using the screening service? The subscription cost represents a fixed cost that lowers your net return.

- Second, consider the length of time that you plan to hold an investment. If you plan on turning over your investments on a monthly basis, weekly updates would be more appropriate than quarterly updates. Likewise, if you plan to hold an investment for a number of years, quarterly updates should be sufficient to meet your needs.

- Thirdly, what is your budget? Costs can escalate rapidly as you increase the data update frequency and the data quantity. Very infrequent screening through an on-line service can be much less costly. In general, data costs are decreasing.

For those who plan to perform screens infrequently, but require up-to-date data, on-line services offer a good alternative to disk-based services. With these on-line services you do not acquire the complete database. Instead, using your computer modem or Internet connection, you connect to another computer that contains the database, input the screening criteria and retrieve the list of companies that pass the screen, along with some of their financial data. Most of the on-line services now offer the ability to research the stocks passing the filter. With some services the cost of obtaining the research is built into the subscription for gaining access to screening; with others the additional costs are levied when performing individual stock research.

For investors who wish to perform sophisticated screening and want the ability to manipulate the complete data directly, the disk-based services tend to be better choices.

Remember when working with fundamental screening programs, data errors will exist. The wider the usage of the program, the more likely it is that data errors will be found quickly and corrected. Realize that screening is merely the first step in the security analysis process. After screening, further in-depth analysis is required.

> **Warning→** Remember when working with fundamental screening programs, data errors will exist. The wider the usage of the program, the more likely it is that data errors will be found quickly and corrected.

Reviews

Disk-Based Services

Market Guide StockQuest	
Performance	4
Usefulness	4
Documentation	3
Ease of Use	3
Value	5

Market Guide StockQuest
by Market Guide, Inc.
Free—Windows
(516) 327-2400
www.marketguide.com

Like many data providers, Market Guide is refining and upgrading its Web and software products in response to the increasingly competitive financial data marketplace. StockQuest is a disk-based screening tool distributed through Market Guide's Web site. The program data is updated daily with updates available after midnight EST. Full program and data downloads are around 3.5M in size, while daily data updates are approximately 2.7M.

StockQuest's emphasis is screening, not company research. StockQuest comes with 75 data items covering the normal range of screening elements such as industry breakdowns, multiples, growth rates, price strength, size, ownership statistics and financial ratios. The program supports the creation of user-defined fields that can be used in screens and reports. The screening editor is more flexible than average applications, allowing you to incorporate mathematical and logical operations into screening criteria (see Figure 5.14).

165

FIGURE 5.14
*Field
categories
available for
screening in
StockQuest.*

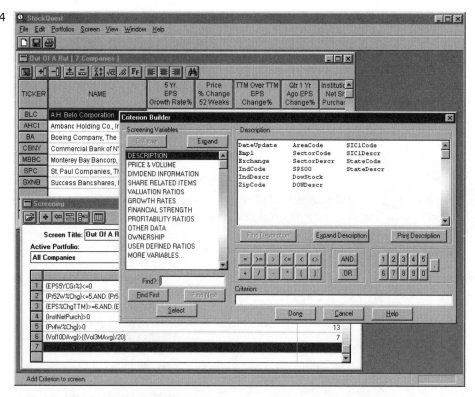

The program does not offer detailed financial data internally, but overcomes this weakness by providing access to free detailed company reports on Market Guide's Web site. Navigation within the site is very straightforward. By entering a company name or ticker, a user can quickly gain access to a broad range of charts, growth rates, ratios, insider transaction data, and detailed financials.

The program is downloaded directly through Market Guide's Web site and does not come with a printed user's guide—it relies on the on-line help, text files, and Web FAQs for documentation. However, the program's operation is fairly clear-cut and is covered adequately through the on-line documentation.

While not as comprehensive as the other disk-based screening services, the program features many of the basic elements that you would typically screen for and includes a powerful screening engine. StockQuest, combined with the Market Guide Web site, produces a very reasonable stock investment decision platform.

Principia Pro for Stocks	
Performance	4
Usefulness	4
Documentation	5
Ease of Use	5
Value	4

Principia Pro for Stocks
by Morningstar, Inc.
$95/yr.–$495/yr.—Windows
(800) 735-0700
www.morningstar.com

Morningstar's stock screening and analysis tool, Principia Pro for Stocks, is positioned toward the professional financial advisor analyzing and constructing a portfolio of stocks, mutual funds, and annuites. Principia Pro for Stocks also integrates with Morningstar's mutual fund and annuity offerings, which are available at additional cost.

FIGURE 5.15 *Morningstar's Principia Pro for Stocks includes an easy-to-use screening editor.*

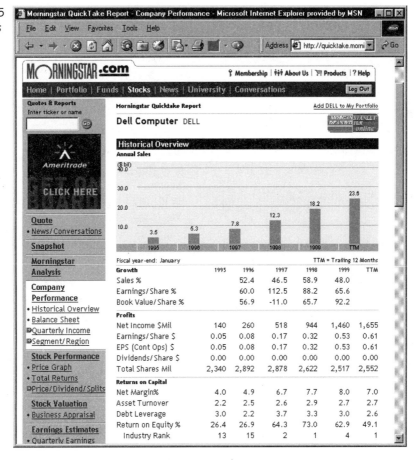

The program provides 600 data fields on 8,000 companies listed on NYSE, Amex and Nasdaq exchanges. One hundred and sixty of the fields can be used in screens. Notably, the program only allows these fields to be compared against hand-entered constants; you cannot make direct comparisons of one field to another. Morningstar tries to work around this limitation by offering additional screening variables for elements such as year-to-year EPS changes.

The database provides a standard set of information for screening and basic analysis. In addition to the program features and data fields displayed, Principia Pro for Stocks provides an industry sector breakdown of each company. The program also provides a listing of the mutual funds that are the largest holders of a particular stock, along with the Morningstar mutual fund ratings of those listed.

Most programs only track lists of stocks in their portfolio module. Principia Pro features a portfolio analysis tool that can combine the holdings of a stock, mutual fund, and variable annuity portfolio and examine the portfolio characteristics. Note that investors must subscribe to a specific asset module in order to analyze its security type in the portfolio module.

Overall, while Principia Pro for Stocks is an above-average company research tool, the program's emphasis is on portfolio construction and analysis. Principia Pro for Stocks is best suited for the investor holding both stocks and mutual funds and looking for a tool that can seamlessly tie these research modules.

Research Wizard	
Performance	4
Usefulness	4
Documentation	5
Ease of Use	3
Value	4

Research Wizard
by Zacks Investment Research
$600/yr.—Windows
(800) 399-6659, (312) 630-9880
www.zacks.com

Zacks is known for its database of consensus earnings estimates and brokerage recommendations, so it is not surprising that Research Wizard has a rich collection of estimates and recommendations. For $600 per year, users are given access to weekly updates and detailed company and research reports from the Zacks Web site.

Research Wizard allows you to study and screen for items such as earnings surprises, estimate revisions, and brokerage recommendations, along with basic company fundamentals. While the program has a slightly dated feel in comparison to recently released programs by vendors such as Morningstar and Value Line, screening and reporting is fairly straightforward. You can employ either a

FIGURE 5.16
*Partial list of
screening
fields available
in Research
Wizard.*

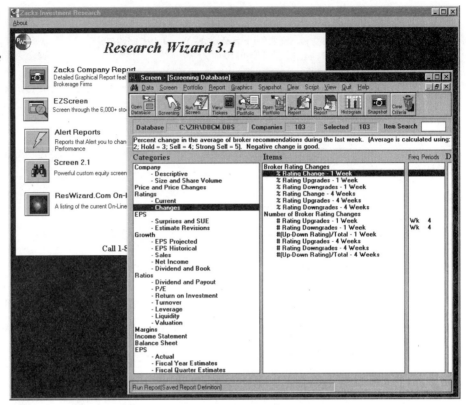

simplified screening module that lets you establish filter parameters from a limited set of popular screening criteria or use the advanced screening tool that provides easy access to all the data fields in the program.

The program provides a one-page "snapshot" report that summarizes key company and industry statistics and graphs factors such as earnings, price, earnings surprises and estimate revisions. Tabular reports can be printed or exported.

Research Wizard is a good choice if you're looking for a screening program with fresh data, a reasonably sized database, and a rich collection of statistics on estimates and recommendations.

Stock Investor Standard
by the American Association of Individual Investors
$148/yr. ($99/yr. for AAII members)—Windows 95/98/NT
(800) 428-2244, (312) 280-0170
www.aaii.com

Editor's note: *Stock Investor is published by the American Association of Individual Investors. Because of the potential conflict of interest, we did not feel it appropriate to rate our program, and hence provide only a factual description.*

FIGURE 5.17
The editor used to create stock screens in Stock Investor Standard.

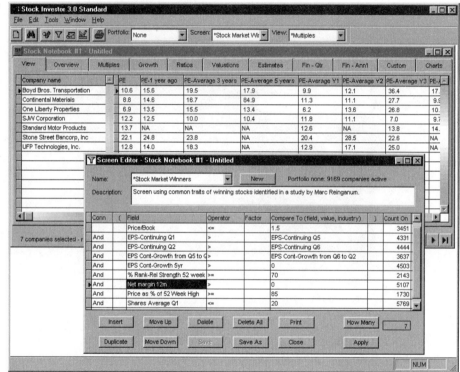

Stock Investor is a quarterly updated program containing fundamental financial data on 9,000 companies. Comparison information on 12 sectors and 100 industry groups is included. The program allows you to look up, analyze and screen for companies meeting specific criteria on over 600 variables. Consensus earnings estimates are provided by I/B/E/S and fundamental data is provided by Market Guide. The income statement data supplied by the program includes eight quarters of sales, earnings and dividend data and five years of sales, cash flow, earnings and dividend figures. The balance sheet data covers eight quarters and three years of operations.

Stock Investor provides over 300 ratios and growth rates and allows the creation of 60 custom variables. Also included is detailed information on company dividend reinvestment plans (DRPs). The screening function enables searches for companies meeting up to 30 criteria using any data field. Screening filters can be performed against constants, other fields, or industry norms. You can create portfolios and print out predefined or custom reports.

Stock Investor Professional
by the American Association of Individual Investors
$247/yr. ($198/yr. for AAII members)—Windows 95/98/NT 4.0
(800) 428-2244, (312) 280-0170
www.aaii.com

Editor's note: *Stock Investor is published by the American Association of Individual Investors. Because of the potential conflict of interest, we did not feel it appropriate to rate our program, and hence provide only a factual description.*

Stock Investor Pro is a monthly updated program running under Windows 95, 98 or NT that contains fundamental data on 9,000 companies. Comparison information on 12 sectors and 100 industry groups is included. The program allows you to look up, analyze and screen for companies meeting specific criteria on over 1,500 variables. Consensus earnings estimates are provided by I/B/E/S and fundamental data is provided by Market Guide.

The program includes detailed income statements, balance sheets and cash flow statements for seven years and eight quarters. Financial statements can be viewed as reported, on a per share basis, on a period-by-period percent change basis, and on a common size basis. Stock Investor Pro provides over 300 ratios and growth rates and allows the creation of 60 custom variables. Also included is detailed information on company dividend reinvestment plans (DRPs).

The screening function enables screening for companies meeting criteria using any data field in the program, along with comparisons to database or industry norms. Predefined screens following the techniques of well-known investors are included in the program. You can create portfolios and print out predefined or custom reports.

FIGURE 5.18
Stock Investor Pro comes with 21 predefined stock filters.

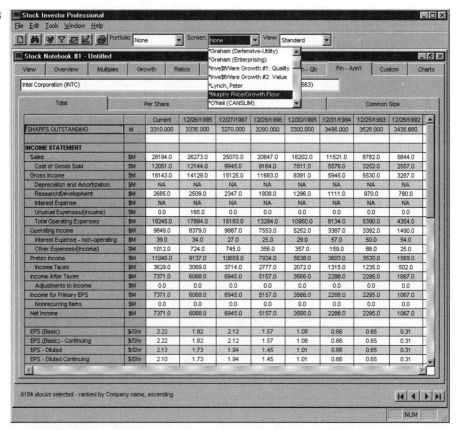

Value Line Investment Survey	
Performance	5
Usefulness	5
Documentation	5
Ease of Use	4
Value	3

Value Line Investment Survey
by Value Line, Inc.
$595–$995/yr.—Windows
(800) 535-8760
www.valueline.com

Investment Survey by Value Line is a strong entry from a company known for its in-depth reports of common stocks. You can select from two subscription options—$595 per year gives you access to the 1,700 companies tracked in the paper-based Value Line Investment Survey, while $995 per year provides you with a broader 5,000-company database. While Value Line's coverage of 5,000 companies is narrower than the more typical 8,000+ universe found in other data services, it still provides coverage of a wide range of firms, including many small-capitalization firms. Both subscription

FIGURE 5.19
Value Line provides 11 years of financial statistics.

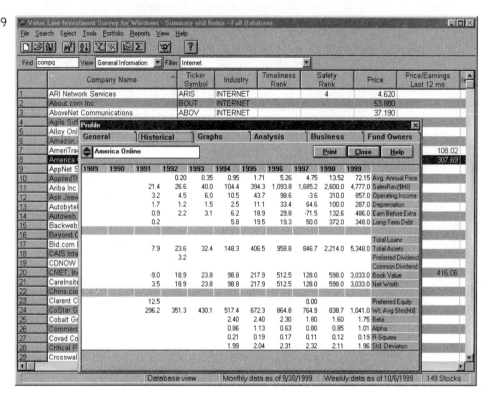

options offer monthly CD-ROM updates by mail, coupled with the option to update data weekly through the Internet, or by phone dial-up. Subscribers of the standard 1,700 company database can choose to receive their updates by floppy disk, but gain access to viewing and printing the full-page reports from the print publication if they opt for the CD-ROM.

As the comparison grid at the end of this chapter reveals, Investment Survey provides a rich database including proprietary Value Line rankings. However, not all data fields displayed in the program are available for screening or export. Notably, screens are limited to using financial statement data items from the current reporting period. While historical and projected growth rates are options in constructing screens, investors who like to construct filters requiring year-by-year increases in earnings or sales will have to look elsewhere. In addition to the elements revealed in the comparison grid, Investment Survey displays the 15 mutual funds that hold the most shares of a company's stock.

As a research tool, the program is above average when judged by the breadth and depth of its database. The ability to access and print the paper-based Value Line reports is a valuable option. As a screening tool, however, the program is a slight disappointment because only a subset of data displayed by the program is available for screening. However, the program overall is a good general-purpose screening and research tool coupled with an up-to-date, easy-to-use interface.

On-Line Services

America Online Stock Screening	
Performance	3
Usefulness	3
Documentation	3
Ease of Use	5
Value	4

America Online Stock Screening
by America Online
$21.95/mo.—Macintosh, Windows
(800) 827-6364
www.aol.com

America Online (AOL) has become the dominant on-line service through an attractive mix of proprietary content, Internet access and competitive pricing. Over the years America Online have signed agreements with a wide range of data providers and established a rich collection of newspapers, business magazines and financial data vendors.

America Online's screening module is simple and presented using AOL's built-in Web browser. Fourteen data fields are available for screening and users can specify minimum and/or maximum values for each of the supported fields. As is typical with on-line services, screens cannot be saved from session to session.

America Online supplies a rich set of stock research from a range of sources including Market Guide, Disclosure, Hoover's, Multex, and Zacks. Over 1,500 bits of information are included for each company in addition to links to SEC company filings.

With over 20 million subscribers, America Online provides a wide range of active message boards. The Motley Fool was created on AOL and still has significant links on the service. The Shark Attack forum provides a forum for more active traders. Separately, individual message folders are provided for a wide range of stocks.

FIGURE 5.20
America Online permits users to construct screens using up to 14 criteria.

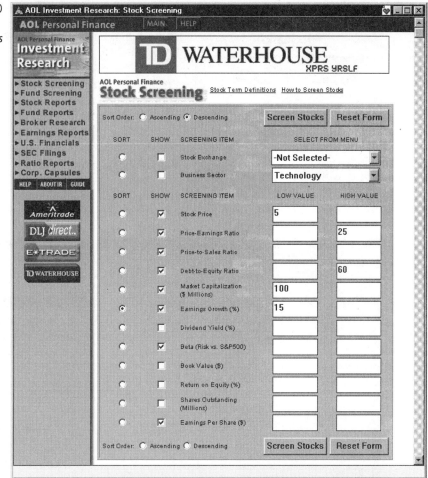

Overall, America Online is an attractive financial service for users primarily concerned with research, not screening. AOL offers a wide range of data directly through its service as well as access to the Internet for additional information, but its screening module is very basic.

TIP@Wallstreet with ProSearch	
Performance	5
Usefulness	5
Documentation	4
Ease of Use	4
Value	2

TIP@Wallstreet with ProSearch
by Telescan, Inc.
$349 + $18/mo. + connect time—Windows
(800) 324-8246
www.wallstreetcity.com

ProSearch is an on-line system that works with Telescan's analysis program, TIP@Wallstreet. The service allows you to search more than 14,000 stocks listed on the NYSE, Amex and Nasdaq using as many as 40 of the 296 fundamental, technical and forecasting criteria. ProSearch is unique in offering a rich set of technical indicators to use for screening along with fundamental elements.

FIGURE 5.21
An illustration of ProSearch's screening editor in action.

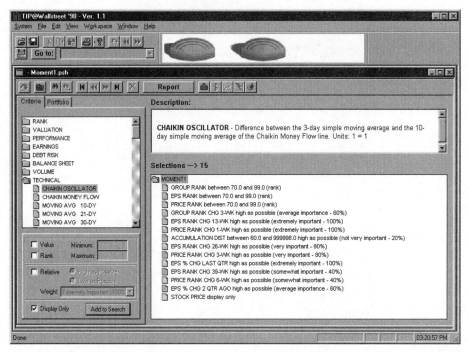

ProSearch allows you to create criteria off-line that you can save for future reference—a common feature for disk-based screening programs, but surprisingly unique for on-line and Internet systems. Since only selected fields of data are displayed at the end of the search, ProSearch allows you to designate lists of fields for display purposes only. When performing a screen, the top 200 securities passing the screen are presented. Data for ProSearch is updated daily, not surprising given its emphasis on technical factors.

Other features of note include ProSearch's ability to weight individual criteria and score any given indicator, enabling you to search for the high and low values. ProSearch also includes the unique ability to test the effectiveness of a strategy historically. ProSearch is a very strong offering, combining access to a wide range of data, frequent data updates and flexible screening.

The Telescan Investors Platform (TIP) software with the ProSearch Module costs $349. The monthly fee to access the screening module is $18 per month, plus connect fees. Telescan offers many subscription options— the most basic costs $9.95 per month, which includes one hour of access time and additional time at $4.80 per hour. Unlimited access runs $34.95 per month.

ProSearch offers above-average screening with a rich array of fundamental and technical factors and backtesting capability. However, detailed company reports must be purchased separately at additional cost. Investors interested in ProSearch's screening capability should also examine Telescan's Web-based Wall Street City service (www.wallstreetcity.com), which segments various ProSearch screening options at different price levels. Overall, ProSearch is best suited for users looking primarily for a screening tool and a fresh, broad database combining technical and fundamental data.

Internet-Based Screening

INVESTools Stock Screening	
Performance	4
Usefulness	4
Documentation	2
Ease of Use	3
Value	3

INVESTools Stock Screening
by INVESTools, Inc.
$9.95/mo.—any PC with Internet access
(800) 567-2683
www.investools.com

INVESTools offers a range of screening and subscription options on its Web site covering basic portfolio management tools, stock and mutual fund analysis and even on-line versions of investment newsletters. [**Editor's Note:** *AAII is a business partner of INVESTools through its on-line publication of Computerized Investing.*] Three levels of screening are available through INVESTools—predefined, basic, and advanced.

FIGURE 5.22
*INVESTools
includes nine
free predefined
screens.*

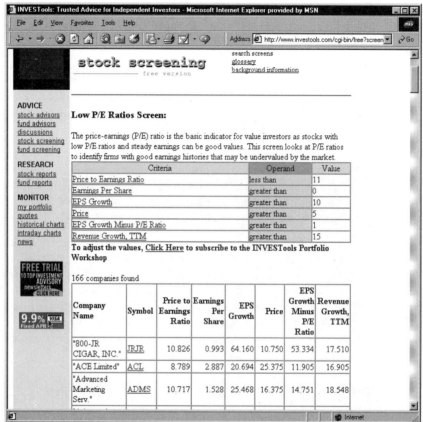

INVESTools offers nine predefined filters (see Figure 5.22) that can be accessed by all Internet users. The free predefined screens cover a reasonable range of growth, value, and capitalization screens. Screening results include company information on each of the variables used in the screen along with links to fundamental data on the companies. Market Guide company snapshots are free, while more detailed reports can be purchased at prices ranging from $1.00 to $6.95 per report. The financial statement comparison grid listing for INVESTools reflects the data found in the most detailed Provestor report, which costs $6.95.

Basic screening is included with INVESTools' $9.95 per month portfolio workshop subscription described in Chapter 8: Financial Information Services. Portfolio workshop includes portfolio monitoring, news, charts, Zacks earnings estimates, and Market Guide Quick Facts reports. The basic screening service allows you to modify the predefined screens to fine-tune their results.

The advanced screening module gives access to 68 different variables spread across a wide range of company statistics, growth rates, and ratios. Comparison can only be made against constants. For some fields, users are given the option of specifying minimum and maximum values, but the majority of the criteria allow for only one comparison value. Notably, screens can be saved for later use.

FIGURE 5.23
INVESTools'
advanced
screening tool.

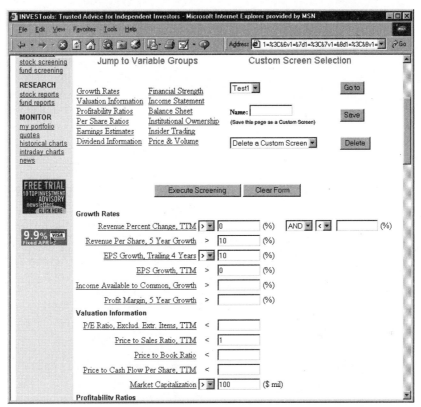

Results of screens are presented in a table consisting of the companies passing the filter and the values for each of the variables used in the screen. The results can be sorted by any of the variables used in the screen. As with the free screening, a link is provided to the free Market Guide snapshot, but detailed reports must be purchased separately.

The site's portfolio workshop section offers subscriptions that provide a good balance between portfolio monitoring and stock research, but combining the portfolio workshop with the advanced stock screening brings the cost to about $20 per month, reducing the value of the service.

Marketguide.com—NetScreen	
Performance	3
Usefulness	3
Documentation	4
Ease of Use	3
Value	5

Marketguide.com—NetScreen
by Market Guide, Inc.
Free—any PC with Internet access
(516) 327-2400
www.marketguide.com

NetScreen is a free, Java-based screening tool available on the Market Guide Web site. The service is limited to screening using 20 common data items. While the construction of screening criteria is more cumbersome than most systems, Market Guide allows for the creation of fairly complex screening criteria. A single line in a filter can include mathematical and logical manipulation. Screening results are displayed in a table that includes the variables used in the filter and links to company reports on the passing companies.

FIGURE 5.24
Screen filter editor for NetScreen is displayed.

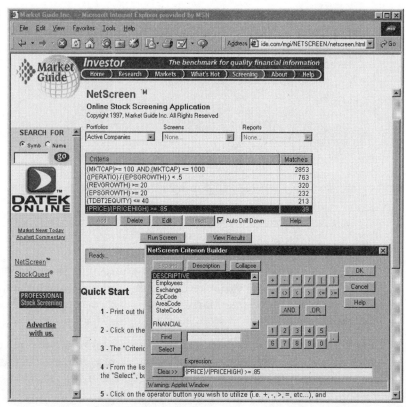

The free company research reports steal the show on the Market Guide Web site. Market Guide is a well-respected supplier of company fundamental and price data. The Market Guide database covers over 9,000 active stocks trading on the New York Stock Exchange, American Stock Exchange, Nasdaq National and Small Cap market, and over-the-counter. Its snapshot and highlight reports are found throughout the Web, but the Market Guide Web site goes further by providing free reports covering earnings estimates, ratio comparisons, insider trading, institutional ownership, company financials, and dividend reinvestment plan details.

FIGURE 5.25
Market Guide provides a useful array of free company reports. A segment of the "Financials Report" is displayed in this screen shot along with links to additional reports.

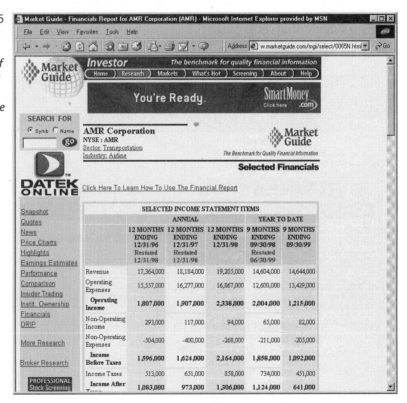

The "What's Hot" segment of the Web site is also worthy of a mention. It provides daily rankings of the best- and worst-performing stocks, industries and sectors. Links are provided to the stocks within a given industry or sector for additional research.

The detailed company and industry data coupled with the free, although basic, NetScreen offering makes the Market Guide Web site worth checking out.

Morningstar.com— Free Service	
Performance	3
Usefulness	3
Documentation	5
Ease of Use	5
Value	5

Morningstar.com
by Morningstar, Inc.
Free–$9.95/mo. or $99/yr.—any PC with Internet access
(800) 735-0700
www.morningstar.com

Morningstar.com is a full-featured investment Web site providing portfolio tracking, market monitoring, stock and fund screening and research, educational articles and message boards. Much of the site is free, with additional research and screening available with a $9.95 per month subscription.

FIGURE 5.26
The editor used to create stock filters and display screening results in Morningstar.com.

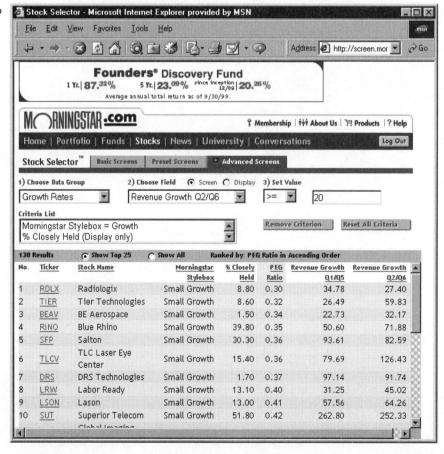

Morningstar.com— Premium Service	
Performance	4
Usefulness	4
Documentation	5
Ease of Use	5
Value	4

Research on the site consists of stock screening coupled with research reports. Free screening is basic; you are limited to using two criteria per screen. For example, you are able to select industry sector and one financial filter such as a price-earnings ratio. The premium screening module is well executed, allowing investors to pick from 125 criteria for stocks, but is limited to performing comparisons against user-entered constant values, and the screens cannot be saved for use at a later time.

FIGURE 5.27 *Morningstar.com features a mix of free and fee-based information. Elements with a plus sign require a subscription.*

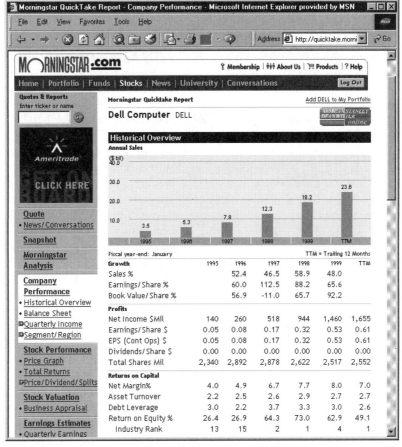

Comprehensive stock reports consist of 10 sections providing an overview snapshot, detailed company profile, financial statements and ratios, a long-term price chart, stock price performance statistics, stock, industry and market multiples, earnings estimates and analyst opinions, industry snapshot, insider and institutional shareholder activity, SEC filings, and news. The financial statement provides five years of income statement items, and current balance sheet data. The premium reports adds details such as a history of cash and stock dividends, regional (international) sales and profit exposures, and earnings estimate surprise statistics.

Articles with a focus on current market issues, interviews and detailed educational features are located throughout the site. Message boards provide a forum for discussion of the many issues brought up in the articles.

Overall the Morningstar.com is a well-organized Web site that provides a diverse and useful set of tools for the stock investor.

MSN MoneyCentral Investor	
Performance	5
Usefulness	5
Documentation	5
Ease of Use	5
Value	5

MSN MoneyCentral Investor
by Microsoft, Inc.
Free—any PC with Internet access
(800) 426-9400
moneycentral.msn.com/investor

Microsoft offers a complete personal finance and investing site through its free MSN Web portal. The investing sections offers portfolio tracking, charts, news, educational articles, stock and mutual fund research, and brokerage services. Access to articles, news, screens, company and mutual fund data, and portfolio tracking is free to all Internet users. The site provides one of the best portfolio managers on the Web with a well thought-out module that tracks your holdings, reports the cost and current value, and alerts you to related news stories when you examine your holdings on-line.

Articles cover a wide range of topics ranging from discussions of current market events to detailed examinations of stock analysis techniques. News articles are posted daily, with historical articles archived by topic.

The research and screening module on the site is also top-notch. As revealed in the comparison grid at the end of this chapter, the company coverage is both broad and deep. Microsoft has pulled together the content of Disclosure, Hoover's, Media General and Zacks into a comprehensive company report. Navigation between the various modules is easy and logical. The screening flexibility

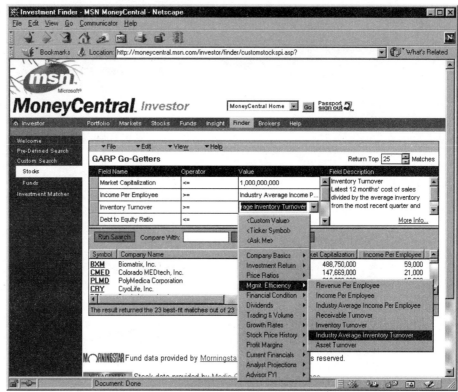

FIGURE 5.28
The editor used to create stock filters and display screening results in MSN MoneyCentral Investor.

is above average among on-line and Internet vendors, even stronger than most of the disk-based services. The screening editor is an ActiveX program that we were able to run on Windows-based systems using either Internet Explorer or Netscape browsers. On Mac systems, however, MSN displays a more basic Web-based screening module.

The research wizard walks an investor through the factors to consider when looking at a stock, including its fundamentals, price history, valuations, catalysts, and competition. Another unique feature is the advisor FYI alerts, which alerts users to factors that may influence a stock's price, such as an earnings estimate revision, a price-earnings ratio in the bottom 25% for its industry, and increasing relative price strength.

Microsoft has made steady improvements to its investment Web site since its introduction and the site is one of the strongest stock research and screening services on the Web.

Quicken.com	
Performance	4
Usefulness	4
Documentation	5
Ease of Use	5
Value	5

Quicken.com
by Intuit Inc.
Free—any PC with Internet access
(800) 446-8848
www.quicken.com

Quicken.com is a free site offering investors a central place for investors to manage many aspects of personal finance, including banking, insurance, retirement planning, and investing.

Quicken.com offers six predefined screens-covering basic growth, value, momentum, and market-capitalization approaches. Results are displayed in a standard table view, but Quicken has a unique on-line feature that allows users to switch between different views, such as financials or growth rates.

FIGURE 5.29
Screen filter editor for Quicken.com.

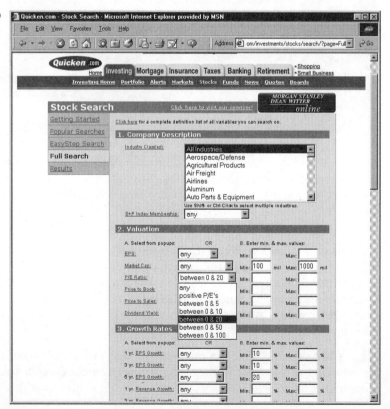

The "Full Search" screening module allows users to construct custom screens using any of the 33 well-chosen elements. Users can select pre-defined ranges for each element or specify a minimum and maximum range.

The site includes all the basic tools required to research those companies passing screens, including quotes, news, portfolio tracking, company fundamentals, links to full SEC filings, insider transactions, and analyst ratings and earnings estimates. Unique features include consensus stock ratings by Quicken.com users and a stock evaluator that highlights elements affecting a company's stock price.

FIGURE 5.30
Quicken.com walks users through a series of variables that may affect the stock price.

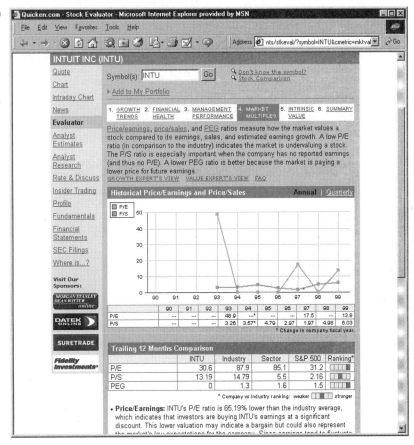

The site is well organized and presents information available for each stock clearly. Quicken.com's features and data exceeds those found on a number of fee-based sites. Most investors will find this free site adequate for their needs.

S&P Personal Wealth	
Performance	4
Usefulness	4
Documentation	5
Ease of Use	5
Value	3

S&P Personal Wealth
by Standard & Poor's
$9.95/mo. or $99/yr.—any PC with Internet access
(800) 823-3209
www.personalwealth.com

Standard & Poor's Personal Wealth is a one-stop investment center that offers financial planning, portfolio management, charting, mutual fund and stock research, and screening at a cost of $9.95 per month, or just less than $100 a year.

FIGURE 5.31
S&P Personal Wealth stock screening module.

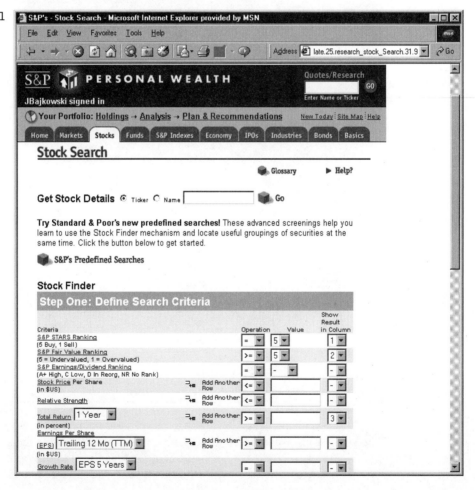

Personal wealth provides five predefined screens as well as a stock screening tool. Both tools are tied strongly to the S&P's proprietary STARS (STock Appreciation Ranking System) rankings and other S&P valuation measures. The screening editor is basic, but covers the major elements used for screening.

The company profiles provide all of the details one would expect. The organization and display of information is well thought out. Unique elements include S&P ratings, informative company and industry write-ups, and 10 in-depth S&P Stock Reports per month.

FIGURE 5.32
S&P Personal Wealth provides detailed company profile reports.

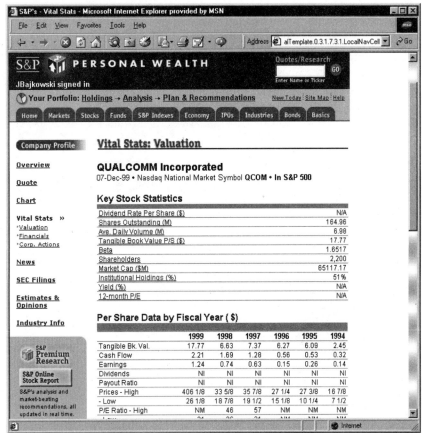

The tools and data are solid and useful, but the information comes with a subscription charge in an era where the market is heading toward free data. The site will appeal most to investors who want easy access to S&P's well-regarded investment analysis.

StockScreener	
Performance	3
Usefulness	3
Documentation	4
Ease of Use	5
Value	5

StockScreener

by Hoover's, Inc.
Free—any PC with Internet access
(800) 486-8666
www.stockscreener.com

Hoover's Inc. has grown to become a good source of company descriptions and financial data. StockScreener is a free service from Hoover's offering screening on approximately 8,000 companies.

The service includes the typical elements expected in a basic screening service. Minimum and maximum elements can be specified for 22 factors such as multiples, ratios, company size and growth rates (see Figure 5.33). Screening results are dis-

FIGURE 5.33
StockScreener allows you to specify minimum and maximum values in its editor.

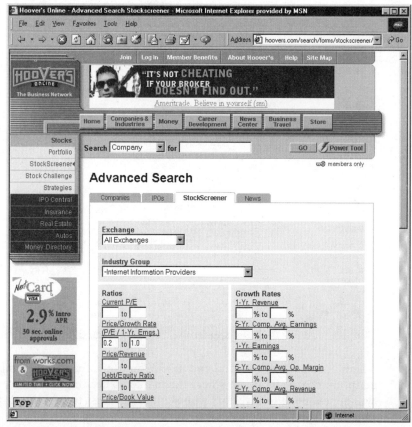

played in a table that also shows the factors used for the screen. Company names are linked to resources such as the SEC Edgar database for further company research. StockScreener is best suited for the investor looking to perform basic screening.

Company profiles are free to all, but Hoover's also offers a membership that includes detailed financials for $109.95 per year. The financial statement comparison grid listing for StockScreener details the data provided through this subscription option.

Thomson Investors Network	
Performance	3
Usefulness	3
Documentation	4
Ease of Use	5
Value	4

Thomson Investors Network
by Thomson Financial Services, Inc.
$34.95/yr.—any PC with Internet access
(301) 545-4999
www.thomsoninvest.net

Thomson Investors Network is a comprehensive investment Web site providing portfolio management, quotes, news, E-mail alerts, stock, mutual fund and muni bond data, screening tools, and even basic investment education. The site is primarily a subscription-based service costing $34.95 per year, although certain elements, such as stock screening, can be done for free.

The screening available on the site is weaker than some of the other on-line and Internet systems. For example, screening is limited to selecting six criteria from the 18 available fields, and comparisons can only be made in relative context (i.e., strong, above average, below average or weak).

Separately, Thomson provides results of basic screens such as low price-earnings companies broken down by market capitalization. As revealed in the comparison grids, the site is above average in terms of the data available for researching companies—exceeding company information found in most free Web sites. The site is best suited for investors looking for individual company research tools, but not strong screening.

FIGURE 5.34
The screening editor in Thomson Investors Network only allows broad ranges to be specified in its filters.

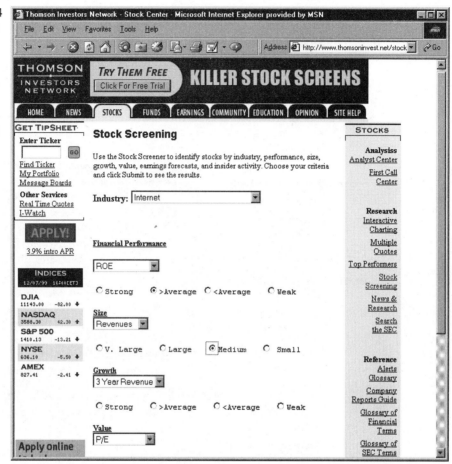

Wall Street City	
Performance	5
Usefulness	5
Documentation	5
Ease of Use	5
Value	4

Wall Street City
by Telescan, Inc.
Free–$149.95/mo.—any PC with Internet access
(800) 324-8246
www.wallstreetcity.com

Wall Street City a comprehensive investment Web site providing a wide range of data and subscription options, ranging from free portfolio tracking, news, market updates and basic search tools to a rich array of charting, screening and company research tools.

The site offers the greatest range of screening tools among the Internet and on-line sites. You can opt for a rich collection of predefined screens using both fundamental and technical approaches, or you can access an on-line version of the ProSearch screening application reviewed on page 176 in this chapter.

FIGURE 5.35
Wall Street City includes the flexible and powerful Java-based screening module that covers a wide range of fundamental and technical factors.

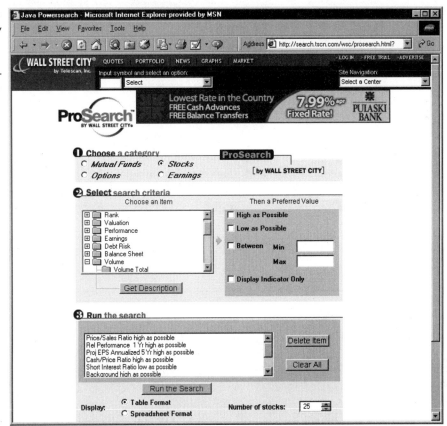

Wall Street City includes a unique backtesting feature that analyzes the historical success of a screen with various holding periods and market capitalization concentrations. Telescan tracks the performance of its predefined screens and reports on the performance of these strategies. Access to features such as the best- and worst-performing stock groups, predefined stock screens, and the "What's Working Now?" center are available. This center is noteworthy for reporting on the success of a wide range of fundamental and technical screening strategies. The predefined screens show the filters that make up the screen, a list of passing companies, historical performance charts, and statistics for the strategy.

FIGURE 5.36
*Example of
top-
performing
stocks screen
from Wall
Street City.*

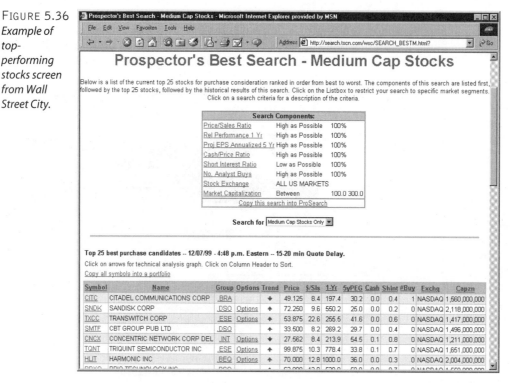

Overall, Wall Street City is a feature- and data-rich site of interest to a wide range
of investors. Wall Street City's tiered pricing allows you to tailor the product subscription to your needs and expand services as your needs develop. With subscriptions ranging from free to $149.95 per month, more advanced levels of news,
charting, screening, and research can be chosen.

Yahoo! Finance	
Performance	3
Usefulness	3
Documentation	3
Ease of Use	4
Value	5

Yahoo! Finance
by Yahoo! Inc.
Free–any PC with Internet access
(408) 731-3300
quote.yahoo.com

Yahoo! Finance brings together a simple, but
reasonable set of free tools for the investor.
Yahoo! offers a very basic stock screening
tool—users can screen on any of the seven
available criteria, but are forced to pick criteria from within preset levels.

FIGURE 5.37
*Screening
module in
Yahoo!
Finance.*

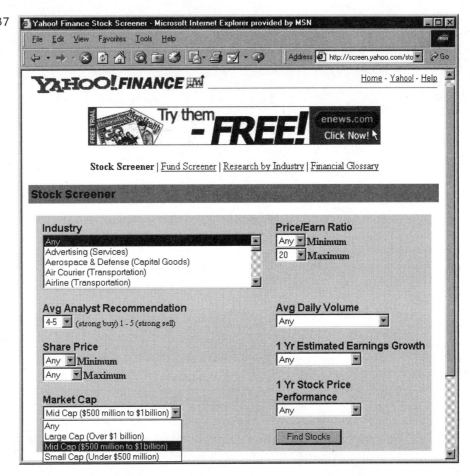

Yahoo! is able to leverage its linking expertise to bring together a reasonable collection of news and research data. Fundamental stock data comes from Market Guide, while Zacks provides earnings estimates and brokerage recommendations. Even insider transactions from CDA/Investnet are available for free, which also provides the mutual fund profiles.

Overall, Yahoo! Finance is good site for keeping track of your portfolio and performing basic company research, but is weak for screening.

Zacks Advisor	
Performance	4
Usefulness	4
Documentation	4
Ease of Use	5
Value	4

Zacks Advisor
by Zacks Investment Research
$150/yr.—any PC with Internet access
(800) 399-6659, (312) 630-9880
www.zacks.com

The Zacks Advisor service offers investors a wide range of investment information and screening options for $150 per year.

With the service, you have access to daily E-mail alerts covering items such as analysts' changes, detailed company financials, brokerage research reports, predefined screens, and custom screening. Zacks offers 13 predefined screens that can be further broken down into market-cap ranges. Custom screening offers control over 100 variables covering the usual range of screening options, along with earnings estimates and brokerage recommendation figures not available through most services. Zacks also allows users to save custom screens for later use.

FIGURE 5.38
Custom screening editor on Zacks Advisor.

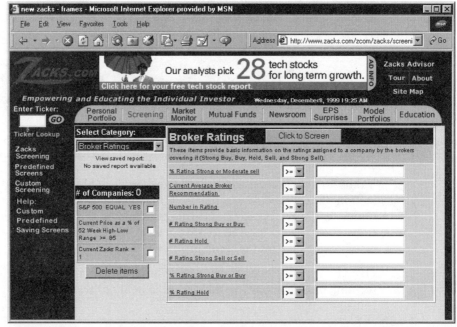

Zacks provides detailed reports on a company's financials, ratios, industry comparisons, consensus earnings estimates, and analyst recommendations. Detailed analyst estimate reports go as far as to list a record of each estimate and recommendation for a given company.

FIGURE 5.39
Zacks offers detailed analyst estimate and recommendation reports.

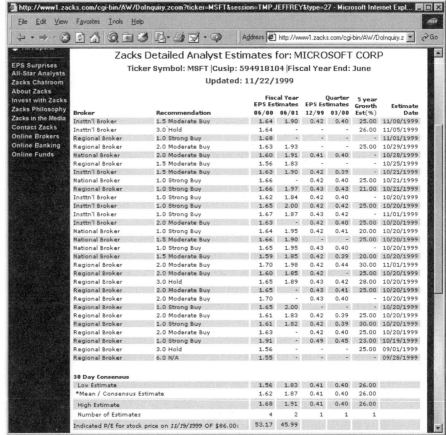

Overall, Zacks offers a wide range of useful tools for those with a stock portfolio. Screening and research is above average and the basic tools necessary to construct a stock portfolio are provided, while the portfolio management module helps keep investors abreast of their holdings.

Comparison Grid

The fundamental stock screening comparison grid features some abbreviations in the section entitled ratios. These abbreviations are used primarily because of space constraints within the grid.

The abbreviations for ratios-related features include the following:

Leverage:

debt/cap: debt to capital

debt/eq: debt to equity

lt debt/cap: long-term debt to capital

lt debt/eq: long-term debt to equity

liab/assets: liabilities to assets

Profitability:

PM: profit margin

ROA: return on assets

ROE: return on equity

Multiples:

P/E: price-earnings ratio

P/B: price-to-book-value ratio

P/S: price-to-sales ratio

P/CF: price-to-cash-flow ratio

P/FCF: price-to-free-cash-flow ratio

Fundamental Stock Screening: Disk-Based		Market Guide StockQuest	Principia Pro for Stocks
Company		Market Guide, Inc.	Morningstar, Inc.
Telephone		(516) 327-2400	(800) 735-0700
Web Address		www.marketguide.com	www.morningstar.com
Delivery Medium (Software/On-line/Internet)		software (Internet)	software (CD)
Update Schedule		weekly	monthly/quarterly/annually
Price (AAII Member Discount)		free	$495/$295/$95
Demo (Cost)			
Platform		Windows	Windows 95/98/NT 4.0+
Data Source		Market Guide	Morningstar, Zacks
Database Content	Number of Stocks	9,600	8,000
	Number of Data Fields	75 (StockQuest)	600
	Create Custom Data Fields	✖	✖
	Number of Data Fields for Sorting	75	160
	Company Information — Address/Phone	✖ (Web Site)	✖
	Company Information — ADR	✖	✖
	Company Information — DRP Plan	✖ (Web Site)	✖
	Company Information — Industry Grouping	✖	✖
	Company Information — Description Length		580 characters
	Earnings Estimates — Source		Zacks
	Earnings Estimates — Quarterly		✖ (2 qtrs)
	Earnings Estimates — Annual		✖ (2 yrs)
	Earnings Estimates — Growth—Long Term		✖ (long-term)
	Ratios — Leverage	debt/eq, lt debt/eq	debt/eq, debt/cap
	Ratios — Liquidity	current	current, quick
	Ratios — Profitability	ROE, ROA, PM	ROE, ROA, PM, net PM
	Ratios — Multiples	P/B, P/S, P/CF, yield	P/E, P/B, P/S, P/CF, yield
	Growth Rates — Periods	✖ (pre-calc)	✖ (1-, 3-yr)
	Growth Rates — Total/Annualized		✖ (annualized)
	Price & Share Data — High/Low/Close/Volume	✖ (52-week)	✖ (52-week)
	Price & Share Data — Relative Strength	✖	✖
	Price & Share Data — Market Cap/Float	✖	✖
	Price & Share Data — % Insider/Institutional Holdings	✖	✖ (Inst'nl % held by mutual funds)
Screening	Number of Data Fields for Screening	75	160
	Any Data Field	✖	
	Against Constant Values	✖	✖
	Against Other Data Fields	✖	
	Against Industry		
	Save Custom Screens/# of Predefined Screens	✖/none	✖/none
Viewing	Browse Table	✖	✖
	Financial Statement Presentation	total $, per share, % change	total $, per share, % chg, common size
	Individual Company Summaries	✖	✖
Reporting	Charts/Graphs		✖
	Export to a File	✖	✖ (text)
	Statistical Summaries (Statistical Data)	high, low, mean (avg)	mean

Fundamental Stock Screening: Disk-Based		Research Wizard	Stock Investor Standard 3.0
Company		Zacks Investment Research	AAII
Telephone		(800) 399-6659, (312) 630-9880	(800) 428-2244; (312) 280-0170
Web Address		www.zacks.com	www.aaii.com
Delivery Medium (Software/On-line/Internet)		software (diskette/Internet)	software (CD)
Update Schedule		weekly	quarterly
Price (AAII Member Discount)		$600/yr.	$99/yr. ($148/yr. non-members)
Demo (Cost)		✖ ($55, 2-month trial)	✖ ($49, $35 member; 1-mo. trial)
Platform		Windows	Windows 95/98/NT
Data Source		Zacks	MarketGuide, I/B/E/S
Database Content	Number of Stocks	6,000	8,000+
	Number of Data Fields	338	600+
	Create Custom Data Fields	✖	✖
	Number of Data Fields for Sorting	338	600+
	Company Information — Address/Phone		✖
	ADR		✖
	DRP Plan		✖
	Industry Grouping	✖	✖ (Market Guide)
	Description Length	na	75 word avg.
	Earnings Estimates — Source	Zacks	I/B/E/S
	Quarterly	✖	
	Annual	✖	✖
	Growth—Long Term	✖	✖
	Ratios — Leverage	debt/eq, lt debt/eq, liab/assets, debt/cap	lt debt/cap, liab/assets
	Liquidity	current, quick, working cap	current, quick
	Profitability	ROE, ROA, PM, net PM	ROE, ROA, net PM, gross PM
	Multiples	P/E, P/B, P/S, P/CF, yield	P/E, P/B, P/S, P/CF, P/FCF, yield
	Growth Rates — Periods	✖	✖ (pre-calc 3-, 5-yr)
	Total/Annualized	✖	✖ (annualized)
	Price & Share Data — High/Low/Close/Volume	✖	✖ (annual 5-yr)
	Relative Strength		✖ (4-, 13-, 26-, 52-week)
	Market Cap/Float	✖ (market cap)	✖
	% Insider/Institutional Holdings	✖	✖
Screening	Number of Data Fields for Screening	338	600+
	Any Data Field	✖	✖
	Against Constant Values	✖	✖
	Against Other Data Fields	✖	✖
	Against Industry	✖	✖
	Save Custom Screens/# of Predefined Screens	✖/none	✖/21
Viewing	Browse Table	✖	✖
	Financial Statement Presentation	total $, per share, % chg, common size	total $, per share, % change, common size
	Individual Company Summaries		✖
Reporting	Charts/Graphs	✖	✖
	Export to a File	✖	✖
	Statistical Summaries (Statistical Data)	high, low, mean, median	high, low, mean, median

Fundamental Stock Screening: Disk-Based		Stock Investor Professional	Value Line Investment Survey
Company		AAII	Value Line, Inc.
Telephone		(800) 428-2244; (312) 280-0170	(800) 535-8760
Web Address		www.aaii.com	www.valueline.com
Delivery Medium (Software/On-line/Internet)		software (CD)	software (CD, on-line)
Update Schedule		monthly	monthly (weekly on-line)
Price (AAII Member Discount)		$198/yr. ($247/yr. non-members)	$595/yr. (1,700 stocks), $995/yr. (5,000)
Demo (Cost)		✖ ($65, $50 member; 1-mo. trial)	✖ (free)
Platform		Windows 95/98/NT	Windows 3.1+
Data Source		Market Guide, I/B/E/S	Value Line
Database Content	Number of Stocks	8,000+	1,700 or 5,000
	Number of Data Fields	1,500+	400
	Create Custom Data Fields	✖	✖
	Number of Data Fields for Sorting	1,500+	200+
	Company Information — Address/Phone	✖	✖
	ADR	✖	✖
	DRP Plan	✖	
	Industry Grouping	✖ (Market Guide, SIC)	✖ (SIC, Value Line-based)
	Description Length	75 word avg.	200 words+
	Earnings Estimates — Source	I/B/E/S	Value Line
	Quarterly	✖	✖ (4 qtrs)
	Annual	✖	✖
	Growth—Long Term	✖	✖
	Ratios — Leverage	debt/eq, lt debt/cap, liab/assets	lt debt/eq, lt debt/cap, liab/assets
	Liquidity	current, quick	current, quick, working capital
	Profitability	ROE, ROA, net PM, gross PM	ROA, ROE, PM, net PM, gross PM
	Multiples	P/E, P/B, P/S, P/CF, P/FCF, yield	P/B, P/S, yield
	Growth Rates — Periods	✖ (pre-calc 1-, 3-, 5-, 7-yr)	✖ (1-, 5-yr)
	Total/Annualized	✖ (annualized)	✖ (annualized)
	Price & Share Data — High/Low/Close/Volume	✖ (monthly 5-yr)	✖ (52-wk high/low/close, 11-yr avg)
	Relative Strength	✖ (4-, 13-, 26-, 52-week)	
	Market Cap/Float	✖	✖ (market cap)
	% Insider/Institutional Holdings	✖	✖
Screening	Number of Data Fields for Screening	1,500+	200+
	Any Data Field	✖	
	Against Constant Values	✖	✖
	Against Other Data Fields	✖	✖
	Against Industry	✖	✖ (stock performance only)
	Save Custom Screens/# of Predefined Screens	✖/21	✖/35
Viewing	Browse Table	✖	✖
	Financial Statement Presentation	total $, per share, % change, common size	total $, per share
	Individual Company Summaries	✖	✖
Reporting	Charts/Graphs	✖	✖
	Export to a File	✖	✖
	Statistical Summaries (Statistical Data)	high, low, mean, median	high, low, mean

Fundamental Stock Screening: On-Line		America Online Stock Screening	TIP@Wallstreet w/ProSearch
Company		America Online	Telescan, Inc.
Telephone		(800) 827-6364	(800) 324-8246
Web Address		www.aol.com	www.wallstreetcity.com
Delivery Medium (Software/On-line/Internet)		on-line	on-line
Update Schedule		daily	daily/weekly/monthly/quarterly/annly
Price (AAII Member Discount)		included with AOL $21.95/mo.	software: $349.00 (10%); $18/mo. + connect
Demo (Cost)		✖ (100 free hours)	✖ (free trial)
Platform		Mac, Windows	Windows
Data Source		Market Guide, Disclosure	Telescan, Market Guide, Zacks
Database Content	Number of Stocks	9,000	14,000
	Number of Data Fields	1,500	296
	Create Custom Data Fields		
	Number of Data Fields for Sorting	1	296
	Company Information — Address/Phone	✖	✖
	ADR	✖	✖
	DRP Plan		✖
	Industry Grouping	Market Guide	✖ (S&P)
	Description Length	900 characters	summary
	Earnings Estimates — Source	Zacks	Zacks
	Quarterly	✖ (2 quarters)	✖ (last 16 quarters)
	Annual	✖ (2 years)	✖ (latest year)
	Growth—Long Term	✖ (5 yrs)	✖ (last 16 quarters)
	Ratios — Leverage	debt/eq, lt debt/eq	debt/eq, lt debt/eq, liab/assets
	Liquidity	current, quick	current, quick, working cap
	Profitability	ROE, ROA, PM, net PM	ROE, ROA, PM, net PM, gross PM
	Multiples	P/E, P/B, P/S, P/CF, yield	P/E, P/B, P/S, yield, P/CF
	Growth Rates — Periods	✖ (1-, 3-, 5-yr)	✖
	Total/Annualized	✖ (annualized)	✖
	Price & Share Data — High/Low/Close/Volume	✖ (last year hi/low/close)	✖ (24-yr)
	Relative Strength		✖ (1-day;1-, 3-, 6-, 18-, 26-wk; 1-, 3-, 5-yr)
	Market Cap/Float	✖ (market cap)	✖
	% Insider/Institutional Holdings	✖ (insider only)	✖
Screening	Number of Data Fields for Screening	14	200+
	Any Data Field		✖
	Against Constant Values	✖	✖
	Against Other Data Fields		
	Against Industry		✖
	Save Custom Screens/# of Predefined Screens		✖/31
Viewing	Browse Table		✖
	Financial Statement Presentation	total $, per share	total $, per share
	Individual Company Summaries	✖	✖
Reporting	Charts/Graphs	✖	✖
	Export to a File		✖
	Statistical Summaries (Statistical Data)		high, low, mean (avg), median

Fundamental Stock Screening: Internet-Based		INVESTools	Marketguide.com—NetScreen
Company		INVESTools, Inc.	Market Guide, Inc.
Telephone		(800) 567-2683	(516) 327-2400
Web Address		www.investools.com	www.marketguide.com
Delivery Medium (Software/On-line/Internet)		Internet	Internet
Update Schedule		weekly	weekly
Price (AAII Member Discount)		Predefined—Free; Advanced—$9.95/mo.	free with any Internet access
Demo (Cost)		✖ (1 month free)	
Platform		any PC with Internet	any PC with Internet
Data Source		Market Guide, Zacks	Market Guide
Database Content	Number of Stocks	9,400	9,600
	Number of Data Fields	68	20
	Create Custom Data Fields		
	Number of Data Fields for Sorting	68	
	Company Information	Address/Phone	✖	
		ADR		✖
		DRP Plan		
		Industry Grouping	✖ (Market Guide)	✖
		Description Length	6 sentences	6 sentences
	Earnings Estimates	Source	Zacks	
		Quarterly	✖ (1 quarter)	
		Annual	✖ (2 years)	
		Growth—Long Term	✖ (5 yrs)	
	Ratios	Leverage	debt/eq, liab/assets	debt/eq
		Liquidity	current, quick	current
		Profitability	ROE, ROI, net PM, gross PM	ROE, ROA, gross PM
		Multiples	P/E, P/B, P/S, P/CF, yield	P/B, P/S, P/CF, yield
	Growth Rates	Periods	✖ (5-yr)	✖ (5-yr)
		Total/Annualized	✖ (annualized)	✖ (annualized)
	Price & Share Data	High/Low/Close/Volume	✖ (latest close)	✖ (52-wk)
		Relative Strength	✖ (4-, 52-week)	
		Market Cap/Float	✖ (market cap)	✖
		% Insider/Institutional Holdings	✖	
Screening	Number of Data Fields for Screening	68	20
	Any Data Field	✖	
	Against Constant Values	✖	✖
	Against Other Data Fields		✖
	Against Industry		
	Save Custom Screens/# of Predefined Screens	✖/9	
Viewing	Browse Table	✖	✖
	Financial Statement Presentation	total $, per share	total $, per share, % change
	Individual Company Summaries	✖	✖
Reporting	Charts/Graphs	✖ (extra cost)	
	Export to a File		
	Statistical Summaries (Statistical Data)		

Fundamental Stock Screening: Internet-Based		Morningstar.com—Free Service	Morningstar.com—Premium Service
Company		Morningstar, Inc.	Morningstar, Inc.
Telephone		(800) 735-0700	(800) 735-0700
Web Address		www.morningstar.com	www.morningstar.net
Delivery Medium (Software/On-line/Internet)		Internet	Internet
Update Schedule		daily	daily
Price (AAII Member Discount)		free with any Internet access	$9.95/month or $99/year
Demo (Cost)			✖ (1 month free)
Platform		Web	Web
Data Source		Morningstar, S&P ComStock, Zacks	Morningstar, S&P ComStock, Zacks, Dow Jones
Database Content	Number of Stocks	8,000+	8,000+
	Number of Data Fields	300	600
	Create Custom Data Fields		
	Number of Data Fields for Sorting	13	125
	Company Information — Address/Phone	✖	✖
	ADR	✖	✖
	DRP Plan		
	Industry Grouping	Morningstar	Morningstar
	Description Length	500 words	500 words
	Earnings Estimates — Source	Zacks	Zacks
	Quarterly	✖ (2 quarters)	✖ (2 quarters)
	Annual	✖ (2 years)	✖ (2 years)
	Growth—Long Term	✖ (5 yrs)	✖ (3, 5 yrs)
	Ratios — Leverage	debt/eq	debt/eq
	Liquidity	current	current
	Profitability	ROE, ROA	ROE, ROA, PM
	Multiples	P/E, P/B, P/S, P/CF, P/FCF, yield	P/E, P/B, P/S, P/CF, P/FCF, yield
	Growth Rates — Periods	✖ (1, 3-yr)	✖ (1, 3-yr)
	Total/Annualized	✖ (annualized)	✖ (annualized)
	Price & Share Data — High/Low/Close/Volume	✖ (monthly 5-year chart)	✖ (daily close 1995+)
	Relative Strength		
	Market Cap/Float	✖ (market cap)	✖ (market cap/float)
	% Insider/Institutional Holdings		✖ (% inst'l held by mutual funds)
Screening	Number of Data Fields for Screening	13	125
	Any Data Field		
	Against Constant Values		✖
	Against Other Data Fields		
	Against Industry		
	Save Custom Screens/# of Predefined Screens		
Viewing	Browse Table		✖
	Financial Statement Presentation	total $, per share, % change, common size	total $, per share, % change, common size
	Individual Company Summaries	✖	✖
Reporting	Charts/Graphs	✖	✖
	Export to a File		✖
	Statistical Summaries (Statistical Data)		

Fundamental Stock Screening: Internet-Based		MSN MoneyCentral Investor	Quicken.com
Company		Microsoft, Inc.	Intuit Inc.
Telephone		(800) 426-9400	(800) 446-8848
Web Address		moneycentral.msn.com/investor	www.quicken.com
Delivery Medium (Software/On-line/Internet)		Internet	Internet
Update Schedule		daily	daily
Price (AAII Member Discount)		free with any Internet access	free with any Internet access
Demo (Cost)			
Platform		any PC with Internet	any PC with Internet
Data Source		Hoovers, Zacks, Media General, and others	S&P, I/B/E/S, Business Wire, PR News, Reuters, Vickers
Database Content	Number of Stocks	8,000+	9,600
	Number of Data Fields	1,500	1,000
	Create Custom Data Fields		
	Number of Data Fields for Sorting	200	8
	Company Information — Address/Phone	✖	✖
	ADR	✖	
	DRP Plan		
	Industry Grouping	✖ (Media General)	✖ (S&P)
	Description Length	500 words	40 words
	Earnings Estimates — Source	Zacks	I/B/E/S
	Quarterly	✖ (2 quarters)	✖ (2 quarters)
	Annual	✖ (2 years)	✖ (2 years)
	Growth—Long Term	✖ (5 yrs)	✖ (5 yrs)
	Ratios — Leverage	debt/eq	debt/eq, assets/eq
	Liquidity	current, quick	current, quick
	Profitability	ROE, PM, net PM, gross PM	ROE, ROA
	Multiples	P/E, P/B, P/S, P/CF, yield	P/E, P/S, Yield
	Growth Rates — Periods	✖ (1-, 5-yr)	✖ (5-yr)
	Total/Annualized	✖ (annualized)	✖ (annualized)
	Price & Share Data — High/Low/Close/Volume	✖ (daily for up to 10 yrs)	✖ (5-yr chart)
	Relative Strength	✖ (1-wk, 1, 3, 6, 12-mo)	
	Market Cap/Float	✖ (market cap)	✖ (market cap)
	% Insider/Institutional Holdings	✖ (institutional only)	✖
Screening	Number of Data Fields for Screening	200	33
	Any Data Field		
	Against Constant Values	✖	✖
	Against Other Data Fields	✖	
	Against Industry	✖	
	Save Custom Screens/# of Predefined Screens	✖/12	/6
Viewing	Browse Table	✖	✖
	Financial Statement Presentation	total $, per share	total $
	Individual Company Summaries	✖	✖
Reporting	Charts/Graphs	✖	✖
	Export to a File	✖	
	Statistical Summaries (Statistical Data)		

205

Fundamental Stock Screening: Internet-Based		S&P Personal Wealth	StockScreener
Company		Standard & Poor's	Hoover's, Inc.
Telephone		(800) 823-3209	(800) 486-8666
Web Address		www.personalwealth.com	www.stockscreener.com
Delivery Medium (Software/On-line/Internet)		Internet	Internet
Update Schedule		daily	daily
Price (AAII Member Discount)		$9.95/month or $99/year	free with any Internet access
Demo (Cost)		✖ (1 month free)	
Platform		any PC with Internet	any PC with Internet
Data Source		S&P, BigCharts	Hoover's, Media General
Database Content	Number of Stocks	9,000	8,000
	Number of Data Fields	400+	22
	Create Custom Data Fields		
	Number of Data Fields for Sorting	28	22
	Company Information — Address/Phone	✖	✖
	ADR	✖	
	DRP Plan		
	Industry Grouping	✖	✖
	Description Length	500 words	100 words
	Earnings Estimates — Source	S&P	
	Quarterly	✖ (1 quarter)	
	Annual	✖ (2 years)	
	Growth—Long Term		
	Ratios — Leverage	debt/eq	debt/eq
	Liquidity	current	current
	Profitability	ROE, ROA, PM	ROE, PM
	Multiples	P/E, yield	P/E, P/B, yield
	Growth Rates — Periods	✖ (5-yr)	✖ (5-yr)
	Total/Annualized	✖ (annualized)	
	Price & Share Data — High/Low/Close/Volume	✖ (5-yrs)	
	Relative Strength		
	Market Cap/Float	✖ (market cap)	✖ (market cap)
	% Insider/Institutional Holdings	✖	
Screening	Number of Data Fields for Screening	28	22
	Any Data Field		✖
	Against Constant Values	✖	
	Against Other Data Fields		
	Against Industry		
	Save Custom Screens/# of Predefined Screens	/5	
Viewing	Browse Table	✖	
	Financial Statement Presentation	total $, per share	
	Individual Company Summaries	✖	
Reporting	Charts/Graphs	✖	
	Export to a File		
	Statistical Summaries (Statistical Data)		

Fundamental Stock Screening: Internet-Based		Thomson Investors Network	Wall Street City
Company		Thomson Financial Services, Inc.	Telescan, Inc.
Telephone		(301) 545-4999	(800) 324-8246
Web Address		www.thomsoninvest.net	www.wallstreetcity.com
Delivery Medium (Software/On-line/Internet)		Internet	Internet
Update Schedule		monthly	daily
Price (AAII Member Discount)		$34.95/year	free–$149.95
Demo (Cost)		✘ (1 month free)	✘ (first 30 days free)
Platform		any PC with Internet	any PC with Internet
Data Source		First Call, CDA, Spectrum, Media General	S&P Comstock, Zacks, Market Guide
Database Content	Number of Stocks	7,300	14,000
	Number of Data Fields	500+	1,000
	Create Custom Data Fields		
	Number of Data Fields for Sorting		1
	Company Information — Address/Phone	✘	✘
	ADR		
	DRP Plan		
	Industry Grouping	✘	✘
	Description Length	one line	25 words
	Earnings Estimates — Source	First Call	Zacks
	Quarterly	✘ (last and current)	✘
	Annual	✘ (2 years)	✘
	Growth—Long Term	✘ (1 yr)	✘
	Ratios — Leverage	debt/eq	lt debt/eq
	Liquidity	current, quick	current
	Profitability	ROE, PM, net PM, gross PM	ROE, ROA, gross PM
	Multiples	P/E, P/B, P/S, P/CF, yield	P/E, P/B, P/S, P/CF, yield
	Growth Rates — Periods	✘ (5-yr)	✘ (custom)
	Total/Annualized	✘ (annualized)	✘ (5-yr total, 1-, 3-, 5-yr annualized)
	Price & Share Data — High/Low/Close/Volume	✘ (52-wk high, low/daily close)	✘ (since 1973)
	Relative Strength	✘ (5-, 200-day, 10-week)	✘
	Market Cap/Float	✘ (market cap)	✘
	% Insider/Institutional Holdings	✘	✘
Screening	Number of Data Fields for Screening	18	300
	Any Data Field		✘
	Against Constant Values	✘	
	Against Other Data Fields		
	Against Industry		
	Save Custom Screens/# of Predefined Screens	/10	✘/50+
Viewing	Browse Table		✘
	Financial Statement Presentation	total $, per share, % chg	total $, per share, % change
	Individual Company Summaries	✘	✘
Reporting	Charts/Graphs	✘	✘
	Export to a File		✘
	Statistical Summaries (Statistical Data)		high, low

Fundamental Stock Screening: Internet-Based			Yahoo! Finance	Zacks Advisor
Company			Yahoo! Inc.	Zacks Investment Research
Telephone			(408) 731-3300	(800) 399-6659, (312)630-9880
Web Address			quote.yahoo.com	www.zacks.com
Delivery Medium (Software/On-line/Internet)			Internet	Internet
Update Schedule			daily	daily
Price (AAII Member Discount)			free with any Internet access	$150/year
Demo (Cost)				✗ (1 month free)
Platform			any PC with Internet	any PC with Internet
Data Source			Market Guide, Zacks	Zacks
Database Content	Number of Stocks		9,000	6,000
	Number of Data Fields		200	1,500
	Create Custom Data Fields			
	Number of Data Fields for Sorting		8	
	Company Information	Address/Phone	✗	
		ADR		✗
		DRP Plan		
		Industry Grouping	✗	✗
		Description Length	6 sentences	50 words
	Earnings Estimates	Source	Zacks	Zacks
		Quarterly	✗ (2 quarters)	✗ (2 quarters)
		Annual	✗ (2 years)	✗ (2 years)
		Growth—Long Term	✗ (1, 5 yr)	✗ (5 yrs)
	Ratios	Leverage	debt/eq	debt/eq, lt debt/eq
		Liquidity	current	current, quick
		Profitability	ROE, ROA, PM	ROE, ROA, PM
		Multiples	P/E, P/B, P/S, yield	P/E, P/B, yield
	Growth Rates	Periods	✗ (5-yr)	✗ (pre-calc)
		Total/Annualized	✗ (annualized)	✗
	Price & Share Data	High/Low/Close/Volume	✗ (chart 1960+)	✗ (high/low/close)
		Relative Strength		✗ (YTD)
		Market Cap/Float	✗	✗ (market cap)
		% Insider/Institutional Holdings		✗
Screening	Number of Data Fields for Screening		8	100
	Any Data Field			
	Against Constant Values		✗	✗
	Against Other Data Fields			
	Against Industry			
	Save Custom Screens/# of Predefined Screens			✗/13
Viewing	Browse Table		✗	✗
	Financial Statement Presentation		total $, per share	total $, per share, % chg
	Individual Company Summaries		✗	✗
Reporting	Charts/Graphs		✗	
	Export to a File			
	Statistical Summaries (Statistical Data)			

Fundamental Stock Screening Services: Financial Data
Number of Quarters (Q) and Number of Years (Y) of Data Provided

Disk-Based Services	Market Guide StockQuest*	Principia Pro for Stocks	Research Wizard
Income Statement			
Sales	16Qs, 4Ys	8Qs, 5Ys	9Qs, 3Ys
Cost of Sales	2Qs, 3Ys		9Qs, 3Ys
Selling & Administrative Expenses			
Research & Development Expenses			
Depreciation, Amortization		3Ys	
Interest			
Non-Operating Income/Expenses	2Qs, 3Ys		
Taxes	2Qs, 3Ys		
Extraordinary Items	2Qs, 3Ys		
Net Income	2Qs, 3Ys	8Qs, 5Ys	9Qs, 3Ys
EPS	16Qs, 4Ys	8Qs, 5Ys	9Qs, 3Ys
Dividends	2Qs, 3Ys	5Ys	9Qs, 3Ys
Balance Sheet			
Cash	2Qs, 3Ys	1Q, 2Ys	3Qs, 3Ys
Accounts Receivable	2Qs, 3Ys		3Qs, 3Ys
Inventory		1Q, 2Ys	3Qs, 3Ys
Total Current Assets	2Qs, 3Ys	1Q, 2Ys	3Qs, 3Ys
Equipment			
Accumulated Depreciation			
Net Plant & Equipment	2Qs, 3Ys		
Investments	2Qs, 3Ys		
Deferred Charges			
Intangible Assets			
Total Long-Term Assets		1Q, 2Ys	
Total Assets	2Qs, 3Ys	1Q, 2Ys	3Qs, 3Ys
Accounts Payable	2Qs, 3Ys		
Accrued Expenses			
Notes Payable			
Current Portion of Long-Term Debt			
Total Current Liabilities	2Qs, 3Ys	1Q, 2Ys	3Qs, 3Ys
Long-Term Debt	2Qs, 3Ys	1Q, 2Ys	3Qs, 3Ys
Total Liabilities	2Qs, 3Ys	1Q, 2Ys	
Preferred Stock	2Qs, 3Ys		3Qs, 3Ys
Total Common Equity	2Qs, 3Ys	1Q, 2Ys	
Total Liabilities & Owner's Equity	2Qs, 3Ys	1Q, 2Ys	
Statement of Cash Flows			
Net Cash from Operations	2Qs, 3Ys	3Ys	
Net Cash from Investing Activities	2Qs, 3Ys		
Capital Expenditures	2Qs, 3Ys	3Ys	
Net Cash From Financial Activities	2Qs, 3Ys		
Free Cash Flow		3Ys	3Ys

Includes company reports from Market Guide Web site.

Fundamental Stock Screening Services: Financial Data
Number of Quarters (Q) and Number of Years (Y) of Data Provided

Disk-Based Services	Stock Investor Standard	Stock Investor Professional	Value Line Investment Survey
Income Statement			
Sales	8Qs, 5Ys	8Qs, 7Ys	10Qs, 11Ys
Cost of Sales	8Qs, 5Ys	8Qs, 7Ys	
Selling & Administrative Expenses			
Research & Development Expenses	8Qs, 5Ys	8Qs, 7Ys	
Depreciation, Amortization			10Qs, 11Ys
Interest		8Qs, 7Ys	
Non-Operating Income/Expenses		8Qs, 7Ys	
Taxes		8Qs, 7Ys	1Y
Extraordinary Items		8Qs, 7Ys	
Net Income	8Qs, 5Ys	8Qs, 7Ys	10Qs, 11Ys
EPS	8Qs, 5Ys	8Qs, 7Ys	11Ys
Dividends	8Qs, 5Ys	8Qs, 7Ys	11Ys
Balance Sheet			
Cash	8Q, 3Ys	8Qs, 7Ys	1Y
Accounts Receivable		8Qs, 7Ys	1Y
Inventory		8Qs, 7Ys	1Y
Total Current Assets	8Q, 3Ys	8Qs, 7Ys	1Y
Equipment			1Y
Accumulated Depreciation			1Y
Net Plant & Equipment	8Q, 3Ys	8Qs, 7Ys	1Y
Investments	8Q, 3Ys	8Qs, 7Ys	
Deferred Charges			
Intangible Assets	8Q, 3Ys	8Qs, 7Ys	
Total Long-Term Assets	8Q, 3Ys	8Qs, 7Ys	
Total Assets	8Q, 3Ys	8Qs, 7Ys	11Ys
Accounts Payable		8Qs, 7Ys	1Y
Accrued Expenses			
Notes Payable			
Current Portion of Long-Term Debt			
Total Current Liabilities	8Q, 3Ys	8Qs, 7Ys	1Y
Long-Term Debt	8Q, 3Ys	8Qs, 7Ys	11Ys
Total Liabilities	8Q, 3Ys	8Qs, 7Ys	
Preferred Stock	8Q, 3Ys	8Qs, 7Ys	11Ys
Total Common Equity	8Q, 3Ys	8Qs, 7Ys	11Ys
Total Liabilities & Owner's Equity	8Q, 3Ys	8Qs, 7Ys	1Y
Statement of Cash Flows			
Net Cash from Operations	8Qs, 5Ys	8Qs, 7Ys	
Net Cash from Investing Activities	8Qs, 5Ys	8Qs, 7Ys	
Capital Expenditures		8Qs, 7Ys	1Y
Net Cash From Financial Activities	8Qs, 5Ys	8Qs, 7Ys	
Free Cash Flow	8Qs, 5Ys	8Qs, 7Ys	1Y

Fundamental Stock Screening Services: Financial Data
Number of Quarters (Q) and Number of Years (Y) of Data Provided

On-Line Services	America Online Stock Screening	TIP@Wallstreet with ProSearch**
Income Statement		
Sales	16Qs, 3Ys	20Qs, 5Ys
Cost of Sales		20Qs, 5Ys
Selling & Administrative Expenses		20Qs, 5Ys
Research & Development Expenses		20Qs, 5Ys
Depreciation, Amortization	2Qs, 3Ys	20Qs, 5Ys
Interest		20Qs, 5Ys
Non-Operating Income/Expenses	2Qs, 3Ys	20Qs, 5Ys
Taxes	2Qs, 3Ys	20Qs, 5Ys
Extraordinary Items	2Qs, 3Ys	20Qs, 5Ys
Net Income	2Qs, 3Ys	20Qs, 5Ys
EPS	16Qs, 3Ys	20Qs, 5Ys
Dividends	2Qs, 3Ys	20Qs, 5Ys
Balance Sheet		
Cash	2Qs, 3Ys	20Qs, 5Ys
Accounts Receivable	2Qs, 3Ys	20Qs, 5Ys
Inventory		20Qs, 5Ys
Total Current Assets	2Qs, 3Ys	20Qs, 5Ys
Equipment		20Qs, 5Ys
Accumulated Depreciation		20Qs, 5Ys
Net Plant & Equipment	2Qs, 3Ys	20Qs, 5Ys
Investments		20Qs, 5Ys
Deferred Charges		20Qs, 5Ys
Intangible Assets		20Qs, 5Ys
Total Long-Term Assets		20Qs, 5Ys
Total Assets	2Qs, 3Ys	20Qs, 5Ys
Accounts Payable	2Qs, 3Ys	20Qs, 5Ys
Accrued Expenses		20Qs, 5Ys
Notes Payable	2Qs, 3Ys	20Qs, 5Ys
Current Portion of Long-Term Debt	2Qs, 3Ys	20Qs, 5Ys
Total Current Liabilities	2Qs, 3Ys	20Qs, 5Ys
Long-Term Debt		20Qs, 5Ys
Total Liabilities	2Qs, 3Ys	20Qs, 5Ys
Preferred Stock	2Qs, 3Ys	20Qs, 5Ys
Total Common Equity	2Qs, 3Ys	20Qs, 5Ys
Total Liabilities & Owner's Equity		20Qs, 5Ys
Statement of Cash Flows		
Net Cash from Operations	2Qs, 3Ys	20Qs, 5Ys
Net Cash from Investing Activities	2Qs, 3Ys	20Qs, 5Ys
Capital Expenditures	2Qs, 3Ys	20Qs, 5Ys
Net Cash From Financial Activities	2Qs, 3Ys	20Qs, 5Ys
Free Cash Flow		20Qs, 5Ys

*Surcharge for company financial reports.

Fundamental Stock Screening Services: Financial Data
Number of Quarters (Q) and Number of Years (Y) of Data Provided

Internet Services	INVESTools**	Marketguide.com—NetScreen*	Morningstar.com
Income Statement			
Sales	16Qs, 4Ys	16Qs, 3Ys	4Qs, 5Ys
Cost of Sales	2Qs, 4Ys	2Qs, 3Ys	
Selling & Administrative Expenses	2Qs, 4Ys		
Research & Development Expenses	2Qs, 4Ys		
Depreciation, Amortization	2Qs, 4Ys		3Ys
Interest	2Qs, 4Ys		
Non-Operating Income/Expenses	2Qs, 4Ys	2Qs, 3Ys	
Taxes	2Qs, 4Ys	2Qs, 3Ys	
Extraordinary Items		2Qs, 3Ys	
Net Income	2Qs, 4Ys	2Qs, 3Ys	4Qs, 5Ys
EPS	16Qs, 4Ys	16Qs, 3Ys	4Qs, 5Ys
Dividends	2Qs, 4Ys	2Qs, 3Ys	5Ys (24Qs Prem.)
Balance Sheet			
Cash	4Qs, 4Ys	2Qs, 3Ys	1Q
Accounts Receivable	4Qs, 4Ys	2Qs, 3Ys	
Inventory	4Qs, 4Ys		
Total Current Assets	4Qs, 4Ys	2Qs, 3Ys	1Q
Equipment	4Qs, 4Ys		
Accumulated Depreciation	4Qs, 4Ys		
Net Plant & Equipment		2Qs, 3Ys	
Investments	4Qs, 4Ys	2Qs, 3Ys	
Deferred Charges			
Intangible Assets			
Total Long-Term Assets			1Q
Total Assets	4Qs, 4Ys	2Qs, 3Ys	1Q
Accounts Payable	4Qs, 4Ys	2Qs, 3Ys	
Accrued Expenses	4Qs, 4Ys		
Notes Payable	4Qs, 4Ys		
Current Portion of Long-Term Debt	4Qs, 4Ys		
Total Current Liabilities	4Qs, 4Ys	2Qs, 3Ys	1Q
Long-Term Debt	4Qs, 4Ys	2Qs, 3Ys	1Q
Total Liabilities	4Qs, 4Ys	2Qs, 3Ys	
Preferred Stock		2Qs, 3Ys	
Total Common Equity	4Qs, 4Ys	2Qs, 3Ys	1Q
Total Liabilities & Owner's Equity	4Qs, 4Ys	2Qs, 3Ys	1Q
Statement of Cash Flows			
Net Cash from Operations	2Qs, 4Ys	2Qs, 3Ys	3Ys
Net Cash from Investing Activities	2Qs, 4Ys	2Qs, 3Ys	
Capital Expenditures	2Qs, 4Ys	2Qs, 3Ys	3Ys
Net Cash From Financial Activities	2Qs, 4Ys	2Qs, 3Ys	
Free Cash Flow			3Ys

*Includes company reports from Market Guide Web site.
**Surcharge for company financial reports.

Fundamental Stock Screening Services: Financial Data
Number of Quarters (Q) and Number of Years (Y) of Data Provided

Internet Services	MSN MoneyCentral Investor	Quicken.com	S&P Personal Wealth
Income Statement			
Sales	12Qs, 10Ys	4Qs, 4Ys	24Qs, 6Ys
Cost of Sales	5Qs, 5Ys	4Qs, 4Ys	
Selling & Administrative Expenses	5Qs, 5Ys		
Research & Development Expenses			
Depreciation, Amortization	5Qs, 10Ys		6Ys
Interest	5Qs, 5Ys	4Qs, 4Ys	6Ys
Non-Operating Income/Expenses	5Qs, 5Ys		
Taxes	5Qs, 5Ys	4Qs, 4Ys	6Ys
Extraordinary Items	5Qs, 5Ys	4Qs, 4Ys	
Net Income	5Qs, 10Ys	4Qs, 4Ys	6Ys
EPS	12Qs, 10Ys	4Qs, 4Ys	24Qs, 6Ys
Dividends	5Qs, 5Ys	1Y	6Ys
Balance Sheet			
Cash	5Qs, 5Ys	4Qs, 4Ys	6Ys
Accounts Receivable	5Qs, 5Ys	4Qs, 4Ys	
Inventory	5Qs, 5Ys	4Qs, 4Ys	
Total Current Assets	5Qs, 10Ys	4Qs, 4Ys	6Ys
Equipment	5Qs, 5Ys		
Accumulated Depreciation	5Qs, 5Ys	4Qs, 4Ys	
Net Plant & Equipment	5Qs, 5Ys	4Qs, 4Ys	
Investments			
Deferred Charges			
Intangible Assets	5Qs, 5Ys		
Total Long-Term Assets	5Qs, 5Ys		
Total Assets	5Qs, 5Ys	4Qs, 4Ys	6Ys
Accounts Payable	5Qs, 5Ys		
Accrued Expenses			
Notes Payable			
Current Portion of Long-Term Debt	5Qs, 5Ys		
Total Current Liabilities	5Qs, 10Ys	4Qs, 4Ys	6Ys
Long-Term Debt	5Qs, 10Ys	4Qs, 4Ys	6Ys
Total Liabilities	5Qs, 5Ys		
Preferred Stock	5Qs, 5Ys	4Qs, 4Ys	
Total Common Equity	5Qs, 5Ys	4Qs, 4Ys	6Ys
Total Liabilities & Owner's Equity	5Qs, 5Ys	4Qs, 4Ys	6Ys
Statement of Cash Flows			
Net Cash from Operations	5Qs, 5Ys		
Net Cash from Investing Activities	5Qs, 5Ys		
Capital Expenditures	5Qs, 5Ys		6Ys
Net Cash From Financial Activities	5Qs, 5Ys		
Free Cash Flow	5Qs, 5Ys		6Ys

Fundamental Stock Screening Services: Financial Data
Number of Quarters (Q) and Number of Years (Y) of Data Provided

Internet Services	StockScreener**	Thomson Investors Network	Wall Street City
Income Statement			
Sales	4Qs, 10Ys	2Qs, 4Ys	4Qs, 2Ys
Cost of Sales	4Qs, 3Ys	2Qs, 4Ys	4Qs, 2Ys
Selling & Administrative Expenses	4Qs, 3Ys	2Qs, 4Ys	4Qs, 2Ys
Research & Development Expenses			4Qs, 2Ys
Depreciation, Amortization	4Qs, 3Ys	2Qs, 4Ys	2Qs, 2Ys
Interest		2Qs, 4Ys	2Ys
Non-Operating Income/Expenses	4Qs, 3Ys	2Qs, 4Ys	2Ys
Taxes	4Qs, 3Ys	2Qs, 4Ys	4Qs, 2Ys
Extraordinary Items		2Qs, 4Ys	2Ys
Net Income	4Qs, 10Ys	2Qs, 4Ys	4Qs, 2Ys
EPS	4Qs, 10Ys	2Qs, 4Ys	4Qs, 2Ys
Dividends	4Qs, 10Ys	2Qs, 4Ys	2Ys
Balance Sheet			
Cash	4Qs, 3Ys	2Qs, 4Ys	4Qs, 4Ys
Accounts Receivable	4Qs, 3Ys	2Qs, 4Ys	4Qs, 4Ys
Inventory	4Qs, 3Ys	2Qs, 4Ys	4Qs, 4Ys
Total Current Assets	4Qs, 3Ys	2Qs, 4Ys	4Qs, 4Ys
Equipment		2Qs, 4Ys	2Ys
Accumulated Depreciation		2Qs, 4Ys	2Ys
Net Plant & Equipment	4Qs, 3Ys	2Qs, 4Ys	
Investments			4Qs, 2Ys
Deferred Charges			2Ys
Intangible Assets		2Qs, 4Ys	2Ys
Total Long-Term Assets		2Qs, 4Ys	4Qs, 2Ys
Total Assets	4Qs, 3Ys	2Qs, 4Ys	4Qs, 4Ys
Accounts Payable	4Qs, 3Ys	2Qs, 4Ys	4Qs, 4Ys
Accrued Expenses			
Notes Payable	4Qs, 3Ys	2Qs, 4Ys	4Qs, 4Ys
Current Portion of Long-Term Debt			
Total Current Liabilities	4Qs, 3Ys	2Qs, 4Ys	4Qs, 4Ys
Long-Term Debt	4Qs, 3Ys	2Qs, 4Ys	4Qs, 4Ys
Total Liabilities	4Qs, 3Ys	2Qs, 4Ys	4Qs, 4Ys
Preferred Stock	4Qs, 3Ys	2Qs, 4Ys	4Qs, 4Ys
Total Common Equity	4Qs, 3Ys	2Qs, 4Ys	4Qs, 4Ys
Total Liabilities & Owner's Equity		2Qs, 4Ys	4Qs, 4Ys
Statement of Cash Flows			
Net Cash from Operations	4Qs, 3Ys	4Ys	2Qs, 4Ys
Net Cash from Investing Activities	4Qs, 3Ys	4Ys	2Qs, 4Ys
Capital Expenditures	4Qs, 3Ys	4Ys	2Qs, 4Ys
Net Cash From Financial Activities	4Qs, 3Ys	4Ys	2Qs, 4Ys
Free Cash Flow			

**Surcharge for company financial reports.

Fundamental Stock Screening Services: Financial Data
Number of Quarters (Q) and Number of Years (Y) of Data Provided

Internet Services	Yahoo! Finance	Zacks Advisor
Income Statement		
Sales	16Qs, 4Ys	8Qs, 5Ys
Cost of Sales	2Qs, 3Ys	8Qs, 5Ys
Selling & Administrative Expenses		8Qs, 5Ys
Research & Development Expenses		8Qs, 5Ys
Depreciation, Amortization		8Qs, 5Ys
Interest		8Qs, 5Ys
Non-Operating Income/Expenses	2Qs, 3Ys	8Qs, 5Ys
Taxes	2Qs, 3Ys	8Qs, 5Ys
Extraordinary Items	2Qs, 3Ys	8Qs, 5Ys
Net Income	2Qs, 3Ys	8Qs, 5Ys
EPS	16Qs, 4Ys	8Qs, 5Ys
Dividends	2Qs, 3Ys	
Balance Sheet		
Cash	2Qs, 3Ys	8Qs, 5Ys
Accounts Receivable	2Qs, 3Ys	8Qs, 5Ys
Inventory		8Qs, 5Ys
Total Current Assets	2Qs, 3Ys	8Qs, 5Ys
Equipment		
Accumulated Depreciation		
Net Plant & Equipment	2Qs, 3Ys	8Qs, 5Ys
Investments	2Qs, 3Ys	8Qs, 5Ys
Deferred Charges		8Qs, 5Ys
Intangible Assets		8Qs, 5Ys
Total Long-Term Assets		
Total Assets	2Qs, 3Ys	8Qs, 5Ys
Accounts Payable	2Qs, 3Ys	8Qs, 5Ys
Accrued Expenses		8Qs, 5Ys
Notes Payable		8Qs, 5Ys
Current Portion of Long-Term Debt		8Qs, 5Ys
Total Current Liabilities	2Qs, 3Ys	8Qs, 5Ys
Long-Term Debt	2Qs, 3Ys	8Qs, 5Ys
Total Liabilities	2Qs, 3Ys	8Qs, 5Ys
Preferred Stock	2Qs, 3Ys	8Qs, 5Ys
Total Common Equity	2Qs, 3Ys	8Qs, 5Ys
Total Liabilities & Owner's Equity	2Qs, 3Ys	8Qs, 5Ys
Statement of Cash Flows		
Net Cash from Operations	2Qs, 3Ys	5Ys
Net Cash from Investing Activities	2Qs, 3Ys	5Ys
Capital Expenditures	2Qs, 3Ys	5Ys
Net Cash From Financial Activities	2Qs, 3Ys	5Ys
Free Cash Flow		5Ys

Chapter 6

TECHNICAL ANALYSIS

In Chapter 5, you were introduced to fundamental analysis—the study of a company's products or services, industry position, management strength, and sales and earnings performance to determine the future price performance. In contrast, technical analysis attempts to forecast price movement in a security—stock, bond, mutual fund, or option—by examining how the market price and volume of market activity behave over time.

Technicians—those who use technical analysis—believe that all fundamental variables are captured in the price of a security. They point to the fact that a company may have strong fundamentals, yet still have a falling stock price as demand for the stock increases. Technical analysis does not concern itself with the *how* or the *why*!

Some investors use technical analysis exclusively, while others combine fundamental and technical analyses. The technician assumes that all market information, including fundamental assessments, are reflected in the security's price; thereby making a separate fundamental assessment redundant. Others use fundamental analysis to identify attractive companies and then use technical tools to determine when to exactly buy and sell the securities. They are hoping that a study of a security's chart will help reveal supply and demand trends for the security itself that are not yet evident through a study of the security's fundamentals.

The most popular tool used in technical analysis is the chart. The roots of price charting can be traced back several centuries. Over time as investment instruments have evolved, so have the charting techniques used. In today's technology-laden society, the computer has become a logical partner in this endeavor. Computers allow you to quickly analyze a wide range of securities using a multitude of time periods. The increasing ease-of-use of technical analysis software packages means that even the computing novice has a tremendous amount of charting capabilities at his disposal. Technical analysis software is an invaluable tool when performing technical analysis, whether it is the relatively basic task of charting or the more complex task of system backtesting.

Just as is the case when performing any task, you need the proper tool for the job. In order to perform the level of analysis you require, and to create those charts that meet your needs, you need to find the proper program to perform these functions. In addition, you need to be able to use the program or have the capacity to learn how to use the tool. It serves no purpose to have a program with multiple functions if you have no use for them. In other words, you need to choose a program that meets your analysis needs as well as one you are comfortable using to make investment decisions. Otherwise, it is money wasted (in terms of both a useless program and perhaps money lost on poor investment decisions), and you

Tip→	Know what type(s) of analysis you will be performing and purchase the program that best meets your needs. Don't be swayed by the bells and whistles of an advanced technical analysis package if you will never use them.

are back at square one. Lastly, it is imperative that you understand the concepts behind stock charts and know what the program is showing you before you invest your money.

Over the past several years, the technical analysis software market has remained relatively static as far as the players in it—a few companies dominate the market while several others exist by differentiating themselves either on price or on unique functionality. The market leaders are constantly updating their software and creating splinter products so as to blanket every niche of the market. This has led to a wide variety of programs from which to choose. Functions offered range from simple price and volume plotting to sophisticated real-time analysis as well as trading system development and testing.

Faced with all these choices, you may find it difficult to decide which technical analysis package is right for you. The aim of this chapter is to familiarize you with the options and functions typically found in technical analysis software and explain the key elements to look for when selecting a program. You will also find personal commentary on the purpose, strengths, and weaknesses of the technical analysis packages compared in this chapter. However, in the end it is up to you to decide on a program that best suits your investment style and needs. The key to making a successful purchase is to be an informed shopper and know what you want from the software package before you buy it.

Data Collection and Management

Technical analysis deals with the analysis of open, high, low, and close prices as well as volume data. With price data as the cornerstone of technical analysis, the quality of the data used dictates how good (or bad) analysis made through the help of a program will be. It is possible to spend several hundred dollars on a technical analysis application and have it rendered all but useless by insufficient, incomplete, or worst of all, incorrect data.

One of the first questions that arises when discussing data is how often you will need updates. The typical options are intraday tick-by-tick (real-time or delayed) or end-of-day. Your investment style or strategy will primarily determine the method that is right for you. If you regularly take a position in a security for only

Warning→	Technical analysis programs are all but useless without accurate and timely data. Be sure you select a data vendor in which you have confidence.

a few days, you will want to watch the intraday tick-by-tick movement of the security. This will require a real-time or delayed data feed and program designed to process intraday data. Be aware that with intraday feeds, you will be receiving more data; tick-by-tick instead of day-by-day with an end-of-day feed. Therefore, you will need more free hard disk space to accommodate this data, with some software makers recommending at least 200M. A tick is a reference to every trade of a security. An intraday feed attempts to post every trading price and volume of a security. The information can be transmitted as soon as the trade occurs (real-time) or with a minimum 15-minute delay (delayed). Exchanges sell price information to data vendors and charge significantly higher rates for immediate, real-time price information. The exchange fee, coupled with the normal premium investors are willing to pay for "fresher" data, makes real-time feeds more expensive than delayed feeds.

Tip→	With real-time feeds, you will be receiving more data; tick-by-tick instead of day-by-day with an end-of-day feed. Therefore, you will need more free hard disk space to accommodate this data.

For those who trade on a less frequent basis, trying instead to capture long-term security and market trends, all you may need is end-of-day or weekly, monthly, or even quarterly data updates. A majority of individual investors cannot effectively compete at the day-trading level because of the time and monetary commitment required. For this reason, many of the programs discussed in this chapter specialize in end-of-day analysis.

After deciding upon the frequency of your data updates, the second consideration you are faced with is the choice of data source. The main avenues of data gathering are manual entry, CD-ROM, downloading, and importing.

Warning→	During periods of extremely heavy market trading, even a real-time data feed ("the tape") can run late if the data vendor does not have the capacity (bandwidth) to transmit every trading price to your system quickly enough.

Manual Entry: Wasted Opportunities?

Manual entry of historical price and volume data, while an option, can be a tedious and time-consuming endeavor. Consider, for example, tracking the 30 stocks of the Dow Jones industrials over five years—a relatively conservative number of securities over a relatively short time frame. Even if you are only interested in the open, high, low, close and volume for each of these 30 stocks over five years, the number of entries is mind-boggling: 30 stocks with five pieces of data per day, 250 trading days per year for five years, leads to over 187,000 entries. Even for the fastest typists, that would take weeks of data entry—time better spent performing actual analysis and finding potential investment opportunities.

Downloading

Downloading is the process of connecting to an outside data provider via modem or the Internet and collecting specific information on an individual security into a file that can be saved on your hard drive or other storage medium. There are dozens of companies that offer downloadable data, each with its own cost structure and data variety. Downloading is the preferred method of data retrieval, although other sources of timely data transfer do exist: cable, satellite, and radio/video. Historically these media were used to retrieve real-time data and required special equipment. Today, real-time Internet feeds are becoming more popular with data vendors. In fact, many data vendors, such as Dial/Data, and Data Broadcasting Corp. are offering Internet-based data retrieval on a real-time, delayed or end-of-day basis. They only require that you have access to the Internet. With most technical analysis programs, data is updated with every download, and price, volume, split, and dividend data are updated daily. The advantages of data downloading are convenience, timeliness, and cost. However, some purchasers of technical analysis software are not aware of the costs associated with data downloading. Since the effectiveness of these programs depends on continual data updating, keep in mind that the data will most likely cost more, over time, than the program itself.

Warning→	Keep in mind that over the life of the technical analysis program, the cost of the data downloading may well surpass that of the program itself.

Data Vendors

The vast majority of technical analysis software is compatible with third-party data providers. The more advanced programs, such as MetaStock from Equis International or SuperCharts from Omega Research, for example, offer data compatibility with several major data vendors. Programs such as these provide you with the flexibility of testing several vendors to find one that best suits your needs and budget. Other programs, such as Worden Brother's TC2000, only support their own internal data sources. While this does not mean that these sources lack content, you are, however, tied to the data they provide and the rates they charge for access. Compare the data vendors supported by each program in the comparison grid starting on page 297 in the section titled data maintenance.

FIGURE 6.0
*Data vendor
compatibility
window from
SuperCharts.*

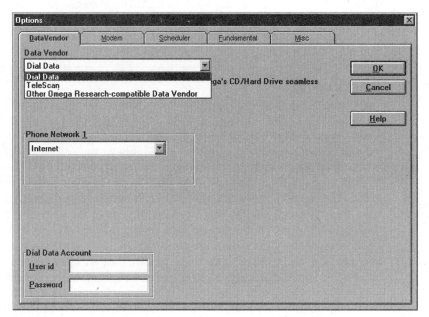

CD-ROM

CD-ROM disks offer a less expensive means of receiving historical data and some companies, such as Momentum (www.momentumcd.com), offer bulk data on CD-ROM with several years of data for several thousand securities (stocks, mutual funds, options, etc.). The data is transferred and saved to your hard drive for use with your technical analysis software. The drawback with this method is that you may be saving vast amounts of data that you never use, sacrificing hard disk space. You can avoid this problem by finding a program that allows you to select and import individual securities. Software manufacturers such as Window on WallStreet and Equis International now offer historical data on CD-ROM that spans three to 25 years of daily historical data for thousands of individual securities (stocks, mutual funds, options, etc.). These applications tend to make more efficient use of hard disk space by letting you save only the data that you are interested in on your hard drive, while the remainder of the data remains on the CD-ROM disk. The resulting advantage is an inexpensive database of historical data, in addition to less hard disk space used.

There are some notable drawbacks to using CD-ROM as your sole source of data. First and foremost, you receive your data on either a monthly or quarterly basis. If you wish to receive more frequent updates, you will have to seek out an additional data source, most likely at added cost. Furthermore, the data you receive may be anywhere from a couple of weeks to perhaps a month or more old. This is due to the time it takes to amass the data and then create the disks themselves. Lastly, since the data on CD-ROM disks is read-only, you cannot alter the data on the disk. With downloading, if data is incorrect, chances are the company will correct the error within a day or two and you can obtain the correction when you perform your next data download. If the data on the CD is incorrect and if you are fortunate enough to discover the error, you will have to manually adjust the data on your hard drive. Furthermore, you are left to adjust for stock splits and dividend payments yourself—two functions typically performed by the on-line data provider. Most programs do allow you to access the raw data in order to make changes, if necessary.

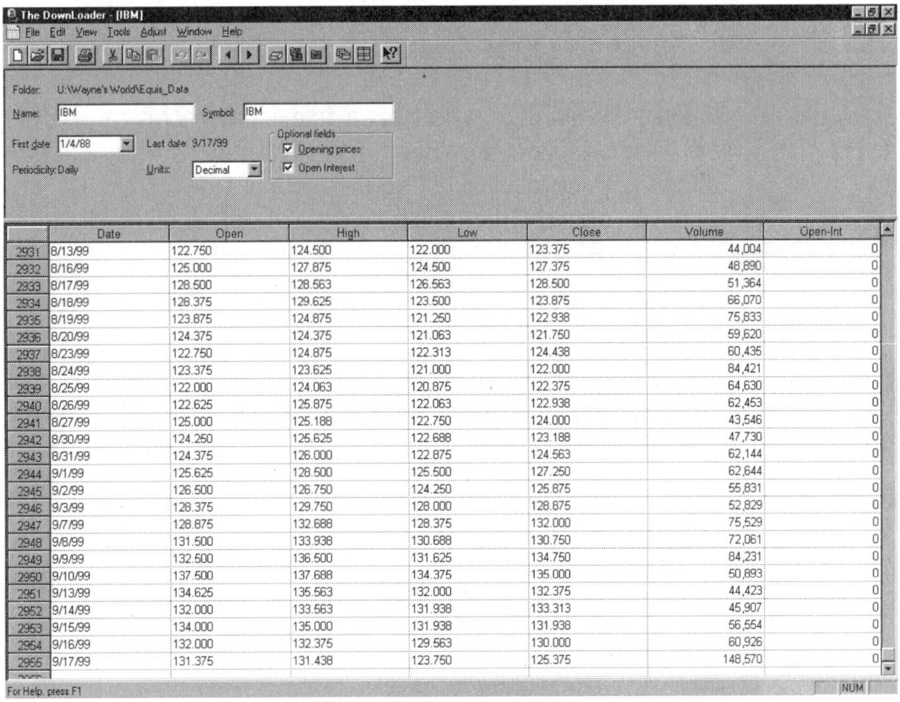

FIGURE 6.1
Data sheet for IBM in Equis' Downloader.

	Date	Open	High	Low	Close	Volume	Open-Int
2931	8/13/99	122.750	124.500	122.000	123.375	44,004	0
2932	8/16/99	125.000	127.875	124.500	127.375	48,890	0
2933	8/17/99	128.500	128.563	126.563	128.500	51,364	0
2934	8/18/99	128.375	129.625	123.500	123.875	66,070	0
2935	8/19/99	123.875	124.875	121.250	122.938	75,833	0
2936	8/20/99	124.375	124.375	121.063	121.750	59,620	0
2937	8/23/99	122.750	124.875	122.313	124.438	60,435	0
2938	8/24/99	123.375	123.625	121.000	122.000	84,421	0
2939	8/25/99	122.000	124.063	120.875	122.375	64,630	0
2940	8/26/99	122.625	125.875	122.063	122.938	62,453	0
2941	8/27/99	125.000	125.188	122.750	124.000	43,546	0
2942	8/30/99	124.250	125.625	122.688	123.188	47,730	0
2943	8/31/99	124.375	126.000	122.875	124.563	62,144	0
2944	9/1/99	125.625	128.500	125.500	127.250	62,644	0
2945	9/2/99	126.500	126.750	124.250	125.875	55,831	0
2946	9/3/99	128.375	129.750	128.000	128.875	52,829	0
2947	9/7/99	128.875	132.688	128.375	132.000	75,529	0
2948	9/8/99	131.500	133.938	130.688	130.750	72,061	0
2949	9/9/99	132.500	136.500	131.625	134.750	84,231	0
2950	9/10/99	137.500	137.688	134.375	135.000	50,893	0
2951	9/13/99	134.625	135.563	132.000	132.375	44,423	0
2952	9/14/99	132.000	133.563	131.938	133.313	45,907	0
2953	9/15/99	134.000	135.000	131.938	131.938	56,554	0
2954	9/16/99	132.000	132.375	129.563	130.000	60,926	0
2955	9/17/99	131.375	131.438	123.750	125.375	148,570	0

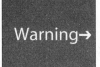

Warning→ Be aware that if you choose to receive your historical data via CD-ROM, you will only be receiving it on a monthly or quarterly basis. In addition, it takes longer to correct data errors and you must make adjustments such as stock splits and dividend payments manually.

Importing and Exporting

For those who already own some type of analysis package, you may already have a database of historical data. In this case, you may not want to spend money to recollect data you already have. Check to see if your existing program allows you to export data and then look for a technical analysis program that offers some type of importing function. This form of gathering data involves the conversion of data already collected but stored in another format. Most programs, such as MetaStock, will allow importing and exporting in the major platform formats in addition to various other forms of ASCII. Importing and exporting also potentially allow you to use your data with other applications, such as financial planners or portfolio management tools. The comparison grid at the end of this chapter notes the importing and exporting formats for each product. A good program will support multiple sources for both downloading and importing. Other programs can read multiple formats directly, which requires no conversion at all.

Tip→ If you are looking to switch from an existing technical analysis program to a new one, you can save time and money by finding a program that allows conversion of existing data to a usable format. Otherwise, the data you already have will be worthless when using the new program.

If you already own a technical analysis program but wish to switch to another, some companies offer competitive upgrades and discounted prices as incentive for users to switch. Remember to ask vendors if they offer a discount to switch to their program.

Program Features

Although technical analysis programs vary greatly in terms of the analysis they perform and their level of complexity, most of the programs perform a base set of functions. Before shopping for a technical analysis application, it is a good idea to familiarize yourself with the common terms associated with technical analysis

FIGURE 6.2
Data conversion screen in Equis' Downloader.

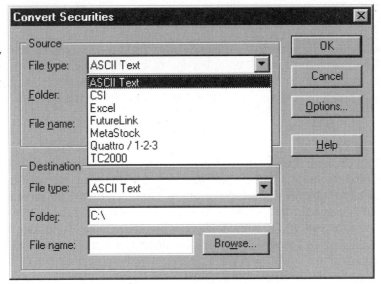

Tip→ If you currently own a technical analysis program, inform other vendors of this fact. Many companies offer competitive upgrades and discounted prices if you switch from a different program.

and the standard options and functions technical analysis programs offer. Doing so will make you a more informed shopper and reduce the risk of purchasing a program you do not need or cannot use.

Tip→ Before shopping for a technical analysis application, it is a good idea to familiarize yourself with the common terms associated with technical analysis and the standard options and functions technical analysis programs offer.

Charting

Charting lies at the very heart of technical analysis: presenting a visual presentation of the price fluctuations of an underlying security. Therefore, it is important that you select a program that offers the chart-types you use.

Virtually every technical analysis program can generate a bar chart that displays the price and volume history for a given security or market for a given period of time. The computer's ability to process large amounts of data required to generate detailed charts makes it well suited for displaying charts.

Charting can be performed using many formats, from the more common bar and line charts, to the more complex charts with multiple indicators and trading systems with buy and sell signals. This array of choices, while increasing your analysis possibilities, requires you to have some idea of the type and complexity of charting you may desire.

Line Chart

The line chart is the simplest type of chart you will use. Also called closing-price charts, the only data input needed to create this type of chart is the closing price of a given security. Each point on the chart represents the closing price of the security for that time period. Dates are displayed along the bottom axis and prices are displayed on the side(s). Using a line chart, you can quickly discern whether the market is positive on a stock (its price is rising) or negative (the price is falling). Mutual funds normally only report daily or closing NAVs, so line charts are the only option for plotting mutual funds.

FIGURE 6.3
An example of a line chart for Black Hills Corp. from SuperCharts.

Bar Chart

Bar charts, a.k.a. open-high-low-close charts, are the most widely used price charts. They provide more in-depth information than line charts, showing the open, high, and low prices in addition to the closing price. Each time period—whether it is a day, week, month, etc.—is represented by a vertical bar. The top of each vertical bar represents the highest price the security traded at during the period while the bottom of the bar represents the lowest price at which it traded. On the right side of each bar is a closing "tick" to signify the last price at which the security traded. If opening prices are available, they are signified by a tick on the left side of the bar. The vertical length of the bar shows the price range for that period.

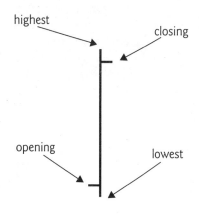

FIGURE 6.4
An example of a bar chart for US West from ProTA Gold.

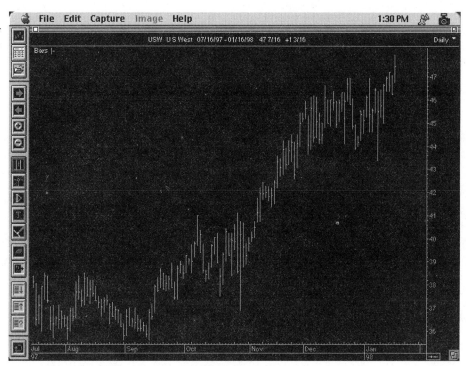

Candlestick Chart

Candlestick charts, developed in Japan during the 1600s to forecast rice prices, display the relationship between the open, high, low and closing prices of a security—similar in format to a bar chart. If you wish to plot candlesticks, be sure your data provider offers open, high, low and close data. Tracking of a security's open has become common only in the last 10 years.

FIGURE 6.5
*A general
description of
a candlestick
chart.*

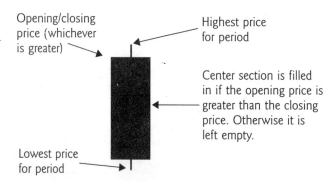

Opening/closing
price (whichever
is greater)

Highest price
for period

Center section is filled
in if the opening price is
greater than the closing
price. Otherwise it is
left empty.

Lowest price
for period

FIGURE 6.6
*Candlestick
chart of
CenturyTel
using
Investor/RT.*

The interpretation of candlesticks primarily deals with patterns and, perhaps more than any other chart, candlesticks exhibit patterns that historically are termed as either bullish or bearish. A full discussion of candlestick patterns would warrant its own book. However, here is a brief discussion of some bullish and bearish candlestick patterns:

Bullish Patterns

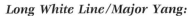

Long White Line/Major Yang:
This is a bullish line. It occurs when the price opens near the low and closes significantly higher and near the period's high.

Hammer/Umbrella Line:
This is a bullish indicator if it occurs after a significant downtrend. If it occurs after a significant uptrend, it is called a hanging man. It signifies a small range between the open and closing prices and a low that is significantly lower than the open, high, and close.

Morning Star:

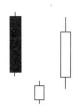

This is a bullish signal indicating a possible bottom. The "star" shows a possible reversal and the bullish empty line supports this. The star can be empty or filled in.

Bearish Patterns

Long Black Line/Major Yin:
This is a bearish line. It occurs when a price opens near the high and closes significantly lower near the period's low.

Hanging Man/Umbrella Line:

These lines are bearish if they follow a significant uptrend. If this pattern follows a significant downtrend, it is called a hammer. They symbolize a small range between the open and closing prices and a low that is significantly lower than the open, high and closing prices. The candle bodies can either be empty or filled in.

Evening Star:

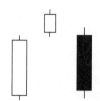

This is a bearish pattern that can symbolize a potential top. The "star" indicates a possible reversal and this is confirmed by the bearish filled-in line. The star can be filled-in or empty.

Many of the programs highlighted in this chapter offer candle charting capabilities. Some of the more advanced programs offer pattern in which basic patterns are automatically identified and marked by the program. These programs include: TIP@Wallstreet, SuperCharts, Personal Hotline, Personal Analyst, Investor/RT, MetaStock, and TradeStation.

FIGURE 6.7
Candlestick recognition capability of Personal Hotline.

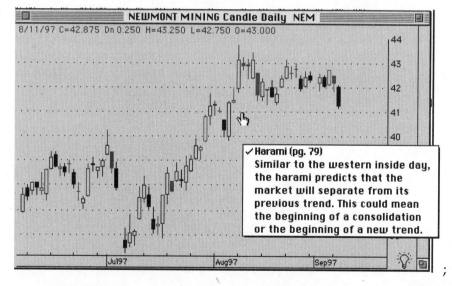

Point and Figure Chart

Point and figure charts were developed in the 1880s by Charles Dow. Just like line charts, they too concern themselves only with the closing price of a security when analyzing daily data. Unlike line charts, however, point and figure charts have no regard for time, or volume for that matter.

Point and figure charts display the underlying supply and demand of a security by tracking the price movement of a security. When supply outweighs demand, prices will fall. When demand is greater than that of supply, prices will rise. Points are only plotted if the price moves a minimum pre-set level, thus measuring the trend and reversal pattern for a security.

In plotting price movements, Xs represent rising prices and Os represent falling prices. When dealing with point and figure charts, there are two important items to consider: box size and reversal amount. The box size is the value assigned to each "box" (X or O) on the chart. It is the minimum amount the price must move in order to continue the current trend. In other words, the amount the price must increase to add an X or the amount the price must fall to add an O to an existing column. As long as the price continues in the same direction, either up or down, Xs and Os are plotted in the same column.

FIGURE 6.8
Point and figure chart of Allegheny Energy with MetaStock.

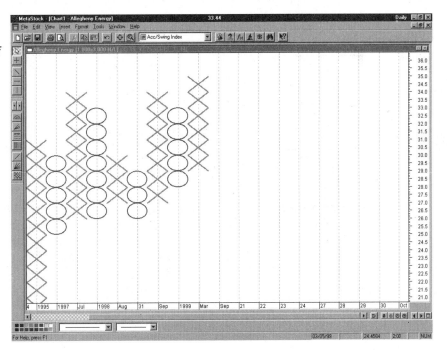

The reversal amount determines how many boxes the price must reverse course in order to move to a new column of Xs or Os. This can be adjusted depending on your individual style, although the typical reversal is the "three box" reversal. Therefore, if the box size is $1, it will take a rise of $3 in the stock price in order to shift from a column of Os (declining prices) to a new column of Xs (rising prices). Price fluctuations of less than $1, in this example, would require no action.

A column of Xs shows that demand is exceeding supply (uptrend) while a column of Os shows that supply is exceeding demand (downtrend). A series of short columns shows that supply and demand are relatively equal (sideways trend).

Equivolume Chart

Equivolume charts, developed by Richard W. Arms, illustrate the relationship between price and volume. Instead of plotting volume in a separate chart or scale below the price chart (as is usually seen on bar charts), equivolume places volume on the same level as price. Price and volume are combined into a two-dimensional box, with the top line indicating the high price for the period and the bottom the low price for the period. The width of the box is an indication of the volume for the period, with a wider width indicating a higher trading volume.

FIGURE 6.9
The components of an equivolume box.

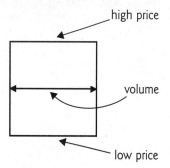

The shape of each box gives a picture of the supply and demand for the security. Short, wide boxes representing heavy volume and little change in price can indicate a turning point in the price trend. Tall, narrow boxes representing light volume and large price movement generally occur in established trends. Insider/TA, MetaStock and TIP@Wallstreet are the only programs reviewed here that offer equivolume charting.

FIGURE 6.10
An illustration of equivolume charting in Insider/TA for Southern Company.

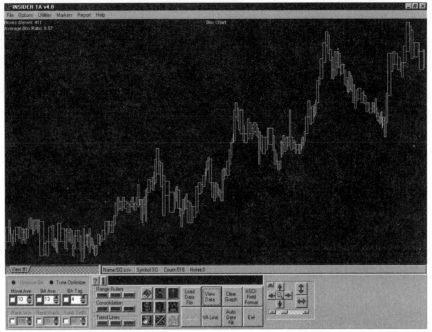

Investing Horizon and Charting

Charting is performed on several levels, the most popular being intraday, daily, weekly and monthly. Generally day traders and brokers perform intraday charting. They typically have ready access to the trading pits of the major exchanges. Day trading, or real-time trading as it is sometimes called, is very hard for the individual investor to practice—mainly due to the time commitment and higher cost of real-time information and transaction costs, in addition to the near-instant accessibility needed to process transactions in the trading pits.

The most common chart form is the daily chart. Daily charts plot the open, high, low and close each day for selected securities. To obtain a broader view of a security's price fluctuation, weekly and monthly charts can be drawn. However, weekly and monthly views are usually just compressed versions of daily charts.

Once your data is gathered in the format you prefer, you can implement the various charting tools and plotting functions offered by your program. Some programs will allow you to choose specific time periods in which to view the data, either by specific date blocks, such as 01/01/98–06/30/99, or by data points, such as the last 200 bars, or days, of data.

FIGURE 6.11
*Data
formatting
window in
SuperCharts.*

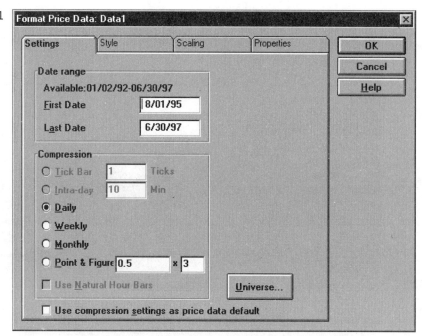

In addition to loading a specific date range or data point for a security, you may also want to change the program's scaling. Scaling refers to the values associated with the Y-axis (vertical). The two basic types are arithmetic, where the prices are plotted on a scale using equal dollar increments, and logarithmic, or more accurately semi-log, where prices are plotted on a scale using equal percentage increments. Logarithmic scaling is sometimes used to compare relative price changes rather than simply dollar changes. A long-term chart with a linear (arithmetic) scale can distort the significance of price changes early in the time series, making them look insignificant in comparison to price changes late in the time series.

Comparing these two graphs (Figure 6.12 and Figure 6.13 on page 235) gives a good example of how the scaling of a graph can impact how data is represented. In the logarithmic graph the larger price changes (whether they are increases or decreases in price) in recent years are shown to have no greater significance than price changes experienced in the past when the index was at much lower levels.

FIGURE 6.12
An illustration of linear scaling for the Dow Jones utilities index over the period 1/2/74 to 9/17/99.

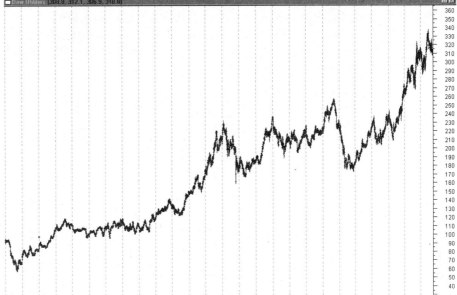

FIGURE 6.13
An illustration of semi-log scaling for the Dow Jones utilities over the period 1/2/74 to 9/17/99.

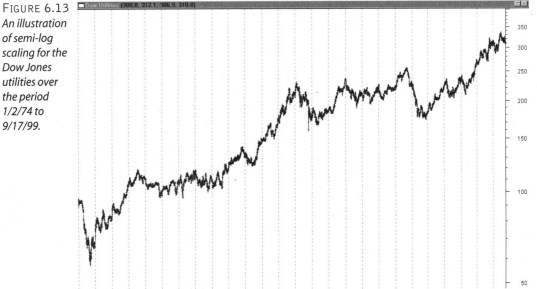

Trendlines

Trend analysis examines the price behavior of a security. Using trend analysis, you attempt to identify if the overall direction of price movement is up, down or sideways. This is accomplished by drawing lines, called trendlines, that connect two or more prices.

FIGURE 6.14
An illustration of the S&P 100 with primary, secondary, and minor trendlines drawn by MacChart.

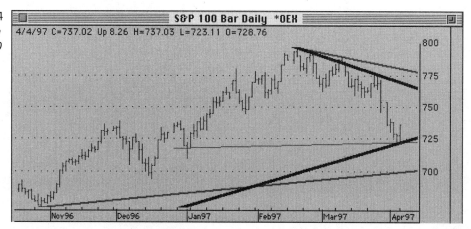

You can use programs to draw, erase, rotate, duplicate and stretch trendlines. Once again, the computer allows you to test and examine a wide variety of scenarios in a manner not practical with only pencil and paper. Trendline analysis has evolved into a large and complex field. If you plan to explore this area beyond a basic level, make sure that the technical analysis program you choose includes the necessary features. Refer to the comparison grid on page 297 to find those programs that offer trendlines.

Indicators

When performing any type of technical analysis, technical indicators will form the backbone of the analysis. In all technical analysis programs, you are provided with a certain number of predefined indicators. The number of technical indicators the program provides is an important consideration when comparing technical analysis programs, especially for new users. Indicators also form the foundation on which you can build new trading systems. The more indicators included with a program, the more diverse a trading strategy you can build. In addition, finding a program with pre-installed indicators saves you from performing the redundant task of creating your own. However, keep in mind that bigger doesn't always mean better. Your needs should be the deciding factor when choosing a technical analysis package. Make sure that the program supports the specific indicators you follow. Furthermore, when viewing the comparison grid that appears later in this chapter, don't automatically write off a program because it seems to offer the least number of technical indicators. Some programs, such as VectorVest by ProGraphics and TC2000 by Worden Brothers, offer their own unique proprietary indicators that, depending on your analysis needs, may suit you better. The table on page 307 shows which popular indicators each program offers.

Tip→	Don't be swayed into paying hundreds of dollars for a package that offers functions you will never use.

Another important consideration is whether the program allows you to modify the pre-installed indicators. Many technicians modify technical indicators to best fit the security being analyzed as well as their investment horizon or style. Being able to modify existing indicators means you can change the time frame associated with the calculation of an indicator. For example, the MACD (moving average convergence/divergence) is usually constructed using a 12-period and 26-period moving average crossover. However, by either increasing or decreasing the values, you can vary the MACD to provide a somewhat longer and smoother, or shorter and more active, trading scope. The comparison grid at the end of the chapter shows which programs allow modification of existing indicators.

FIGURE 6.15
Indicator formatting window in TC2000.

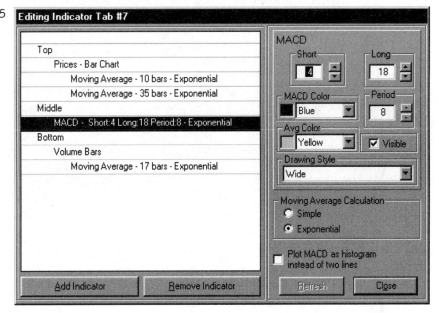

When performing any type of security analysis, it is always helpful to be able to compare multiple indicators at the same time. Furthermore, most investors track more than one indicator at a time. It is important to select a program that allows you to plot indicators directly on top of an existing chart, in addition to plotting them in their own windows. Good programs will allow you to save individual security plots with their respective indicators, as well as allow you to save a group of securities (such as your portfolio of holdings or securities you are tracking) with their underlying indicators. This feature saves you time as you can avoid re-plotting indicators every time you wish to view a security or group of securities, and saves you from having to open multiple security files.

Tip→	It is important to select a program that allows you to plot indicators directly on top of an existing chart, in addition to plotting them in their own windows.

FIGURE 6.16
International Business Machines' 50-day and 200-day moving averages overlaid using MegaTech.

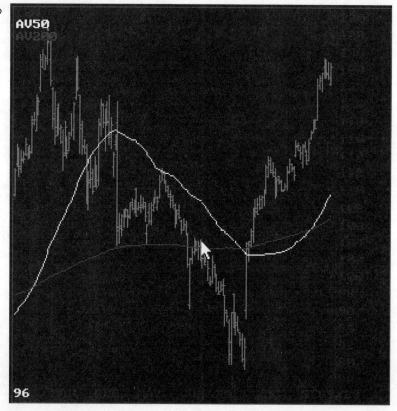

Custom Indicators

Depending on your level of expertise in technical analysis, you may follow your own custom variables not found pre-installed on a program. To give you added flexibility, some programs allow you to create your own custom indicators. Typically you are given a range of functions to use as well as the ability to "cannibalize" pre-installed indicators and implement them into your own technical indicators. The flexibility afforded to you in the endeavor varies greatly across

FIGURE 6.17
Using EasyLanguage from Omega-Research, you can create your own custom variables in either SuperCharts or TradeStation 2000i.

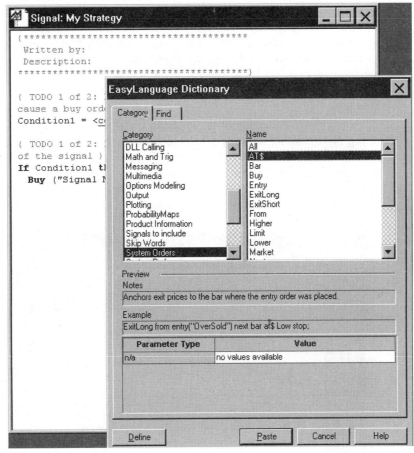

programs. Some programs, such as MetaStock, SuperCharts, and TradeStation, have proprietary programming "languages" you use. Other programs use more common spreadsheet-like functions. Beyond creating custom variables, you should also be able to plot these custom indicators on charts and, if the program has the functionality, be able to use custom indicators in the creation of trading systems.

Chart Templates

Some programs provide the user with a host of predefined chart templates. These templates enable you to view historical data in any number of formats. Some of the more basic formats are the standard bar, line, and candle charts. More advanced templates include multiple indicators with alerts that provide quick scanning of a number of securities where the same sets of indicators are applied. The program should also allow you to create your own templates with your favorite indicators and customized alerts. If you often use the same indicators or trading systems on multiple securities, this is a valuable feature to look for in a program.

Merging

Merging securities is useful for creating your own specialized indexes (such as merging several technology stocks together to create a modified technology index). You can create an index by merging the stocks in a portfolio and then compare the individual issues against the portfolio index (see Figure 6.18). Refer to the comparison grid on page 297 to see which programs allow you to create custom indexes by combining securities and/or indexes.

FIGURE 6.18
Creating a composite index of Duke Energy and Dominion Resources using Equis' Downloader.

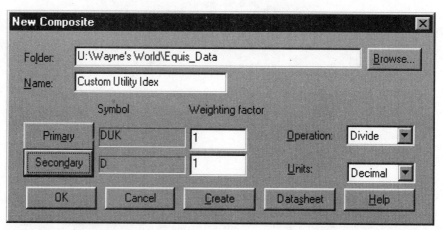

Trading Systems

A trading system is defined as an indicator or group of indicators used to generate buy and sell signals. Backtesting is the method used for identifying how well (profit-wise) a certain trading system performed during a given time period. This helps you see the different transactions that would have taken place if the system had been in use as well as whether or not the investing strategy was successful. It is important to try to simulate real market conditions when testing a trading strategy. For example, commissions should be charged with every transaction. "Slippage" of price and time may occur between the point when a trading signal is generated and when the order is placed and executed. Other details include stop/loss methods, user-defined entry and exit signals, and whether you want to trade on long positions, short positions or both. The more "real" you are able to make a trading system, the more reliable the results may be.

Tip→	When selecting software that offers backtesting capabilities, be sure to check that it includes features that will make the test results more realistic.

Many programs also include predefined trading systems that can be used as is, or in combination with other methods. In fact, many of the trading systems work by including specific functions (such as a type of relative strength index or stochastics) that you can modify in order to let you develop a trading system with a minimal amount of programming, in addition to giving you outright programming control if you so desire.

Warning→	Be aware that just because a trading system is profitable using past data is no guarantee that it will return a profit in the future.

Bear in mind that trading systems should be tested with at least 10 years of data. The longer the time period over which a system is tested, the more market conditions the data will capture. If you use programs to "tweak" a system so that it works perfectly over a fixed range of past dates, it might not perform as well in the future because it has not been tested over a variety of market conditions. You should include a hold-out period, which is not used to optimize the strategy. After a strategy is developed and tested, it should be run against the data in the hold-out period to see if it continues to work. Furthermore, you are optimizing it to market activity from the past. Be wary of so-called "black box" trading systems that claim you don't need any knowledge of the markets or technical analysis to make lots of money. If a system seems too good to be true, it probably is.

FIGURE 6.19
*Trading
system format
options
available with
TradeStation
2000i.*

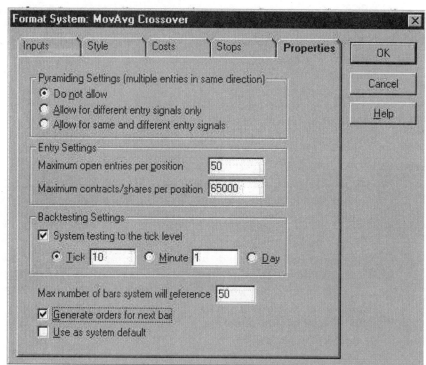

> Warning→ Be wary of so-called "black box" trading systems that claim you don't need any knowledge of the markets or technical analysis to make lots of money. If a system seems too good to be true, it probably is.

Custom Trading Systems

Just as with custom indicators, you may wish to create your own trading systems. Usually the process is similar to that followed when creating custom indicators. You should be able to specify entry and exit points based on pre-installed and custom indicators. Once again, the comparison grid at the end of the chapter shows which programs reviewed here allow you to create custom trading systems.

Once you have picked out the trading system(s) in which you are interested, you will probably want to see how they will fare in varying market conditions. To help you with this, programs may offer profit reports. These reports outline information such as the total number of trades, the number of profitable trades, the

FIGURE 6.20
*Rule Builder
window in
Trading Expert
Pro.*

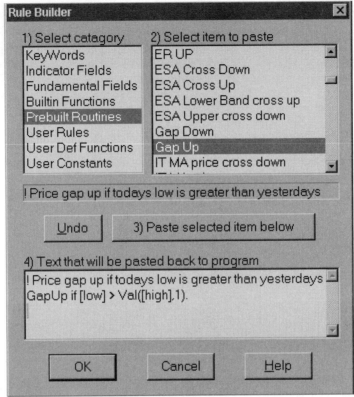

number of losing trades, and the maximum drawdown (lowest account value). These reports allow you to see how a trading system performs and also allows for head-to-head comparisons of different trading systems.

Another valuable feature of a technical analysis program is the ability to directly rank or compare a trading system's performance. This is very useful in illustrating the consequences and profit or loss when commissions are factored into your trading system.

Technical Screening

For those who follow a large number of securities, the process of analyzing each one can take a long time. Some programs have features that enable you to automate this process, particularly if you use the same indicator(s) for each security.

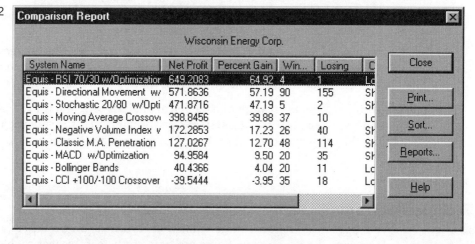

System Test Report

SUMMARY

Total Net Profit:	$16793.28	Average trade gain/loss ($):	$4198.32
Total percentage gain/loss:	335.87%	Average trade gain/loss (%):	50.66%
Annualized rate of return:	39.12%		

SUMMARY WITHOUT BEST AND WORST TRADES

Total Net Profit:	$7572.03	Average trade gain/loss ($):	$3786.01
Total percentage gain/loss:	151.44%	Average trade gain/loss (%):	52.11%
Annualized rate of return:	17.64%		

TRADE STATISTICS

Total no. of trades:	4	Percentage profitable trades:	75.00%
No. Profitable Trades:	3	No. Losing Trades:	1
Amount of profitable trades:	$16529.86	Amount of losing trades:	$-398.57
Largest profitable trade:	$9619.82	Largest losing trade:	$-398.57
Average profitable trade:	$5509.95	Average losing trade:	$-398.57
No. of stop hits:	1	Average gain/loss per stop:	$-398.57

LONG/SHORT BREAKDOWN

Number of Long trades:	4	Number of Short trades:	0
No. profitable Long trades:	3	No. profitable Short trades:	0
Average Long gain/loss:	$4032.82	Average Short gain/loss:	$0.00

TRADE DURATIONS

Total no. periods in test:	2238	Number of days in test:	3134
Most consecutive wins:	3	Most consecutive losses:	1
Amt. of consecutive wins:	$16529.86	Amt. of consecutive losses:	$-398.57

Trades   Print...   Copy   Close

Comparison Report

Wisconsin Energy Corp.

System Name	Net Profit	Percent Gain	Win...	Losing	C
Equis - RSI 70/30 w/Optimization	649.2083	64.92	4	1	Lc
Equis - Directional Movement w/	571.8636	57.19	90	155	Sh
Equis - Stochastic 20/80 w/Opti	471.8716	47.19	5	2	Sh
Equis - Moving Average Crossov	398.8456	39.88	37	10	Lc
Equis - Negative Volume Index v	172.2853	17.23	26	40	Sh
Equis - Classic M.A. Penetration	127.0267	12.70	48	114	Sh
Equis - MACD w/Optimization	94.9584	9.50	20	35	Sh
Equis - Bollinger Bands	40.4366	4.04	20	11	Lc
Equis - CCI +100/-100 Crossover	-39.5444	-3.95	35	18	Lc

Close   Print...   Sort...   Reports...   Help

These features are collectively referred to as technical screening. The concept is the same as any other type of screening: You specify one or more sets of conditions to a group of securities, and the computer sifts through that group to find only those companies that match your set of conditions. Depending on the program, you may be given pre-installed screens or scans and/or the ability to create your own.

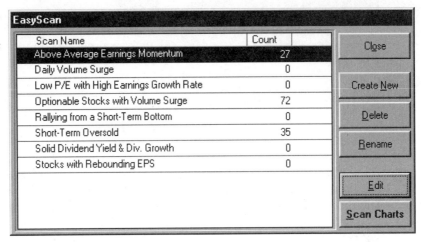

You need access to a database that contains historical data for securities in order to perform technical screening. This database can either exist locally (on your hard drive or CD-ROM) or remotely (with an on-line service). With the CD-ROM, you have the responsibility of maintaining the data for such things as dividend payments and stock splits and updating the information, whereas the data vendor handles this if you use an on-line service.

Along with filtering, a good technical screening program will provide you with the ability to sort data and generate reports that include data not used in the screening conditions.

Reviews

While the main focus of each of the programs mentioned in this chapter is technical analysis, several programs offer an expanded array of features and analysis capabilities. Many programs offer company and industry news, company reports, and other useful information. Programs such as Internet Trader Pro and Day Trader Internet offer substantial fundamental information to complement the technical aspect. Furthermore, this program, along with TIP@Wallstreet and MetaStock, offer extensive Web integration—a feature that should grow in popularity as the Internet further positions itself in the realm of investing. The following are reviews and ratings of the key players in the technical analysis arena.

Behold!	
Performance	4
Usefulness	5
Documentation	4
Ease of Use	3
Value	4

Behold! 2.8
by Investors' Technical Services (NTECH)
$795—Macintosh
(512) 367-4626
www.bhld.com

Behold! is one of the more advanced technical analysis programs on the market for the Macintosh. Designed by Investors' Technical Services, it allows you to develop, test, and optimize technical trading systems.

Trading Models

Behold! deals exclusively with the development and analysis of trading models. A trading model consists of three parts: worksheet, the chart, and the system rules. The worksheet contains the original price data of a security and any adaptations thereof—moving averages or indexes—as well as the formulas that calculate those moving averages and indexes. In creating items such as moving averages or stochastics, you can use either built-in functions or those you create yourself. The charting module is straightforward—it is used to display the original data, moving averages, and/or indexes. Lastly, the system rules are the trading rules you wish the program to test.

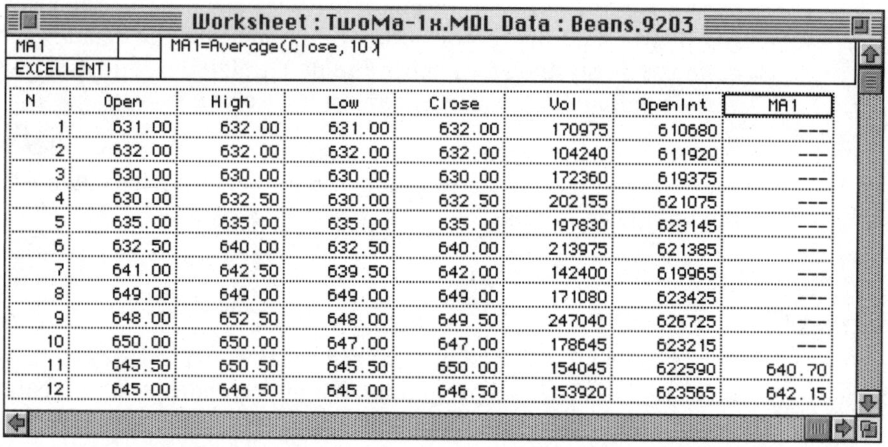

FIGURE 6.24
Worksheet in Behold!

Worksheet : TwoMa-1x.MDL Data : Beans.9203

MA1   MA1=Average(Close, 10)
EXCELLENT!

N	Open	High	Low	Close	Vol	OpenInt	MA1
1	631.00	632.00	631.00	632.00	170975	610680	---
2	632.00	632.00	632.00	632.00	104240	611920	---
3	630.00	630.00	630.00	630.00	172360	619375	---
4	630.00	632.50	630.00	632.50	202155	621075	---
5	635.00	635.00	635.00	635.00	197830	623145	---
6	632.50	640.00	632.50	640.00	213975	621385	---
7	641.00	642.50	639.50	642.00	142400	619965	---
8	649.00	649.00	649.00	649.00	171080	623425	---
9	648.00	652.50	648.00	649.50	247040	626725	---
10	650.00	650.00	647.00	647.00	178645	623215	---
11	645.50	650.50	645.50	650.00	154045	622590	640.70
12	645.00	646.50	645.00	646.50	153920	623565	642.15

Historical Testing

Once you have created your trading model, you can have Behold! test the profitability of the model. When you test a model, you also specify the type of report you wish the program to generate—trade-by-trade, one-line summary, or performance summary. The trade-by-trade report shows the entry and exit dates and prices for each trade, the one-line summary is a customizable report, and the performance summary is an in-depth, one-page trade summary.

System Optimization

Behold! gives users the ability to optimize their trading models in the attempt to make them more profitable. The Optimizer function in Behold! allows the user to test a range of values for a given criterion to find the value that generated the greatest profit or lowest loss. You are able to optimize up to three variables or criteria per trading model. You simply select those variables you wish to optimize and the range of values you wish to test for each variable. When optimizing a trading system with Behold!, you are provided with a graphical representation of how the changes you make impact the profitability of the system. This Optigraph shows the net effect the optimization had on the system.

FIGURE 6.25
Optigraph from Behold! The lighter squares shows the combinations of variables that make a system more profitable.

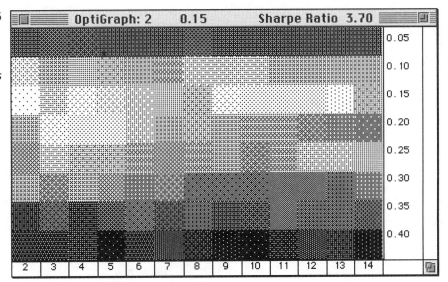

AutoRun

The AutoRun function within Behold! applies the active trading model. After scanning the data, Behold! generates a report that tells you what your current position should be as well as stop method suggestions for active trades. These reports can then be screened to show only those securities with an open position, those that require a new position, or those exiting a trade. Another unique feature found in Behold! is the ability to create scripts (macros) that allow the program to automate calculations, charting, printing, etc.

Data

Behold! can read a variety of data formats, including Compu Trac, Trendsetter (TickerWatcher), and Market Analyzer. It also comes with built-in converters for text data and a built-in file updater for MJK, a data provider.

Compared to other Mac-based technical analysis programs, Behold! is not the prettiest and isn't the easiest to use right out of the box. However, for the patient user, a run through the manual's tutorial will get you acclimated to the program's key features. Behold! is also geared more toward the seasoned technician—someone who is willing to roll up their sleeves and create their own trading systems. If you are looking for a Mac-based system on which you can create, test, and optimize your own trading systems at a fair price, you will want to take a strong look at Behold!

Day Trader Internet Internet Trader Pro	
Performance	5
Usefulness	5
Documentation	5
Ease of Use	5
Value	5

Day Trader Internet 7.5
Internet Trader Pro 7.5
by Window on WallStreet, Inc.
$1,495.95 for Day Trader Internet; $499.95 for Internet Trader Pro—Windows
(888) 375-8522
www.windowonwallstreet.com

The past two years has seen a flurry of activity from Window on WallStreet. In late 1999, they were purchased by one of their competitors, Omega Research. The impact of this acquisition remains to be seen. Last year they released the completely redesigned Day Trader program and the new Internet Trader Pro package. This year they released an upgrade to both programs—version 7.5—with added features. Like many other software manufacturers, Window on WallStreet offers several technical analysis packages to meet the varying needs of investors.

Internet Trader Pro ($499.95), previously known as Professional Investor, offers end-of-day and real-time intraday data and analytics, charting, fundamentals, and some trading system development capabilities. Day Trader Internet ($1,499.95) is designed for the day trader with added system trading functions.

New Features

Both programs now offer Nasdaq Level 2 display screens that allow you to see market activity at the market maker level. Secondly, option analysis tools have also been added. The programs feature option analytics such as the Black-Scholes pricing model, option over/under pricing, historical & implied volatility, historical & implied option Greeks—delta, gamma, theta, and vega. With the customizable filtering and sorting capabilities, users are able to locate options that meet their individual criteria and then sort them. Day Trader offers all of the capabilities included with Internet Trader Pro as well as enhanced, real-time analysis capabilities.

Indicators

Both programs offer 150 indicators—fundamental and technical. Window on WallStreet is one of the few companies that combine technical and fundamental analysis. Their "rational analysis technology expert" (RATE) system combines price and volume movements with earnings per share data to give you over 20 indicators. As with most programs, you have the capability to customize existing indicators, or you can create you own.

FIGURE 6.26
An example desktop in Internet Trader Pro.

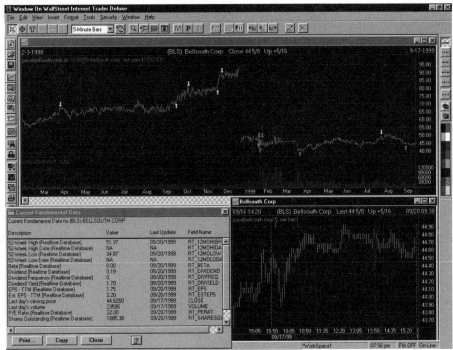

Trading System Testing and Development

Internet Trader Pro and Day Trader have over 15 pre-installed trading systems that you can use. Each program's profit-testing system allows you to test the profitability of a system. To add reality to a given system, you can specify such things as commissions, system stops, margin trading, and idle interest. You can have the programs scan one or several systems and rank them by profitability. Window on WallStreet's formula language, although not as powerful as Easy-Language from Omega Research (see the review of TradeStation and Super-Charts page 277), allows you to create and test your own trading systems.

Screening

The SmartScan feature available with both programs allows you to specify both fundamental and technical criteria, at which point the programs will scan either the entire universe of securities or, if you wish, smaller groups such as a specific industry for securities passing the criteria. Searches can be performed on either an end-of-day or real-time intraday basis using over 60 fundamental factors and technical indicators.

FIGURE 6.27
The results of a SmartScan from Internet Trader Pro.

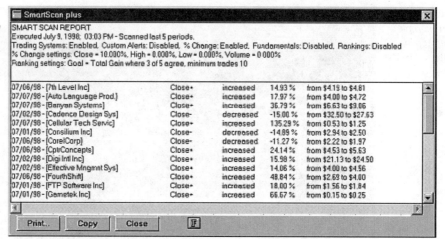

Internet Integration

As the Internet grows in prominence as a research tool, more and more companies are integrating Internet-based tools into their programs. Window on Wall-Street is no exception. The SmartBrowse feature allows you to search for news and content on a specific symbol via the Internet. In addition, both programs allow program updating via the Internet—the programs automatically download the latest enhancements and revisions available.

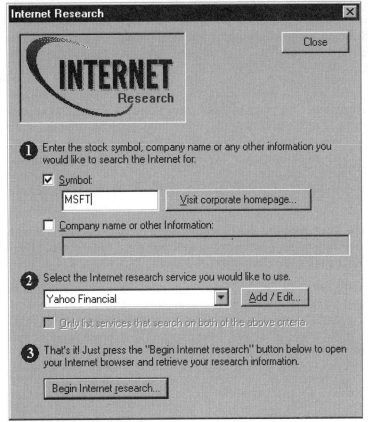

FIGURE 6.28
The SmartBrowse window found in both Internet Trader Pro and Day Trader Internet.

Day Trading

Day Trader—with its more advanced features—is better suited for those looking for a day trading platform. All analysis techniques from indicator alerts to trading systems are recalculated in real time. You are alerted during the trading day as trading systems generate buy/sell signals. The time and sales windows keep you up-to-date on the securities you trade—letting you track your order execution—and are dynamically updated. Day Trader lags behind some other day trading systems by not offering testing of intraday systems.

Data Management and Support

A common complaint among users of technical analysis programs is the time spent downloading data before the analysis can even take place. Internet Trader Pro ships with a CD containing a historical price, volume, and fundamentals database. The program will first retrieve data from the CD and then fill in the missing data from the Window on WallStreet Internet site. The CD is shipped on a quarterly basis, covers over 15,000 securities, and has data such as historical price, volume, earnings per share, and dividend data, as well as over 60 fundamental data elements.

Both Internet Trader Pro and Day Trader Internet use Window on WallStreet's Internet-based market data service—Financial Data Cast Network (FDCN). With free basic service you can track up to 20 securities and indexes a day, receive intraday price updates, end-of-day histories, and one market ranking from your choice of exchange for most active, top gainers, losers, etc. For fees starting at $14.95 and going up to $179.95, you can track a larger universe of securities and indexes and retrieve news headlines and SEC abstracts, time and sales data, and even tick-by-tick data. Month-to-month real-time subscriptions begin at $69.95.

If you already have a data feed, chances are it is compatible with both programs. The programs support such popular real-time and delayed feeds such as DTN, DBC Signal, S&P Comstock, and BMI.

Overall, Window on WallStreet programs offer something for almost all technicians and the Internet integration adds an element few programs are offering yet. The programs' on-line help systems make them well-suited for the technical novice, while their power and functionality make them suited for all but the most seasoned of day traders.

FastBreak FastGraph	
Performance	4
Usefulness	3
Documentation	3
Ease of Use	3
Value	4

FastBreak 2.6
FastGraph 2.6
by Edge Ware, Inc.
$299 for FastBreak; $199 for FastGraph;
$399 for both—Windows 95/98/NT
(703) 691-7913, (614) 475-5449
www.edge-ware.com

FastBreak and FastGraph are stock and mutual fund trading strategy software for use with FastTrack mutual fund and stock data (www.fasttrack.net). FastBreak requires the FastTrack service. FastBreak is a stock and mutual fund trading program that generates buy and sell signals based on relative price trends. FastGraph is a graphical program that allows users to analyze FastBreak data files.

FastBreak

In FastBreak, you have several options and techniques to choose from when devising a trading strategy. Options include ranking based on gain over a specified time period and the slope of the price chart in relation to the slope for all other funds in the family. A more involved strategy based upon the "AccuTrak" proprietary indicator compares funds two at a time to find the "stronger" fund in relation to the AccuTrak value. Once this process is completed for all the funds in a given fund family, the funds are ranked from strongest to weakest. There are three strategies that combine price gains and ranks for a fund over a specified period and rank them based on the results.

Once you have selected the trading strategy you wish to test, you can further customize the system by dictating how you wish the system to be tested. You can specify the time period to test, whether to short the fund based upon the relative strength of a fund compared to other funds in the trading family, the number of days to hold a fund, the number of days between when a trade is signaled and when it is actually made, and the maximum drawdown.

FIGURE 6.29
*Outlining the
strategy
specifics in
FastBreak.*

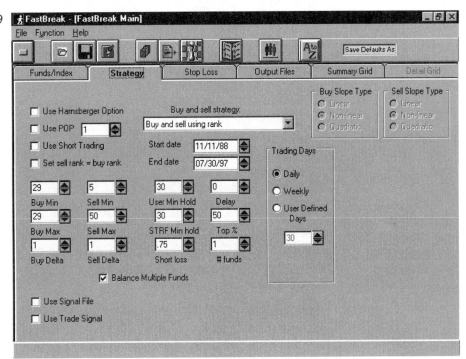

Once the selected funds have been tested, FastBreak will generate a summary file, which contains the results from each test case. The report contains information such as the compound annual return for the strategy, maximum draw-down, risk, and the average gain on winning trades as well as loss on losing trades.

FastGraph

FastGraph can be used to analyze and graphically illustrate FastTrack and Fast-Break data. You are able to plot simple line charts for a single fund or multiple funds. Using FastBreak summary files, you are also able to see the effects of changing a parameter on the returns of a trading strategy.

FIGURE 6.30
Correlation graph for two mutual funds in FastGraph.

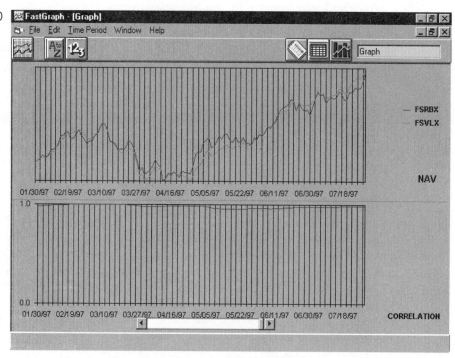

As a tandem, FastGraph and FastBreak are less of a technical analysis suite and more of a trading strategy testing platform. In this regard it is well suited for those who pursue an active trading strategy in either stocks or mutual funds.

Insider TA Standard Insider TA Pro	
Performance	4
Usefulness	3
Documentation	4
Ease of Use	3
Value	4

Insider TA Standard 4.0
Insider TA Pro 4.0
by Stock Blocks, Inc.
$199 (Standard); $295 (Pro)—Windows
(800) 697-1617
www.stockblocks.com

Stock Blocks offers a niche program focused on one key technical element: volume.

Charting

Insider TA provides both candlestick and box charts. Box charting, also referred to as equivolume, focuses on volume to analyze a stock. The vertical height of a given box is the price range for the period while the horizontal x-axis is a sequence of periods that grows wider as volume increases and narrower as volume decreases. The resulting chart consists of rectangular shapes that represent price in the height and volume in the width. The shapes, and their corresponding height-to-width ratio, can then be used as forecasting signals for future price movement.

Volume-Oriented Analysis

To aid in the volume analysis process, Insider TA offers four volume-related tools—consolidation mapping, box analyzer (BA), volume analyzer, and VA rank. When viewing a stock chart, a period of consolidation is determined when there is little vertical movement to the price. The stock trades in a narrow range until, typically, it breaks out of this range—either to the upside or to the downside. When viewing a box chart, consolidation is identified by a range of boxes with a somewhat constant height (price range), yet generally wide—reflecting large trading volume. Over time, this volume tends to diminish, which is often an indication of an impending breakout. Once this breakout, or divergence, begins volume tends to rise and the price is driven away from the previous trading range. At this point, consolidation mapping comes into play: Assuming all those who bought during the consolidation period are now selling, the sum of shares traded during the consolidation period will approximate the sum of the shares traded during the breakout. Insider TA's consolidation mapping tool allows you to select a period of consolidation and extend the chart into the future to the next potential trending or consolidation period. The box analyzer (BA) feature attempts to identify trends in box shapes and price movement. Based on these trends, Insider TA then produces buy and sell tags that indicate where a reverse in price movement may take place. Furthermore, the program gives you a performance summary of how, based on the buy and sell tags, the trades would have performed. You are able to optimize the box settings to find those that best fit an individual security. However, be aware that, as is the case with system optimization functions, past performance is not a guarantee of what will happen in the future.

Insider TA's volume analyzer (VA) is a derivation of on-balance volume (OBV). An "accumulator" function counts volume based on "up" and "down" days. Put in simple terms, VA attempts to measure the demand for a stock. When the volume signal is increasing, this is a sign of potential interest in the stock while a falling volume indicator could signal a lack of, or waning, interest. Building on the VA function, Insider TA then measures the relationship between a stock's price and its respective volume indicator level, generating buy and sell signals from the observed relationships.

FIGURE 6.31
Box chart of American Electric Power Co. with VA line and BA function plotted by Insider TA.

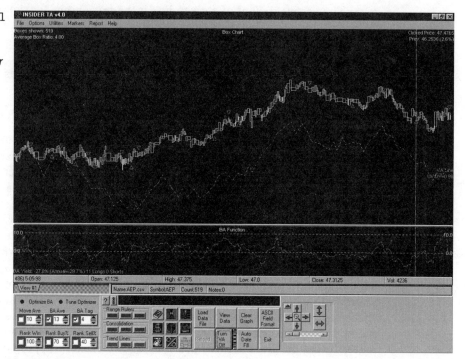

Insider TA Pro

Insider TA Pro offers additional features beyond the standard release, such as stop-loss and trailing stop signaling, MetaStock and TC2000 data compatibility, and a file scan utility where you can scan portfolios of stocks to find those that meet your individual criteria. The stop-loss and trailing-stop signals attempt to protect you in the event of an unexpected turn in a stock's price. You can set a stop-loss signal at some percentage below the buy tag price and set trailing stops to preserve a certain percentage of your profits. Trailing-stop signals are generated automatically once a specific price is met.

FIGURE 6.32
The File Scan utility in Insider TA Pro allows you to search for stocks that meet certain volume-based criteria.

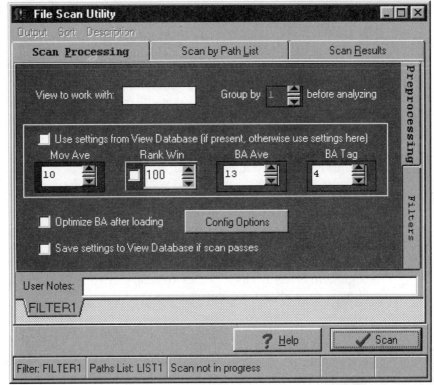

While Stock Blocks produces programs that provide solid analysis tools for those interested in a specific area of technical analysis, they are not as complete as other technical analysis programs. The programs are easy to navigate, especially with the Windows interface that was introduced with version 4.0. The on-line tutorials and manuals allow users to conduct their analysis with ease. The bottom line is: If you are looking for a program to conduct volume-based analysis but are not interested in all the bells and whistles (as well as the price tag that comes with them), the Insider TA series may be just the fit.

Investor/RT 3.8	
Performance	4
Usefulness	4
Documentation	4
Ease of Use	4
Value	2

Investor/RT 3.8
by Linn Software, Inc.
$995—PowerMac, Windows 95/98/NT
(800) 546-6842
www.linnsoft.com

Investor/RT is one of the more unique technical analysis programs on the market today. While offering an impressive array of technical indicators, charting features, portfolio management module, and data compatibility, Investor/RT stands alone in its ability to run on either PowerMac or Windows-based systems.

Charting
Investor/RT offers an impressive array of chart types—bar, candlestick, point and figure, line, market profile, and volume profile. Each chart window can contain multiple securities and technical indicators. There are no limits as to the time periods that may be plotted. You can view charts in either an intraday, daily, weekly, or monthly format. For easy viewing of several charts, the program's slide show feature allows you to set the viewing time for each chart and sit back and let the program do the rest. Investor/RT also provides candlestick pattern recognition. Select from any of the over 30 predefined patterns and the program will mark each pattern's occurrence on the display.

Scans
With Investor/RT, you have the capability to identify trading signals using the scan function. You can choose from over 160 technical indicators as well as prices, fundamental elements, and historical or current data. The program's "scan request language" supports arithmetic, relational, and logical operations of varying complexity. A scan can be run on daily, weekly, monthly, tick, or minute bar data. Once the program has completed its search, it offers up the results in a separate table. A scan can be scheduled to run automatically at regular intervals during the course of a trading day.

Portfolio Manager
For any trader it is important to track open positions. Having portfolio management within your analysis package is an added convenience. Investor/RT can track long or short positions, gains and losses on stock, mutual funds, futures,

FIGURE 6.33
You can create a scan object in Investor/RT to identify the securities that meet your characteristics.

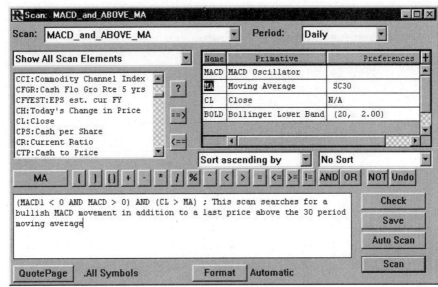

and equity/index options. The system also tracks transactions such as cash, dividends, commissions, and interest in order to calculate the annualized rate of return for each open position. However, it does not provide year-end tax reporting.

FIGURE 6.34
Portfolio objects in Investor/RT track those instruments in which you have an open position.

Ticker	Last	Value	Net G/L	Qty	Cost Basi	Open Dat	Open Pos	% G/L	Annualized	Commis	
IBM	167 11/16	16,768.75	3,937.75	100	12,831.00	10/09/98	127 3/4	30.69%	76.72%	50.00	
CA	39 5/8	7,925.00	4,698.25	200	3,226.75	10/09/98	16 1/16	145.60%	364.01%	8.00	
AAPL	34.13	3,412.50	-89.25	100	3,501.75	10/09/98	34.94	-2.55%	-6.37%	8.00	
T	82 7/8	8,287.50	2,385.75	100	5,901.75	10/09/98	58 15/16	40.42%	101.06%	8.00	
NSC	27 9/16	2,756.25	-181.64	100	2,937.89	10/09/98	28 7/8	-6.18%	-15.46%	50.00	
XON	65	6,500.00	-593.75	100	7,093.75	10/09/98	70 7/16	-8.37%	-20.93%	50.00	
LU	99 3/8	9,937.50	3,662.50	100	6,275.00	10/09/98	62 1/4	58.37%	145.92%	50.00	
EK	63 9/16	6,356.25	-2,018.75	100	8,375.00	10/09/98	83 1/4	-24.10%	-60.26%	50.00	
Mkt Value		61,943.75			50,142.89						
Cash (Debt)		49,857.11									
Equity		$111,800.86	$11,800.86								

Data Support
Investor/RT is compatible with several of the most popular data feeds—both real-time and delayed—available today. Those that are supported include Signal,

eSignal, DTN Spectrum and Real-Time, InterQuote, myTrack, and Dial/Data. Having so many data vendors allows you to "shop around" for the service that best suits your needs and pocketbook.

New Features
Linn Software has released several upgrades to Investor/RT recently. Some of these include Nasdaq Level II display screens, raw-tick charts for showing tick-by-tick activity, and statistical and arithmetic scan functions. They have also increased the number of technical indicators supported, such as the tick velocity indicator that tracks the trading velocity of an instrument in ticks per minute.

Each year Linn Software adds features to Investor/RT at a rate much higher than most other technical analysis programs. With each release, the program grows in its usefulness and power and comes closer to the upper-echelon of programs. Mac users will find its power and functionality among the best, which can be said for Windows users as well. One drawback is that Investor/RT does not offer system testing or indicator creation, which it should based on its cost. Despite these shortcomings, Investor/RT is a serious contender in the technical analysis field. If you aren't interested in such extras, Investor/RT is a worthy candidate.

MacChart	
Performance	4
Usefulness	3
Documentation	4
Ease of Use	4
Value	3

MacChart 3.0
Personal Analyst 4.0
Personal Hotline 8.0
by Trendsetter Software, Inc.
$129/$349/$495—Macintosh
(800) 825-1852
www.trendsoft.com

Perhaps more than any other investment-related software area, Macintosh users have a bit of a selection when it comes to technical analysis programs. Historically, this has been aided by Macintosh's superiority when it comes to graphical display.

Trendsetter Software has established itself as the premier producer of technical analysis programs for the Macintosh. While other companies have attempted to make their programs cross-platform compatible (able to run on both Macintosh and Wintel systems), Trendsetter has focused its energies on Macs alone and, in doing so, has created quality products for Mac users. As is typically the case with vendors that offer multiple software packages, all of Trendsetter's products offer the same core capabilities. Progressing through their product line, the number of features increases.

Personal Analyst	
Performance	4
Usefulness	4
Documentation	4
Ease of Use	4
Value	4

Trendsetter is aware of the dilemma faced by technical analysis beginners—you buy a basic program that you outgrow and then you have to buy a new program. In the attempt to allay those fears, the company offers a "buy-back" program—whereby it will pay 75% of the original purchase price and credit that amount toward the purchase of one of its more advanced programs.

MacChart—Technical Analysis for the Beginner

MacChart ($129) has replaced Analyst Lite in the Trendsetter lineup. While the name has changed, the program itself has remained basically the same. MacChart is designed for those who are looking to increase their knowledge of technical analysis without spending a lot of money or getting a lot of features they will not need right away. The program offers a wide array of technical studies from noted market experts such as Welles Wilder and John Bollinger and offers charting capabilities—including candlesticks—to satisfy most users. In all, there are over 20 technical indicators and studies.

Personal Hotline	
Performance	4
Usefulness	5
Documentation	4
Ease of Use	4
Value	5

Personal Analyst ($395) is a somewhat more advanced product than MacChart. Just as with MacChart, you can create line, bar, and candlestick charts. In addition, you are given 50 technical indicators and studies.

Pattern Recognition

Beyond plotting candlesticks, Personal Analyst has the added feature of being able to recognize popular candlestick patterns. The program scans the price data of a given security and will identify the patterns for you on the chart. With the "pop-up" discussions, you can easily learn about the chart patterns being identified.

Technical Screening

Both Personal Analyst and Personal Hotline—Trendsetter's high-end program— offer technical screening. You are able to specify the criteria in which you are interested and the program will scan its database for those stocks that meet all the rules. For example, if you are interested in companies with a relative strength index (RSI) value of less than 30, you can have both programs search out those companies.

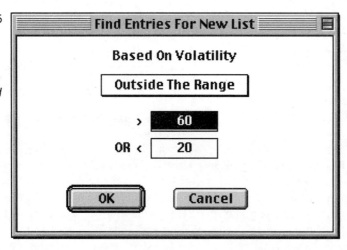

Charting

Personal Analyst and Personal Hotline both offer point and figure charting as well as three unique chart templates—equiview, multiview, and general market. The equiview template displays two years of price data, which is useful for viewing seasonal tendencies. Multiview displays two separate securities on the same chart for easy comparison. Lastly, the general market template displays an advance/decline line, up volume versus down volume, the TRIN, McClellan oscillator, and summation index.

Trade Tracking and Analysis

Personal Hotline ($695) offers all the features available with Personal Analyst plus five additional features designed for the serious technical analyst. With the personal trade tracking function, Personal Hotline summarizes your open positions on a daily basis and analyzes your trading results. For those looking for powerful trade analysis, Personal Hotline serves as the expert trading model. The program scans a security's price data and, by using different combinations of buy, sell, and stop-loss levels, produces a summary of the historical trading results. In addition it can track theoretical performance and allows you to view past trading results such as winners versus losers, average gain and loss, net profit after commissions, and maximum drawdown. The day trader system gives dai-

FIGURE 6.36
*Create point &
figure charts
using Personal
Analyst and
Personal
Hotline
(displayed).*

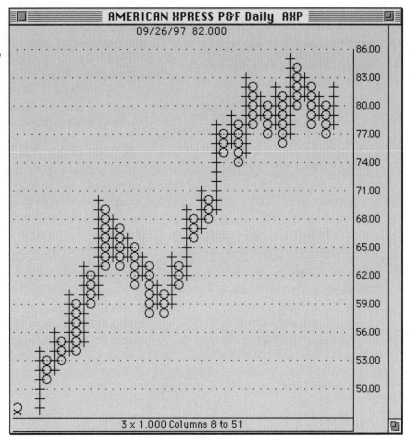

ly recommendations for commodities and stocks. Lastly, candle pattern alerts inform you when new candlestick patterns form and personal system alerts let you define buy and sell alerts based on 30 technical elements.

All of Trendsetter's products are easy to use and, with the help of the well-written manuals, easy to learn. By offering such a variety of programs, Trendsetter offers something for every technician—from the novice to the veteran day trader.

MegaTech Chart System	
Performance	3
Usefulness	4
Documentation	4
Ease of Use	3
Value	3

MegaTech Chart System
by Ret-Tech Software
$175—DOS, Windows 3.x/95
(847) 382-3903
www.rettech.com

MegaTech stands alone as the only DOS-based technical analysis program reviewed in the chapter. The program has remained static over the past several years while the computing world has seemingly passed it by. While it is a DOS-based system, it does attempt to shed the misconception that DOS programs are cumbersome and difficult to use. The commands to create windows, add price data and apply technical indicators have been reduced to a few simple keystrokes. In case you get confused, both the manual and on-line technical indicator directory provide guidance.

While the program offers most of the functions the average user needs, it does lack some of the more advanced features, such as backtesting. However, it makes up for this by including several unique features of its own. One such feature is its indicator plotting—rather than saving the entire collection of price data and the underlying indicators, it saves only the relative references. This is useful if you lack significant free hard disk space. You can save several pages of securities with different indicators without duplicating the large amount of space taken up by the historical data.

Indicators
With 50 technical indicators and studies, MegaTech offers analysis capabilities to satisfy all but the savviest technical investors. With the "tech on tech" feature, you can create your own technical studies based on the results of other technical studies. For example, after plotting a relative strength indicator, you can take the underlying data results and create a moving average of the relative strength.

Charts
MegaTech allows you to create as many as 16 charts on your screen simultaneously. Each chart may use daily, weekly, or monthly formats. Depending on your system's memory, you can display almost 15 years of daily data, 70 years of weekly data and monthly charts dating back to the 1880s. When you update your data, the program automatically updates any charts you have created.

FIGURE 6.37
IBM price plots and 10-day moving average of RSI created with MegaTech's "tech on tech" function.

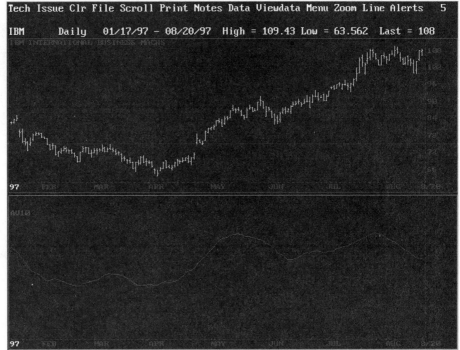

Other features and functions include customizable alerts for high and low price or volume breakouts and the spread feature, which enables you to create multi-issue spreads on various options.

Data Sources

MegaTech supports a variety of data sources. The program can access the Ret-Tech BBS and provide availability to various utility programs that can be used to handle different data formats. A utility for Dial/Data, Radio Exchange, Signal and Final Markets from Knight-Ridder can be obtained from Ret-Tech for free. ASCII text file importing and exporting is also available.

MegaTech is surprisingly easy to use for a DOS program. It only takes a few key-strokes to create a chart and overlay a variety of technical indicators and studies. The well-developed manual provides in-depth descriptions of the indicators offered. If you're looking for a strong technical analysis program and prefer DOS, MegaTech Chart System may be for you.

MetaStock 6.5 MetaStock Professional	
Performance	5
Usefulness	5
Documentation	5
Ease of Use	5
Value	5

MetaStock 6.5
MetaStock Professional
by Equis International
$349 for 6.5; $1,495 for Professional—
Windows 95/98/NT
(800) 822-3040
www.metastock.com

Equis International is one of the most influential and innovative companies offering technical analysis software. Its two flagship programs—MetaStock 6.5 and MetaStock Professional—are among the most complete technical analysis packages on the market today. Along with providing an impressive array of indicators and trading systems, it's also as easy to use as Microsoft Office products such as Word or Excel. Being completely object-oriented, MetaStock allows you to modify and move every on-screen object with a simple "point and click" of the mouse. With the introduction of MetaStock Professional, Equis also offers a Windows-based real-time analysis package.

Charting and Analysis
Both versions of MetaStock have an arsenal of over 100 technical indicators and line studies. If this isn't enough, or if you wish to modify an existing indicator, you can use the indicator builder. Here you can choose from over 200 mathematical, statistical, and technical functions for designing your own custom indicators. Furthermore, you are able to reference existing custom indicators when creating new ones. Unlike some other systems that offer custom indicators and system design, MetaStock's is not a true programming environment. Compared to Omega Research's EasyLanguage, it is easier to learn and, consequently, easier to create your own indicators and systems. However, it does not offer the flexibility that EasyLanguage does.

MetaStock offers an extensive collection of charting styles and unparalleled charting capabilities. Nine different charting styles are available—bars, candlesticks, line, point and figure, and candlevolume. MetaStock charts can also plot 32,000 data points—over 100 years of daily price data! Another useful feature of MetaStock is the data that is packaged with the program: five years' worth of historical data on over 21,000 securities.

You can easily manipulate and customize charts using MetaStock's drag and drop feature. Price plots, indicators and chart windows can be moved within charts by simply clicking on the elements and dropping them into another chart or window.

FIGURE 6.38
The Help system in MetaStock offers instruction on how to interpret the various indicators supplied with the program. The interpretation for the Bollinger bands plotted on the candlestick chart of Edison International is displayed here.

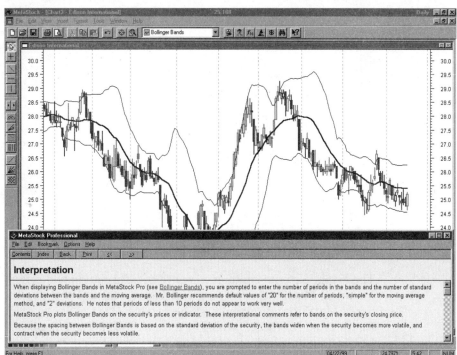

Explorer

The explorer function that comes with the program allows you to compare, filter, rank, search, and list multiple indicator values for multiple securities. You can view a list of securities that are generating either buy or sell signals or that have broken some predefined barrier in terms of price or technical indicator.

Internet Connectivity

Recognizing the growing importance of the Internet in investing and analysis, MetaStock includes Internet integration for obtaining up-to-date information. With just a few mouse clicks, you have access to 20-minute delayed quotes and current news and information on every security in the MetaStock database. Through the Reuters Money Network Web site, you get free portfolio tracking and fundamental information as well.

FIGURE 6.39
The pre-installed screening strategies available with Equis' Explorer.

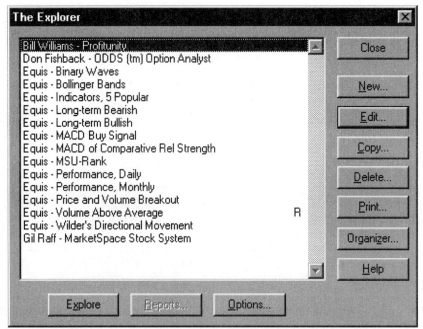

The Equis Web site contains a wealth of information and educational material—including MetaStock Online, a Web-based, scaled-down version of the software-based MetaStock program, and the complete text of Steve Achelis' (founder of Equis) book "Technical Analysis From A to Z." The book is an excellent way to learn about the technical indicators you run across in the programs. The site also offers a collection of market commentaries, troubleshooting tips, and technical support.

Expert Advisors
To help users get a handle on what a technical indicator is telling them, Equis includes 27 Expert Advisors—a collection of technical commentaries based on the current technical condition of a given security. These commentaries were designed by such industry experts as John Bollinger, Greg Morris, and Martin Pring. When you open an Expert Advisor, buy and sell signals are plotted on the chart in question. You can also create your own Market Advisors using the Indicator Builder.

FIGURE 6.40
Attaching an Expert System to a given stock will generate buy and sell signals according to the specific system. Here Martin Pring's Long-Term Momentum System has been applied to CMS Energy.

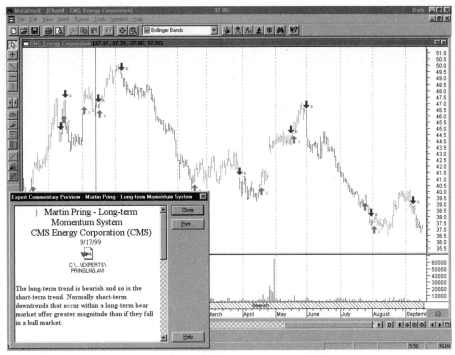

System Building and Backtesting

MetaStock offers several predefined trading systems, and allows you to create your own systems, all of which can be backtested. For the more advanced technical analysts, MetaStock allows you to write and backtest trading systems. You can set entry/exit conditions, commission amounts and other details, and the system tester tests the security to calculate how much real money would have been made or lost using the trading system. MetaStock can also optimize trading systems to help determine which parameters work best for a given trading system and compare systems to see which would be more profitable.

Data Compatibility

MetaStock includes a single-vendor version of the Downloader software. This data collection program automatically collects price updates, tests data for accuracy, checks for data errors, adjusts for stock splits and reinvests mutual fund dividends. You have access to either Dial/Data or Reuters Trend Datalink for data downloading.

If you are not sure which data vendor you want to use, MetaStock gives you tremendous latitude when it comes to selecting one. A six-vendor version of the Downloader is available for an additional $59, which allows downloading from CompuServe, DBC Signal, Dial/Data, Dow Jones, Reuters Datalink, and Telescan.

MetaStock Professional

Of the top contenders in the real-time analysis forum, MetaStock Professional is the leader in value. All of the features outlined here are found on both version 6.5 and Professional. However, Professional provides you with tick-by-tick analysis capability, whereas MetaStock 6.5 offers analysis on an end-of-day basis.

MetaStock 6.5 is one of the strongest offerings on the technical analysis software market today for end-of-day analysis, as is the case with MetaStock Professional in the arena of real-time analysis. Both programs offer comprehensive collections of technical indicators and trading systems to satisfy almost any trader. The wealth of tutorials makes it well suited for technical analysis neophytes. MetaStock's technical screening, system creation, and testing capabilities make it a powerful tool for seasoned technicians. Its ease-of-use allows you to begin your analysis almost right out of the box. If you do get stuck, MetaStock comes with exceptional documentation that walks you through virtually every function of the program. These factors make the program well worth its higher price. If you are looking for strong real-time analysis at a reasonable price, you will be hard pressed to find a competitor to top MetaStock Professional.

OmniTrader	
Performance	4
Usefulness	4
Documentation	5
Ease of Use	4
Value	4

OmniTrader 4.0
by Nirvana Systems, Inc.
Stocks Edition $395/Futures Edition $695/
Real-time $1,995—Windows 95/98/NT
(800) 880-0338
www.nirv.com

For those who are interested in following a system trading approach but do not want to deal with the hassle of creating systems, OmniTrader may be your platform of choice. OmniTrader attempts to automate the entire analysis and trading process—it collects data on a real-time, delayed, or end-of-day basis, tests over 120 trading systems against a database of over 12,000 securities, generates buy/sell signals, processes trade orders, and tracks your positions. As with all programs that offer their own trading systems, be sure you understand the various systems before you commit your own money to trading them.

Analysis Tools

Using Nirvana Systems' adaptive reasoning model, OmniTrader adapts to each security's personality. As the program tests its trading systems on the database of securities, it will only select the systems that are performing the best in the current market condition. Those systems generate signals that OmniTrader uses to form a consensus trading signal.

After OmniTrader has made its buy/sell signals, it provides a breakdown of the analysis. By clicking on any of the signals displayed on the chart, a trading adviser reports which trading system(s) generated the signal. Trading assistants automatically categorize and display patterns such as automatic trendlines, candle patterns, and automatic support and resistance levels. By clicking on the assistant's tag, the trading adviser highlights the pattern and its importance.

FIGURE 6.41
A daily candlestick chart for Minnesota Power & Light with the automatic trendlines drawn. The Focus List on the left illustrates the overall signals being generated for each stock.

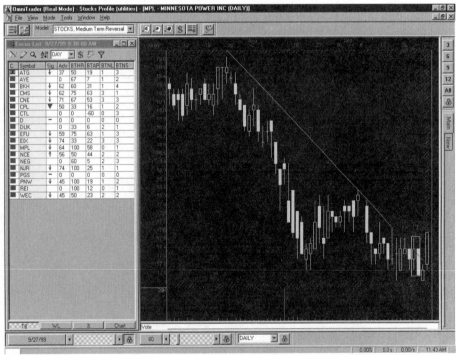

To further the analysis process, the to-do list automatically retrieves data, updates the current positions in the portfolio manager, tests the trading systems to find those that are the most profitable for each security, and calculates signals for a focus list. The focus list is a summary of each day's trading signals. With it, you are given a variety of statistics including the percentage of winning trades, number of long and short trades, etc. You can configure the list so that only the information that interests you is displayed. A portfolio manager tracks an unlimited number of accounts, maintains the current valuation of your trading positions, and can even generate a Schedule D for tax purposes.

Trading Simulators

In order to help you become more familiar with the program and to become more confident in your trading skills, OmniTrader offers two trading simulators. The first, called the trading game, allows you to practice trading a single security. The second, called the lab mode, allows you to practice trading a portfolio of securities.

The trading game and lab mode trading simulations test your theories without risking your money. The trading game simulates market conditions by recreating the true market activity of a single security. The lab mode recreates the experience of trading a portfolio of securities. While using these systems, a "bank" holds your trading capital and an equity curve tracks your results against time.

FIGURE 6.42
An illustration of the "game" mode in OmniTrader.

Futures Trading

For traders interested in futures, OmniTrader also comes in a Futures Edition. Just as it does with stock and mutual funds, this version automates the analysis process for futures. It will roll over to the next contract automatically, build continuous contracts, and provide alerts to first notice days. You also get free access to commitment of traders (COT) data via the Nirvana Systems Web site. COT data, which is published every two weeks by the Commodity Futures Trading Commission (CFTC), contains the long and short positions in the futures market. Traders use this data to determine if trends are developing. Lastly, you receive seasonality graphs that show you the seasonal tendencies of contracts.

Real-Time Option

Nirvana released a real-time version of OmniTrader that can be used with intraday delayed and real-time data services. It offers all of the features and capabilities of both the Stocks and Futures editions in real-time.

OmniTrader offers one of the most extensive collections of technical trading systems of any technical analysis software package. Using the simulation labs to test systems without risking your own money is an invaluable educational tool. The backtesting capabilities and signal generation make it a tool well suited for experienced traders. There is an assumption, however, that you do not want to perform more personalized analysis. You are not given the flexibility to customize trading indicators or strategies that you have with other programs. While you can alter and optimize systems, you are not able to generate systems from scratch. Compared to some other technical analysis packages, OmniTrader does take some getting used to. However, Nirvana provides you with concise documentation that should help you learn the functionality of the program.

ProTA 2.11 ProTA Gold	
Performance	5
Usefulness	5
Documentation	5
Ease of Use	5
Value	5

ProTA 2.11
ProTA Gold
by BeeSoft
ProTA $59; ProTA Gold $199—Macintosh
(800) 840-3588
www.beesoft.net

ProTA from BeeSoft is a relative newcomer to the technical analysis field. However, over its short life it has made great strides that now make it a serious competitor for Mac-based technical analysis platforms.

Charting and Analysis

For the analysis of stocks, mutual funds, indexes, futures, options, and bonds, ProTA has all of the popular chart types—close, bar, point and figure, and candlesticks. In addition, it offers over 40 fully customizable technical indicators and line studies. Users can also save chart templates with their preferences for display, indicators, etc., as well as run an automated "slide show" of charts.

Portfolio Tracking and Management

ProTA's portfolio sheets provide you with up to 20 columns of information in a spreadsheet-like format. You can keep track of such trade-specific information as purchase data, number of shares or contracts purchased, commissions, etc. The portfolio automatically calculates statistics including cost basis, profit/loss, and return on investment. You can track technical information such as moving average values and volume activity, as well as enter trade entries and exits and track overall performance.

ProTA Gold

ProTA Gold has all of the same functions as ProTA 2.11, as well as some advanced features found on high-end technical analysis packages. If you aren't satisfied with the existing library of technical indicators, ProTA Gold gives you the added flexibility of creating an unlimited number of your own custom indicators. Users can also download custom indicators from the BeeSoft Web site and install them into their program or post their own creations.

FIGURE 6.43
Specifying entry conditions for a simple moving average system in ProTA Gold.

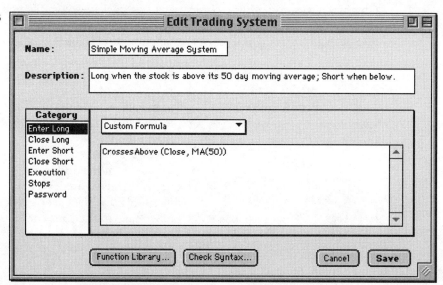

For those of you who are interested in creating your own trading systems, ProTA Gold offers that functionality. You can specify trading rules for entering and exiting both long and short trades. Once you have created your trading systems, you can plot buy/sell points of a chart, generate trade lists and summary statistics, and optimize the system.

ProTA Gold will scan for securities that meet your criteria. You can specify one or several technical and performance-based values and the program can scan the database or a portfolio to find those securities that fit the parameters. Those securities that pass the screen are then placed in a portfolio sheet where you can view and/or rank the results.

FIGURE 6.44
Creating scan criteria in ProTA Gold.

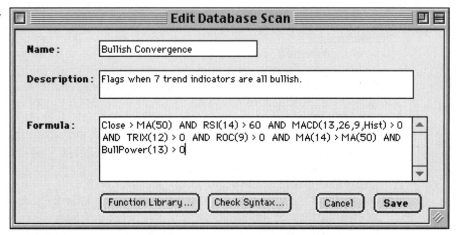

BeeSoft has two quality programs with ProTA 2.11 and ProTA Gold. The programs themselves are intuitive and easy to use and the documentation should steer you straight should any confusion arise. With ProTA, the charting capabilities and collection of technical indicators you are given make it an exceptional value. With the addition of custom indicator building, trading system, testing, and screening you have a robust program that could easily cost hundreds of dollars more.

SMARTrader	
Performance	4
Usefulness	5
Documentation	4
Ease of Use	3
Value	5

SMARTrader

by Stratagem Software International, Inc.
$299—Windows
(504) 885-7353
www.stratagem1.com

The lineage of SMARTrader can be traced back to one of the fixtures of early technical analysis programs—CompuTrac. While CompuTrac has faded from the field, SMARTrader lives on as a platform for charting, technical analysis, and trading system testing.

SpecSheet

Similar to Behold!, SMARTrader is built around what is called a "specsheet" (short for specification sheet), which is divided into the definition window and the spreadsheet. The definition window is where you specify the information you wish the spreadsheet to calculate—such as data files, indicators, and entry and exit rules. The spreadsheet is where the actual raw data, studies, formulae, and profit results are calculated and displayed. In addition, a specsheet can have a "ChartFamily," where spreadsheet values are displayed in graphical form.

SmartSearch and SmartView

SMARTrader allows you to automate tasks using SmartSearch and SmartView. With SmartSearch, the program will search the database to find securities that meet user-defined criteria. Securities that meet the criteria are placed on a "hot list" and SMARTrader will draw price charts using indicators you specify. The SmartView function allows you to draw price charts and view them. "Browse" mode cycles through the charts automatically using a time interval of your choice.

QuickCharts

SMARTrader includes quickcharts, a simple charting utility that allows you to chart securities and select from a few basic technical indicators to overlay.

Some of the other features that come with SMARTrader include a formula builder for creating custom technical variables, a profitability testing system that tracks all open and closed positions, and a portfolio manager that tracks all open positions of a trade.

FIGURE 6.45
Point & figure chart, specsheet, and data window for the S&P 500 in SMARTrader.

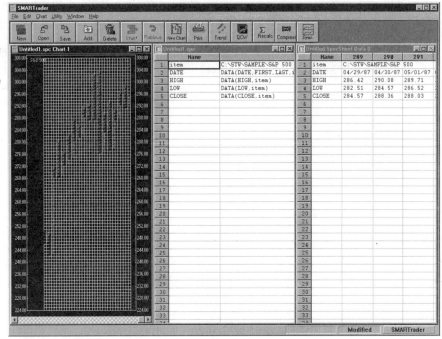

While SMARTrader offers many of the functions and features of today's more advanced technical analysis packages, it is not as polished as most. The specsheets seem a bit cumbersome when you first start, but after building several systems, you begin to see the intuition behind it. These two factors may not make it a package of choice for the aspiring technical analyst. However, if you are familiar with technical analysis and are willing to put forth the effort, SMARTrader offers solid analysis and testing capabilities without the platinum price.

SuperCharts	
Performance	5
Usefulness	5
Documentation	5
Ease of Use	5
Value	5

SuperCharts 4.0
TradeStation 2000i
by Omega Research
$395 for SuperCharts (end-of-day); $1199.40 (real-time)—Windows; $2,399.40 for TradeStation—Windows 95/98/NT
(800) 556-2022
www.omegaresearch.com

Omega Research caters to a myriad of investors with its two products, SuperCharts and TradeStation. SuperCharts is geared toward end-of-day traders (though a real-time version is available) looking for in-depth analysis capabilities, trading system development, and testing at a reasonable price. TradeStation 2000*i* (formerly called TradeStation 5.0) is completely redesigned and rebuilt from TradeStation 4.0. Arguably the most advanced trading analysis system on the market, it is intended for investors who trade for a living, either on a commercial or personal level, and want to follow some sort of systematic approach in their trading. At $2,399, the program is an investment in itself and requires substantial computing resources as well.

Trading and Analysis Tools

TradeStation 2000*i*	
Performance	5
Usefulness	5
Documentation	5
Ease of Use	5
Value	4

SuperCharts is a strong contender in the technical analysis field. With one of the larger technical indicator libraries available—over 80—you have the ability to modify existing indicators and create your own. The program comes with expert analyst indicators that help explain what the indicators mean. In addition to defining the indicator, it discusses what each indicator is looking for, and in which market it should work best. The expert analyst indicator, when applied to a chart, identifies which indicators should work best in the charted market conditions, applies those indicators to the chart, and even reports whether the market is bearish, bullish, or neutral based on the indicator. You also have the capability of creating up to 1,000 custom indicators and studies.

System Building and Testing

With SuperCharts you can create your own trading systems and backtest them to see how they would have performed on a historical basis. After backtesting, the program will generate a system performance report so that you can see how well it would have performed. You can optimize trading systems as well. The program will test a range of parameters for a trading system and optimization reports will show you which values produced the largest and smallest profits.

Screening

Along with paintbar and show-me studies, users can have SuperCharts examine their charts and notify them of trendline breakouts, special chart patterns, moving average crossovers—any buy or sell opportunity you specify. Show-me and paintbar studies allow you to spot certain market conditions on a chart. They mark the bars on a chart that meet specific criteria by either plotting colored dots on the bar or by painting an on-line bar a certain color. With both, you are able to specify the conditions you are looking for. You specify the technical indicators that interest you and the program will analyze the symbols being tracked and generate a report that indicates which symbols triggered alerts. It will also mark the points at which various criteria are met on the charts.

FIGURE 6.46
SuperCharts'
SmartScan
feature cycles
through
portfolios,
directories,
etc., checking
for alerts.

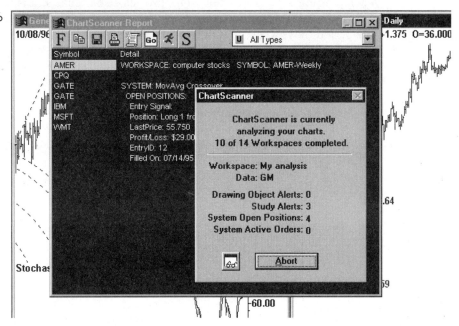

Real-Time
As mentioned, SuperCharts is also available in a real-time version. All of the features mentioned above are also found in the real-time version. In addition, with the quickwindow and quickmonitor features, you are able to access instant price quotes on any security at any point during the trading day. The newsmonitor application retrieves news headlines, full news stories, and even images and displays them on your screen.

TradeStation 2000i
Omega Research has taken one of the most widely-used real-time investment analysis packages on the market and has rebuilt it from the ground up for TradeStation 2000*i*. This high-end program is designed for those who wish to follow some form of systematic trading, whether it is fundamental or technical.

With the program's new research desktop, you are able to create and save workspaces with TradeStation and other Omega products as well as any other applications such as Internet browsers or spreadsheets.

Charting

When plotting with most open, high, low, close bar charts, it is impossible to know if the market had been trending upward or downward within a single bar's time period (day, week, month, etc.). In other words, given a standard open, high, low, close price chart, you cannot discern where the high or low price was hit first through the course of trading nor can you tell where the majority of the volume for the period took place. In TradeStation 2000i, you are able to view trading activity at the tick level and look at each individual trade that was made during the period using the "look inside a bar" system.

FIGURE 6.47
Daily bar chart of Microsoft from TradeStation 2000i with buy and sell signals generated by a moving average crossover trading system.

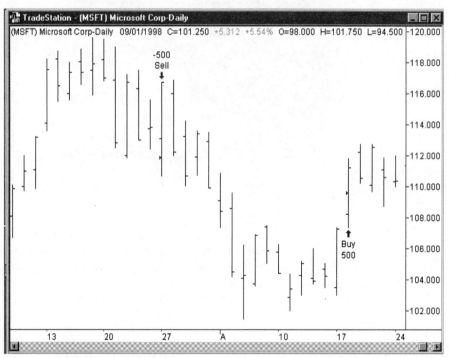

Figure 6.47 shows a standard bar chart. Beyond giving you the open, high, low, and closing price of Microsoft, it does nothing to tell you about the trading activity over the period. With the ActivityBar chart illustrated in Figure 6.48, how-

FIGURE 6.48
An hourly ActivityBar chart for Microsoft using TradeStation 2000i.

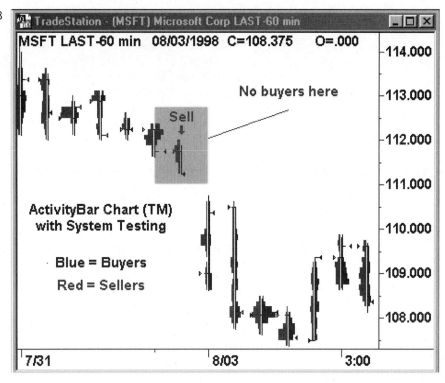

ever, you are able to see exactly at which prices Microsoft was being bought and sold at as well as the trading activity at the different price levels. These charts are dynamically updated when used in conjunction with a data feed.

Indicators

TradeStation provides charting and analysis tools that allow users to display charts and quote windows on their screen. More than 200 technical indicators are included that users can overlay on any chart. Users can create charts based on any user-defined period of time, number of transactions, or trade volume. The expert analyst indicators provide you with the expertise of Larry Williams and Tom DeMark, two top industry experts. You can use these indicators to analyze your charts and then read—in the experts' own words—what trends or significant tops or bottoms may be developing on the chart.

TradeStation also allows users to set alerts for specific patterns or market conditions. Users can set alerts on trendlines so an audio or visual alarm will sound when a trendline is penetrated by market activity.

System Building and Testing

Both SuperCharts and TradeStation allow users to write indicators, studies, or trading systems using the "EasyLanguage" PowerEditor. Omega Research claims that EasyLanguage, while a programming language, was designed with the non-programmer in mind. It does take some getting used to and is not as intuitive as one might be led to believe. However, EasyLanguage is an industry standard, so it is not uncommon to run across systems written in EasyLanguage being described in popular investment publications such as Technical Analysis of Stocks and Commodities.

FIGURE 6.49

The PowerEditor window in TradeStation 2000i.

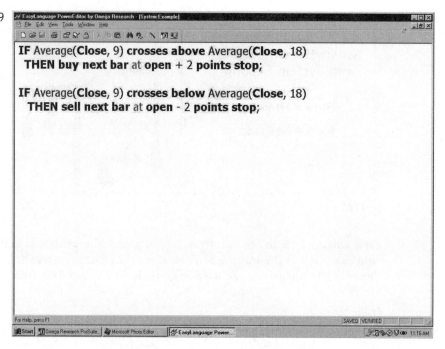

If you are uncomfortable with the idea of writing your own systems and studies, TradeStation 2000*i* provides the EasyLanguage wizard that allows you to create trading systems, indicators, show-me studies and paintbar studies by simply "picking and clicking." The program includes over 500 built-in functions you can use to get you started. TradeStation 2000*i* comes loaded with over 100 pre-written entry and exit conditions.

Once you have designed a system, you test and optimize the system and receive system performance summaries that contain information such as total net profit, total number of winning and losing trades, and return on account. In all, Trade-

Station 2000*i* offers over 100 performance ratios and graphs to determine the profitability of your portfolio. With the ability to "look inside" bars with TradeStation, you can test systems right down to the tick. The expanded system reports allow you view the test by trade, day, month, or year.

Data

Also new to TradeStation 2000*i* is the Omega GlobalServer that allows you to collect data for every symbol sent by any compatible data provider. You are given data collection templates that you can choose from and the program will automatically download the specified issues, the time interval (one minute, hour, day, etc.), and the time period. The number of data providers from which you can choose has been expanded and includes DBC Signal and BMI, Signal Online, StockEdge Online, InSite, PC Quote and PC Quote Online, and DTN. With the browser function, you can select a symbol and automatically access Internet information for the symbol from numerous information providers.

Both products incorporate a historical database of securities (which includes up to 25 years of historical stock, mutual fund, index and futures data). The enormous storage capacity available with the CD-ROM means that the amount of hard disk space needed is significantly low. The historical data is saved and accessed through the CD; only new data is stored on your hard drive. When displayed, the program merges the historical data on the CD-ROM and the new data from the hard drive. With some other CD-ROM-based data services, all pertinent data must be transferred to your hard drive, thus taking up more space.

Trade Placement and Fulfillment

TradeStation 2000*i*'s increased Internet integration allows you to place orders on-line. If your analysis indicates either a buy or sell opportunity, TradeStation can be linked with your on-line broker. The program will ask if you want to place the trade, place the trade for you, and will automatically inform you when the order is filled and report the price at which it was filled.

Computing Needs

Just as TradeStation is for the serious investor, it also requires some serious computing power. Most of the programs in this chapter can operate on today's average computer with a Pentium processor, 16 to 32 megabytes of memory (RAM) and anywhere from 10 to 75 megabytes of free hard disk space. However, to get the best performance from TradeStation 2000*i*, Omega recommends at least 48 megabytes of RAM and anywhere from 130 to 230 megabytes of free hard disk space, depending on whether or not you are using a real-time data feed.

FIGURE 6.50
With TradeStation 2000i's Internet integration, you can retrieve company research or place trades.

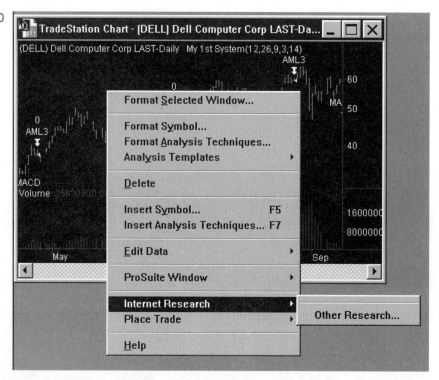

TradeStation Chart - [DELL] Dell Computer Corp LAST-Da...

(DELL) Dell Computer Corp LAST-Daily   My 1st System(12,26,9,3,14)

Format Selected Window...

Format Symbol...
Format Analysis Techniques...
Analysis Templates   ▶

Delete

Insert Symbol...   F5
Insert Analysis Techniques... F7

Edit Data   ▶

ProSuite Window   ▶

Internet Research   ▶
Place Trade   ▶   Other Research...

Help

> **Warning→**   TradeStation 2000*i* requires a system with above-normal computing power. You should have a system with a Pentium processor, at least 48M of memory, and at least 130M of free hard disk space.

Omega Research is definitely a market leader in investment analysis software. Both SuperCharts and TradeStation are well-designed platforms that cater to the more casual, end-of-day trader, as well as the serious day trader. If you aren't interested in real-time capabilities, SuperCharts offers extensive charting and testing. The redesign of TradeStation places it at the top for those looking for a real-time analysis tool. Its price and stockpile of analysis tools make it suited for the serious day trader who trades for a living. If you are looking for real-time analysis but are leery of TradeStation's price tag, SuperCharts Real-Time gives you a middle-of-the-road alternative. All of Omega Research's programs can be used practically right out of the box; they are highly intuitive and also provide in-depth documentation and on-line tutorials. The level of analysis both programs offer is among the best in the market, making the programs well worth the price.

TC2000	
Performance	4
Usefulness	4
Documentation	5
Ease of Use	5
Value	5

TC2000 4.2
by Worden Brothers, Inc.
Free—Windows 95/98/NT
(800) 776-4940
www.tc2000.com

When discussing high-end technical analysis systems, chances are you will run across companies such as Omega Research, Equis International, and Window on WallStreet. The programs these companies provide, as already shown, can cost hundreds and even thousands of dollars and can do practically everything you can ask for in technical analysis. However, for those looking for a simple, easy-to-use technical analysis and charting system for a reasonable price, the one name that consistently appears at the top of the list is Worden Brothers and its TC2000 program.

Indicators

When compared to other technical analysis programs, TC2000 does not provide as extensive a technical indicator library. However, when TC2000 was released as a Windows program in 1998, Worden increased the number of indicators that come with the program—now at 12. Along with this expanded library of indicators are the proprietary indicators: balance of power (BOP), moneystream, and time segmented volume. The balance of power indicator provides insight into the underlying action of a security's price movement. It depicts a trend of systematic buying or selling of a security. Moneystream is a price/volume indicator, resembling the on-balance volume indicator. Bullish and bearish messages are signaled by divergences in the indicator.

Analysis

To help in the analysis process, TC2000 provides you with "Worden Notes." These notes are based upon the trading ideas of Don and Peter Worden. You can view the charts they used and learn from their indicator choices and analysis ideas. The notes are delivered to you throughout, as well as at the end of, the trading day.

Lists

So that you do not have to sift through the nearly 10,000 stocks in the TC2000 database, you are given 384 lists from which to choose to narrow down the active set of companies. These lists include industry groups (Worden and Media Gener-

FIGURE 6.51
Illustration of TC2000's moneystream and balance of power indicators for GTE Corp.

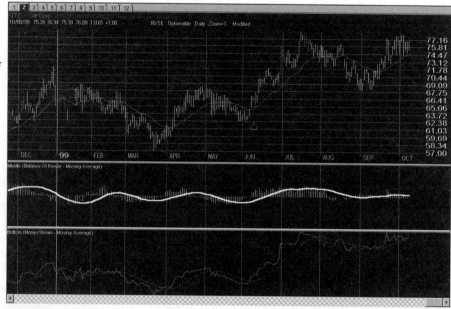

al classifications), indexes, or trading opportunities. Once presented with a list of stocks, you can then sort the list by one of over 50 fundamental criteria or by price performance.

EasyScan

Using the easyscan feature in TC2000, you are able to locate those symbols that meet your custom criteria. Simultaneously you can scan for long-term technical and/or fundamental conditions, as well as intraday conditions. In all, you have over 40 pre-installed scans from which to choose, although you are also able to build your own. The process is relatively easy and straightforward—select the data elements in which you are interested and their respective ranges and let the program go to work. Once you have created a scan, the program can show you the individual criteria and how many companies passed each one. This way you can easily see those criteria that are too stringent and those that are too lax.

Data

Worden Brothers has offered data along with its analysis program from its start. Industry publications such as Technical Analysis of Stocks & Commodities hail the service as being "clean" and inexpensive. As a data provider alone TC2000 is a good value—less than $30 a month for unlimited downloads. At just over $1 a day users can download data as often as they want. Many users export the data

FIGURE 6.52
Desktop for TC2000. The watchlist on the top left allows you to sort the database hundreds of different ways. At the bottom left are the Worden Notes—commentary on what is happening with a given company.

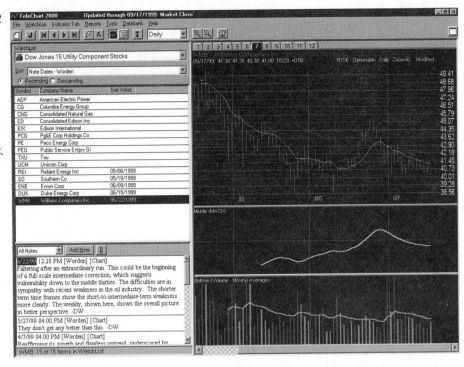

for use with other programs. However, one shortcoming to purchasing the data alone is that most other programs do not directly download from TC2000. Data must be imported, thus adding an extra step to the process.

Although TC2000 lacks the extensive charting, backtesting and analysis capabilities that many of the programs discussed in this chapter offer, for simple graphing and introductory analysis work TC2000 is unrivalled in the area of introductory technical analysis software. In addition, it is hard to ignore that Worden is giving away the program. The documentation and short-cut keys make for easy navigation. For those looking for simple charting and solid analysis capabilities in a clean, easy-to-use format, TC2000 should meet your needs.

TIP@Wallstreet	
Performance	5
Usefulness	5
Documentation	5
Ease of Use	4
Value	5

TIP@Wallstreet 1.2
by Telescan, Inc.
$199 ($349 w/ProSearch)—Windows
(800) 324-8246
www.wallstreetcity.com

In discussing other technical analysis programs such as MetaStock and Internet Trader Pro, you can clearly see the growing importance the Internet is playing in investing. Over the past few years, more and more companies have started integrating the Internet into their programs. Telescan was one of the first companies to take this step when it introduced TIP@Wallstreet. This program combines the fundamental and technical analysis capabilities of the Telescan Investor's Platform (TIP) as well as the news, information, and analysis available at the Wall Street City Web site (www.wallstreetcity.com). The marriage of these two entities creates a package that offers the fundamental and technical analysis and charting capabilities of the TIP software with the comprehensive research offered at the Wall Street City Web site.

Charting
The program offers charting capabilities as well as technical and fundamental analysis. TIP@Wallstreet is unique in that you download the charts from Telescan, not the data. The auto-run function allows you to create lists of securities and then download graphs with a single command. You can specify the time frame of the graph and the indicator, if any, to be plotted. This saves you significant on-line time since you are not downloading raw data. TIP allows you to plot multiple indicators of the same graph. With the autologon feature, you can program the system to automatically retrieve portfolio data, company and market news, and download graphs.

Indicators
Over 80 technical indicators are provided including stochastics, MACD, Bollinger bands, candlesticks and more. With profitability testing and optimizing testing, you can use the program to test the effectiveness of buy/sell signals generated by technical indicators. Optimizing identifies the combination of indicators that produce the best results. By selecting the "best" indicators in terms of predicting profitable trends, you can create a trading system that, in theory, is more profitable.

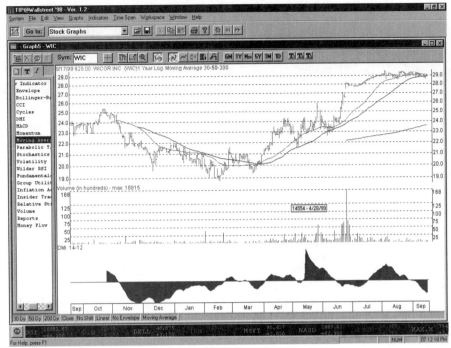

FIGURE 6.53
Price and volume plots of WICOR with 25-, 50-, and 200-day moving averages and DMI indicator using TIP@Wallstreet.

ProSearch Module

Telescan's ProSearch Module is one of the most powerful stock screening features available with a technical analysis program. Whether you are using one of the 30 sample searches or creating your own using as many as 40 of the over 280 technical and fundamental criteria, you can find the top-ranked stocks based on value, growth, technical, momentum, etc. Furthermore you can backtest the results of the screens to see how the various search strategies would have performed over time. Using the ProSearch builder feature, you can select a stock and have the program find similar performing stocks.

For active traders, ProSearch alerts scans thousands of stocks and alerts you to technical breakouts—in real-time. Every five minutes alerts scans the Telescan database based on over 100 technical criteria and displays the results.

Data

With TIP, you have access to one of the most comprehensive databases for historical statistical and textual information. It covers over 8,000 stocks, 2,000 mutual funds, 256 industry groups, 100 market indexes and 40,000 options. Historical price and volume data dates back 25 years and 20-minute delayed

FIGURE 6.54
*Screening
criteria using
the ProSearch
module of
TIP@Wallstreet.*

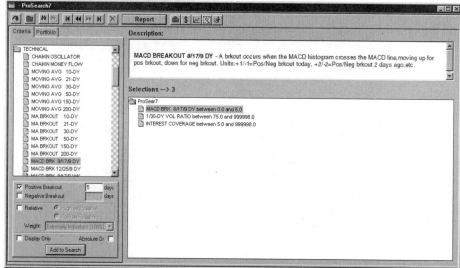

quotes are provided for securities listed on the New York Stock Exchange, the American Stock Exchange and Nasdaq. Twenty-four-hour news coverage and an archive of stories are also maintained for over 7,000 companies.

The imbedded Web browser gives you access to additional information from such sources as Zacks Investment Research, Market Guide, S&P MarketScope, and Macro*World Outlook reports.

For those who like to combine both technical and fundamental analysis when making investment decisions, TIP@Wallstreet is one of the best programs on the market. For the full range of analysis and information provided, the program is very reasonably priced. It is an easy program to use—however, as with all information-based services, you can rack up a substantial bill depending on the types of services used and the time spent on-line.

TradingExpert Pro	
Performance	5
Usefulness	5
Documentation	5
Ease of Use	4
Value	5

TradingExpert Pro
by AIQ Systems
$995—Windows
(800) 332-2999
www.aiq.com

TradingExpert Pro from AIQ Systems is a market timing and stock screening application that combines charting, technical analysis, system design and testing, as well as portfolio management into one package for the serious technician. The artificial intelligence program provides you with expert systems that analyze stocks in order to find those that may be technically ready to move either up or down. The expert systems are programmed using the rules of technical experts.

Market Timing
For market timing, TradingExpert offers its expert rating, which signals possible changes in the market direction. The market timing model compares the Dow to the activity of the broad market, which is represented by the New York Stock Exchange market breadth and the number of NYSE stocks reaching new highs and lows. Each chart you create with the program will have, among other things, a daily expert rating. For those interested in sector and group analysis, TradingExpert Pro has a group/sector report that ranks groups by trend score.

Indicators
When you create a chart, you are given an area that lists the values of over 50 indicators in the program, providing you with an assessment of the technical indicators. Using red and green arrows, you can see indications of a strong uptrend or downtrend, respectively. Arrows in yellow zones show signs of strength or weakness.

System Building
The expert design studio module that comes with TradingExpert Pro allows you to design, backtest, and optimize your own trading systems. The report writer screens data using your trading systems and generates customized reports listing the information and securities that meet your trading criteria. To get you started, the expert design studio gives you a wide selection of trading systems that you can use or modify to meet your own needs and trading behavior. For those interested in fundamental elements, you can purchase AIQ's fundamental module

FIGURE 6.55
TradingExpert Pro's 'color barometer' shows you the status of the technicals for a given company.

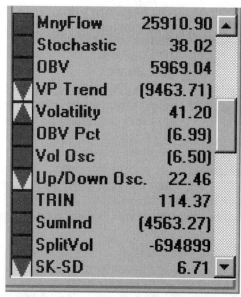

MnyFlow	25910.90	▲
Stochastic	38.02	
OBV	5969.04	
VP Trend	(9463.71)	
Volatility	41.20	
OBV Pct	(6.99)	
Vol Osc	(6.50)	
Up/Down Osc.	22.46	
TRIN	114.37	
SumInd	(4563.27)	
SplitVol	-694899	
SK-SD	6.71	▼

(for an additional $88) that gives you up to 300 fundamental factors to use with the expert design studio. Any of the systems you create or that come with the program can then be backtested.

With TradingExpert, you can condense the information into one- and two-page reports. These reports are customizable and include weighted action lists that consist of stocks that are poised for a technical move, group and sector reports, trendline breakouts that alert you when a stock, sector/group, or mutual fund crosses a trendline, and price and volume reports.

Data Compatibility
TradingExpert Pro is compatible with several popular data services, including Dial/Data, TrackData's myTrack, and eSignal from DBC. Subscribers to myTrack can add support of TradingExpert Pro to their subscription for as low as $59 for delayed data and $79 for real-time. Users of eSignal can add TradingExpert to their service for $49 a month, plus a one-time registration fee.

TradingExpert offers a well-designed market timing and analysis program. The artificial intelligence rules programmed into it offer you more extensive and powerful analysis capabilities. Despite the program's advanced nature, the programmers were thoughtful in making it easy to navigate and use. The documentation

FIGURE 6.56
*ExpertSystem
for the Dow in
TradingExpert
Pro.*

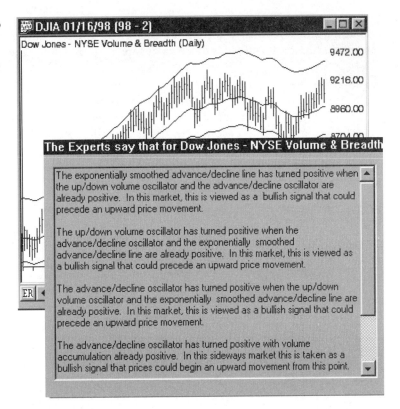

is first-rate, allowing you to become familiar with the program's features. Also included is the technical indicators manual, which explains each indicator in detail. In addition, the monthly payment option eases the financial burden.

VectorVest ProGraphics	
Performance	4
Usefulness	4
Documentation	4
Ease of Use	4
Value	4

VectorVest ProGraphics 5.0
by VectorVest, Inc.
$39-$49/mo.–$545/yr.—Windows
(888) 658-7638
www.vectorvest.com

VectorVest ProGraphics provides a combination of fundamental and technical analysis as well as unique indicators based on a stock's value, safety, and timing. The uniqueness accounts for the apparent lack of technical indicators you see when viewing the comparison grid at the end of this chapter. This stock analysis and graphics system allows you to analyze, sort, screen, search, rank and graph stocks, industry groups and sectors by any of 29 investment parameters, including pre-installed indicators of safety, timing and value.

Navigation

At the heart of ProGraphics is a stock viewer feature, providing analysis of value, safety, timing, volume, price, earnings and dividends on over 6,000 stocks, 190 industry groups, and 50 business sectors.It contains 65 days of daily history and 52 weeks of weekly history. With the stock viewer, you can analyze, sort, screen, search and rank all stocks, industry groups and business sectors in both the daily and weekly modes.

FIGURE 6.57
Illustration of ProGraphic's stock viewer.

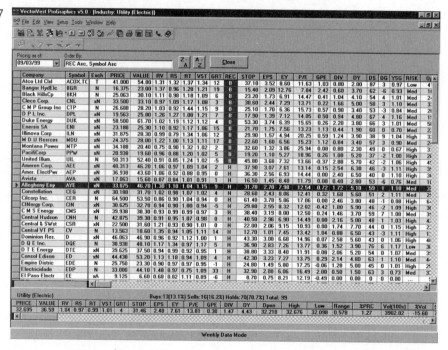

Analysis

Fundamental factors provided by VectorVest include dividend, dividend yield, earnings per share, price-earnings ratio, risk, and industry. Technical factors provided include price (open, high, low, close), relative strength, relative timing, stop, volume, and average volume.

Each stock followed by ProGraphics is given a daily buy, sell or hold recommendation. Any stock whose price rises above the stop price gets a buy or hold rating. Stocks whose prices fall below their stop prices get a sell rating. The VectorVest views, which are obtained with your data downloads, offer a weekly commentary of the financial markets. They also offer opinions on whether the market is overvalued or undervalued as well as the market's overall trend.

FIGURE 6.58
VectorVest's stock analysis gives you insight into how a particular stock is performing and may perform based on ProGraphics proprietary indicators.

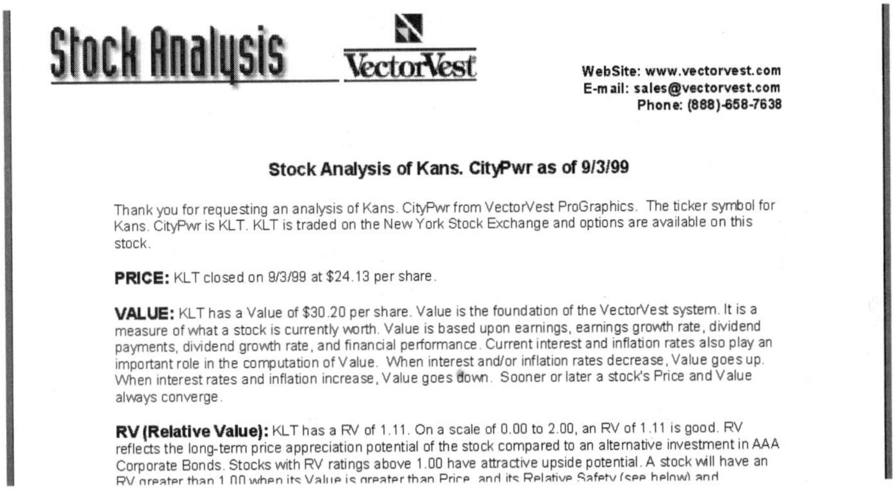

Stock Analysis

VectorVest

WebSite: www.vectorvest.com
E-mail: sales@vectorvest.com
Phone: (888)-658-7638

Stock Analysis of Kans. CityPwr as of 9/3/99

Thank you for requesting an analysis of Kans. CityPwr from VectorVest ProGraphics. The ticker symbol for Kans. CityPwr is KLT. KLT is traded on the New York Stock Exchange and options are available on this stock.

PRICE: KLT closed on 9/3/99 at $24.13 per share.

VALUE: KLT has a Value of $30.20 per share. Value is the foundation of the VectorVest system. It is a measure of what a stock is currently worth. Value is based upon earnings, earnings growth rate, dividend payments, dividend growth rate, and financial performance. Current interest and inflation rates also play an important role in the computation of Value. When interest and/or inflation rates decrease, Value goes up. When interest rates and inflation increase, Value goes down. Sooner or later a stock's Price and Value always converge.

RV (Relative Value): KLT has a RV of 1.11. On a scale of 0.00 to 2.00, an RV of 1.11 is good. RV reflects the long-term price appreciation potential of the stock compared to an alternative investment in AAA Corporate Bonds. Stocks with RV ratings above 1.00 have attractive upside potential. A stock will have an RV greater than 1.00 when its Value is greater than Price, and its Relative Safety (see below) and

Indicators

You can create graphs using VectorVest parameters and indicators or classic price, volume and moving average data. The program also offers a "trend-setter" function including pattern recognition, the ability to backtest strategies, and a portfolio manager feature.

The bulk of VectorVest's analysis revolves around a company's value, safety, and timing. By analyzing a company's earnings, earnings growth, dividends, and profitability, the program attempts to determine a relative value figure for that company. This denotes the growth potential of the stock price. A company's safety has to do with whether or not the growth potential of the stock price justifies the risk involved in investing in the company. Lastly, timing involves when to buy, sell, or hold a given stock. After calculating these individual variables, VectorVest ProGraphics combines them into a master indicator called the VST-Vector. This provides a common denominator to compare stocks—those with a high VST-Vector have the best combination of value, safety and timing as determined by VectorVest.

FIGURE 6.59
You are able to create line graphs for a stock's price as well as plot the VectorVest indicators to see how they fluctuate over time.

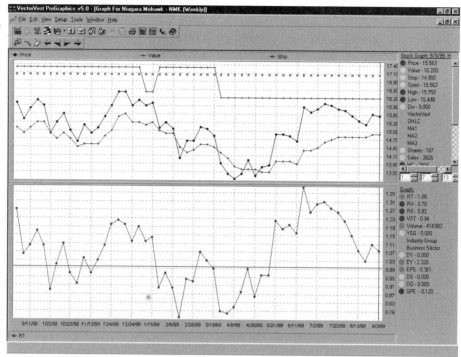

Data

Depending on the subscription, data can be downloaded on either a daily or weekly basis from VectorVest's own database, via the Internet or toll-free number. The fee structure is unique for this program in that the data costs are included in the cost of the program. Whether you subscribe on a yearly or monthly basis, you know how much the program will cost to operate since you will not accrue additional costs for the data.

While ProGraphics does not offer the extensive collection of technical indicators that most of the other programs here offer, it does offer some unique proprietary indicators. The platform of the program is not strictly technical, nor is it fundamental. Rather, ProGraphics focuses on three measures—timing, value and safety—to compare stocks. The program is rather easy to navigate and use and, to help you get started, you are provided with a multitude of tips on how to select stocks using the program.

Technical Analysis Program		Behold! 2.8	Day Trader Internet 7.5
Company		Investors' Technical Services	Window on WallStreet, Inc.
Telephone		(512) 367-4626	(800) 375-8522
Web Address		www.bhld.com	www.windowonwallstreet.com
E-mail		info@bhld.com	wowinfo@wallstreet.net
Price (AAII Discount)		$795	$1,499.95
Platform(s)		MacOS 7.5+	Windows 95/98/NT
Indicators	Number of predefined indicators	90	150
	Allows modification of pre-existing indicators	✖	✖
	Allows creation of new indicators	✖	✖
	Choice of indicator overlay or plot in new window	✖	✖
Charting Elements	Chart types: B=bar, C=candle, CV=candlevolume EV=equivolume, L=line, P&F=point and figure	B, C, L	B, C, L, P&F
	Number of predefined charts (chart templates)	14	40
	Create templates of indicators/trading systems	✖	✖
	Moveable trendlines	✖	✖
	Security merge feature	✖	✖
	Maximum number of charts displayed on screen	unlimited	limited only by memory
	Maximum number of data points per chart	unlimited	limited only by memory
Trading Systems	Backtesting	✖	✖
	Number of predefined trading systems	14	17
	Create & save custom trading systems	✖	✖
	Rank/compare systems against each other		✖
	Generate profit report of trading system	✖	✖
	Indicates maximum drawdown	✖	✖
	System stop methods: (trailing, max-loss, breakeven, profit target, etc.)	trailing, max-loss, breakeven, profit target	trailing, max-loss, breakeven
	Pre-defined entry/exit signals (black box)		✖
	User-defined entry/exit signals (by price, indicator)	✖	✖
	Considers trade position (long/short)	✖	✖
	Accounts for slippage/commission	✖	✖
Help Functions	On-line help	✖	✖
	Indicator interpretation help	✖	✖
Data Maintenance	Sources of data download	CSI, MJK	DTN, FDCN, DBC Signal, S&P Comstock, BMI
	Auto download feature	✖	✖
	Import formats	Trendsetter, ProTA, CompuTrac, ASCII	CSI, MetaStock, TC2000, ASCII, AIQ
	Export formats	ASCII	MetaStock, ASCII
	Handles distributions and splits	✖	✖
	Data conversion/merge feature	✖	✖
	Historical database included	✖	✖
Batch printing		✖	✖

Technical Analysis Program		FastBreak 2.6/ FastGraph 2.6	Insider TA Pro 4.0
Company		Edge Ware, Inc.	Stock Blocks, Inc.
Telephone		(703) 691-7913, (614) 475-5449	(800) 697-1617
Web Address		www.edge-ware.com	www.stockblocks.com
E-mail		info@edge-ware.com	insiderta@stockblocks.com
Price (AAII Discount)		FastBreak $299, FastGraph $199, Both $399	$295
Platform(s)		Windows 95/98/NT	Windows 3.x/95/98/NT
Indicators	Number of predefined indicators	7	4
	Allows modification of pre-existing indicators	✖	✖
	Allows creation of new indicators		
	Choice of indicator overlay or plot in new window	✖	✖
Charting Elements	Chart types: B=bar, C=candle, CV=candlevolume EV=equivolume, L=line, P&F=point and figure	B, C, L, P&F	B, C, EV
	Number of predefined charts (chart templates)	7	4
	Create templates of indicators/trading systems	✖	✖
	Moveable trendlines		✖
	Security merge feature	✖	
	Maximum number of charts displayed on screen	1	4
	Maximum number of data points per chart	34,000	2,600
Trading Systems	Backtesting	✖	✖
	Number of predefined trading systems	12	5
	Create & save custom trading systems	✖	✖
	Rank/compare systems against each other	✖	✖
	Generate profit report of trading system	✖	✖
	Indicates maximum drawdown	✖	✖
	System stop methods: (trailing, max-loss, breakeven, profit target, etc.)	trailing, profit target	trailing, max-loss, profit target
	Pre-defined entry/exit signals (black box)		✖
	User-defined entry/exit signals (by price, indicator)	✖	✖
	Considers trade position (long/short)	✖	✖
	Accounts for slippage/commission	✖	commission
Help Functions	On-line help		✖
	Indicator interpretation help		✖
Data Maintenance	Sources of data download	Investors FastTrack	QuotesPlus
	Auto download feature		
	Import formats	Investors FastTrack, ASCII	ASCII, MetaStock, TC2000, Quotes Plus
	Export formats		ASCII
	Handles distributions and splits	✖	✖
	Data conversion/merge feature		✖
	Historical database included		
Batch printing			

Technical Analysis Program		Internet Trader Pro 7.5	Investor/RT 3.8
Company		Window on WallStreet, Inc.	Linn Software, Inc.
Telephone		(800) 375-8522	(800) 546-6842
Web Address		www.windowonwallstreet.com	www.linnsoft.com
E-mail		wowinfo@wallstreet.net	sales@linnsoft.com
Price (AAII Discount)		$499	$995 (10%)
Platform(s)		Windows 95/98/NT	Windows 95/98/NT, MacOS 8.5
Indicators	Number of predefined indicators	150	75
	Allows modification of pre-existing indicators	✖	✖
	Allows creation of new indicators	✖	✖
	Choice of indicator overlay or plot in new window	✖	✖
Charting Elements	Chart types: B=bar, C=candle, CV=candlevolume EV=equivolume, L=line, P&F=point and figure	B, C, L, P&F	B, C, L, P&F
	Number of predefined charts (chart templates)	40	2
	Create templates of indicators/trading systems	✖	
	Moveable trendlines	✖	✖
	Security merge feature	✖	✖
	Maximum number of charts displayed on screen	limited only by memory	unlimited
	Maximum number of data points per chart	limited only by memory	unlimited
Trading Systems	Backtesting	✖	
	Number of predefined trading systems	17	10
	Create & save custom trading systems	✖	✖
	Rank/compare systems against each other	✖	
	Generate profit report of trading system	✖	
	Indicates maximum drawdown	✖	
	System stop methods: (trailing, max-loss, breakeven, profit target, etc.)	trailing, max-loss, breakeven	
	Pre-defined entry/exit signals (black box)	✖	
	User-defined entry/exit signals (by price, indicator)	✖	
	Considers trade position (long/short)	✖	
	Accounts for slippage/commission	✖	
Help Functions	On-line help	✖	✖
	Indicator interpretation help	✖	✖
Data Maintenance	Sources of data download	DTN, FDCN, DBC Signal, S&P Comstock, BMI	Signal, eSignal, BMI, DTN, Dial/Data, Interquote, myTrack
	Auto download feature	✖	✖
	Import formats	CSI, MetaStock, TC2000, ASCII, AIQ	ASCII
	Export formats	MetaStock, ASCII	ASCII
	Handles distributions and splits	✖	✖
	Data conversion/merge feature	✖	✖
	Historical database included	✖	
Batch printing		✖	

Technical Analysis Program		MacChart 3.0	MegaTech Chart System
Company		Trendsetter Software, Inc.	Ret-Tech Software
Telephone		(800) 825-1852	(847) 382-3903
Web Address		www.trendsoft.com	www.rettech.com
E-mail		sales@trendsoft.com	rettger@sprynet.com
Price (AAII Discount)		$129 ($30)	$175
Platform(s)		MacOS 7.0+	DOS, Windows 95
Indicators	Number of predefined indicators	22	50
	Allows modification of pre-existing indicators	✖	✖
	Allows creation of new indicators		
	Choice of indicator overlay or plot in new window	✖	✖
Charting Elements	Chart types: B=bar, C=candle, CV=candlevolume EV=equivolume, L=line, P&F=point and figure	B, C, L	B, C, L, P&F
	Number of predefined charts (chart templates)		
	Create templates of indicators/trading systems	✖	✖
	Moveable trendlines	✖	
	Security merge feature		✖
	Maximum number of charts displayed on screen	unlimited	16
	Maximum number of data points per chart	65,000	3,000
Trading Systems	Backtesting		
	Number of predefined trading systems		
	Create & save custom trading systems		
	Rank/compare systems against each other		
	Generate profit report of trading system		
	Indicates maximum drawdown		
	System stop methods: (trailing, max-loss, breakeven, profit target, etc.)		
	Pre-defined entry/exit signals (black box)		
	User-defined entry/exit signals (by price, indicator)		
	Considers trade position (long/short)		
	Accounts for slippage/commission		
Help Functions	On-line help	✖	
	Indicator interpretation help	✖	✖
Data Maintenance	Sources of data download	Dial/Data	Knight-Ridder, Prodigy, Radio Exchange, Signal
	Auto download feature	✖	✖
	Import formats	ASCII	ASCII, PRO
	Export formats	ASCII	ASCII
	Handles distributions and splits	✖	✖
	Data conversion/merge feature	✖	✖
	Historical database included	✖	
Batch printing		✖	✖

Technical Analysis Program		MetaStock 6.5/ MetaStock Professional	OmniTrader 4.0
Company		Equis International	Nirvana Systems, Inc.
Telephone		(800) 882-3040	(800) 888-0338
Web Address		www.metastock.com	www.nirv.com
E-mail		sales@equis.com	sales@nirv.com
Price (AAII Discount)		MetaStock 6.5 $349/ Professional $1,495	Stocks Edition $395/Futures Edition $695/Real-Time $1,995
Platform(s)		Windows 95/98/NT	Windows 95/98/NT
Indicators	Number of predefined indicators	108	120
	Allows modification of pre-existing indicators	✖	✖
	Allows creation of new indicators	✖	
	Choice of indicator overlay or plot in new window	✖	✖
Charting Elements	Chart types: B=bar, C=candle, CV=candlevolume EV=equivolume, L=line, P&F=point and figure	B, C, CV, EV, L, P&F	B, C, L
	Number of predefined charts (chart templates)	14	
	Create templates of indicators/trading systems	✖	✖
	Moveable trendlines	✖	
	Security merge feature	✖	
	Maximum number of charts displayed on screen	limited only by memory	unlimited
	Maximum number of data points per chart	65,000	unlimited
Trading Systems	Backtesting	✖	✖
	Number of predefined trading systems	11	120
	Create & save custom trading systems	✖	✖
	Rank/compare systems against each other	✖	✖
	Generate profit report of trading system	✖	✖
	Indicates maximum drawdown	✖	
	System stop methods: (trailing, max-loss, breakeven, profit target, etc.)	trailing, max-loss, breakeven, profit target	trailing, max-loss, breakeven, profit target
	Pre-defined entry/exit signals (black box)	✖	✖
	User-defined entry/exit signals (by price, indicator)	✖	✖
	Considers trade position (long/short)	✖	✖
	Accounts for slippage/commission	✖	✖
Help Functions	On-line help	✖	✖
	Indicator interpretation help	✖	✖
Data Maintenance	Sources of data download	CompuServe, Dial/Data, Signal, Reuter's, Telescan, eSignal, BMI	Telescan, Interquote, Quote.com, eSignal
	Auto download feature	✖	✖
	Import formats	ASCII, CSI, Excel, Futurelink, Quattro, Lotus 1-2-3, TC2000, AIQ	MetaStock, CSI, AIQ, TC2000
	Export formats	ASCII, DIF, Excel, Quattro, Lotus 1-2-3	
	Handles distributions and splits	✖	✖
	Data conversion/merge feature	✖	
	Historical database included	✖	✖
Batch printing		✖	✖

Technical Analysis Program		Personal Analyst 4.0	Personal Hotline 8.0
Company		Trendsetter Software, Inc.	Trendsetter Software, Inc.
Telephone		(800) 825-1852	(800) 825-1852
Web Address		www.trendsoft.com	www.trendsoft.com
E-mail		sales@trendsoft.com	sales@trendsoft.com
Price (AAII Discount)		$349 ($50)	$595 ($100)
Platform(s)		Macintosh	Macintosh
Indicators	Number of predefined indicators	50	50
	Allows modification of pre-existing indicators	✖	✖
	Allows creation of new indicators		
	Choice of indicator overlay or plot in new window	✖	✖
Charting Elements	Chart types: B=bar, C=candle, CV=candlevolume EV=equivolume, L=line, P&F=point and figure	B, C, L, P&F	B, C, L, P&F
	Number of predefined charts (chart templates)		
	Create templates of indicators/trading systems	✖	✖
	Moveable trendlines	✖	✖
	Security merge feature	✖	✖
	Maximum number of charts displayed on screen	unlimited	unlimited
	Maximum number of data points per chart	65,000	65,000
Trading Systems	Backtesting		✖
	Number of predefined trading systems		6
	Create & save custom trading systems		✖
	Rank/compare systems against each other		✖
	Generate profit report of trading system		✖
	Indicates maximum drawdown		✖
	System stop methods: (trailing, max-loss, breakeven, profit target, etc.)		trailing, profit target
	Pre-defined entry/exit signals (black box)		✖
	User-defined entry/exit signals (by price, indicator)		✖
	Considers trade position (long/short)		✖
	Accounts for slippage/commission		✖
Help Functions	On-line help	✖	✖
	Indicator interpretation help	✖	✖
Data Maintenance	Sources of data download	Dial/Data	Dial/Data
	Auto download feature	✖	✖
	Import formats	ASCII	ASCII
	Export formats	ASCII	ASCII
	Handles distributions and splits	✖	✖
	Data conversion/merge feature	✖	✖
	Historical database included	✖	✖
Batch printing		✖	✖

Technical Analysis Program		ProTA 2.11/ProTA Gold	SMARTrader
Company		BeeSoft	Stratagem Software International, Inc.
Telephone		(800) 840-3588	(504) 885-7353
Web Address		www.beesoft.net	www.stratagem1.com
E-mail		support@beesoft.net	stratagem1@aol.com
Price (AAII Discount)		ProTA 2.0 $59; Gold $199	$299 (15%)
Platform(s)		MacOS 7.0+	Windows 95/98/NT
Indicators	Number of predefined indicators	45	101
	Allows modification of pre-existing indicators	✖	✖
	Allows creation of new indicators	Gold	✖
	Choice of indicator overlay or plot in new window	✖	✖
Charting Elements	Chart types: B=bar, C=candle, CV=candlevolume EV=equivolume, L=line, P&F=point and figure	B, C, L	B, C, L, P&F
	Number of predefined charts (chart templates)	4	68
	Create templates of indicators/trading systems	✖	✖
	Moveable trendlines	✖	✖
	Security merge feature	Gold	✖
	Maximum number of charts displayed on screen	250	10
	Maximum number of data points per chart	32,768	2,000
Trading Systems	Backtesting	Gold	✖
	Number of predefined trading systems	4	23
	Create & save custom trading systems	Gold	✖
	Rank/compare systems against each other	Gold	
	Generate profit report of trading system	Gold	✖
	Indicates maximum drawdown	Gold	✖
	System stop methods: (trailing, max-loss, breakeven, profit target, etc.)	trailing, max-loss, profit target	trailing, max-loss
	Pre-defined entry/exit signals (black box)	Gold	
	User-defined entry/exit signals (by price, indicator)	Gold	
	Considers trade position (long/short)	Gold	✖
	Accounts for slippage/commission	Gold	✖
Help Functions	On-line help	✖	✖
	Indicator interpretation help	✖	✖
Data Maintenance	Sources of data download	Dial/Data, AOL, Quote.com, BeeSoft	
	Auto download feature	✖	
	Import formats	ASCII	MetaStock, TC2000, ASCII
	Export formats	MetaStock, ASCII	ASCII
	Handles distributions and splits	✖	
	Data conversion/merge feature	✖	
	Historical database included	✖	
Batch printing		✖	✖

Technical Analysis Program		SuperCharts 4.0/ SuperCharts Real-Time	TC2000 4.2
Company		Omega Research	Worden Brothers, Inc.
Telephone		(800) 556-2022	(800) 776-4940
Web Address		www.omegaresearch.com	www.tc2000.com
E-mail		sales@omegaresearch.com	support@worden.com
Price (AAII Discount)		End-of-day $395/Real-Time $1,199.40	Free
Platform(s)		Windows	Windows 95/98/NT
Indicators	Number of predefined indicators	83	12
	Allows modification of pre-existing indicators	✖	✖
	Allows creation of new indicators	✖	
	Choice of indicator overlay or plot in new window	✖	✖
Charting Elements	Chart types: B=bar, C=candle, CV=candlevolume EV=equivolume, L=line, P&F=point and figure	B, C, L, P&F	B, C, L
	Number of predefined charts (chart templates)	23	12
	Create templates of indicators/trading systems	✖	✖
	Moveable trendlines	✖	
	Security merge feature	✖	
	Maximum number of charts displayed on screen	24	2
	Maximum number of data points per chart	13,000	500
Trading Systems	Backtesting	✖	
	Number of predefined trading systems	16	
	Create & save custom trading systems	✖	
	Rank/compare systems against each other		
	Generate profit report of trading system	✖	
	Indicates maximum drawdown	✖	
	System stop methods: (trailing, max-loss, breakeven, profit target, etc.)	trailing, max-loss, breakeven, profit target, trading & inactivity	
	Pre-defined entry/exit signals (black box)	✖	
	User-defined entry/exit signals (by price, indicator)	✖	
	Considers trade position (long/short)	✖	
	Accounts for slippage/commission	✖	
Help Functions	On-line help	✖	✖
	Indicator interpretation help	✖	✖
Data Maintenance	Sources of data download	Dial/Data, Telescan	Worden Brothers, Inc.
	Auto download feature	✖	✖
	Import formats	AIQ, ASCII, CompuTrac, CSI, KR, MegaTech, MetaStock, TC2000, Tick Data	
	Export formats	ASCII	MetaStock, TC2000 3.0, ASCII
	Handles distributions and splits	✖	✖
	Data conversion/merge feature	✖	
	Historical database included	✖	✖
Batch printing		✖	

Technical Analysis Program		TIP@Wallstreet 1.2	TradeStation 2000i
Company		Telescan, Inc.	Omega Research
Telephone		(800) 324-8246	(800) 556-2022
Web Address		www.telescan.com	www.omegaresearch.com
E-mail		sales@telescan.com	sales@omegaresearch.com
Price (AAII Discount)		$249 (10%)	$2399.40 ($199.95/mo. for 12 mos.)
Platform(s)		Windows 95/98/NT	Windows 95/98 or NT 4.0
Indicators	Number of predefined indicators	80+	100+
	Allows modification of pre-existing indicators	✖	✖
	Allows creation of new indicators		✖
	Choice of indicator overlay or plot in new window	✖	✖
Charting Elements	Chart types: B=bar, C=candle, CV=candlevolume EV=equivolume, L=line, P&F=point and figure	B, C, CV, EV, L, P&F	B, C, L, P&F
	Number of predefined charts (chart templates)		5
	Create templates of indicators/trading systems	✖	✖
	Moveable trendlines	✖	✖
	Security merge feature		✖
	Maximum number of charts displayed on screen	4	unlimited
	Maximum number of data points per chart	limited only by memory	unlimited
Trading Systems	Backtesting	✖	✖
	Number of predefined trading systems	80+	25+
	Create & save custom trading systems		✖
	Rank/compare systems against each other	✖	
	Generate profit report of trading system	✖	✖
	Indicates maximum drawdown		✖
	System stop methods: (trailing, max-loss, breakeven, profit target, etc.)		trailing, max-loss, breakeven, progit target, trading & inactivity
	Pre-defined entry/exit signals (black box)		✖
	User-defined entry/exit signals (by price, indicator)		✖
	Considers trade position (long/short)		✖
	Accounts for slippage/commission		✖
Help Functions	On-line help	✖	✖
	Indicator interpretation help	✖	✖
Data Maintenance	Sources of data download	Telescan	Dial/Data, Telescan, DBC Signal, Signal Online, BMI, DTN, PC Quote
	Auto download feature	✖	✖
	Import formats	AIQ, MetaStock	AIQ, ASCII, CompuTrac, CSI, Knight-Ridder, MegaTech, MetaStock, TC2000
	Export formats		ASCII
	Handles distributions and splits	✖	✖
	Data conversion/merge feature	✖	✖
	Historical database included	✖	✖
Batch printing		✖	✖

Technical Analysis Program		TradingExpert Pro	VectorVest ProGraphics 5.0
Company		AIQ Systems	VectorVest, Inc.
Telephone		(800) 332-2999	(888) 658-7638
Web Address		www.aiq.com	vvww.vectorvest.com
E-mail		aiqonline@aol.com	sales@vectorvest.com
Price (AAII Discount)		$1,295	$39-$49/month
Platform(s)		Windows 95/98/NT	Windows 3.x/95/98/NT
Indicators	Number of predefined indicators	60+	36
	Allows modification of pre-existing indicators	✖	✖
	Allows creation of new indicators	✖	
	Choice of indicator overlay or plot in new window	✖	
Charting Elements	Chart types: B=bar, C=candle, CV=candlevolume EV=equivolume, L=line, P&F=point and figure	B, C, L, P&F	B, C, L
	Number of predefined charts (chart templates)	12	
	Create templates of indicators/trading systems	✖	
	Moveable trendlines	✖	✖
	Security merge feature	✖	
	Maximum number of charts displayed on screen	unlimited	1
	Maximum number of data points per chart	20 years	unlimited
Trading Systems	Backtesting	✖	✖
	Number of predefined trading systems	200+	30
	Create & save custom trading systems	✖	✖
	Rank/compare systems against each other	✖	✖
	Generate profit report of trading system	✖	✖
	Indicates maximum drawdown	✖	
	System stop methods: (trailing, max-loss, breakeven, profit target, etc.)	trailing, max-loss, breakeven, profit target	trailing
	Pre-defined entry/exit signals (black box)	✖	✖
	User-defined entry/exit signals (by price, indicator)	✖	
	Considers trade position (long/short)	✖	
	Accounts for slippage/commission	commission	
Help Functions	On-line help	✖	✖
	Indicator interpretation help	✖	✖
Data Maintenance	Sources of data download	Dial/Data, Interactive Data, Telescan, myTrack, Signal, BMI	VectorVest
	Auto download feature	✖	✖
	Import formats	MetaStock, TC2000, ASCII	
	Export formats	ASCII, MetaStock, TC2000	ASCII, Excel, Lotus
	Handles distributions and splits	✖	✖
	Data conversion/merge feature	✖	
	Historical database included	✖	✖
Batch printing		✖	

Technical Analysis Indicators

	Behold! 2.8	Day Trader Internet 7.5	FastBreak 2.6/FastGraph 2.6	Insider TA 4.0	Internet Trader Pro 7.5	Investor/RT 3.8	MacChart 3.0	MegaTech Chart System	MetaStock 6.5/Professional	OmniTrader 4.0	Personal Analyst 4.0	Personal Hotline 8.0	ProTA 2.11/Gold	SMARTrader	SuperCharts 4.0/Real-Time	TC2000 4.2	TIP@Wallstreet 1.2	TradeStation 2000i	TradingExpert Pro	VectorVest ProGraphics 5.0
Moving Averages																				
Simple	✗	✗		✗	✗	✗	✗	✗	✗		✗	✗	✗	✗	✗	✗	✗	✗	✗	✗
Exponential	✗	✗	✗		✗	✗	✗	✗	✗	✗	✗	✗	✗	✗	✗	✗	✗	✗	✗	
Weighted	✗	✗	✗		✗	✗	✗		✗		✗	✗	✗	✗	✗			✗	✗	✗
Chart Features																				
Andrews Pitchfork	✗	✗			✗				✗		✗	✗		✗						
Bollinger Bands	✗	✗	✗		✗	✗	✗	✗	✗	✗	✗	✗	✗	✗	✗	✗	✗	✗	✗	
Cycle Rules		✗	✗		✗			✗	✗		✗	✗	✗		✗			✗	✗	
Fibonacci Studies	✗	✗			✗	✗			✗	✗	✗	✗	✗	✗	✗			✗	✗	
Gann Analysis		✗			✗			✗	✗		✗	✗			✗			✗		
Horizontal Lines	✗					✗	✗	✗	✗		✗	✗	✗	✗						
Moving Average Bands	✗					✗		✗	✗				✗	✗			✗		✗	
Open Interest	✗	✗			✗	✗	✗	✗	✗		✗	✗	✗	✗			✗		✗	
Parallel Lines	✗					✗			✗				✗				✗			
Linear Regression	✗	✗			✗	✗	✗		✗		✗	✗	✗	✗	✗	✗	✗	✗		
Tick Volume	✗					✗								✗						
Tirone Levels									✗							✗		✗		
Trendlines	✗	✗		✗	✗	✗	✗	✗	✗		✗	✗	✗	✗	✗	✗	✗	✗	✗	
Vertical Lines	✗					✗	✗		✗		✗	✗					✗			
Volume	✗	✗		✗	✗	✗	✗	✗	✗	✗	✗	✗	✗	✗	✗	✗	✗	✗	✗	✗
Built-In Indicators																				
Absolute Breadth Index																✗		✗		
Accumul./Distrib. (Chaikin)	✗	✗			✗	✗		✗	✗	✗	✗	✗	✗	✗	✗	✗	✗	✗	✗	
Accumulation Swing Index		✗			✗				✗							✗		✗		
Advance/Decline Ratio		✗			✗	✗		✗			✗	✗	✗	✗			✗	✗	✗	
Arms Index (TRIN)		✗			✗	✗		✗	✗		✗	✗	✗	✗					✗	✗
Average True Range	✗	✗			✗	✗			✗		✗	✗	✗	✗	✗					
Beta		✗			✗				✗							✗				
Chaikin Oscillator	✗	✗		✗	✗	✗		✗	✗	✗	✗	✗	✗	✗	✗	✗	✗	✗	✗	
Commodity Channel Index	✗	✗			✗	✗		✗	✗	✗	✗	✗	✗	✗	✗		✗	✗	✗	
Commodity Selection Index	✗	✗			✗				✗						✗					
Demand Index	✗	✗			✗				✗				✗					✗		
Directional Movement Index	✗	✗			✗	✗	✗	✗	✗	✗	✗	✗	✗	✗			✗		✗	
Ease of Movement		✗		✗	✗	✗			✗							✗		✗	✗	
Herrick Payoff Index	✗	✗			✗				✗							✗		✗		

Technical Analysis Indicators	Behold! 2.8	Day Trader Internet 7.5	FastBreak 2.6/FastGraph 2.6	Insider TA 4.0	Internet Trader Pro 7.5	Investor/RT 3.8	MacChart 3.0	MegaTech Chart System	MetaStock 6.5/Professional	OmniTrader 4.0	Personal Analyst 4.0	Personal Hotline 8.0	ProTA 2.11/Gold	SMARTrader	SuperCharts 4.0/Real-Time	TC2000 4.2	TIP@Wallstreet 1.2	TradeStation 2000i	TradingExpert Pro	VectorVest ProGraphics 5.0
Built-In Indicators (cont'd)																				
MACD	✗	✗			✗	✗	✗	✗	✗	✗	✗	✗	✗	✗	✗	✗	✗	✗	✗	
Market Facilitation Index	✗							✗	✗					✗						
Mass Index		✗			✗				✗		✗	✗				✗			✗	
McClellan Oscillator		✗			✗	✗		✗	✗		✗	✗	✗	✗	✗		✗	✗	✗	✗
McClellan Summation Index		✗			✗	✗		✗	✗		✗	✗	✗	✗			✗	✗	✗	✗
Momentum	✗	✗			✗	✗		✗	✗	✗	✗	✗	✗	✗	✗	✗	✗	✗		✗
Money Flow		✗			✗	✗		✗	✗	✗			✗	✗	✗	✗	✗	✗	✗	
Negative Volume Index		✗			✗			✗	✗		✗	✗							✗	✗
On-Balance Volume	✗	✗		✗	✗	✗	✗	✗	✗		✗		✗	✗	✗	✗	✗	✗	✗	
Parabolic SAR	✗	✗	✗		✗		✗	✗	✗	✗	✗		✗	✗	✗			✗		
Percent Retracement		✗			✗	✗	✗	✗	✗		✗	✗			✗					
Positive Volume Index		✗			✗			✗	✗		✗	✗						✗	✗	✗
Price Oscillator	✗	✗			✗				✗		✗	✗	✗	✗	✗	✗	✗	✗	✗	
Put/Call Ratio													✗							
Rate of Change	✗	✗			✗	✗	✗	✗	✗	✗	✗	✗	✗	✗	✗	✗			✗	✗
Relative Strength Index	✗					✗	✗	✗	✗	✗	✗	✗	✗	✗	✗	✗	✗	✗	✗	✗
Speed Resistance		✗			✗				✗		✗	✗		✗				✗		
Standard Deviation	✗	✗			✗	✗			✗		✗	✗	✗	✗			✗	✗	✗	✗
Stochastics	✗	✗			✗	✗	✗	✗	✗	✗	✗	✗	✗	✗	✗	✗	✗	✗	✗	✗
Swing Index	✗	✗			✗				✗					✗	✗	✗			✗	
Trade Volume Index									✗											
TRIX	✗	✗			✗	✗			✗	✗	✗	✗	✗	✗					✗	
Ultimate Oscillator		✗			✗				✗		✗	✗			✗	✗			✗	
Volatility (Chaikin)		✗			✗	✗	✗	✗	✗	✗			✗	✗	✗	✗	✗	✗	✗	
Volatility (Wilder)	✗	✗			✗	✗							✗							
Volume Oscillator	✗	✗			✗	✗		✗	✗		✗	✗	✗			✗	✗	✗	✗	
Wilder's RSI	✗	✗			✗	✗	✗	✗	✗		✗	✗	✗	✗	✗	✗			✗	
Williams' % R	✗	✗			✗	✗		✗	✗	✗	✗	✗	✗	✗	✗				✗	✗
Williams' Accumul./Distrib.		✗			✗	✗		✗	✗		✗	✗	✗	✗	✗					
Zig Zag		✗			✗				✗					✗					✗	✗
Proprietary Indicators	0	0	2	1	0	3	0	0	0	5	2	2	0	12	0	3	0	0	10	12
Total Number of Indicators (Not All Listed Here)	90	150	7	4	150	75	22	50	108	120	50	50	45	101	83	22	80+	100+	60+	36

Chapter 7

MUTUAL FUND ANALYSIS

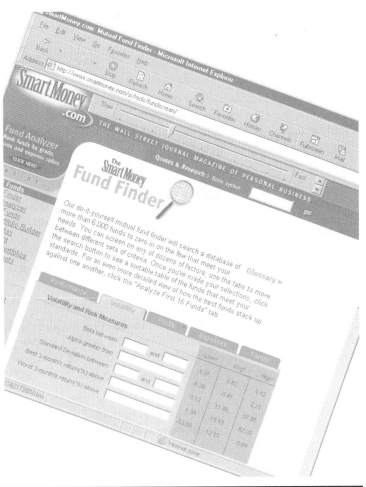

Mutual funds allow investors to pool their money into large portfolios for cost-effective, professional money management. Mutual funds free investors from the work involved in selecting and managing a portfolio of individual stocks and bonds, but the explosion of mutual fund choices has made it more difficult to select and monitor the funds themselves. While you can turn to an investment adviser or financial planner for advice on selecting mutual funds, mutual fund analysis programs provide the necessary tools for the investor willing to do his homework.

The focus of this chapter is on mutual fund screening services—filtering and analysis programs combined with mutual fund data. While these services can range greatly in their level of sophistication, their basic goal is to provide you with the tools and data necessary to select and monitor your personal portfolio of mutual funds.

Mutual Fund Screening

The thought of sifting through thousands upon thousands of mutual funds to select a single fund (appropriate for your portfolio) can be quite an imposing task. With the number of mutual funds approaching the number of publicly traded stocks, how can you narrow the scope? One answer is screening.

Screening involves setting up a list of parameters, or criteria, that you can use to find a group of securities or funds that have similar characteristics. While you could use a financial newspaper, magazine or book to perform basic screens, the screening process is best accomplished using a computer and a software program. Software packages offer some form of data service with the screening capability built into the software. Subscribers receive periodic data updates. While a software program may be included, it is worthless without these data updates. Likewise, the data is only as useful as the flexibility and power of the program's screening function.

Recent Internet developments allow investors to perform screening on-line. The software is either downloaded to your computer in an invisible fashion or the screens are filled out through forms on your Web browser. Your screen is actually performed on a central computer and the screening and ranking results sent back to your computer.

Mutual fund screening systems enable an investor to quickly filter through a large universe of funds to locate a chosen few that meet your risk, return and management style needs. For example, if you determine that your portfolio is lacking international stock diversification, a screening program can quickly come up with a list of no-load mutual funds with consistent performance above the average for international equity funds, acceptable risk and below average expenses.

The screening criteria dictate how the database is filtered. It is important to select a system that provides the flexibility to create effective screening criteria along with a database that provides a rich set of data fields suitable for screening. Most systems give a running tally of the number of funds that pass each successive search criterion. The more criteria you input into the screen or the tighter you make the values for each, the fewer funds that will pass your filter.

Critical elements to consider when choosing a mutual fund screening application include:

- number of funds in the complete universe

- number and types of fields that can be used for screening and sorting

- conditions and values that can be specified for each field

Tip→	Critical elements to consider when selecting a mutual fund screening application include number of funds, number and types of fields for screening, and conditions and values that can be specified.

For example, a screen might consist of an investment objective equal to aggressive growth, an annual five-year return greater than 15.0%, a front-end load equal to zero and an expense ratio less than 1.50%. If this screen provides too many candidates, requiring a 20.0% annual five-year return or adding a risk measure, for example, can tighten the criteria and, therefore, decrease the number of passing funds. Once the universe of funds has been narrowed sufficiently, individual fund analysis follows.

Monitoring and Performance Comparison

The key function performed by mutual fund applications is monitoring, or the comparison of a fund's performance. While performance comparison is primarily done through screening during the selection process, a worthwhile feature of any good mutual fund analysis system is the ability to easily and clearly present how well your fund investment did against other funds or benchmarks for funds within your portfolio.

Tip→	A valuable feature of any good mutual fund screening program is the ability to present how well your fund did against other funds.

Increasingly more systems offer sophisticated charting and graphics, reports for specific time periods, and fund comparison reports that make monitoring easier and more comprehensive. In the most powerful programs, the performance of an index, an average for a fund investment objective, and the performance of other similar funds can all be displayed in color along with the performance of a particular fund using line graphs and bar charts for any period selected. Some applications even offer basic mutual fund portfolio management capabilities.

FIGURE 7.0
This bar chart featured in Mutual Fund Expert provides a performance comparison of the Fidelity Select: Brokerage & Investment Portfolio fund.

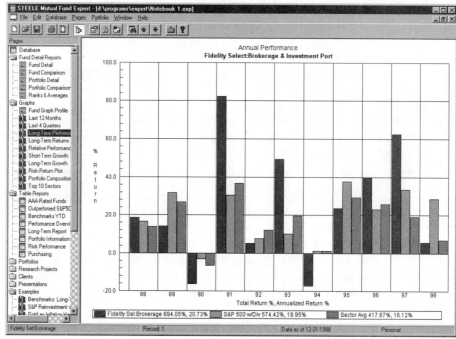

Size and Depth of the Database

The analysis of an individual fund and the examination of fund details hinge on the amount and organization of information presented. Basic requirements in regard to mutual fund information include:

- the universe of funds

- the depth of the data

- frequency of data updates

<table>
<tr><td>Tip→</td><td>Basic requirements to check for in any potential candidate include the universe of funds, the depth of the data, and how frequently the data is updated.</td></tr>
</table>

Universe of Funds

A comprehensive data set should cover the universe of non-money market mutual funds—currently exceeding 8,000.

Alternatively, the universe should match the universe of funds that you consider for your portfolio such as no- or low-load funds. In the comparison grid (starting on page 351), the section entitled database content shows the number of funds and indexes tracked by each program, the number of data fields reported, and the number of fields that can be used for screening and sorting.

Depth of Data

Along with the size of the data set, you also want to consider how comprehensive the data is on each fund. If the application does not at least have performance returns for one, three, five, and 10 years, along with monthly or quarterly returns, then the data set is really not that competitive. Annual returns for specific years allow you to gauge performance during different market environments. Throw in similar data for index benchmarks and investment objective categories along with absolute and relative risk measures, and most performance questions can be answered. The chapter comparison grid reports the performance statistics, risk-related features, and portfolio information included in each system.

Portfolio information probably varies the most from application to application. However, at the very least the fund manager and the portfolio asset composition should be present; this information, along with the fund's top holdings, are increasingly becoming the standard. Calculated summaries of price-earnings ratios, price-to-book-value ratios, earnings growth rates, median market capitalization, and dividend yields are a bonus.

<table>
<tr><td>Warning→</td><td>Portfolio information will vary widely from application to application. However, the fund manager and the portfolio asset composition should be present.</td></tr>
</table>

While most major applications cover fund services and operations equally well, a fund description and analysis write-up is still rare and useful, but not really the primary purpose of these systems. While more data is better, extensive analysis is typically only available with a higher subscription cost. It's your job to balance the need for specific fund information with your budget.

Frequency of Updates

Mutual fund screening programs and services are typically sold as subscriptions. Typical update schedules are monthly and quarterly. A monthly update schedule means that you will receive an update once each month for a total of 12 in one year. With a quarterly schedule, you will receive an update once each quarter for a total of four in one year. As expected, a subscription with monthly updates will cost more than one with quarterly updates. Your interest in monitoring the performance of your mutual funds, your desire to screen for new funds and, finally, your budget will ultimately steer your decision. The comparison grid indicates the data update schedules available for each application along with the associated costs of each. Note that the mutual fund performance data on most on-line services is updated only monthly. Items such as price charts and net asset value may be updated daily, but most other data elements are tied to a monthly mark-to-the market.

Fund Information to Look For

The analysis of an individual fund and the examination of fund details hinge on the amount and organization of information presented. Information generally falls into four main categories:

- performance statistics

- risk-related features

- fund portfolio information

- fund operations and services

Performance Statistics

Performance statistics usually include annual total returns and annualized total returns over three-, five- and 10-year periods and longer. Returns for shorter periods, usually year-to-date, one month, three months and the last 12 months are also common. Performance is also often reported as a difference from an index, such as the S&P 500, or from a category average. Percentile or decile ranks for performance are sometimes displayed to put the absolute performance differences into perspective (see Figure 7.1).

FIGURE 7.1
*Steele Systems'
Mutual Fund
Expert
provides an
extensive
performance
statistics page.*

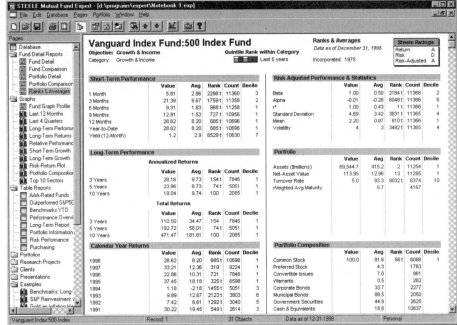

Risk-Related Features

Risk measures range from standard deviation and beta to risk indexes and risk deciles. Risk-adjusted returns using return-to-risk ratios such as the Sharpe ratio or Treynor ratio may be included. Alpha, another risk-adjusted performance measure, and R-squared, a measure of diversification, are usually grouped with beta (see Figure 7.2). For fixed-income funds, average portfolio maturity is usually reported, while some services also report the average credit quality of the bond holdings.

Fund Portfolio Information

Fund portfolio information can be very expansive or quite meager, but more often than not is just a brief synopsis. At the extreme, a program might offer details resembling a typical annual report along with calculated portfolio statistics that attempt to capture the portfolio manager's investment style and approach. Portfolio breakdowns by percentage in cash, stocks, etc., are minimal descriptions of

FIGURE 7.2
*Risk-related
features for
Mutual Fund
Survey from
Value Line
include beta
and the
Sharpe ratio.*

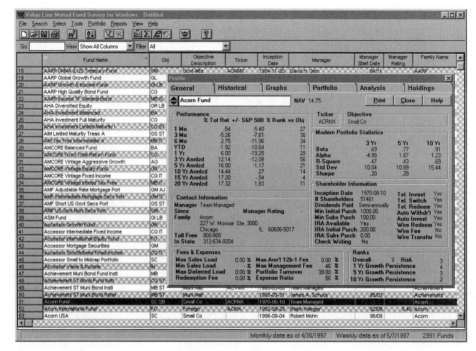

portfolio position. A listing of top stock holdings with portfolio percentage representation and a portfolio breakdown by sector or industry weights is useful in understanding investment strategy. The most comprehensive programs also include average price-earnings ratio, price-to-book-value ratio, earnings growth and dividend yield for all stocks in the portfolio. For bond funds, weighted average coupon, maturity and credit rating are reported.

Fund Operations and Services
Fund operations and services describes loads, fees and expenses—along with the fund's initial and subsequent investment minimums. You may also find the fund manager's name and tenure in addition to the fund telephone number and other fund features, such as automatic withdrawal and investment programs (see Figure 7.4).

FIGURE 7.3
The top ten holdings of the Acorn Fund, presented in a fund quote on the Stockpoint Web site.

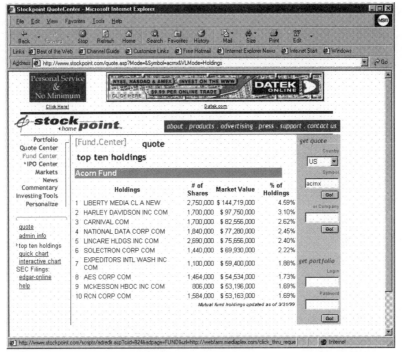

FIGURE 7.4
Fund portfolio details, including operations and services, as presented by Principia Pro from Morningstar.

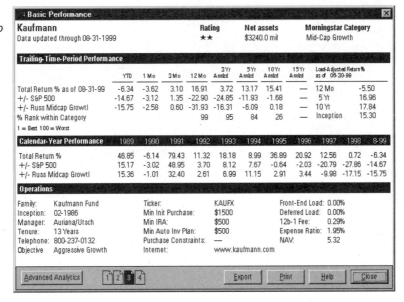

Key Screening Elements

In order to properly screen and sort mutual funds, the program you select should include these key elements:

- return

- risk

- load

First of all, if the program you are considering does not allow you to screen or sort on almost all of the various return, risk, and fee/expense/load variables available, then it is probably not as flexible as you need.

FIGURE 7.5
An aggressive growth screen created using Value Line's Mutual Fund Survey shows the return screening criteria choices.

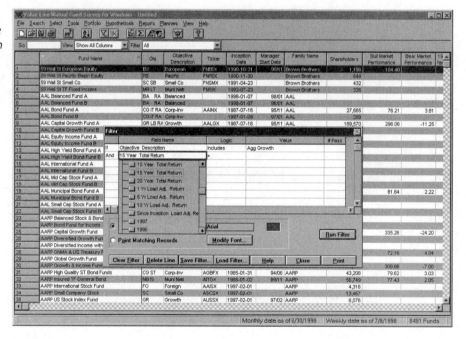

You should also be able to set the values for screening criteria at any reasonable and appropriate numerical value in combination with the common operations—greater than, less than, equal to, etc. The criteria should be easy to string together to create an effective overall screen. The screening section of the comparison grid details the possible screening options for mutual fund software.

> **Warning→** If you can't screen or sort on almost all of the various return, risk, and fee/expense/load variables available, the program is probably not as flexible as you need.

Distribution Methods

Mutual fund data delivery choices include CD-ROM, diskette and modem updates. When the data is distributed via CD-ROM or diskette, it is stored on your computer and screening and analysis information is at your disposal. Obviously a CD-ROM package can store much more data than diskette versions. Some applications store some information on the CD-ROM to keep from overburdening your hard disk. On-line or Internet screening programs can either send data to your computer for screening or allow you to perform the screen on-line and send only the results to your computer.

Mutual fund analysis programs using modem or on-line delivery usually offer more limited screening power and somewhat reduced data sets. However, some of the recent Web-based entries from vendors such as Microsoft and Morningstar provide combinations of detailed data and versatile screening.

> **Warning→** Mutual fund analysis programs using modem or on-line delivery usually offer limited screening power and somewhat reduced data sets.

The Standouts

The standout applications in the area of mutual fund screening are disk-based and include Steele Systems' Mutual Fund Expert family of programs and the two Principia Pro programs from Morningstar. Mutual Fund Expert and Principia Pro for Mutual Funds are clearly the leaders in this field. They are both powerful screening tools offering comprehensive databases and extensive screening options. Both programs rise above their peers with crisp, seamless and easy-to-use interfaces.

Of the Internet offerings, the MSN MoneyCentral Investor Web site and the Quote.com advanced Mutual Fund Center sit atop the polls, along with Morningstar's advanced screens. These services are solid and rank among the best mutual fund screening software packages. Some of the Internet-based screening tools serve merely as a supplement to the more advanced screening systems, yet these three can stand on their own and replace the disk-based services for the typical mutual fund investor.

Reviews

Disk-Based Services

Because these programs are delivered on a disk or CD-ROM, they offer deep data sets and sophisticated screening and reporting capabilities. Look for CD-ROM-based software to offer the most in terms of depth and range of data due to their large storage capacity. Accordingly, disk-based programs also carry higher costs than on-line and Internet services. When comparing these programs, keep in mind how much data and screening functionality you actually need.

Mutual Fund Expert— Personal	
Performance	5
Usefulness	5
Documentation	3
Ease of Use	4
Value	5

Mutual Fund Expert 6.0

by Steele Systems, Inc.
$95–$599—Windows
(800) 379-0679
www.mutualfundexpert.com

Mutual Fund Expert from Steele Systems comes in three versions: a Personal version, a Pro version, and a Pro Plus version. The three programs, now available on CD-ROM, include an impressive database of over 11,600 mutual funds (including money market mutual funds and multiple class funds) and are available in monthly and quarterly updates. The main difference between the three is in the detail of information supplied for each fund.

Mutual Fund Expert—Pro	
Performance	5
Usefulness	5
Documentation	3
Ease of Use	4
Value	4

The Personal version features a roster of 89 data fields and performance returns for the last 12 months, last four quarters, and the last 10 years, as well as three-, five- and 10-year annualized returns. Personal includes the risk-related measures of beta, standard deviation, and average maturity. However, it offers no portfolio information. Quarterly updates run $95 for a one-year subscription, while monthly updates cost $185.

The Pro program includes the same set of performance returns as Personal and 208 data fields for screening and ranking. Pro and Pro Plus feature greater risk-return related coverage—including both the Sharpe and Treynor ratios. The only portfolio information provided with the Pro version is fund manager. Quarterly Pro updates cost $299 for a one-year subscription and monthly updates are $499.

FIGURE 7.6
*Screening
criteria is
selected to
create an
aggressive
growth filter in
Mutual Fund
Expert.*

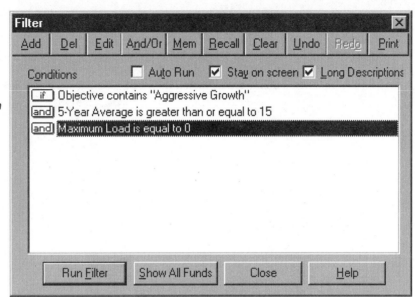

Mutual Fund Expert— Pro Plus	
Performance	5
Usefulness	5
Documentation	3
Ease of Use	4
Value	5

Pro Plus offers a more robust 592 data fields and has complete performance returns from 1962 to the present. Pro Plus portfolio details include information on the fund manager and the fund's portfolio composition. With Pro Plus, a quarterly subscription costs $399. A subscription for monthly updates will run you $599.

Screening and reporting capabilities are strong for each of the respective Expert programs, with all three allowing investors to perform any and all necessary filters in order to select funds. The programs are easy to work with and all have the same interface. If you are comfortable working with multi-page (multiple tab) worksheets, then you will find it easy to navigate through the information supplied by these programs. The Expert family of programs also features a unique quick-reference toolbar on the main database page of each program for easy navigation. Overall, the Mutual Fund Expert programs are top-notch fund screening applications and perform the necessary tasks for effective fund analysis.

FIGURE 7.7
Resulting window after aggressive growth screen is applied in Mutual Fund Expert.

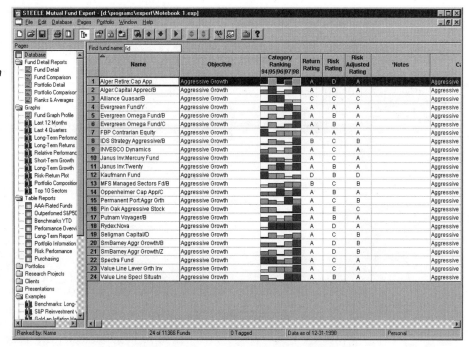

Mutual Fund Survey	
Performance	4
Usefulness	4
Documentation	4
Ease of Use	5
Value	4

Mutual Fund Survey 2.0
by Value Line, Inc.
$395/yr.—Windows
(800) 535-8760
www.valueline.com

Mutual Fund Survey for Windows is a CD-based screening program from Value Line. Based on the printed Value Line Mutual Fund Survey, this electronic version includes a larger database (10,000-plus funds) of both load and no-load funds. Mutual Fund Survey's old stable mate, The No-Load Analyzer, has been dropped from the team in favor of offering one slimmed-down model. Mutual Fund Survey now offers both a monthly and quarterly update schedule.

FIGURE 7.8
Mutual Fund Survey illustrates the growth of $10,000 for the Janus Balanced fund.

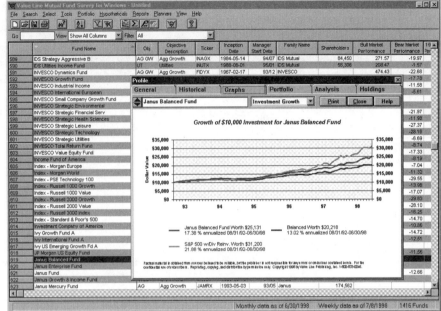

Mutual Fund Survey includes performance returns for the latest month and last two quarters; annualized returns for one, three, five, 10, 15, and 20 years; and individual returns from 1977 to the present. Mutual Fund Survey includes a formidable amount of risk-related statistics and portfolio information, such as the largest holding of the fund and the percentage of the fund in foreign securities. It also offers extensive screening and complete reporting capabilities. With an easy-to-use interface and seamless drop-down menu toolbar, Mutual Fund Survey performs sound fund analysis.

Principia Pro	
Performance	5
Usefulness	4
Documentation	4
Ease of Use	5
Value	5

Principia Pro for Mutual Funds 4.1
by Morningstar, Inc.
$295–$895—Windows
(800) 735-0700
www.morningstar.com

Principia Pro for Mutual Funds is now the lone fund screening program from Morningstar. The Windows-based Principia program has recently received another upgrade and Morningstar has once again re-formatted its roster of programs. The company is no longer updating the old Ascent program. Morningstar is, however, still supporting the two versions of Principia—Principia Pro and Principia Pro Plus.

FIGURE 7.9
Principia Pro's
filter window
for selecting
screening
criteria.

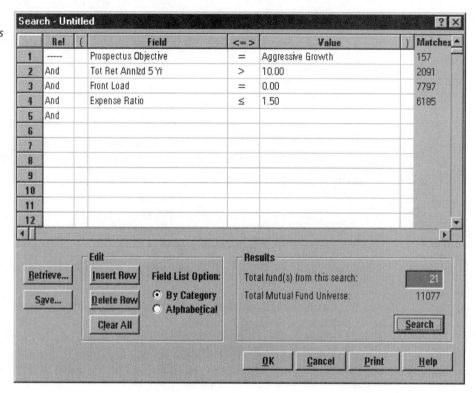

Both programs cover 10,800 funds. Principia Pro provides over 140 fields, all of which are available for screening and ranking. Principia Pro Plus is their top-of-the-line program—geared more toward professional investors and investment advisers—featuring more than 300 data fields, with over 140 available for screening and sorting. Principia Pro Plus also comes complete with the Advanced Analytics package, providing "under the hood" details and insightful information, as well as a feature new last year on Principia Pro—Portfolio Developer, a presentation tool that allows users to construct hypothetical illustrations of client portfolios. Principia Pro includes integration with a new stock screening program sold separately, allowing users to analyze a portfolio of stocks and funds.

The Principia programs offer an annualized return for the trailing 12-month period and individual performance returns for the last 10 years for Pro and the last 15 years for Pro Plus, and the latest month and quarter. The programs

FIGURE 7.10
Resulting mutual funds that pass the aggressive growth screen in Principia Pro.

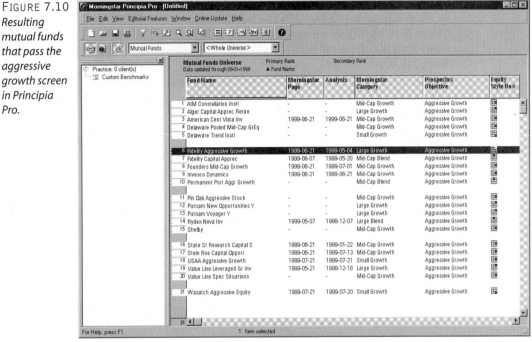

include R-squared and the Sharpe ratio as part of their risk-related measurements. Portfolio information such as unrealized capital gains and portfolio composition are also included for both applications. The Principia programs' screening capabilities are the most comprehensive of the products reviewed in this chapter, and both applications provide complete reporting options.

Both Principia Pro programs include an easy-to-use on-screen filtering utility and even display Morningstar's equity and fixed-income style boxes in their main database pages. The team of Principia Pro programs does an excellent job of fund screening and analysis and continues to solidify Morningstar's position as an industry leader in the world of mutual fund screening applications.

Quarterly Low-Load Mutual Fund Update
by the American Association of Individual Investors
$50/yr. ($39 for AAII members)—DOS, Macintosh
(800) 428-2244, (312) 280-0170
www.aaii.com

Editor's Note: *Quarterly Low-Load Mutual Fund Update is published by the American Association of Individual Investors. Because of the potential conflict of interest, we do not feel it appropriate to rate our program, and hence, provide only a factual description.*

The Quarterly Low-Load Mutual Fund Update is AAII's entry in the mutual fund screening software arena. Supported by the Association since January 1992, the diskette-based Quarterly Update is a basic screening tool available for the DOS and Macintosh platforms.

Focusing its attention on no- and low-load funds, the Quarterly Update program features a database of over 1,100 funds and 76 data fields. It offers quarterly performance returns for the last three quarters; one-, three-, and five-year annualized returns; and individual-year performance returns for each of the last 10 years. Beta, standard deviation and average maturity are the risk-related data provided by the program. It also provides information on the fund manager along with the fund's investment styles and types of securities held. The Quarterly Update program does not provide any type of detailed reports.

FIGURE 7.11
A standard report view for the Acorn Fund taken from AAII's Quarterly Low-Load Mutual Fund Update.

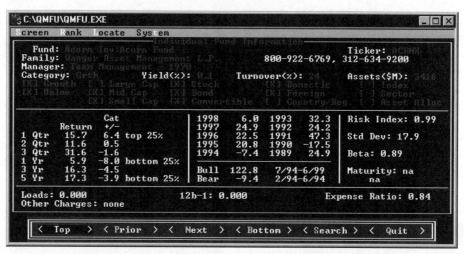

On-Line Services

On-line, or modem-based, screening modules package a software interface and a data set together a little bit differently than the traditional software vendors discussed in the previous section. These on-line services allow users to connect to a current mutual fund database via their modems in order to conduct screening and analysis. Access to this data is granted with a subscription to the services, most often for a monthly fee. Software is either provided for free or purchased in addition to a subscription.

If you subscribe to an on-line service, be sure to check out the mutual fund services it offers, but keep in mind that you will probably need to supplement it with a dedicated program to do any substantial screening of mutual funds on a regular basis.

In the past, on-line services such as America Online (AOL), CompuServe, and Prodigy Classic offered mutual fund screening interfaces to their subscribers as part of a package of investment services—either free or at an additional cost. AOL is the only one of the original "Big Three" to continue to provide such a service to its subscribers, as CompuServe discontinued its FundWatch Online service some time ago and Prodigy Classic is no more after its recent shutdown. The screening interface currently available on AOL is almost identical to the module available on the AOL Web site, which borrows its interface from Intuit's Quicken.com Web site. See the Quicken.com review under the Internet offerings on page 338 for AOL's package of fund screening tools.

TIP@Wallstreet with Mutual Fund Search	
Performance	4
Usefulness	4
Documentation	5
Ease of Use	4
Value	5

TIP@Wallstreet w/Mutual Fund Search 1.2
by Telescan, Inc.
$349—DOS, Windows
(800) 324-8246
www.wallstreetcity.com

TIP@Wallstreet—TIP stands for Telescan Investor's Platform—is a multi-purpose, on-line investment analysis application; the Mutual Fund Search module is an additional, separate screening tool that can be packaged with the TIP@Wallstreet software and the Wall Street City Web site (www.wallstreetcity.com). (The Wall Street City Web site has its own screening module reviewed in the Internet section on page 347.) This product combines software with a dial-up service to provide mutual fund screening and analysis as well as extensive fund information. Data updates can be obtained quarterly, monthly, weekly, and even daily.

FIGURE 7.12
*TIP@Wallstreet
with Mutual
Fund Search
from Telescan
screens for no-
load mutual
funds.*

At the core of the mutual fund screening process is Mutual Fund Search. With a screening interface similar to that of the disk-based services, Mutual Fund Search is menu-driven. After submitting your search criteria, the program goes on-line to execute the filter and returns an output report of the passing funds. Establishing screens and analyzing the results can be done off-line at no cost.

TIP@Wallstreet includes a 9,000-fund database and 82 data fields available for both screening and ranking. It features annualized performance returns for the last 15 years as well as 15 years of individual annual returns. Quarterly returns are provided for the last four quarters. Monthly returns are not furnished. The program contains the basic risk-related features and comes with a comprehensive list of portfolio information elements, including unrealized capital gains and the percentage of foreign investment in the fund. Screening capabilities are quite comprehensive as well. The Mutual Fund Search module is a solid screening tool for effective fund analysis.

The TIP@Wallstreet software package, including Mutual Fund Search, costs $349. Data for the program costs $12 per month, in addition to connect charges. Telescan offers many access plans, including a $9.95 per month option that provides one hour of access, with additional hours billed at $4.80 each.

Internet Services

Of the 11 Internet-based mutual fund screening services listed here, seven are completely free. Free screening capabilities are available at the Morningstar.com site as well as fee-based screens. Two different screening modules are present at the Quote.com site—both of which are free. Today, mutual fund screening is even free at Microsoft's MSN MoneyCentral Investor site, formerly a subscription-based service.

Screening functions found on the Internet tend to be more extensive than what is offered through on-line services. However, the depth and range of data varies. Those sites that provide free mutual fund screening require you to register with the site. While these sites offer convenience, they still don't outrank the available disk-based services in terms of breadth of data and screening flexibility.

Morningstar.com Free Service	
Performance	2
Usefulness	2
Documentation	2
Ease of Use	5
Value	2

Morningstar.com—Free Service
by Morningstar, Inc.
Free—any PC with Internet access
(800) 735-0700
www.morningstar.com

Morningstar.com includes both free access as well as a fee-based service plan called Premium Service (discussed as a separate service in the next review). Premium Service subscribers gain access to a deeper data set and more powerful screening.

For mutual fund screening, the Fund Selector screening module is divided into three sections: Basic Screens, Preset Screens—both of which are free—and Advanced Screens. Preset Screens is a group of pre-packaged mutual fund screens with such names as "Small and Strong" and "Bargain Bin." The Advanced Screens filtering tool and functionality are described in the next review as part of the Premium Service.

In the free screening area, the Fund Selector module inside the Basic Screens tab is the same tool that frequent users of the site have become accustomed to using. This general-purpose application offers the basics in fund screening criteria and is known for its simplistic user interface. The Basic Screens Fund Selector allows for only two pieces of criteria per screen—one of which has to be a fund category (U.S. stock funds would be one example)—and the other can be any one of nine data fields. This second group of criteria features a list that includes such data points as annualized performance returns and a Morningstar rating. The criteria limitations, however, lower the Basics Screens' overall grade.

FIGURE 7.13
The two-criteria fund screening interface for Morning-star.com's Fund Selector—Basic Screens.

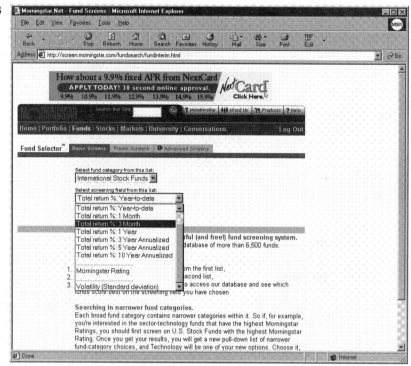

The screening capabilities for the free service are quite limited, and this is not just due to the fact that only two pieces of criteria can be stipulated per screen. For example, screen results supply only the passing funds' ticker, name, and the numbers for the chosen data field; and the results can only be ranked on that selected field. Nevertheless, the Basic Screens tab offers some performance return content that the fee-based service does not. For example, Basic Screens includes returns for both the latest month and latest quarter, and it allows you to screen using those two fields. These screening capabilities are not present with Premium Service, which offers no monthly return data—one clear advantage of the free service.

The free segment of Morningstar.com includes over 200 pieces of data per mutual fund. The information is presented as a multi-tabbed mutual fund Quicktake report. These proprietary Morningstar reports provide everything from fund details to risk and return statistics to portfolio sector weightings. These reports also feature net asset value charts and Morningstar style boxes. These Quicktake reports help in offering complete relative performance coverage, solid risk-related features, and mounds of portfolio information.

FIGURE 7.14
Screen results for an international stock fund using Morningstar.com's Fund Selector— Basic Screens.

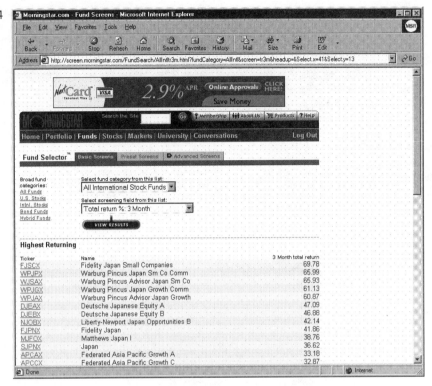

If you are looking for very basic mutual fund screening, the free services at the Morningstar.com Web site should suit you just fine. However, if you are looking for more in-depth data and multi-dimensional screening capabilities, check out the Premium Service on Morningstar.com and its Advanced Screens.

Morningstar.com Premium Service	
Performance	3
Usefulness	3
Documentation	2
Ease of Use	5
Value	3

Morningstar.com—Premium Service
by Morningstar, Inc.
$9.95/mo.—any PC with Internet access
(800) 735-0700
www.morningstar.com

The Morningstar.com Web site includes a subscription-based service plan entitled Premium Service. Premium Service costs $9.95 per month or users can sign up for one year at a cost of $99—and the first two weeks are free. Functionality available only with Premium Service is identified throughout the site by yellow plus signs. Basically, Premium Service expands upon all of the site's free services—in this instance, mutual fund screening capabilities and mutual fund research data.

FIGURE 7.15
Screen criteria and fund results for a domestic stock fund screen using Premium Service's Fund Selector—Advanced Screens.

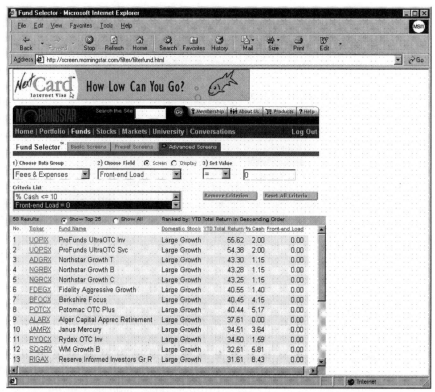

The Premium Service features a more robust screening tool, offering a greater total number of data fields (400+ compared to 200+) and more data fields for screening (70 compared to 10) versus the site's free service. The screening tool here also offers far more flexibility in creating filters. Multiple criteria can be selected in any screen and the results appear on the same page, directly below the criteria. Columns for each selected piece of criteria are listed among the passing fund names. In order to rank results on a certain field, simply click on any one of the column headings.

The Premium Service's Advanced Screens functionality also feature Morningstar Quicktake reports. The Quicktake reports in the Advanced Screens tab include the same information as that found in the Basic Screens tab, as well as some additional fund data and information, most notably expanded return data and portfo-

FIGURE 7.16
Morningstar Style Box details for the Fidelity Aggressive Growth fund as shown in the expanded Morningstar Quicktake report.

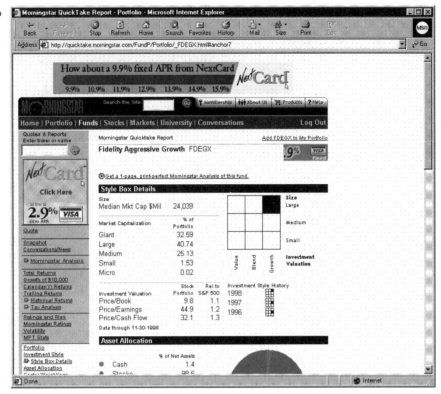

lio holding details. The Advanced Screens' Quicktake report features both a list of the top 25 stock holdings for each mutual fund and several investment style statistics, including total market capitalization of the fund's holdings. It reports seven years of annual return data—like the Basic Quicktake report does, but, in addition, provides quarterly performance returns for the last 24 quarters.

However, there are some negatives to the fee-based fund-screening module. The biggest weakness is missing monthly return data. Potential subscribers need to weigh the huge amount of data along with the more advanced screening capabilities against the missing short-term return data and, of course, the monthly fees when making a decision between the two Morningstar offerings. The fees, like those charged by other sites, bring the value grade down for the Morningstar.com fee-based mutual fund screening tool.

A Premium Service subscription adds value to many areas of the Morningstar.com site, not just to the mutual screening tool. Nevertheless, the Advanced Screens are indeed where the most value has been added, along with the expanded Quicktake reports. Yet the free areas of the site should be sufficient for the analysis needs of the average individual investor. Browse through the free areas of the Morningstar.com site, and if you feel you require more, sign up for Premium Service and test it out for free for two weeks.

MSN MoneyCentral Investor Investment Finder	
Performance	4
Usefulness	4
Documentation	4
Ease of Use	5
Value	4

MSN MoneyCentral Investor— Investment Finder
by Microsoft, Inc.
Free—any PC with Internet access
(800) 426-9400
moneycentral.msn.com/investor

The MSN MoneyCentral Investor site offers a powerful on-line mutual fund screening tool, Investment Finder, as part of its set of additional on-line modules. Fund data is supplied for over 8,000 funds by top resources Morningstar and Value Line; data is updated monthly. MSN MoneyCentral Investor features the most data fields by far (300—100 of which are available for screening) of all the free Internet applications discussed in this chapter and comes close to, if not surpasses, the totals of many software programs in the area.

MSN MoneyCentral Investor, until not too long ago, was a fee-based site costing $9.95 a month for full access to the Web site and all of its trappings. Formerly known to our readers as the fee-based Microsoft Investor Web site, the site was recently redesigned and renamed. One of a few sites considered a "one-stop" multi-dimensional investment center, the MSN MoneyCentral Investor site is currently free to all registered users.

Developing a screen here mirrors the process done in a software interface. Screening criteria are selected from a menu of nine different categories and input one at a time. The results are displayed directly below the screening module, allowing you to easily adjust screening criteria or any additional filters. And as with software, users can save screens. Users can either design their own screens or select from a list of 12 pre-packaged screens.

The Investment Finder offers performance returns for the latest quarter and one-, three-, five-, and 10-year annualized returns. One glaring weakness is that the site does not offer returns for individual years. However, MSN MoneyCentral Investor does have a solid roster of screening options and reporting choices.

FIGURE 7.17
When selecting screening criteria using MSN MoneyCentral Investor Investment Finder module, a description appears for each field.

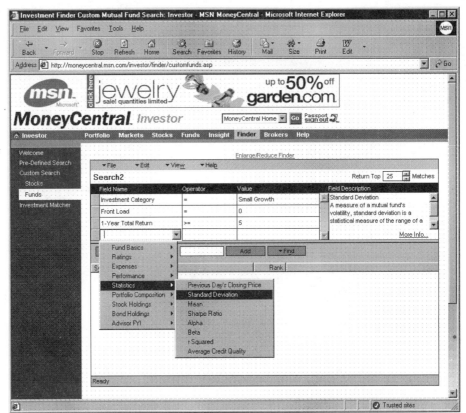

The MSN MoneyCentral Investor site is a multi-dimensional powerhouse site designed to meet the needs of the individual investor. Its numbers—8,000 funds and 300 data fields—are quite impressive, as is its screening proficiency. The fact that its data and extensive screening capabilities are available for free is a bonus. This is the only Web site that can compete on the level of the software programs. In fact, it can excel on that level—a quite suitable stand-alone screening application. In addition, a similar stock screener and an on-line portfolio management system are also found on the site. Access to broad news archives, consensus earnings estimates and analyst recommendations, and company and fund reports are also provided.

FIGURE 7.18
A list of passing funds screened by the MSN MoneyCentral Investor Web site's Investment Finder module.

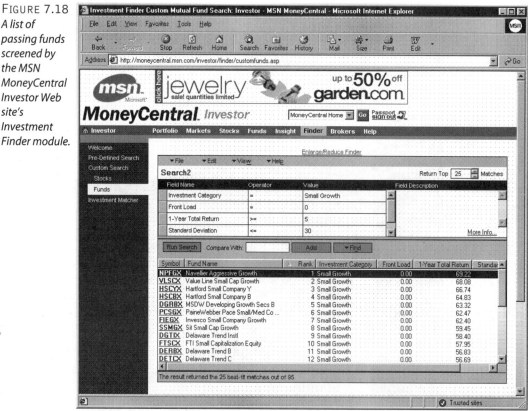

Mutual Funds Online Fund Selection System	
Performance	3
Usefulness	3
Documentation	4
Ease of Use	3
Value	3

Mutual Funds Online—
Fund Selection System
by Mutual Funds Magazine
$9.99/mo.—any PC with Internet access
(800) 442-9000
www.mfmag.com

Mutual Funds magazine hosts two unique mutual fund screening tools at their Web site (www.mfmag.com): Quick & EZ and Advanced screening. Collectively, both tools are referred to as the Fund Selection System. Both can only be accessed by subscription, which costs $9.99 a month.

FIGURE 7.19
*The General
Info screening
tab as found
on the Mutual
Funds
Magazine site.*

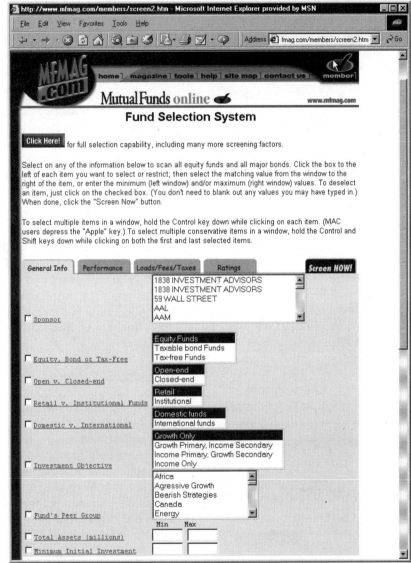

The Quick & EZ screener is designed for users who want to get in, conduct their simple screens, get out, and go forward—fast and simple, as the name conveys. The Quick & EZ module is a simplified version of the Advanced screener—it is scaled down in terms of data points and stripped of certain enhancements and features found in the Advanced section.

For example, Quick & EZ allows you to select up to three possible total return criteria and one fund all-star rating. While Advanced offers five possible total return criteria, it also provides five fund returns minus (percentage gain over) category, five returns minus (percentage gain over) an index, five fund percentile rankings, as well as five all-star ratings choices.

Fund profile reports offer 180 pieces of data per fund, with Quick & EZ providing 58 data fields available for screening and Advanced providing over 190 screenable fields. One drawback of both screening applications is that screen results are only given ranked alphabetically by fund name. Fund reports and data content are the same for each application and Advanced screening has slightly more filtering options available to it. Fund reports are updated daily and include peer group and S&P return numbers, fund returns, and four different price charts.

Subscribers also gain access to the top 10 best- and worst-performing fund lists and a total return performance calculator, as well as the ability to browse current and back issues of the Mutual Funds Magazine. The Mutual Funds' site is a great resource for mutual fund information and it offers some nice add-on tools and a lot of flexibility, not to mention solid fund screening capabilities. The price charged for access is a little steep for what you get, considering the site is geared toward mutual funds and mutual fund analysis only, but it is good at what it does. For the individual who invests only in mutual funds, Mutual Funds Magazine's Fund Selection System is an excellent choice.

Quicken.com Mutual Fund Finder	
Performance	2
Usefulness	3
Documentation	2
Ease of Use	4
Value	3

Quicken.com—Mutual Fund Finder
by Intuit Inc.
Free—any PC with Internet access
(800) 446-8848
www.quicken.com

Intuit, Inc., maintains a mutual fund screening application, Mutual Fund Finder, at the Quicken.com Web site (www.quicken.com). The same exact screening tool can be found at several investment Web sites including CNNfn, AOL.com, and Prodigy Internet. A similar tool based upon this Quicken.com model, is also available on America Online's Personal Finance proprietary content channel.

Supplied with data by Morningstar, this continually revamped site is updated weekly and includes an impressive 9,400-fund database. In the past at this site, finding funds that matched your investment criteria meant selecting categories and merely entering upper and lower limits for fund performance and loads. With this most recent update, users now have access to multiple criteria—over 20 total—for use in a single screen.

FIGURE 7.20
Screen results as represented by the Mutual Fund Finder at the Quicken.com Web site.

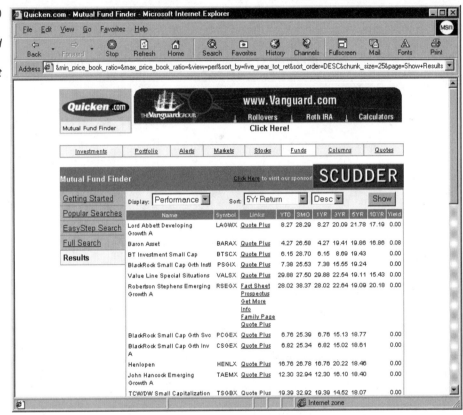

The site offers performance returns for the last quarter and individual returns for the last 15 years along with annualized returns for one, three, five, 10, and 15 years. Quicken.com offers a fair amount of screening choices as well as charting and portfolio management capabilities. The site offers extensive risk-related measures including alpha, beta, and R-squared. The coverage in terms of portfolio information is quite competitive as well; fund manager, asset composition and the largest holdings of the fund are provided. Quicken.com also features a group of screens based on popular investing strategies as well as a step-by-step search module designed to help novice screeners create meaningful fund screens.

Mutual Fund Finder on Quicken.com is a basic filtering application for mutual funds. Screening capabilities are below average but get the job done. For an individual looking to perform basic fund screening and analysis at no cost, this is a site worth browsing.

Quote.com Mutual Fund Center	
Performance	3
Usefulness	4
Documentation	3
Ease of Use	4
Value	4

Quote.com—Mutual Fund Center

by Quote.com, Inc.
Free—any PC with Internet access
(800) 498-8068
www.quote.com

The Mutual Fund Center on the Quote.com Web site (www.quote.com) features two separate screening modules, both of which are free to registered users. The basic screens area is for users requiring quick-and-to-the-point screening. Those looking for more detailed, in-depth screening can also find advanced screens at the same site. The two screening tools feature the same data set, a slightly reduced Morningstar database of over 7,500 funds.

Basic screening provides 11 data fields, while the advanced section offers a more robust 110 fields. The filtering options available with advanced screening include expanded time frames and more performance returns. Advanced screening includes the risk measurement beta. Both screening modules provide standard portfolio information, with advanced screening including the percentage of the fund's investments in foreign securities. With advanced screening, you can also establish up to 12 unique fund screening profiles. These profiles can be run manually or set up to run automatically, with the results E-mailed to the user.

The two screening applications include formidable amounts of screening options and both offer charting functions. Lipper and Morningstar reports are available for free. If you are looking for cheap, rudimentary fund screening, check out Quote.com's basic fund screens. However if you are seeking progressive screening, be sure to see what the advanced screens offer.

FIGURE 7.21
Screening criteria selected using the Quote.com Mutual Fund Center Basic screening interface.

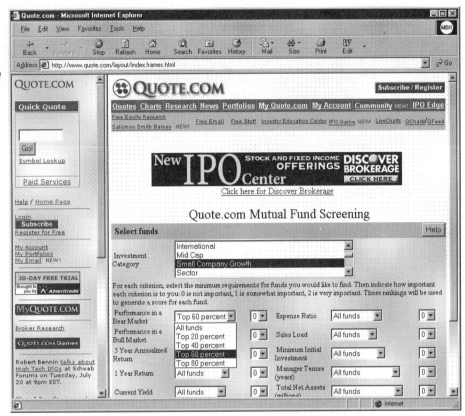

S&P Personal Wealth— Mutual Fund Finder	
Performance	3
Usefulness	4
Documentation	4
Ease of Use	3
Value	3

S&P Personal Wealth— Mutual Fund Finder
by Standard & Poor's
$9.95/mo.–$99.95/yr.—any PC with Internet access
(800) 823-3209
www.personalwealth.com

Standard & Poor's one-stop investment center Web site, Personal Wealth, features its own mutual fund filtering tool, Mutual Fund Finder.

As part of its Premium Service, Mutual Fund Finder presents the basic fund screening interface and comes with a nice "add another row" feature for each of its screening fields. With this add-on function, multiple returns can be stipulated and several risk measures can be utilized in one screen. Mutual Fund Finder includes 34 screenable categories, and up to five columns of data can be used for sorting results.

FIGURE 7.22
With the Mutual Fund Search module on the Personal Wealth site, an "add another row" function allows users to set multiple returns.

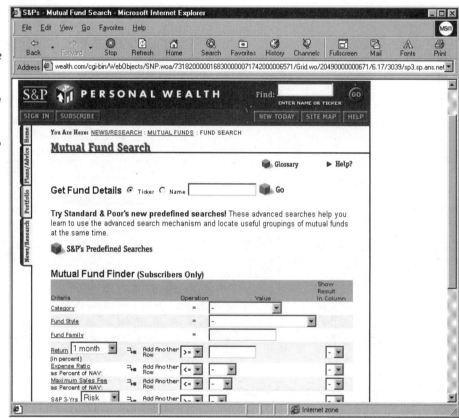

Returns available here include: performance total returns for the latest month and second quarter; annualized returns for one, three, five, and 10 years; and individual annual returns for each of the last five years. Relative performance comparisons are merely versus fund peer group and versus the S&P 500. Risk-related features are quite formidable—with R-squared and the Sharpe ratio as part of its roster—and portfolio information includes five years of dividends and capital gains as well as a fund asset allocation breakdown and a list of the fund's top 10 holdings. S&P Personal Wealth, along with Microsoft Investor, are the only Internet offerings to provide complete screening capabilities. Personal Wealth also comes with a set of five pre-packaged S&P screens.

The site's six-page reports feature a Big Charts module that can plot 14 different price chart time frames, compare the fund to an index, and apply simple moving averages to the charts.

Personal Wealth is a comprehensive site offering solid mutual fund analysis tools and excellent fund reports. This Premium Service, like the plan from Morningstar, comes at a cost of $9.95 per month, or just less than $100 a year.

SmartMoney.com Fund Finder	
Performance	3
Usefulness	3
Documentation	4
Ease of Use	5
Value	3

SmartMoney.com—Fund Finder
by SmartMoney Magazine
Free—any PC with Internet access
www.smartmoney.com

SmartMoney (www.smartmoney.com) has entered the arena of on-line screening with its free Fund Finder. A Java-based application that loads directly within your browser, Fund Finder offers users a unique screening experience. A crisp, five-tab module guides you through the creation of screens and offers assistance by providing low, average, and high statistics for applicable fields, like historical returns. These statistics are based upon all funds in the current database. The site also prepares six different top 25 screens based on total returns—updated daily.

Lipper provides the Fund Finder with data on over 6,000 funds including latest month and latest quarter total returns, and one-, three-, and five-year annualized returns. Individual year returns and a year-to-date return are two performance returns missing from the site. Fund Finder has 26 available fields for screening and results can be sorted on 13 of those fields—all of which are displayed in the results window. One drawback of the Fund Finder is that results are only posted once the screen has filtered the database down to a respectable viewing level—under 50 funds, according to our trials.

The results window also has a very interesting secondary tab that allows for detailed analysis of the top 15 funds from any screen. Continuing with the dynamic Java capabilities, this tab shows how each fund in the top 15 of your screen falls into a high/low visual distribution range for one of 15 data categories, like returns and risk measures. This one-of-a-kind feature includes points plotted along the range as well as the specific number for each fund. The beauty of this tab's display is that it allows users to quickly pick out the outliers and find the norm for each value.

FIGURE 7.23
The screening module found on the Smart-Money.com site provides users with low, average, and high statistics for applicable screening fields.

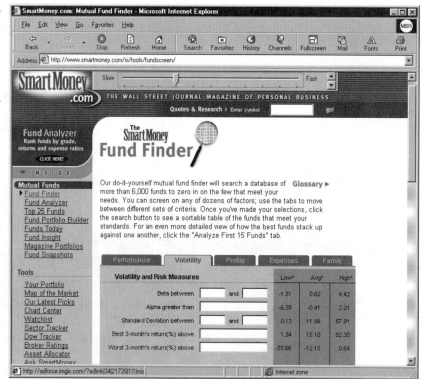

Another unique feature available on the SmartMoney site is the Fund Finder snapshot report. Setting themselves apart yet again, these unique reports provide not only the basic data and information but they also highlight any unusually high or low numbers—marking them with "favorable" (like a high total return), "unfavorable" (like a very low return), and "take note" symbols (for instance, any unusual number SmartMoney thinks you should note).

The SmartMoney Fund Finder is a unique application and quite sharp, to say the least. The screening capabilities are nice, but it is the data interpretation that sets this Web site apart from the competition and makes it a site worth checking out.

Stockpoint Fundfinder Pro	
Performance	2
Usefulness	2
Documentation	2
Ease of Use	4
Value	2

Stockpoint—Fundfinder Pro
by Stockpoint, Inc.
Free—any PC with Internet access
(415) 394-6800
www.stockpoint.com

Stockpoint, Inc., offers a free fund screening package at its Web sitecalled Fundfinder Pro. A very basic screening tool, Fundfinder Pro features a respectable Value Line database of over 7,500 funds. However, this tool offers only very basic screening capabilities—15 screenable data fields, limited database content, and few screening options. Missing from the data roster are monthly and quarterly total returns and individual year returns. Fundfinder Pro can only screen on a fund's category, three different performance returns, an expense ratio, two kinds of loads, and a fee.

FIGURE 7.24
Some of the screening criteria available with the Stockpoint Fundfinder Pro tool.

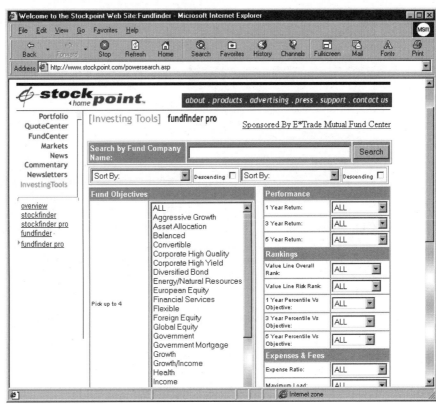

345

The service does include a nice feature called search tips. For the novice screener, these tips can be very handy and may help alleviate the frustrations of many investors who are new to screening and whose first screens result in zero funds.

Stockpoint also provides a set of pre-packaged top 25 screens for over 70 different categories at a Fundfinder link on the site. A major bonus of the Fundfinder application is the site's charts. Fundfinder reports feature both simple, quick charts as well as advanced interactive charts. The free interactive charts allow you to plot seven different technical indicators, including Bollinger bands and stochastics. You can add seven different comparison indexes to its charts and choose from three different chart types, including line and candlestick. These charts are interactive via a Java-based "Zoom In and Zoom Out" function, which allows for fine-tuned analysis. Charts are updated daily.

Fundfinder Pro is a very simple screening tool, but the charting functions add the most value. If you are looking to do basic screening, check out Stockpoint, but everyone should log onto this Web site to test-drive its charts.

Thomson Investor Network Mutual Fund Center	
Performance	2
Usefulness	3
Documentation	2
Ease of Use	3
Value	3

Thomson Investors Network— Mutual Funds Center
by Thomson Financial Services, Inc.
Free—any PC with Internet access
(301) 545-4999
www.thomsoninvest.net

Thomson Financial Services is now offering free mutual fund research and a screening application at their updated Thomson Investors Network site (www.thomsoninvest.net). The application is called Mutual Funds Center, and it features a database covering 9,900+ funds. Mutual fund data is provided by CDA/Wiesenberger. Mutual fund information exceeds 300 data points per fund and 35 data fields are available for screening. The Mutual Funds Center offers basic fund screening criteria including fund objectives; expenses; and performance returns for the latest month and latest quarter; a year-to-date return; and one-, three-, five-, and 10-year annualized returns.

Thomson Investors Network also features pre-defined mutual fund screens, updated every month. Categories include: three-month return; year-to-date return; one-, three-, five-, and 10-year returns; and six sub-category groups (stock, sector, balanced, international, taxable bond, tax-free bond). The site also offers net asset value charts.

FIGURE 7.25
Results of an aggressive growth screen created on the Thomson Investors Network site.

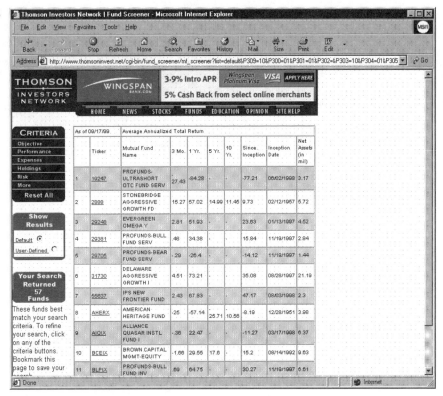

The Thomson Investors Network site does a fine job of mutual fund screening and research. The screening tool's functionality leaves something to be desired but, overall, it is a good source for elementary fund filtering.

Wall Street City—Mutual Fund Java Powersearch	
Performance	3
Usefulness	4
Documentation	2
Ease of Use	5
Value	3

Wall Street City— Mutual Fund Java Powersearch

by Telescan, Inc.
$34.95/mo.—any PC with Internet access
(800) 324-8246
www.wallstreetcity.com

Telescan's home on the Web, the Wall Street City site (www.wallstreetcity.com), features a Java-based ProSearch-style module called Java Powersearch.

Offering a software-like appearance, Powersearch's interface includes five field-picker categories like general characteristics, performance, and composition. Powersearch features solid fund reports from J&J Financial. These reports offer over 70 pieces of data, including percentile rank versus all funds and percentile rank versus category.

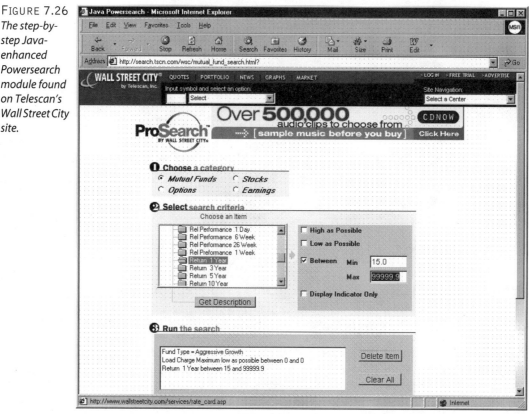

Telescan, famous for its charting and technical analysis software programs, has set the same standard here on Wall Street City. Ten different technical indicators—Bollinger bands, moving average convergence-divergence (MACD), and on-balance volume just to name a few—can be plotted for almost any time frame, from as short as a month to as complete as 15 years. Historical quotes for any of the funds in the Telescan database are also available. Daily, weekly, monthly, quarterly, yearly, and intraday quotes can be accessed and are available for exporting via eight different formats.

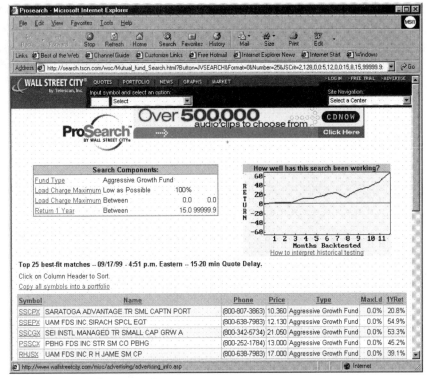

FIGURE 7.27
The passing funds page from the Wall Street City Powersearch module offers a backtesting chart of the current screen.

Database content is quite solid, especially in terms of performance where latest month and quarter returns are provided as well as a year-to-date return and one-, three-, five-, seven-and-half-, and 10-year annualized returns. However, much of this data is missing in the Powersearch module itself, where return criteria is only available for the annualized years. This miss is a little odd and a clear negative of the site's screening tool.

Most of Wall Street City's tools and data content is part of the fee-based Premium Service, which costs $34.95 a month. This includes the customizable Powersearch screens, along with a group of backtested best- and worst-performing searches. A set of pre-determined mutual fund search results, updated throughout the day, are available for free. A free 30-day trial of the Premium Service is available.

The Wall Street City site as a comprehensive investment center has a lot to offer its subscribers—but looking at the site strictly as a mutual fund screening tool, it is rather pricey compared to the other fee-based services. A lower subscription price would definitely raise the Java Powersearch's value grade.

Comparison Grid

The mutual fund screening comparison grid features some abbreviations in the sections entitled risk-related features and portfolio information. These abbreviations are used primarily because of space constraints within the grid.

The risk features abbreviations include the following:

a: alpha, market risk-adjusted performance figure

avg mat: average maturity (for bond funds)

B: beta, a measure of market risk

R-sq: R-squared, proportion of beta related to market

st dev: standard deviation, volatility of fund's return

S: Sharpe ratio, standard deviation-adjusted measure of performance

T: Treynor ratio, beta-adjusted measure of performance

The portfolio information abbreviations include:

comp: portfolio asset composition

foreign: percentage of fund in foreign securities

lg hold: largest holding of fund

mgr: portfolio manager and tenure

cap gains: unrealized capital gains

Mutual Fund Analysis: Disk-Based Services		Mutual Fund Expert 6.0 Personal	Mutual Fund Expert 6.0 Pro
Company		Steele Systems, Inc.	Steele Systems, Inc.
Telephone		(800) 379-0679	(800) 379-0679
Web Address		www.mutualfundexpert.com	www.mutualfundexpert.com
E-mail		mutualexp@aol.com	mutualexp@aol.com
Delivery Medium (Software/Internet/On-line)		software (CD-ROM)	software (CD-ROM)
Update Schedule		monthly/quarterly	monthly/quarterly
Price (AAII Member Discount)		$185/$95 (20%)	$499/$299 (20%)
Platform		Windows	Windows
Data Source		Standard & Poor's Micropal	Standard & Poor's Micropal
Database Content	Number of Funds/Indexes	11,600+/66	11,600+/66
	Number of Data Fields	89	208
	Number of Data Fields for Screening	89	208
	Number of Data Fields for Ranking	89	208
	Performance — Monthly Total Returns	last 12 months	last 12 months
	Quarterly Total Returns	last 4 quarters	last 4 quarters
	Annualized Returns	3/5/10 years	3/5/10 years
	Return for Individual Yrs.	last 10 years	last 10 years
	YTD Return	✖	✖
	Relative	% rank, +/- category, +/- index	% rank, +/- category, +/- index
	Risk-Related Features	B, st dev, avg mat	a, B, R-sq, st dev, avg mat, S, T
	Portfolio Information		mgr
Screening	Any Data Field	✖	✖
	Category	✖	✖
	Monthly Returns	✖	✖
	Quarterly Returns	✖	✖
	Annualized Returns	✖	✖
	Calendar Year Returns	✖	✖
	YTD Return	✖	✖
	Relative Performance	✖	✖
	Risk	✖	✖
	Portfolio Information	✖	✖
	Fees/Expenses/Loads	✖	✖
Reporting	Charts	✖	✖
	Specific Time Periods	✖	✖
	Predefined/Custom Formats	✖	✖
	Export to a File	✖	✖

Mutual Fund Analysis: Disk-Based Services			Mutual Fund Expert 6.0 Pro Plus	Mutual Fund Survey 2.0
Company			Steele Systems, Inc.	Value Line, Inc.
Telephone			(800) 379-0679	(800) 535-8760
Web Address			www.mutualfundexpert.com	www.valueline.com
E-mail			mutualexp@aol.com	vliswin@valueline.com
Delivery Medium (Software/Internet/On-line)			software (CD-ROM)	software (CD-ROM)
Update Schedule			monthly/quarterly	monthly/quarterly
Price (AAII Member Discount)			$599/$399 (20%)	$395/$149
Platform			Windows	Windows
Data Source			Standard & Poor's Micropal	Value Line
Database Content	Number of Funds/Indexes		11,600+/66	10,000+/17
	Number of Data Fields		592	175
	Number of Data Fields for Screening		592	175
	Number of Data Fields for Ranking		592	175
	Performance	Monthly Total Returns	1962 to present	latest month
		Quarterly Total Returns	1962 to present	last 2 quarters
		Annualized Returns	1962 to present	1/3/5/10/15/20 years
		Return for Individual Yrs.	1962 to present	1977 to present
		YTD Return	✖	✖
		Relative	% rank, +/- category, +/- index	% rank, +/- category, +/- index
	Risk-Related Features		a, B, R-sq, st dev, avg mat, S, T	a, B, R-sq, st dev, avg mat, S
	Portfolio Information		mgr, comp	mgr, comp, lg hold, cap gain, foreign
Screening	Any Data Field		✖	✖
	Category		✖	✖
	Monthly Returns		✖	✖
	Quarterly Returns		✖	
	Annualized Returns		✖	✖
	Calendar Year Returns		✖	✖
	YTD Return		✖	✖
	Relative Performance		✖	✖
	Risk		✖	✖
	Portfolio Information		✖	✖
	Fees/Expenses/Loads		✖	✖
Reporting	Charts		✖	✖
	Specific Time Periods		✖	✖
	Predefined/Custom Formats		✖	✖
	Export to a File		✖	✖

Mutual Fund Analysis: Disk-Based Services			Principia Pro for Mutual Funds 4.1	Principia Pro Plus for Mutual Funds 4.1	Quarterly Low-Load Mutual Fund Update
Company			Morningstar, Inc.	Morningstar, Inc.	AAII
Telephone			(800) 735-0700	(800) 735-0700	(800) 428-2244
Web Address			www.morningstar.com	www.morningstar.com	www.aaii.com
E-mail			productssup-portweb@mstar.com	productssup-portweb@mstar.com	quarterly@aaii.com
Delivery Medium (Software/Internet/On-line)			software (CD-ROM)	software (CD-ROM)	software (diskette)
Update Schedule			monthly/quarterly	monthly/quarterly	quarterly
Price (AAII Member Discount)			$495/$295	$895/$595;	$50 (22%)
Platform			Windows	Windows	DOS, Mac
Data Source			Morningstar	Morningstar	Standard & Poor's Micropal
Database Content	Number of Funds/Indexes		10,000+/175	10,000+/175	1,100+/31
	Number of Data Fields		140+	300+	76
	Number of Data Fields for Screening		140+	140+	63
	Number of Data Fields for Ranking		140+	140+	14
	Performance	Monthly Total Returns	latest month	latest month	
		Quarterly Total Returns	latest quarter	latest quarter	last 3 quarters
		Annualized Returns	trailing 12 months	trailing 12 months	1/3/5 years
		Return for Individual Yrs.	last 10 years	last 15 years	last 10 years
		YTD Return	✖	✖	
		Relative	% rank, +/- category, +/- index	% rank, +/- category, +/- index	% rank, +/- category
	Risk-Related Features		a, B, R-sq, st dev, avg mat, S	a, B, R-sq, st dev, avg mat, S	B, st dev, avg mat
	Portfolio Information		mgr, comp, lg hold, cap gain, foreign	mgr, comp, lg hold, cap gain, foreign	mgr
Screening	Any Data Field		✖	✖	
	Category		✖	✖	✖
	Monthly Returns		✖	✖	
	Quarterly Returns		✖	✖	✖
	Annualized Returns		✖	✖	✖
	Calendar Year Returns		✖	✖	
	YTD Return		✖	✖	
	Relative Performance		✖	✖	✖
	Risk		✖	✖	✖
	Portfolio Information		✖	✖	
	Fees/Expenses/Loads		✖	✖	
Reporting	Charts		✖	✖	
	Specific Time Periods		✖	✖	
	Predefined/Custom Formats		✖	✖	
	Export to a File		✖	✖	

Mutual Fund Analysis: On-Line Services		TIP@Wallstreet with Mutual Fund Search 1.2
Company		Telescan, Inc.
Telephone		(800) 324-8246
Web Address		www.wallstreetcity.com
E-mail		webmaster@telescan.com
Delivery Medium (Software/Internet/On-line)		on-line
Update Schedule		daily/weekly/monthly/quarterly
Price (AAII Member Discount)		$349.00 (10%) for software plus access fees
Platform		DOS, Windows
Data Source		Telescan
Database Content	Number of Funds/Indexes	9,000+/450+
	Number of Data Fields	82
	Number of Data Fields for Screening	82
	Number of Data Fields for Ranking	82
	Performance	Monthly Total Returns	
		Quarterly Total Returns	last 4 quarters
		Annualized Returns	last 15 years
		Return for Individual Yrs.	last 15 years
		Year-to-Date Return	
		Relative	% rank, +/- category, +/- index
	Risk-Related Features	a, B, R-sq, st dev, avg mat
	Portfolio Information	mgr, comp, lg hold, cap gain, foreign
Screening	Any Data Field	✖
	Category	✖
	Monthly Returns	✖
	Quarterly Returns	
	Annualized Returns	✖
	Calendar Year Returns	
	Year-to-Date Return	
	Relative Performance	✖
	Risk	✖
	Portfolio Information	✖
	Fees/Expenses/Loads	✖
Reporting	Charts	✖
	Specific Time Periods	
	Predefined/Custom Formats	
	Export to a File	✖

Mutual Fund Analysis: Internet-Based Services			Morningstar.com— Free Service (Basic Screens)	Morningstar.com—Premium Service (Advanced Screens)
Company			Morningstar, Inc.	Morningstar, Inc.
Telephone			(800) 735-0700	(800) 735-0700
Web Address			www.morningstar.com	www.morningstar.com
E-mail			joe@morningstar.com	joe@morningstar.com
Delivery Medium (Software/Internet/On-line)			Internet	Internet
Update Schedule			monthly	monthly
Price (AAII Member Discount)			free w/Internet access	$9.95/month or $99.00/year
Platform			any PC with Internet	any PC with Internet
Data Source			Morningstar	Morningstar
Database Content	Number of Funds/Indexes		8,000+/NA	8,000+/NA
	Number of Data Fields		200+	400+
	Number of Data Fields for Screening		10	70
	Number of Data Fields for Ranking		10	70
	Performance	Monthly Total Returns	latest month	
		Quarterly Total Returns	latest quarter	1992 to present
		Annualized Returns	1/3/5/10 years	1/3/5/10 years
		Return for Individual Yrs.	1991 to present	1991 to present
		YTD Return	✖	✖
		Relative	% rank, +/- category, +/- index	% rank, +/-category, +/- index
	Risk-Related Features		a, B, r-sq, st dev, avg mat, S	a, B, r-sq, st dev, avg mat, S
	Portfolio Information		mgr, comp, lg hold, foreign	mgr, comp, lg hold, foreign
Screening	Any Data Field		✖	✖
	Category		✖	✖
	Monthly Returns		✖	
	Quarterly Returns		✖	
	Annualized Returns		✖	✖
	Calendar Year Returns			
	YTD Return		✖	✖
	Relative Performance			✖
	Risk		✖	✖
	Portfolio Information		✖	✖
	Fees/Expenses/Loads		✖	✖
Reporting	Charts		✖	✖
	Specific Time Periods			
	Predefined/Custom Formats			
	Export to a File			

355

Mutual Fund Analysis: Internet-Based Services		MSN MoneyCentral Investor—Investment Finder	Mutual Funds Online—Fund Selection System
Company		Microsoft, Inc.	Mutual Funds Magazine
Telephone		(800) 426-9400	(800) 442-9000
Web Address		moneycentral.msn.com/investor	www.mfmag.com
E-mail		webmaster@msn.com	webmaster@mfmag.com
Delivery Medium (Software/Internet/On-line)		Internet	Internet
Update Schedule		monthly	daily
Price (AAII Member Discount)		free w/Internet access	$9.99/ month
Platform		any PC with Internet	any PC with Internet
Data Source		Morningstar, Value Line	Mutual Funds Magazine
Database Content	Number of Funds/Indexes	8,000+/24	10,000+/NA
	Number of Data Fields	300+	180
	Number of Data Fields for Screening	100+	196 (58 for Quick & EZ)
	Number of Data Fields for Ranking	100+	1
	Performance — Monthly Total Returns		latest month
	Quarterly Total Returns	latest quarter	last two quarters
	Annualized Returns	1/3/5/10 years	1/3/5/10 years
	Return for Individual Yrs.		1981 to present
	YTD Return	✖	
	Relative	% rank, +/- category, +/- index	+/- category, +/- index
	Risk-Related Features		a, B, st dev, avg mat
	Portfolio Information	mgr, comp, lg hold, cap gain	mgr
Screening	Any Data Field	✖	✖
	Category	✖	✖
	Monthly Returns	✖	✖
	Quarterly Returns	✖	✖
	Annualized Returns	✖	✖
	Calendar Year Returns	✖	✖
	YTD Return	✖	
	Relative Performance	✖	✖
	Risk	✖	✖
	Portfolio Information	✖	✖
	Fees/Expenses/Loads	✖	✖
Reporting	Charts	✖	✖
	Specific Time Periods	✖	
	Predefined/Custom Formats	✖	
	Export to a File	✖	

Mutual Fund Analysis: Internet-Based Services		Quicken.com— Mutual Fund Finder	Quote.com— Mutual Fund Center-Basic
Company		Intuit Inc.	Quote.com, Inc.
Telephone		(800) 446-8848	(800) 498-8068
Web Address		www.quicken.com	www.quote.com
E-mail			info@quote.com
Delivery Medium (Software/Internet/On-line)		Internet	Internet
Update Schedule		monthly	weekly
Price (AAII Member Discount)		free w/Internet access	free w/Internet access
Platform		any PC with Internet	any PC with Internet
Data Source		Morningstar, Value Line	Lipper
Database Content	Number of Funds/Indexes	9,400+/NA	7,500+/NA
	Number of Data Fields	100+	100+
	Number of Data Fields for Screening	20	11
	Number of Data Fields for Ranking	6	10
	Performance — Monthly Total Returns		
	Quarterly Total Returns	latest quarter	
	Annualized Returns	1/3/5/10/15 years	5 years
	Return for Individual Yrs.	last 15 years	latest year
	YTD Return	✖	
	Relative	+/- index	% rank
	Risk-Related Features	a, B, R-sq, st dev	
	Portfolio Information	mgr, comp, lg hold	mgr, comp, lg hold
Screening	Any Data Field	✖	✖
	Category	✖	✖
	Monthly Returns		
	Quarterly Returns	✖	
	Annualized Returns	✖	✖
	Calendar Year Returns		✖
	YTD Return	✖	
	Relative Performance	✖	✖
	Risk		✖
	Portfolio Information	✖	✖
	Fees/Expenses/Loads	✖	✖
Reporting	Charts	✖	✖
	Specific Time Periods		
	Predefined/Custom Formats		
	Export to a File		✖

Mutual Fund Analysis: Internet-Based Services			Quote.com—Mutual Fund Center-Advanced	S&P Personal Wealth—Mutual Fund Finder
Company			Quote.com, Inc.	Standard & Poor's
Telephone			(800) 498-8068	(800) 823-3209
Web Address			www.quote.com	www.personalwealth.com
E-mail			info@quote.com	
Delivery Medium (Software/Internet/On-line)			Internet	Internet
Update Schedule			weekly	daily
Price (AAII Member Discount)			free w/Internet access	$9.95/month or $99.95/year
Platform			any PC with Internet	any PC with Internet
Data Source			Morningstar, Lipper	Standard & Poor's Micropal
Database Content	Number of Funds/Indexes		7,500+/NA	10,000+/NA
	Number of Data Fields		110	110
	Number of Data Fields for Screening		110	34
	Number of Data Fields for Ranking		110	5
	Performance	Monthly Total Returns	latest month	latest month
		Quarterly Total Returns	latest quarter	second quarter
		Annualized Returns	1/5/10 years	1/3/5/10 years
		Return for Individual Yrs.		1994 to present
		YTD Return	✖	✖
		Relative	% rank	+/- category, +/- index
	Risk-Related Features		B	a, B, R-sq, st dev, avg mat, S
	Portfolio Information		mgr, comp, lg hold, foreign	mgr, comp, lg hold, cap gain
Screening	Any Data Field		✖	✖
	Category		✖	✖
	Monthly Returns			✖
	Quarterly Returns			✖
	Annualized Returns		✖	✖
	Calendar Year Returns		✖	✖
	YTD Return		✖	✖
	Relative Performance		✖	✖
	Risk		✖	✖
	Portfolio Information		✖	✖
	Fees/Expenses/Loads		✖	✖
Reporting	Charts		✖	✖
	Specific Time Periods			
	Predefined/Custom Formats			
	Export to a File		✖	

Mutual Fund Analysis: Internet-Based Services		SmartMoney.com— Fund Finder	Stockpoint—Fundfinder Pro
Company		SmartMoney Magazine	Stockpoint, Inc.
Telephone			(415) 394-6800
Web Address		www.smartmoney.com	www.stockpoint.com
E-mail		support@smartmoney.com	webmaster@stockpoint.com
Delivery Medium (Software/Internet/On-line)		Internet	Internet
Update Schedule		daily	monthly
Price (AAII Member Discount)		free w/Internet access	free w/Internet access
Platform		any PC with Internet	any PC with Internet
Data Source		Lipper	Value Line
Database Content	Number of Funds/Indexes	6,000+/NA	7,500+/NA
	Number of Data Fields	52	48
	Number of Data Fields for Screening	26	15
	Number of Data Fields for Ranking	13	14
	Performance — Monthly Total Returns	latest month	
	Quarterly Total Returns	latest quarter	
	Annualized Returns	1/3/5 years	1/3/5/10 years
	Return for Individual Yrs.		
	YTD Return		✖
	Relative	+/- category	% rank
	Risk-Related Features	a, B, R-sq, st dev	
	Portfolio Information	mgr, comp, lg hold	mgr, comp, lg hold, cap gain
Screening	Any Data Field	✖	✖
	Category	✖	✖
	Monthly Returns		
	Quarterly Returns	✖	
	Annualized Returns	✖	✖
	Calendar Year Returns		
	YTD Return	✖	
	Relative Performance		
	Risk	✖	
	Portfolio Information		
	Fees/Expenses/Loads	✖	✖
Reporting	Charts	✖	✖
	Specific Time Periods		
	Predefined/Custom Formats		
	Export to a File		

Mutual Fund Analysis: Internet-Based Services		Thomson Investors Network—Mutual Funds Center	Wall Street City—Mutual Fund Java Powersearch
Company		Thomson Financial Services, Inc.	Telescan, Inc.
Telephone		(301) 545-4999	(800) 324-8246
Web Address		www.thomsoninvest.net	www.wallstreetcity.com
E-mail		custserv1@thomsoninvest.net	webmaster@wallstreetcity.com
Delivery Medium (Software/Internet/On-line)		Internet	Internet
Update Schedule		monthly	daily
Price (AAII Member Discount)		free w/Internet access	$34.95/month
Platform		any PC with Internet	any PC with Internet
Data Source		CDA/Wiesenberger	Telescan, J&J Financial Co.
Database Content	Number of Funds/Indexes	9,900+/NA	9,000+/NA
	Number of Data Fields	300+	71
	Number of Data Fields for Screening	35	83
	Number of Data Fields for Ranking		83
	Performance	Monthly Total Returns	latest month	latest month
		Quarterly Total Returns	latest quarter	latest quarter
		Annualized Returns	1/3/5/10 years	1/3/5/7.5/10 years
		Return for Individual Yrs.		
		YTD Return	✖	✖
		Relative	% rank, +/- category, +/- index	% rank, % rank category
	Risk-Related Features		
	Portfolio Information	comp	mgr, comp
Screening	Any Data Field	✖	✖
	Category	✖	✖
	Monthly Returns	✖	
	Quarterly Returns	✖	
	Annualized Returns	✖	✖
	Calendar Year Returns		
	YTD Return	✖	
	Relative Performance	✖	✖
	Risk	✖	✖
	Portfolio Information	✖	✖
	Fees/Expenses/Loads	✖	✖
Reporting	Charts	✖	✖
	Specific Time Periods		
	Predefined/Custom Formats		
	Export to a File		✖

Chapter 8

FINANCIAL INFORMATION SERVICES

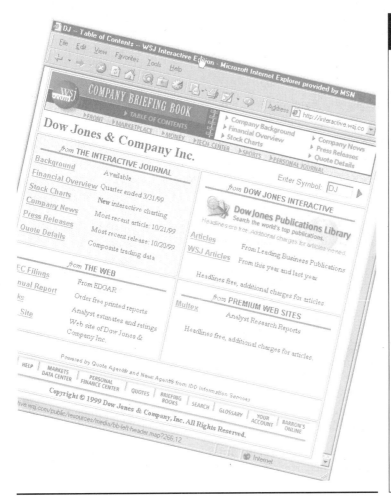

The tremendous growth in financial information services has created a windfall of choices for the individual investor. Financial information services continue to blossom over the Internet—providing a broader range of financial data more affordably. Information services allow you to study a larger group of securities using a wider set of analytical techniques more quickly and consistently by gathering a broad range of data in one spot. Communities of on-line investors gather regularly to swap stock ideas and gain new perspectives on the forces moving closely followed stocks. Free financial information flows throughout.

In this chapter we explore the financial information market as it applies to three primary functions—monitoring your investment portfolio and the general market, performing fundamental stock analysis, and performing technical analysis and charting. We compare the offerings of the major dial-up on-line services and report on the best general-purpose Internet sites for investors.

The Internet

This chapter provides a focus on on-line financial information services—services that you can access through phone and modem. However, before we discuss the information available on-line, an examination of connection options is in order.

Traditionally investors used on-line service companies such as America Online and CompuServe for news, quotes, data, message boards and data downloads. Each on-line service offered its proprietary mix of dial-up software and content, and competed against each other to attract subscribers. The on-line services collected and organized their content for their subscribers. Each service had a unique look and feel. Navigational controls often differed dramatically from service to service. Subscribers could send electronic mail (E-mail) to other subscribers on the same service, but not to someone on a competing service. The development of the Internet as a mass communications medium has changed the on-line game.

The Internet is essentially a means of linking computer networks and individual networks across the globe—an interconnecting network of computers. This includes government, university, commercial, public and private computers, and networks. A wide range of firms are selling Internet connections to consumers, including local and long-distance phone companies, cable television companies, independent Internet service providers (ISPs) and traditional on-line service companies like America Online.

Unlike the traditional on-line services, the Internet is not a centralized system—there is no single information provider. Instead, information is contained on a number of sites. This is both an advantage and a disadvantage—the loose organization has allowed for the rapid growth of a wide range of sites offering extensive information to those who can find it. But the information can be so scattered that searching, finding and filtering the information can be a challenge.

Over the years a number of standard protocols have developed to view and exchange information. Many of these protocols have fallen out of favor. Currently, the popular protocols cover E-mail, Usenet newsgroups, file transfer protocol (FTP), and the World Wide Web.

E-Mail

Virtually all types of on-line accounts have electronic mail, better known as E-mail. Communication takes place in the form of electronic letters that can be composed and sent to an individual or a group, as well as received from other people. The Internet allows you to exchange E-mail with other people that have Internet access and also with users of traditional on-line services.

FIGURE 8.0
Electronic messages ready for review.

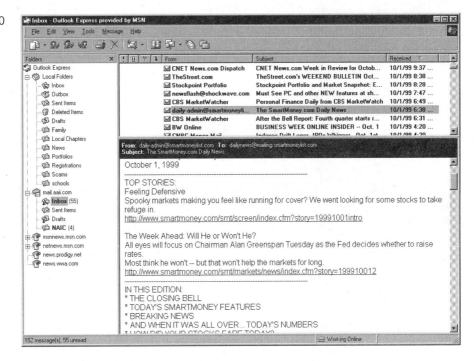

E-mail works by sending a message to the computer (server) of your Internet service provider, which then routes the message to the recipient. Mail sent to you actually ends up on the computer of your ISP, to be downloaded to your personal computer when you log on and retrieve your messages (see Figure 8.0). Messages typically take a few minutes to reach their final destination. However, when you send a message, there is no guarantee that the person receiving the message will ever log on and actually retrieve the message.

World Wide Web

The most popular method of navigating the Internet is through the World Wide Web, a graphical system that allows you to view information contained on the many different Web sites and easily navigate between the sites. Web addresses such as www.aaii.com appear on product labels, publications, print ads, commercials and even billboards.

FIGURE 8.1
Web home page of the AAII.

Web documents, or pages, are located and viewed through browsers that can display text and graphics and link to other Web pages. Netscape and Microsoft are the leading publishers of Web browsers. With the appropriate hardware and software add-ins, Web browsers can play music and radio broadcasts, run video and animations, and even exchange real-time chats.

Web pages are accessed through Web addresses known as URLs, or uniform resource locators. These URLs can be entered directly into the Web browser or accessed through a link embedded into a Web page. Web browsers provide the ability to "bookmark" pages, which saves the URL so you can visit the site in the future without typing in the address again.

Most Web pages contain links that can take you to other sites. Typically these links are presented as underlined or color text or graphical buttons. Clicking on such a link will call up the address of the linked site and send you directly to that site.

The home pages of most Internet service providers contain links to Web search engines. These valuable Internet services allow you to locate Web pages that contain matching key words. Electronic and print directories of Web sites are also available to help locate sites of interest. The appendix on page 421 contains a comprehensive list of finance-related Web sites.

Usenet Newsgroups

Newsgroups provide individuals with areas where they can post questions and answers on a great deal of topics. Although this sounds a lot like E-mail, the main difference is that the messages posted in a newsgroup are available to the entire public, while messages sent by E-mail are only available to their recipients. These groups closely resemble the forum/message areas of on-line services, but differ in being open systems that are not moderated by any single party.

Tens of thousands of newsgroups exist covering a wide range of topics. ISPs must maintain a server (computer) that stores and maintains the Usenet newsgroup messages. Newsgroups are divided into standard and alternative newsgroups. Standard newsgroups should be available on all Usenet newsgroup services, while there is no assurance as to which alternative newsgroups will be tracked by any given ISP.

There are six standard newsgroup categories:

comp—for discussions on computer related issues

misc—for miscellaneous discussions on a variety of topics including investments

news—for discussions about the newsgroups

rec—for discussions on recreation

sci—for discussions about the sciences

soc—for discussions regarding society

Several newsgroups cover topics relating to investing and personal finance. Misc.invest is one such group that has a large number of subscribers and has, consequently, spawned several newsgroups including:

- misc.invest.canada

- misc.invest.commodities

- misc.invest.financial-plan

- misc.invest.funds

- misc.invest.futures

- misc.invest.mutual-funds

- misc.invest.real-estate

- misc.invest.stocks

- misc.invest.stocks.ipo

- misc.invest.stocks.penny

- misc.invest.technical

Several tools exist for working with these newsgroups; however they are not easy for the uninitiated to use. Microsoft's Internet Explorer and Netscape Communicator include newsreaders, but you may need to enter the proper parameters to access the newsgroups. Your service provider should provide you with a list of tools that can be used to access Usenet newsgroups and set-up instructions to use these tools.

For those who enjoy the conversation that takes place on newsgroups, but are turned off by the need for a newsgroup reader, Deja.com offers an alternative. Formerly Deja News, Deja.com offers access to newsgroups via a Web-based platform—meaning all you need is a Web browser. The service currently has around 45,000 discussion forums—Deja member forums as well as those derived from Usenet newsgroups—and boasts over one million registered users.

The investing newsgroups are a good place to learn about related resources available through the Internet. However, keep in mind that Internet newsgroups are not moderated. They contain many advertisements and you can never be sure of the motivation driving a particular posting. Read any post on the newsgroups with a healthy sense of skepticism. Just as message boards and newsgroups have

FIGURE 8.2
The misc.invest. stocks newsgroup provides a public area where individuals can discuss stocks, investment ideas, and computer tools with other investors.

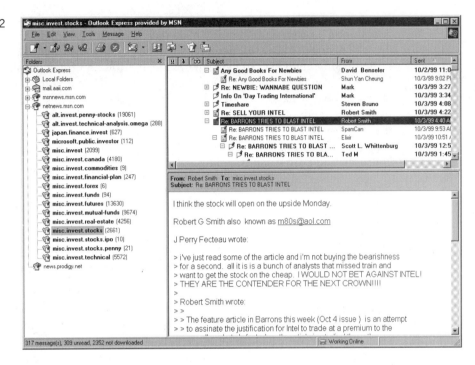

become a popular destination for investors, they have also become a spawning ground for spammers and scam artists. The ability to reach a large audience at relatively low costs is both an advantage and a burden for the Internet. Stock schemes that once required "bucket shops" with hundreds of operators trying to manipulate a penny stock can be duplicated with ease on-line.

Posters at a message board have a wide range of investment expertise and a variety of motives. Moreover, because message boards provide a degree of anonymity, it is difficult to know whether the poster is attempting to manipulate the price or is passing along an honest opinion.

Warning→ Keep in mind that Internet newsgroups are not moderated. They contain many advertisements and you can never be sure of the motivation driving a particular posting. Read any post on the newsgroups with a healthy sense of skepticism.

Pumping and Slamming

A common concern is that many message posters are trying to manipulate the price of a stock. This is particularly the case when it comes to the more thinly traded penny and OTC stocks, where information and financial statements are harder to come by. Since a majority of posters to an individual stock's message boards probably have a stake in the company, they have a vested interest in the price movement of that stock. In the end, they would like others to buy the stock that they own. Likewise, they would prefer people to sell those stocks in which they have a short position. Two activities that have grown through the message board medium are stock pumping and stock slamming.

Stock pumping involves hyping up a stock to create enough interest, and excitement, so that others will buy it—thus driving up the price. If the person succeeds, they profit as the price is bid upward. As is often the case, however, the pumper sells when he senses that the momentum is slowing or that potential investors realize the hype is just that. While the "hypester" profits from the movement, it is invariably the investors sucked in by the hype who lose out as the stock price deflates once the momentum is lost.

Stock slamming is simply the opposite of pumping. An investor who has a short position in a stock, that is, sells borrowed stock with the hope of covering or reversing the short position by buying stock at a later date at a lower price, will begin posting negative comments about the company. The slammer reports that earnings will come in well below expectations or that someone in upper management, such as the CEO, has resigned. These postings are aimed at creating a wave of selling. As the stock price falls, the slammer lines his or her pockets while others exit positions on bogus news.

Message Boards

Message boards are similar to newsgroups, but rely on Web browsers for interaction between users. This allows for greater control and management by the site hosting the message boards. Message boards often feature more focused and better-organized discussion topics than newsgroups. The more popular investment message boards boast discussion for every U.S. publicly traded company, although there is no guarantee this means active discussion.

Message boards tend to give the user more flexibility than standard newsgroup readers when it comes to locating and filtering out specific postings or posters. Many of the larger services allow you to locate postings containing keywords or those made by specific people.

FIGURE 8.3
Yahoo!
Finance offers
a discussion
thread for
virtually every
U.S. publicly
traded stock.

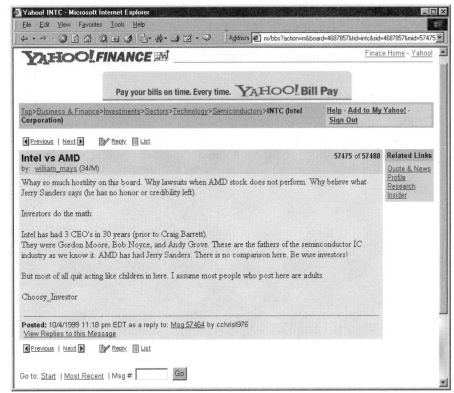

Lastly, message boards are generally more regulated than newsgroups. Boards such as those at the Motley Fool (www.fool.com) site have moderators that monitor postings to make sure messages are on the up-and-up. In addition, services such as Raging Bull (www.ragingbull.com) allow users to report those who violate their terms of service by posting inappropriate messages.

Some sites such as Company Sleuth (www.companysleuth.com) consolidate a range of information about a given company including message postings in one easy-to-access report. Company Sleuth searches the Internet for current financial events, business news, and message postings on a range of boards and sends users daily E-mail reports highlighting recent activity.

Transferring Files
Another action performed on the Internet is the exchange of files. The standard tool used is FTP, which stands for file transfer protocol. This protocol allows you to download files from the Internet or upload files to other computers. File ac-

cess on most servers requires an account and a password, but some systems allow you to view lists of files and download files with an anonymous FTP log-in. Most Web browsers allow users to display and download files, but specialized FTP programs may be required to access and transfer files between secure computers.

FIGURE 8.4
An Internet FTP program by Ipswitch logged into the Microsoft public FTP directory.

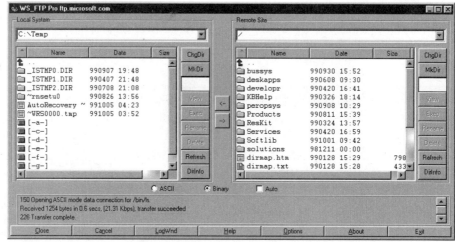

Connection Options

Life would be easy if you had only one choice when accessing the Internet. In reality there are a myriad of ways to connect: dial-up, ISDN, dedicated line, satellite, cable, and DSL.

> **Tip→** When selecting an Internet service provider (ISP), factors that you need to consider include your needs, geographic location, and budget.

All of the general-purpose on-line services, such as America Online and Prodigy, offer Internet services as part of their overall package of services. These services represent a very good starting point for someone using financial information services for the first time. They feature software that installs all the necessary communications programs to access the service's proprietary content as well as the Internet. The services offer their own collection of financial data, while also organizing Internet resources for their subscribers.

The Internet-only ISP options include local firms offering dial-up access, cable-companies promising warp speed access, and national providers with slick software toolkits to get you going. Look for an ISP that gives you cost effective connection with all the necessary software including a dialer, browser, E-mail program, FTP software and a newsgroup reader. The software should follow general standards that allow you to use other Internet software as your needs and preferences develop.

If you are establishing an on-line account for your whole family, look for the option to create multiple E-mail accounts. This capability was first popularized by general-purpose on-line services such as Prodigy and America Online, but lately more Internet service providers have also started to offer this feature as well. If your ISP only offers a single E-mail address, a number of free Web-based E-mail systems such as Hotmail allow users to establish mail accounts separate from your ISP E-mail account.

The ISP should carry the full range of Usenet newsgroups and provide enough storage space to allow a sufficient history of messages to be available before scrolling away.

If you are interested in establishing personal Web pages for your friends and family to access, look for a provider that sets aside storage space for its customers and provides some tools, documentation and support to get you off the starting blocks. If you are new to computers and on-line services, explore the field using a national, general-purpose service such as America Online. Once you know the ins and outs of the Internet and on-line communications in general, you may consider using a pure Internet service provider.

Tip→	If you are new to computers and on-line services, you may want to explore using a national, general-purpose service such as America Online. Once you are more familiar with the Internet and on-line communications in general, you may consider using a pure Internet service provider.

Speed and Reliability

Nothing is more frustrating than becoming dependent on the Internet to supply you with financial data, access your brokerage account, and function as a communication tool only to have your service frequently slow down to a crawl or break down completely. Look for an ISP that does not have a history of outages and delays. Word of mouth is important in this area—check with your computer-literate friends for recommendations. Levels of services can vary from city to city for a single vendor.

The size of the "pipe" that connects you to your ISP and then the ISP to the Internet backbone determines how many customers can comfortably access the Internet and how much data they can pass through. This is referred to as bandwidth—the larger the network connection line, the greater and faster the information flow.

Modem Dial-Up

The vast majority of those connecting to the Internet use standard dial-up connections over plain old telephone (POT) lines. Modem dial-up offers "universal" availability: If you are in an area with telephone lines, then you can access the Internet.

Modems with a speed of 56Kbps (kilobits per second) can be found on most new computers today. While in theory these modems should allow downstream (receive) transfer rates of up to 56Kbps, FCC regulations limit them to 53Kbps. Maximum upstream (sending) rates that can be achieved are 33.6Kbps. Also limiting the rate at which you connect is your phone line: The "cleaner" your phone line (the lower the electrical interference), the higher the rates at which you will be able to connect. Taking into account the quality of most phone lines, realistic connection rates drop to about 46.6Kbps. Your phone line must also be capable of supporting V.90 semi-digital connections above 33.6Kbps. Phone company wiring, amplifiers, volume balancers (pads), and even your home wiring can prevent V.90 connections.

The key drawback of analog modems is that you achieve the lowest transfer rates compared to alternative methods of connecting. Furthermore, unless you add an additional telephone line, you will not be able to make or receive telephone calls while on-line. However, standard modems offer the least expensive method of connecting. The average cost of a new V.90 56K modem is between $70 and $240. Monthly fees for unlimited access from your Internet service provider will cost between $20 and $30.

Make sure that you can connect to your ISP with a local call. Get a list of available dial-up numbers and check with your local phone company as to whether any "meter" will be running while dialing the ISP. Calls within the same area code may not be considered local phone calls.

Check that the dial-up numbers support your modem speed. Also, look for multiple dial-up numbers for your area. During peak periods it may be difficult to avoid a busy signal. Service loads vary with the seasons—usage tends to be higher in winter than in summer.

Digital Speed with ISDN

When the ISDN (Integrated Services Digital Network) modem entered the marketplace a few years ago, many thought it would become the choice for fast Internet access. However, ISDN's days may be numbered as alternate, higher-speed, competitively priced methods become more mainstream.

Compared to a standard 56Kbps modem, ISDN does offer faster speeds—128Kbps coupled with a pure digital connection upstream and downstream. However, price is a definite factor when considering installing an ISDN line. The first thing you need is an ISDN modem, which can run from $100 to $400. Then you must install the ISDN line, which costs extra. Finally, you can expect to pay monthly service fees averaging $50 to $100, which do not guarantee you unlimited service. You typically pay a flat fee for a set number of hours and if you exceed these hours, you are charged an hourly rate.

The other downside to ISDN is that it is not available in all areas. You need to check with your local phone company to see if they install ISDN lines.

A new version of ISDN is in the works, although it will be some time before it achieves nationwide availability. Always On/Dynamic ISDN (AO/DI) provides full-time, low-speed access to your Internet service provider. AO/DI initially connects at 9.6Kbps, but as your traffic needs increase the speeds are automatically bumped to 64Kbps and 128Kbps. The main issue that will slow its deployment is that it requires software updates for both phone companies and Internet service providers. Since your system is always connected to the Internet, AO/DI allows for remote-access to your home system, a feature not available with a standard dial-up connection or traditional ISDN.

Beaming Data via Satellite

If you live in a remote area where other means of Internet connection are unavailable, a satellite connection may be your only high-speed option. If you have a clear line to the southern sky, you can install a small dish over which you can receive data at up to 400Kbps. This works fine if you are looking to just surf the Web. However, if you wish to send data upstream, or transmit E-mail or large files, you will still need a standard dial-up line that works in connection with the downstream satellite feed. The upstream phone connection tells the satellite service what to send your way. There is talk that, in the future, satellite service with two-way access will eliminate the need for the dial-up modem.

Like ISDN, satellite service can be expensive. The hardware itself, such as the dish, can be as much as $700. Monthly fees, which will generally give you a fixed number of access hours, can go as high as $129.

Cable: Not Just for TV

Cable modems currently offer one of the cheapest and fastest ways to connect to the Internet. The catch is that there are only about 20 million households in the U.S. that can currently get cable modem service. New England, which has the highest cable modem penetration of any geographic region in the country, still only has a user rate of just over 2%.

Despite its limited availability, there were almost 500,000 new cable modem users in 1998. Furthermore, Forrester Research, an industry research firm, puts the number of users at two million by the end of 1999 and 80% of the high-speed market by 2002.

While cable modem service providers claim download speeds of up to 30Mbps (megabits per second), speeds of up to 10Mbps are more practical. Upload speeds range from 200Kbps to 2.5Mbps. In addition, the connection is constant. There is no need to dial in to a server or establish a connection.

Outside of its limited availability, there are other problems with cable modems. One issue has to do with security. Cable modem service providers divide up a connection "pipe" between you and other users in your area, or "node." Since you are sharing a connection, there is the possibility of others accessing your computer. While this should not scare you away from considering a cable modem, it is important to protect yourself. Settings in Windows 95 and 98 allow you keep outside users from accessing your system.

Furthermore, since a fixed capacity is being divided up among the users in a node, more users going on-line within your node can affect performance. Cable modem companies downplay this, claiming that if the problem gets out of hand, they can simply add capacity.

If you enjoy your current Internet service provider, be prepared to give it up if you decide upon a cable modem. Your cable service package will include a high-speed communications line and Internet access complete with E-mail, message groups, etc.

In terms of costs, cable modems are inexpensive, given their connection fees. Purchase and installation costs range from $100 to $200 and monthly fees are between $30 and $65.

Digital Subscriber Lines (DSL)

DSL uses the same copper wires used for your telephone service but potentially offers downstream (receive) rates of up to 32Mbps and upstream (send) rates of over 1Mbps.

Regional telephone companies such as Bell Atlantic, Pacific Bell, and US West have started to roll out DSL service. The overall opinion is that phone companies will increase their deployment of DSL in an attempt to stave off the push being made by cable modem service.

There is a lack of continuity in pricing with DSL. Prices range from over $800 a month from US West (excluding Internet access) to just under $200 per month from Bell Atlantic, which includes Internet access. DSL modems and setup can cost up to $600, but again it varies greatly from region to region. There are hopes that eventually monthly fees will fall in line with other services, such as ISDN. However, it is too early to tell whether this will become reality.

Where to Get Connected

For services such as dial-up, ISDN, and DSL, you may wish to contact your local telephone company to see which options are available to you and at what cost. Two of the more prominent cable modem services are Excite@Home (www.home.com) and MediaOne Express (www.mediaoneexpress.com). For further information on cable modems, you may want to check out the cable modem newsgroup: comp.dcom.modems.cable. Lastly, Hughes DirecPC satellite service (www.direcpc.com) is an industry leader for satellite modem service.

Internet.com maintains a searchable list of ISPs around the world at thelist.internet.com (see Figure 8.5). The site allows you to search for an ISP within your area code and shows the type of access speeds and connections offered. Contact information, basic features and systems are detailed along with direct links to each ISP to perform additional research. If you do not currently have Internet access to check this site, you may wish to contact your local library or university to see if they provide an Internet terminal for residents to use.

Tip→	To search for an Internet service provider, try the Internet.com Web site at thelist.internet.com for a list of ISPs around the world.

FIGURE 8.5
The Web site,
thelist.internet.
com, provides
you with a
complete list of
Internet
service
providers
around the
world.

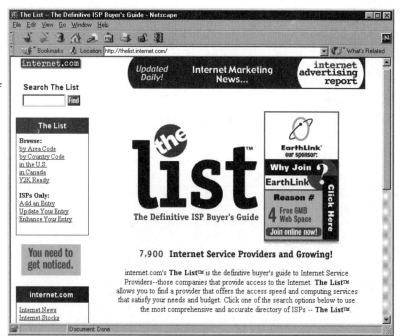

Monitoring Your Investment Portfolio

From the very earliest days of financial markets, the gathering and processing of information has been crucial. The stock exchanges have used state-of-the-art communications networks to transmit the latest security quotes to investors. However, the process of portfolio monitoring extends beyond just obtaining the latest quote. With financial data services, investors can also calculate their portfolio value and asset allocation, obtain any pertinent news on securities that are being tracked, follow the activity of the financial markets, and exchange ideas with other investors. Your options range from real-time feeds that provide up-to-the-second bid/ask quotes to end-of-day services that provide information for all of the publicly traded stocks.

Quotes

Fresh, accurate information is critical for the investor holding volatile securities or possessing a short-term investing horizon. Markets are absorbing and reacting to information more quickly than ever. The active investor carefully monitoring the markets cannot afford a delay in the delivery of critical data.

Quotes are an integral part of an investor's set of tools, especially when charted or plotted. They provide the investor with a map of how a stock's price has traveled and possibly serve as a guide toward future price direction.

A current price quote provides the price of buying a security—the ask—and the price at which you can sell the security—the bid. The difference between the market's best offer to buy a stock (bid) and the best offer to sell the same stock (ask) is known as the spread. Coupled with the trading commissions and tax liabilities, it represents the cost of trading a security. Spreads represent costs to investors and profits to market makers and dealers. Spreads are typically wider for small-capitalization stocks with low trading volume. For example, on October 14, 1999, Dick Clark Productions (ticker: CDPI) was trading with a bid price of 11 and an ask price of $12\frac{1}{4}$. Buying at the spread would mean paying $12.25 per share (if you ignore commissions). If you were to sell your shares of Dick Clark Productions stock the same day you would only obtain $11 per share—one dollar and a quarter, or about 10%, less than what you paid for the stock (see Figure 8.6). Before placing a trade, investors should always examine the bid/ask spread and consider its cost in moving into and out of a security.

The last trading price is also often referred to as a quote. The last price conveys the price at which a security was sold, but does not reveal if the trade represented the purchase of a security by an investor from the market or the sale of a security by an investor to the market. The reported last trading price of securities with wide spreads often repeatedly bounces up and down as transactions move back and forth between the bid and ask price.

Tip→	Before placing a trade, investors should always examine the bid/ask spread and consider its cost in moving into and out of a security.

Delayed Quotes

Delayed quotes are updated throughout the day, but lag the transactions in the market by at least 15–20 minutes. The majority of on-line services—such as America Online, CompuServe and Prodigy—along with most Web sites will report delayed quotes to their customers. The majority of delayed services provide a price snapshot, which can only be updated through another quote request. Figure 8.6 is an example of a delayed quote from The MSN MoneyCentral Investor. However, some vendors offer continuous quote streams on a delayed basis in which the prices of tracked securities are updated during the course of the day. For example, Thomson Investors Network's "LiveTicker" appears in a small browser window and displays periodically updated quotes in a scrolling list.

FIGURE 8.6
*Delayed
quotes
showing the
bid/ask spread
of Dick Clark
Productions in
MSN
MoneyCentral
Investor.*

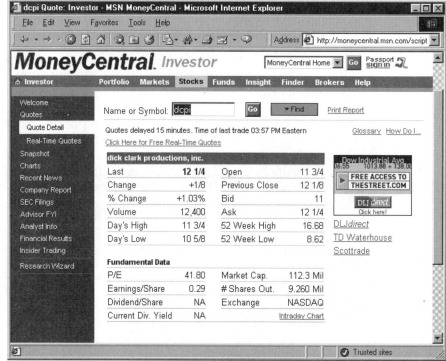

Delayed quotes typically focus on actual transaction prices, not current bid/ask prices. They provide a fairly current snapshot of recent price activity, but may require further investor research before placing a trade during a quickly moving market or when transacting in a volatile security.

Many on-line brokers provide real-time quotations complete with bid/ask spread and size prior to placing a trade. A growing number of Web sites are also offering a limited number of free real-time quotes to their subscribers. These sites absorb the exchange fees investors must pay for the privilege of obtaining real-time quotes, so the sites typically limit the number of quotes available to a customer to around 50 per day. Exchanges make a significant amount of money selling quotes to their customers and charge higher rates to professional investors. To get free quotes customers must fill out a form that confirms their status as an individual investor. A system combining delayed intraday prices with real-time quotes is suitable for the majority of investors with intermediate- to long-term holding horizons.

Portfolio Values

The majority of on-line services and financial information Web sites provide security price quotes. Most of these services also feature portfolio tracking so you can get quotes on all of your securities with a single request. Typically, these services will also allow you to enter the purchase price so the portfolio value and gain or loss can be tracked. Figure 8.7 displays a portfolio report from the Quicken.com Web site. Some Web sites give subscribers the option of receiving portfolio price updates through E-mail.

FIGURE 8.7
A portfolio view on the Quicken.com Web site.

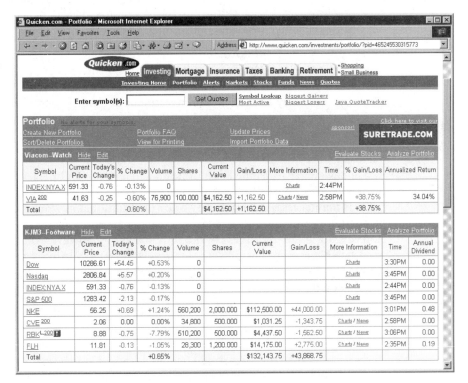

Price updates for stocks and mutual funds are common. If you invest directly in bonds, options or futures you need to make sure the service provides quotes for these securities. This information is revealed in the comparison grid at the end of this chapter. You may also want to check on how a security can be referenced. Ticker symbols are well-suited for stock price searches, but a CUSIP reference may be a preferable identification method for pricing bonds.

News Updates

In addition to tracking the prices of your securities and current value of your portfolio, it is important to keep abreast of news affecting your securities. Staying up-to-date in sector, industry and economic news, as well as individual company news is vital when actively participating in the equities markets.

News can be obtained from a variety of sources, ranging from newspapers and trade publications to financial network television broadcasts such as CNBC and Money Line. These are excellent sources of industry, sector and economic information—however, they lack the customization for individual securities that is needed by the active investor.

Often, an overload of information is more of a problem for investors than a lack of information. It is therefore necessary to establish an account with a general-purpose or Internet service that uses a newswire to provide this timely data, filtered appropriately to match your investment decision process. Check out the news sources and make sure your data service uses a reliable industry standard to provide news. Some of the better-known newswires include Reuters, Knight-Ridder, Bloomberg and Dow Jones.

These newswires form the basis of news delivery for on-line services. For example, INVESTools uses Reuters as its primary business wire. With newswires, more is not necessarily better. Any one of the national news sources above should be adequate. Any more than that will usually result in duplication of information, negating the usefulness of the product. Note, however, that the newswires are available at different subscription levels, offering various levels of detail and frequency. As with quotes, you should match up your needs for timely information with data supply costs.

Investors must manage these news services according to their trading style. Active investors may want an alarm when news comes across the wire on a stock in their watch list. This requires a constant log-on to see if any relevant news items crossed the wire. The long-term, buy-and-hold investor may prefer an electronic clipping service, which collects news stories that can be read at leisure. To set up these clipping files you must establish filters that indicate which topics and newswires interest you. Some services require you to log onto the service to see the filtered articles, while other services such as the Wall Street Journal Interactive edition provide the option of delivering the news stories to you via E-mail (see Figure 8.8).

Most services also allow you to check for news on a specific company. The differences lie in which specific newswire is searched and the storage depth (backdating) of that service.

FIGURE 8.8
Set-up page used by The Wall Street Journal Interactive edition for subscribers to determine the type of E-mail updates to receive.

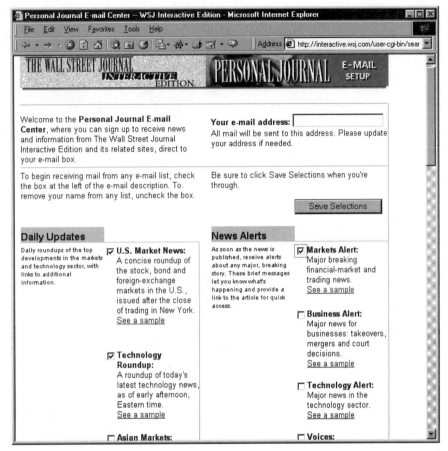

Tip→

When considering an on-line service or a financial data Web site, find out which sources it uses to provide news. Make sure it is an industry standard such as Dow Jones or Reuters.

Market News

It is important to stay informed with events impacting the overall market as well. On-line services and financial data Web sites have much to offer for the individual investor. Updates during the course of the market as well as end-of-day wrap-ups have become the norm.

However, some services provide a more structured approach than others. For example with its recent redesign, America Online allows you to examine market activity in great detail, section-by-section, with the service guiding you along the way.

FIGURE 8.9
America Online organizes daily market statistics and news for quick review.

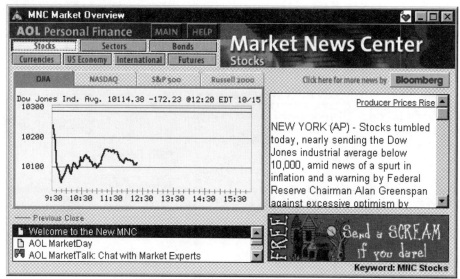

Technical Analysis

Chapter 6: Technical Analysis (see page 217) provides a focus on technical analysis and charting programs. Technical analysis is dependent upon large quantities of historical price and volume data. A few big services such as CompuServe offer decades of pricing on every stock, mutual fund, options and futures contract, and index ever invented. These databases allow you to log onto their system and download open/high/low/close pricing and trading volume. These are the basic ingredients needed to produce a variety of charts. As you can imagine, entering the five required data points for a two-year chart would require a major time investment, as well as rendering dirty fingers from digging through the newspaper archives. Gathering your data electronically allows you to run analysis rather than worry about data collection, providing you with a better opportunity to understand your investments.

A growing number of Web sites are using licensed modules from services such as BigCharts to supply their subscribers with on-line charts. These services offer users a basic set of technical indicators and data that typically covers at least a 10-year period, as well as intraday charts.

FIGURE 8.10
Stock chart from the CBS MarketWatch Web site.

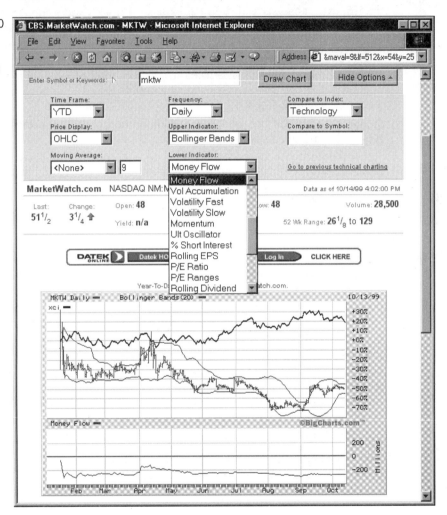

Fundamental Analysis

Researching company fundamentals is an exciting option that is becoming easier, cheaper and more powerful through financial information services. Most of the data services are offering financial statements, earnings estimates, company and industry analysis and even education on stock valuation techniques. Chapter 5: Fundamental Stock Analysis (see page 137) explores financial services that supply databases suitable for fundamental screening, including a number of services evaluated in this chapter. But financial information services go beyond just screening to provide information and analysis needed for valuation. Web sites such as AAII's (www.aaii.com) provide educational articles for stock valuation. The U.S. Securities and Exchange Commission operates a Web site (www.sec.gov) that provides free and instant access to full annual and quarterly reports for all listed companies. The Motley Fool Web site features news and active discussion groups on the attractiveness of specific stocks. The reviews of financial services in this chapter cover the most powerful and useful traditional online services and Internet Web sites. The appendix on page 421 offers a more comprehensive listing of Web sites geared toward investors.

Analyzing Your Goals

All of these options require you to balance your needs, wants, time constraints and budget. When choosing a pricing plan and data retrieval service, it is important to be realistic about what you are trying to accomplish with your investing. If you have a large portfolio that you are actively trading, requiring timely data for a wide range of securities, then you can justify the subscription to several data sources to help in your decision-making processes. If you need a data service to update the pricing in your portfolio once a week, you have no need for real-time data feeds, although you may still need the same amount of data depending on the size of your portfolio. Another investor may want all of this data, but the size of his investment portfolio and respective time horizon simply do not match—the cost of this mismatch will eat up profits.

Also, be wary of "analysis paralysis"—you can do so much research on so many topics from so many data sources that it can consequently inundate your normal routine with too much clutter to make a clear decision.

| Warning→ | Don't clutter your analysis needs with too much research from so many data services that you can't make clear decisions. |

Rating Criteria

Each product is rated on a few key points of interest. While some of these items are subjective, others are readily quantified once you compare the services. The rating criteria change slightly for this chapter because financial information services encompass such a broad range of topics.

Ratings Criteria	
Portfolio Monitoring	5
Fundamental Analysis	5
Mutual Fund Analysis	5
Technical Analysis	5
Performance	5
Ease of Use	5
Value	5

Separate ratings for *portfolio monitoring, fundamental stock analysis, mutual fund analysis* and *technical analysis* are provided. Some services do not provide coverage for all of the investment areas, so they are not rated on that area, resulting in an "na." As in other sections of the book, higher numbers indicate better ratings.

The *performance* ranking accounts for the speed, accuracy and delivery of the data.

Ease of use refers to the organization of the data categories and system navigation.

Value of the service is judged on the overall quality and usefulness of the service relative to the cost of subscribing to the service.

Reviews

General Purpose On-Line Services

America Online	
Portfolio Monitoring	4
Fundamental Analysis	4
Mutual Fund Analysis	4
Technical Analysis	3
Performance	3
Ease of Use	4
Value	5

America Online
by America Online
$21.95/mo.—Macintosh, Windows
(800) 827-6364
www.aol.com

America Online (AOL) is the leading Internet service provider with over 17 million subscribers. No longer the price leader in the category, AOL is still able to attract and retain its members because of its simple Internet access and mix of proprietary content. AOL separates its content offerings into distinct blocks of information called channels. The personal finance channel brings together a rich collection of newspapers, business magazines, and financial data vendors.

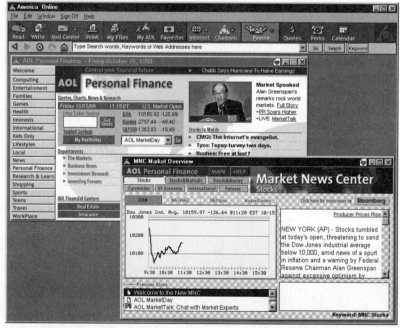

FIGURE 8.11
The personal finance channel of America Online offers a broad array of business related offerings.

America Online provides all of the tools for tracking your portfolio, including multiple portfolios, quotes, news, charts, and a deep collection of discussion groups and chat areas to exchange ideas with other investors. America Online also supplies an abundant set of stock and mutual fund research from a range of sources including Morningstar, Market Guide, Disclosure, and Zacks. Unfortunately, the presentation suffers from the range of formats used to present the information. Screening is basic compared to the better Internet offerings. Overall, America Online is an attractive financial service for a variety of users—offering a wide range of data directly through its service as well as access to the Internet for additional information.

FIGURE 8.12
A portfolio view and security quote snapshot from America Online.

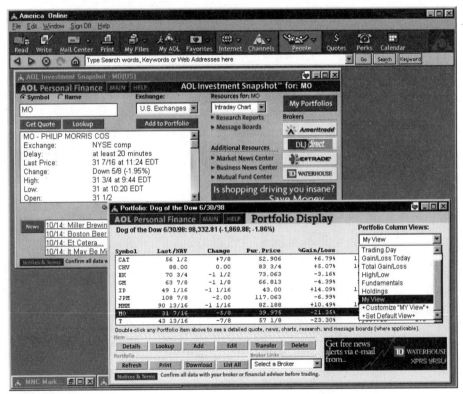

CompuServe	
Portfolio Monitoring	3
Fundamental Analysis	4
Mutual Fund Analysis	3
Technical Analysis	5
Performance	4
Ease of Use	3
Value	3

CompuServe
by CompuServe Corp.
$24.95/mo.—Macintosh, Windows
(800) 848-8990
www.compuserve.com

CompuServe is an on-line service with a gallant history but an uncertain future. CompuServe was developed in the era of text-based on-line services, providing data on an à la carte basis. It has developed a comprehensive collection of proprietary data, but much of it is only available at extra cost. CompuServe has no equal as a single source for hard-to-find data, but you must be willing to pay for it. America Online, the current owner

FIGURE 8.13
Sample of investment-related features found on CompuServe.

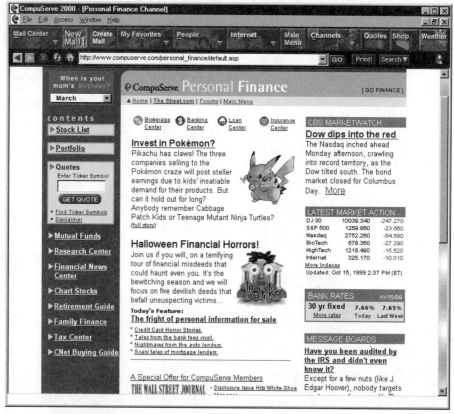

of CompuServe, has expressed the desire to maintain CompuServe's position as the primary service for tech-savvy computer users. Recently, CompuServe has tried to buy new customers with rebate offers attached to purchases of new computers in return for a long-term subscription agreement.

CompuServe's latest interface is rolled up into a version of Microsoft's Internet Explorer Web browser. The segments of the service that were redesigned for the browser are very attractive and combine data from vendors such as CBS Market-Watch and BigCharts. Specialized databases such as historical prices and dividend histories are examples of proprietary data elements that operate in text-emulation mode only, requiring you to enter text at prompts to navigate. CompuServe offers a good interface for its forums, allowing easy access to message threads and file downloads, but the boards do not seem quite as active now that the Internet offers numerous discussion forums.

FIGURE 8.14
The resource center on CompuServe does a nice job organizing investment resources found throughout the Internet.

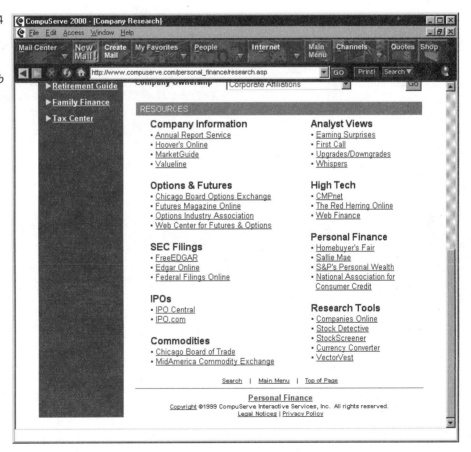

389

Prodigy	
Portfolio Monitoring	4
Fundamental Analysis	4
Mutual Fund Analysis	4
Technical Analysis	4
Performance	5
Ease of Use	5
Value	4

Prodigy

by Prodigy Services Corp.
$19.95/mo.—Macintosh, Windows
(800) 776-3449
www.prodigy.com

Citing year 2000 programming costs, Prodigy has shut down its Prodigy Classic on-line service, which required the use of a proprietary software program and network. All of Prodigy's efforts are currently focused on Prodigy Internet, which functions as an Internet service provider (ISP) that combines full Internet access, coupled with limited proprietary content using standard Web protocols and browsers. Prodigy Internet has linked up with

FIGURE 8.15
Prodigy uses Quicken.com to supply its subscribers with financial information. This stock screen reveals a portfolio view supplied by Quicken.com.

390

Excite and Quicken.com to run its business and investing section. Like the Quicken.com site, the service offers portfolio management, quotes, news, alerts, charts, as well as company and mutual fund snapshots and screening.

Prodigy offers fast, reliable Internet access at an attractive rate. Prodigy does not add any proprietary investment information to the mix, instead it makes use of financial data provided by Quicken.com. Prodigy will appeal to the investor planning on using a wide range of Internet tools and looking for basic, cost-effective, dial-up Internet access.

Internet Sites

CBS MarketWatch	
Portfolio Monitoring	3
Fundamental Analysis	3
Mutual Fund Analysis	3
Technical Analysis	4
Performance	4
Ease of Use	4
Value	5

CBS MarketWatch
by MarketWatch.com, Inc.
Free—any PC with Internet access
(415) 733-0500
cbs.marketwatch.com

CBS MarketWatch began by combining the newsroom of CBS with the financial data of Data Broadcasting Corp. It has developed in a very strong resource for company and market news coupled with a growing set of company and mutual fund data.

CBS MarketWatch sets itself apart from other information services with its staff of reporters that provide headlines, stories, and analysis throughout the trading day. Regular columns cover topics such as IPOs and technology stocks. Tables provide details on events such as stock splits, volume alerts, insider stock sales, and share buybacks. Beyond news, CBS MarketWatch offers free multiple personal portfolios, market and company research, stock screening, charting, and mutual fund data. Mid-day and end-of-day E-mail updates provide summaries of market activity coupled with links to major market stories.

Separately, MarketWatch.com offers two fee-based services. CBS MarketWatch RT is a $34.95/month service offering real-time snapshot quotes and deeper historical and fundamental data and research tools. CBS MarketWatch Live is a branded version of DBC's StockEdge Online. This service starts at $79/month and is geared toward the active trader with its combination of dynamically updated charts, tickers, and quote screens.

FIGURE 8.16
CBS
MarketWatch
offers timely
and insightful
review of
market and
company
activities.

INVESTools	
Portfolio Monitoring	4
Fundamental Analysis	3
Mutual Fund Analysis	1
Technical Analysis	4
Performance	4
Ease of Use	4
Value	5

INVESTools
by INVESTools, Inc.
$9.95/mo.—any PC with Internet access
(800) 567-2683
www.investools.com

INVESTools is a well-rounded Web site offering a rich array of subscription options ranging from portfolio management tools to investment newsletter subscriptions. The site's Portfolio Workshop section offers subscription options that provide a good balance between portfolio monitoring and stock research.

The portfolio module of INVESTools tracks U.S. and Canadian listed stocks and mutual funds. Three portfolio views are available that provide extended quotes, portfolio values, and a summary of fundamental data. As is common for Web portfolio managers, security listings are linked to charts and news. The premium subscription provides access to the Reuters newswire. News and price trigger alerts, as well as end-of-day portfolio updates, can be E-mailed to your Internet account.

INVESTools features above-average charting complete with standard intraday charts found throughout the Internet, as well as technical charts that allow you to establish parameters for chart types and technical studies and then save the chart type.

FIGURE 8.17
A chart from INVESTool's Portfolio Workshop subscription.

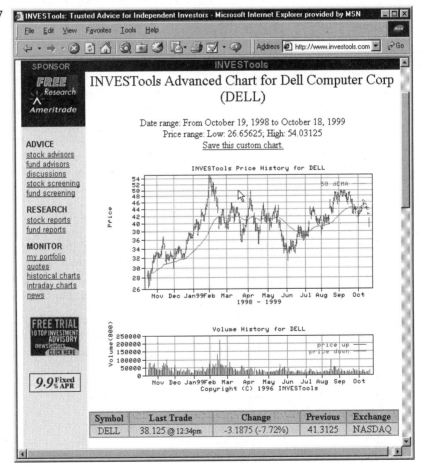

The research and screening on INVESTools is geared toward stocks. The basic screen lets you use predefined filters or establish custom parameters to filter the database of 8,400 companies. Subscribers have unlimited access to Zacks earnings estimates and Market Guide's Quick Facts company reports. Detailed company reports must be purchased separately from Baseline, Market Guide or Standard and Poor's.

Additional resources such as Morningstar Fund Reports ($5 each) and investment newsletters are available, but the premium portfolio feature provides all the basic portfolio tracking and research needed if you're only focusing on stocks.

Morningstar.com	
Portfolio Monitoring	5
Fundamental Analysis	4
Mutual Fund Analysis	5
Technical Analysis	2
Performance	5
Ease of Use	5
Value	4

Morningstar.com
by Morningstar, Inc.
Free (Basic); $9.95/mo. (Premium)—any PC with Internet access
(800) 735-0700
www.morningstar.com

Morningstar.com is a full-featured investment Web site providing portfolio tracking, market monitoring, stock and fund screening and research, educational articles and message boards. Much of the site is free, with additional research and screening available through the Premium Service for $9.95 per month.

Morningstar.com allows you to track stock and mutual fund portfolios as well as analyze its holdings and overall composition. It provides details on items such as security pricing information, security and portfolio gains and losses, basic security fundamentals and news alerts—all the basic elements for portfolio monitoring. Portfolio X-Rays help to analyze the asset allocation of the portfolio and valuation level of the portfolio.

Research on the site consists of stock and fund screening coupled with research reports. Free screening is basic—you are limited to using two criteria per screen. For example, mutual fund screening is limited to selecting from broad fund categories coupled with a single performance indicator or risk ranking. The premium screening module is well executed, allowing investors to pick from 125 criteria for stocks and 70 criteria for funds.

Comprehensive stock reports consist of 10 sections providing an intraday and long-term price chart, company profile, financial statements, stock price performance statistics, current stock and market multiples, earnings estimates, industry

FIGURE 8.18
*The Stock
Selector
screening
module for
Morning-
star.com's
Premium
Service.*

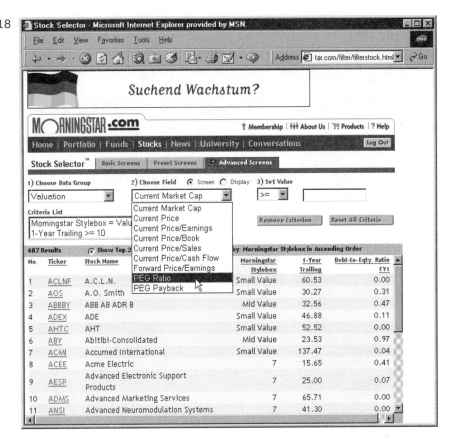

statistics, fund/insider ownership statistics, SEC documents, and news. The
financial statements provide five years of income statement items, three years of
cash flow data and two years of balance sheet data. The financial statements
emphasize ratios and analytical information data over raw line items. The premium reports add details such as a quarterly data, business segment breakdowns,
history of cash and stock dividends, regional (international) sales and profit
exposures, earnings estimate and surprise figures, and detailed listings of historical multiples.

Mutual fund reports provide returns for the past seven years, along with a comparison of performance to a market index and against funds with the same investment objective. Risk measures and Morningstar ratings are included for various
time periods. The portfolio section of the report details items such as the fund
style, top holdings, asset and industry breakdowns, and percentage of foreign
holdings. Morningstar analysis rounds out the report.

FIGURE 8.19
A snapshot of the Acorn fund on Morningstar.com.

Articles with a focus on current market issues, interviews, and detailed educational features are located throughout the site. Message boards provide a forum for discussion of the many issues brought up in the articles.

Overall, the Morningstar.com site provides a diverse set of tools for the stock and mutual fund investor, contained in a well-organized site that features clear navigation. Notably, most investors will find the free portion of the site adequate for many of their needs unless they desire detailed stock and mutual fund screening and research.

396

Motley Fool	
Portfolio Monitoring	4
Fundamental Analysis	2
Mutual Fund Analysis	na
Technical Analysis	4
Performance	4
Ease of Use	4
Value	5

Motley Fool
by The Motley Fool, Inc.
Free—any PC with Internet access
www.fool.com

The Motley Fool site on America Online and the Internet is hugely successful because of its unique combination of basic stock market monitoring and fundamental research with an irreverent, amusing and cocky attitude. Motley Fool presents a free Web site that offers company research, quotes, news, education, and a community of stock investors.

The site includes access to company snapshots that provide company descriptions from Hoover's, a stock price chart service from BigCharts, basic financial statement data and ratios from Media General, and earnings estimates from I/B/E/S. While the information is not as comprehensive as that found on fee-based services, it is good enough to provide a quick view to determine whether a company merits further analysis. Links are provided for investors who wish to purchase more detailed reports.

Motley Fool offers market and company news, earnings announcements, and replays of conference calls directly on their site as well as via an E-mail update. The site includes a set of screens that investors can use as starting points for further analysis.

The site also provides basic investment education. The Motley Fool does a wonderful job of taking basic investment principles and putting an appealing, entertaining spin on otherwise dry, academic information. The heart of the site, however, is the active message boards, with their continual flow of stock investment discussions. Motley Fool more actively monitors the activity in the various discussion groups than most other services. Chat moderators are constantly on the lookout for inappropriate or abusive postings. In addition, in an attempt to avoid problems with stock pumping, Motley Fool prohibits discussion of micro-cap stocks.

Overall, Motley Fool provides a healthy balance of news, education, analysis and investment tools. However, keep in mind that the site, much like INVESTools, is predominantly geared toward stock coverage.

FIGURE 8.20
The Motley Fool provides a range of recommended portfolios.

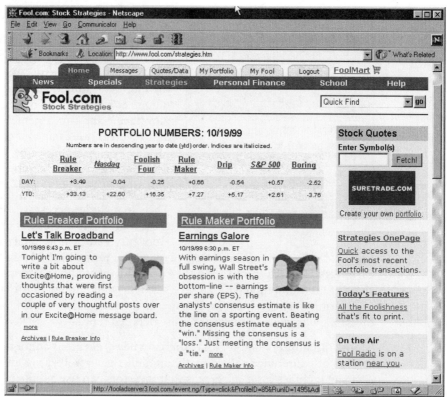

MSN MoneyCentral Investor	
Portfolio Monitoring	5
Fundamental Analysis	5
Mutual Fund Analysis	4
Technical Analysis	4
Performance	5
Ease of Use	4
Value	4

MSN MoneyCentral Investor
by Microsoft, Inc.
Free—any PC with Internet access
(800) 426-9400
moneycentral.msn.com/investor

MSN MoneyCentral Investor has responded to the growing offerings of free information over the Internet by making all of its content free as well. Formerly know as Microsoft Investor, the site features market monitoring, portfolio tracking, financial articles, message boards and chats, charting, stock and mutual fund screening, consensus earnings estimates and analyst recommendations from Zacks, detailed financial statements from Media General, and mutual fund data from Morningstar and Value Line.

FIGURE 8.21
MSN MoneyCentral Investor offers a flexible and powerful portfolio management module.

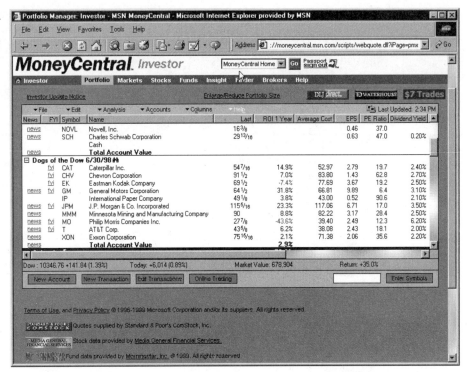

MoneyCentral Investor offers one of the most advanced on-line portfolio managers. It tracks your portfolio value, reports gains and losses, calculates rates of return, alerts users to news stories, and provides direct links to research and charts. A useful feature provides alerts when a stock or fund passes MoneyCentral Investor-created filters such as earnings upgrades or moving average crossovers. MoneyCentral Investor even allows you to import portfolio data from Quicken and link to five brokers for portfolio updates.

The site provides useful charts with options to control time periods, plot multiple securities, and overlay basic indicators such as moving averages. Chart data can be exported easily into Microsoft Excel where it can be saved for use in other programs.

The site offers flexible mutual fund and stock screening coupled with in-depth research that meets the research needs of the typical investor. Reported information on mutual funds includes data on investment objectives, Morningstar and Value Line ratings, performance statistics, portfolio composition and characteristics, and expenses.

The research section's company information includes earnings estimates, company profile, financial ratios, financial statements, industry comparisons, charts, and news. The information is very detailed and well organized to allow quick navigation.

FIGURE 8.22
*Financial
highlights for
Microsoft, Inc.,
from MSN
MoneyCentral
Investor.*

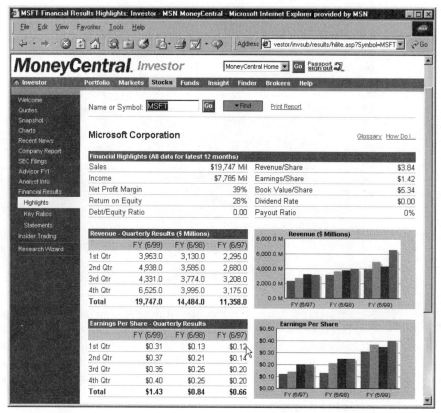

Quicken.com	
Portfolio Monitoring	4
Fundamental Analysis	5
Mutual Fund Analysis	4
Technical Analysis	4
Performance	5
Ease of Use	5
Value	5

Quicken.com
by Intuit Inc.
Free—any PC with Internet access
(800) 446-8848
www.quicken.com

Quicken.com is a free site offering investors a central place to manage many aspects of personal finance including banking, insurance, retirement planning, and investing.

The site includes all the basic tools required to monitor an investment portfolio—quotes, news, charts, portfolio tracking, basic stock and fund screening, stock and fund fundamentals, estimates, and SEC filings. Unique

FIGURE 8.23
Quicken.com invites users to rate stocks and posts the consensus viewpoint for a given stock.

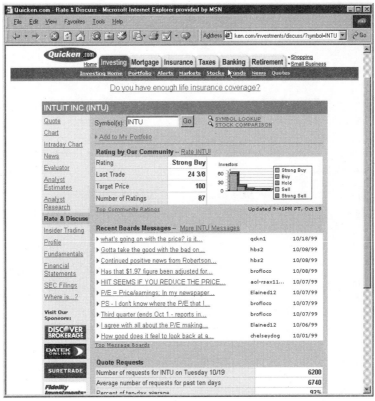

features include stock picks from mutual fund managers and investment advisors as well as consensus stock ratings gathered from Quicken.com users. Quicken.com even includes a simple worksheet for estimating the intrinsic value of a stock. A section titled "The Self-Reliant Investor" serves as an educational reference on the ABCs of investing.

The site is well organized and presents information available for each stock and mutual fund clearly. Most investors will find this free site adequate for their needs.

Quote.com	
Portfolio Monitoring	4
Fundamental Analysis	4
Mutual Fund Analysis	3
Technical Analysis	5
Performance	4
Ease of Use	4
Value	3

Quote.com

by Quote.com, Inc.
$9.95/mo. (Basic)—any PC with Internet access
(800) 498-8068
www.quote.com

Quote.com combines free- and fee-based information in a cafeteria-style approach to selecting investment information. Options range from free quotes, basic portfolio tracking, charts, and stock and mutual fund snapshots to fee-based real-time streaming quotes and charts. As you work your way up the subscription ladder, more detailed reports, portfolio managers capable of tracking a larger number of securities, customizable charts, earnings estimates, and real-time quotes become available. Many options have a 30-day trial.

Quote.com does a very good job of bringing a wide range of tools to the investor, but the à la carte pricing mode makes certain portions of the site expensive compared to sites such as MSN MoneyCentral Investor or Quicken.

FIGURE 8.24
*Free elements
found within
Quote.com
include quotes,
news, charts,
portfolio
tracking,
E-mail reports,
company
snapshots, SEC
filings,
research, and
investment
education.*

S&P Personal Wealth	
Portfolio Monitoring	4
Fundamental Analysis	5
Mutual Fund Analysis	4
Technical Analysis	4
Performance	4
Ease of Use	4
Value	3

S&P Personal Wealth
by Standard & Poor's
**$9.95/mo. or $99.95/yr.—any PC with Internet
access**
(800) 823-3209
www.personalwealth.com

Standard & Poor's Personal Wealth is a one-stop investment center that offers financial planning, portfolio management, charting, mutual fund and stock research, and screening at a cost of $9.95 per month, or just less than $100 a year. Unique elements include S&P ratings on stocks and funds, informative company and industry write-ups, and 10 in-depth S&P Stock Reports per month.

FIGURE 8.25
*S&P Personal
Wealth
provides
proprietary
rankings and
estimates for
its subscribers.*

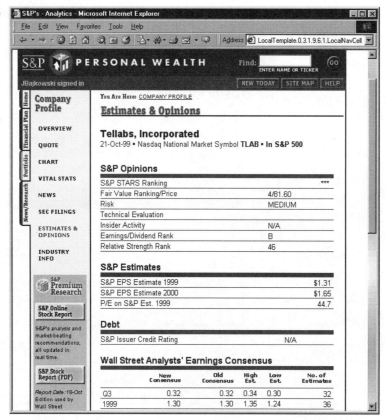

E-mail market updates go beyond descriptions of market activity to present specific investment ideas, stock recommendations, and recommended portfolio allocation changes. Personal Wealth leverages its S&P connections to provide regular updates on changes to the makeup of the S&P indexes.

The tools and data are solid and useful, but the information comes with a subscription charge in an era where the market is heading toward free data. The site will appeal most to investors who want easy access to S&P's well-regarded investment analysis.

SmartMoney.com	
Portfolio Monitoring	4
Fundamental Analysis	4
Mutual Fund Analysis	4
Technical Analysis	4
Performance	4
Ease of Use	4
Value	5

SmartMoney.com
by SmartMoney Magazine
Free—any PC with Internet access
www.smartmoney.com

SmartMoney combines the high-grade editorial content of its magazine with a rich array of useful investment tools and research. The free site covers all of the bases—portfolio management, market news and updates, charting, company and mutual fund research, mutual fund screening, as well as educational articles on financial planning and investment analysis.

The site features a unique set of analytical tools that go beyond the standard set of repackaged data found at most investment Web sites. For example, the charting

FIGURE 8.26
Smart-Money.com offers a number of unique analytical tools coupled with the editorial resources of its publication within its free site.

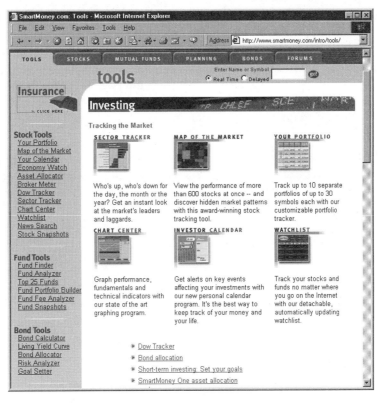

module covers a wide range of technical and fundamental factors. Its Java-based mutual fund screening offers a five-tab module that guides you through the creation of screens and offers assistance by providing low, average, and high statistics for applicable fields, like historical returns. Daily and weekly E-mail updates provide a handy notice of new articles posted to the Web site. SmartMoney's unique, but useful, collection of investment tools makes this site worth checking out.

Stockpoint	
Portfolio Monitoring	3
Fundamental Analysis	3
Mutual Fund Analysis	3
Technical Analysis	4
Performance	4
Ease of Use	4
Value	5

Stockpoint
by Stockpoint, Inc.
Free—any PC with Internet access
(415) 394-6800
www.stockpoint.com

Stockpoint, Inc., offers a portfolio manager, news, stock and mutual fund research, and a stock and fund screening package for free at its Web site. The site features both simple, quick charts as well as advanced interactive charts. The interactive charts allow you to plot seven different technical indicators, including Bollinger bands and stochastics. You can add seven different comparison indexes to its charts and choose from three different chart types, including line and candlestick. These charts are interactive through a Java-based "Zoom In and Zoom Out" function, which allows for fine-tuned analysis.

Stock and fund data, as well as screening, are adequate, but basic. Portfolio E-mail updates are available twice a day. Stockpoint offers a well-organized collection of basic, but helpful tools.

FIGURE 8.27
Stockpoint offers free mutual fund profiles from Value Line coupled with charting and screening.

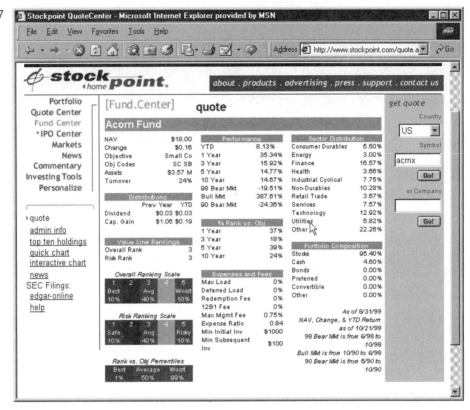

Thomson Investors Network	
Portfolio Monitoring	4
Fundamental Analysis	4
Mutual Fund Analysis	4
Technical Analysis	4
Performance	4
Ease of Use	5
Value	4

Thomson Investors Network
by Thomson Financial Services, Inc.
$34.95/yr.—any PC with Internet access
(301) 545-4999
www.thomsoninvest.net

Covering stocks, mutual funds and municipal bonds, Thomson Investors Network is a comprehensive investment Web site that offers portfolio tracking, news, E-mail alerts, charts, educational articles, research data, and screening. For a flat fee of $34.95 per year, subscribers can receive updates on market indexes, economic statistics and company news.

FIGURE 8.28
A report displaying the consensus buy/sell recommendations for Starbucks on Thomson Investors Network.

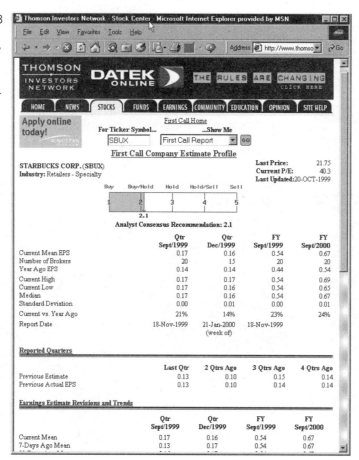

Company data supplied by the site includes items such as consensus earnings forecasts and recommendations, detailed financial statements and ratios, company and industry performance statistics, and insider trading activity.

Thomson is one of the few investment sites to provide information on bonds. Thomson offers a daily updated bond analysis and news section, regional coverage of municipal issues, and a calendar of new bond offerings.

Mutual fund investors will find a wealth of data, including market commentary on current issues and trends within the mutual fund community. Mutual fund reports and basic mutual fund screening are also included.

Overall, Thomson Investors Network is another source of well-organized investment information.

Wall Street City	
Portfolio Monitoring	4
Fundamental Analysis	5
Mutual Fund Analysis	4
Technical Analysis	5
Performance	4
Ease of Use	4
Value	4

Wall Street City
by Telescan, Inc.
Free–$149.95/mo.—any PC with Internet access
(800) 324-8246
www.wallstreetcity.com

Wall Street City is a comprehensive investment Web site that offers a wide selection of data and subscription options ranging from free portfolio tracking, news, market updates, and basic search tools to a rich array of subscription-based tools that provide charting, screening, and research. Wall Street City's tiered pricing allows you to tailor the product subscription to your needs and expand services as needs develop. More advanced levels of news, charting, screening, and research can be chosen for prices ranging from $9.95 to $149.95 per month.

FIGURE 8.29
A one-year bar chart for Telescan on the Wall Street City Web site.

Multiple portfolios can be set up to retrieve portfolio news and price alerts (which can be received via E-mail), quotes and more. Price and news alerts can be received via E-mail. Company news from Reuters and Comtex is available. A keyword search of these resources can retrieve articles of interest.

The site offers the most comprehensive set of screening tools among the Web sites reviewed here, including a range of predefined and user-defined screening modules. These modules cover both fundamental and technical factors for stocks, options and mutual funds. The site even offers 80 in-depth, on-line calculators for financial planning and investment decisions. Stock reports are detailed and include standard data from the income statement, balance sheet, and cash flow statement as well as Vickers insider trading statistics and Zacks earnings estimates.

Wall Street City is an appealing site for sophisticated investors looking for advanced tools necessary for fundamental and technical analysis of stocks and bonds.

Wall Street Journal Interactive Edition	
Portfolio Monitoring	3
Fundamental Analysis	3
Mutual Fund Analysis	3
Technical Analysis	3
Performance	5
Ease of Use	3
Value	4

Wall Street Journal Interactive Edition
by Dow Jones & Company
$59/yr.—any PC with Internet access
(800) 369-2834
wsj.com

The Wall Street Journal Interactive site is really two sites combined into one—the Wall Street Journal Interactive and Barron's Online. An annual fee of $59 ($29 for subscribers to any of the print versions of these publications) gives you full access to the content of these publications coupled with a wide range of stock, fund, economic, and general news; stock, mutual fund, index, and bond data; portfolio management; and charts.

A custom news retrieval option provides you with news based on your preferences. You can elect to have E-mail news alerts and select stories from Barron's and the Wall Street Journal sent automatically. Users can also search an archive of past news and articles. The portfolio manager, charts, and company and fund snapshots are basic, but adequate. Fifty free real-time quotes per day are available, but not tied into the portfolio view or standard quote lookup.

FIGURE 8.30
The Wall Street Journal Interactive briefing book outlines the available information for a given security.

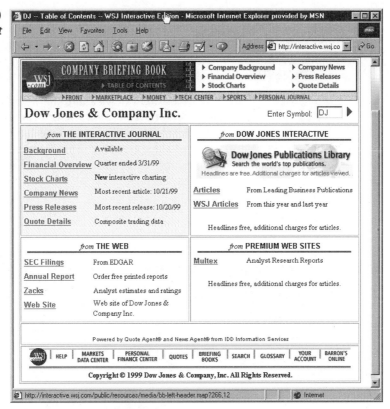

Yahoo! Finance	
Portfolio Monitoring	4
Fundamental Analysis	3
Mutual Fund Analysis	4
Technical Analysis	3
Performance	5
Ease of Use	4
Value	5

Yahoo! Finance
by Yahoo! Inc.
Free—any PC with Internet access
(408) 731-3300
<u>quote.yahoo.com</u>

Yahoo! Finance brings together a basic, but reasonable set of free tools for the investor. All the necessary tools for monitoring a stock or mutual fund portfolio are in place, but execution is fairly simple. Once registered, users can customize the default display of information.

Yahoo! leverages its linking expertise to bring together news from sources such as Reuters, S&P, the Associated Press, CNN, CBS MarketWatch, PR News, and the Business

Wire. Market and stock commentary from popular Web sites such as the Motley Fool and TheStreet.com help to round out the offerings. Fundamental stock data comes from Market Guide, while Zacks provides earnings estimates and brokerage recommendations. Even insider transactions from CDA Investment Technologies are available for free, which also provides the mutual fund profiles.

Beyond offering comprehensive investment news and data, Yahoo! Finance also offers some of the most popular message boards on the Internet. Not only does this site have boards for over 7,700 stocks, but it also boasts boards devoted to brokerage firms' IPOs, options, and short-term trading. The message boards in the stock area are divided into industry groups such as basic materials, energy, financial, and utilities. You can also perform a search for message boards based on keywords.

Overall, Yahoo! Finance is a good site for keeping track of your portfolio and performing basic company research.

FIGURE 8.31
*Detailed quote
on Yahoo!
Finance.*

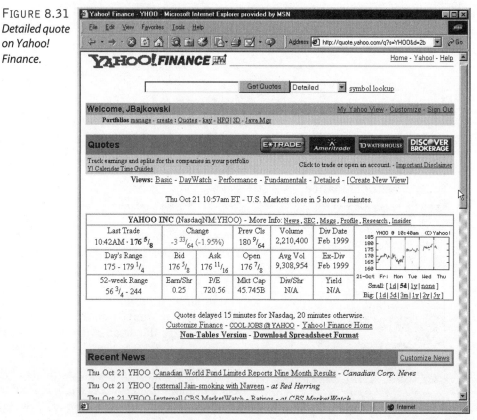

Financial Information Service		America Online	CompuServe
Company		America Online	CompuServe Corp.
Telephone		(800) 827-6364	(800) 848-8990
Web Address		www.aol.com	www.compuserve.com
Monthly Fee for Basic Access (Additional Hours)		$9.95 for 5 hours ($2.95)	$9.95 for 5 hours ($2.95)
Monthly Fee for Unlimited Access		$21.95	$24.95
Portfolio Monitoring	Pricing	part of normal charges	part of normal charges
	Current Quotes (Securities)	stocks, funds, options, futures	stocks, funds, bonds, indexes, options, futures
	Automatic Portfolio Updates		
	Real-Time Quotes		
	Maximum Portfolios / Securities	20/100	1/200
	Alerts (News, Price, Rating, Vol)	✖ (Price, News)	✖ (News)
	E-Mail (Mrk Summary, Portfolio)		
	News Search (Primary News Wires)	✖ (Reuters, AP, Bloomberg, PR News, Business Wire)	✖ (CBSI, Reuters, AP, PR News, Business Wire)
	Message Areas	✖	✖
	Software Library	✖	✖
Fundamental Analysis	Special Products (Additional Costs)	Disclosure, Hoover's, MarketGuide, Zacks	screening part of normal fees, Disclosure reports—$20/co.
	Number of Companies	8,000+	12,000+
	Number of Data Fields	1,000+	700
	Number of Years of Data	4	10
	Ratios	✖	✖
	Financials	✖ (MarketGuide, Disclosure)	✖
	SEC Filings	✖	✖
	EPS Estimates/Ratings	✖ (Zacks: EPS Est, Rec)	✖ (I/B/E/S at extra cost)
	Industry Comparisons	✖ (Market Guide: Basic Ratios)	
	Insider Activity		
	Screening (Number of Data Fields)	✖ (14)	✖ (39)
Technical Analysis	Pricing	part of normal charges	Charts are part of normal charges, downloads are $7.50 per year, $.03 per quote
	Securities Covered	stocks, funds	stocks, indexes, funds, options, futures
	Charts	✖ (1987+)	✖ (1985+)
	Technical Indicators		
	Historical Prices	✖ (1987+)	✖ (1973+)
Mutual Fund	Pricing (Source)	part of normal charges (Morningstar Mutual Funds)	part of normal charges (Morningstar Mutual Funds)
	Number of Funds Followed	8,000	8,800
	Number of Data Fields	100	94
	Screening (Number of Data Fields)	✖ (13)	✖ (39)
	Ranking (Number of Data Fields)	✖	✖

Financial Information Service		Prodigy	CBS MarketWatch
Company		Prodigy Services Corp.	MarketWatch.com, Inc.
Telephone		(800) 776-3449	(415) 733-0500
Web Address		www.prodigy.com	cbs.marketwatch.com
Monthly Fee for Basic Access (Additional Hours)		$9.95 for 10 hours ($2.50)	
Monthly Fee for Unlimited Access		$19.95	free
Portfolio Monitoring	Pricing	part of normal charges	free
	Current Quotes (Securities)	stocks, funds, indexes	stocks, funds, options, futures
	Automatic Portfolio Updates	✖ (Internet Explorer)	✖ (every 5 minutes)
	Real-Time Quotes		MarketWatch RT ($35/mo.)
	Maximum Portfolios / Securities	50/100	unlimited/200
	Alerts (News, Price, Rating, Vol)	✖ (News, Price, Rating, Vol)	
	E-Mail (Mrk Summary, Portfolio)		✖ (Market)
	News Search (Primary News Wires)	✖ (Dow Jones, Business Wire, PR News, Briefing.com, TheStreet.com)	✖ (AP, Business Wire, CBSI, Reuters, PR News, Reuters, UPI)
	Message Areas	✖	✖
	Software Library	✖	
Fundamental Analysis	Special Products (Additional Costs)	part of normal charges	BaseLine ($5/mo.), Hoover's, Market Guide, Multex, Zacks
	Number of Companies	9,600+	12,000+
	Number of Data Fields	1,000	100+
	Number of Years of Data	8	5
	Ratios	✖	✖
	Financials	✖	
	SEC Filings	✖	✖
	EPS Estimates/Ratings	✖	✖ (Zacks)
	Industry Comparisons	✖	
	Insider Activity	✖	✖
	Screening (Number of Data Fields)	✖ (50+)	✖ (22)
Technical Analysis	Pricing	free;	free (BigCharts)
	Securities Covered	stocks, indexes, funds	stocks, indexes, funds
	Charts	✖	✖ (1985+)
	Technical Indicators		✖
	Historical Prices	✖ (5 years)	
Mutual Fund	Pricing (Source)	part of normal charges (Morningstar, Value Line)	free (Lipper)
	Number of Funds Followed	6,000+	8,000+
	Number of Data Fields	80	50
	Screening (Number of Data Fields)	✖ (20)	
	Ranking (Number of Data Fields)	✖ (6)	✖

Financial Information Service		INVESTools	Morningstar.com
Company		INVESTools, Inc.	Morningstar, Inc.
Telephone		(800) 567-2683	(800) 735-0700
Web Address		www.investools.com	www.morningstar.com
Monthly Fee for Basic Access (Additional Hours)			
Monthly Fee for Unlimited Access		Advanced Portfolio–$9.95	Basic–free; Premium–$9.95
Portfolio Monitoring	Pricing	part of normal charges	free/additional Premium features
	Current Quotes (Securities)	stocks, funds, indexes	stocks, funds
	Automatic Portfolio Updates		
	Real-Time Quotes		
	Maximum Portfolios / Securities	1/100	10/50
	Alerts (News, Price, Rating, Vol)	✖ (Price Limits, News)	✖ (News, Price, Rating, Vol)
	E-Mail (Mrk Summary, Portfolio)	✖ (Portfolio)	✖ (Market, Portfolio)
	News Search (Primary News Wires)	✖ (Reuters)	✖ (Basic–PR News, Business Wire, Premium–Reuters, Dow Jones)
	Message Areas		✖
	Software Library		
Fundamental Analysis	Special Products (Additional Costs)	part of normal charges; Screening $9.96/month	free with additional data and screening for Premium option
	Number of Companies	9,400+	8,000+
	Number of Data Fields	200	300+
	Number of Years of Data	4	5
	Ratios	✖	✖
	Financials	✖	✖
	SEC Filings		✖
	EPS Estimates/Ratings	✖	✖
	Industry Comparisons		✖
	Insider Activity		✖
	Screening (Number of Data Fields)	✖ (basic–30; advanced–68)	✖ (Basic–2; Premium–125)
Technical Analysis	Pricing	part of normal charges	free
	Securities Covered	stocks, indexes, funds	stocks, funds
	Charts	✖ (6 years)	✖
	Technical Indicators	✖	
	Historical Prices		
Mutual Fund	Pricing (Source)	$5 per report (Morningstar Mutual Funds OnDemand)	free with additional data and screening for Premium option
	Number of Funds Followed	8,000	8,000
	Number of Data Fields	500	100+
	Screening (Number of Data Fields)		✖ (Basic–10; Premium–70)
	Ranking (Number of Data Fields)		✖ (Basic–10; Premium–70)

Financial Information Service		Motley Fool	MSN MoneyCentral Investor
Company		The Motley Fool, Inc.	Microsoft, Inc.
Telephone			(800) 426-9400
Web Address		www.fool.com	moneycentral.msn.com/investor
Monthly Fee for Basic Access (Additional Hours)			
Monthly Fee for Unlimited Access		free	free
Portfolio Monitoring	Pricing	free	free
	Current Quotes (Securities)	stocks, funds, indexes	stocks, funds, bonds, indexes, options, futures
	Automatic Portfolio Updates		✖
	Real-Time Quotes		✖
	Maximum Portfolios / Securities	unlimited	50/100
	Alerts (News, Price, Rating, Vol)	✖ (News)	✖ (News, Price, Rating, Vol)
	E-Mail (Mrk Summary, Portfolio)	✖ (Market)	
	News Search (Primary News Wires)	✖ (Reuters, PR News, Business Wire, UPI)	✖ (MSNBC, Business Wire, PR News, Reuters)
	Message Areas	✖	✖
	Software Library		
Fundamental Analysis	Special Products (Additional Costs)	free	free
	Number of Companies	8,000+	8,000+
	Number of Data Fields	80	1,500
	Number of Years of Data	4	10
	Ratios	✖	✖
	Financials	✖	✖
	SEC Filings	✖	✖
	EPS Estimates/Ratings	✖	✖
	Industry Comparisons		✖
	Insider Activity	✖	✖
	Screening (Number of Data Fields)		✖ (200)
Technical Analysis	Pricing	free	free
	Securities Covered	stocks, funds, indexes	stocks, indexes, funds
	Charts	✖ (1985+)	✖ (10 years)
	Technical Indicators		✖
	Historical Prices		✖ (10 years)
Mutual Fund	Pricing (Source)		free (Morningstar, Value Line)
	Number of Funds Followed		7,500+
	Number of Data Fields		100+
	Screening (Number of Data Fields)		✖ (100+)
	Ranking (Number of Data Fields)		✖ (100+)

Financial Information Service		Quicken.com	Quote.com
Company		Intuit Inc.	Quote.com, Inc.
Telephone		(800) 446-8848	(800) 498-8068
Web Address		www.quicken.com	www.quote.com
Monthly Fee for Basic Access (Additional Hours)			
Monthly Fee for Unlimited Access		free	basic free, plus ($25/month)
Portfolio Monitoring	Pricing	free	free
	Current Quotes (Securities)	stocks, funds, indexes	stocks, funds, futures, indexes, options
	Automatic Portfolio Updates	✖ (Internet Explorer)	✖ (fee)
	Real-Time Quotes		✖ (fee)
	Maximum Portfolios / Securities	50/100	1/10 (free), 12/100 (fee)
	Alerts (News, Price, Rating, Vol)	✖ (News, Price, Rating, Vol)	✖ (Price Limits, News)
	E-Mail (Mrk Summary, Portfolio)		✖ (Portfolio)
	News Search (Primary News Wires)	✖ (Dow Jones, Business Wire, PR News, Briefing.com, TheStreet.com)	✖ (AP, S&P, Newsbytes, Business Wire, PR News, Reuters)
	Message Areas	✖	✖
	Software Library	✖	
Fundamental Analysis	Special Products (Additional Costs)	free	part of basic, many additional options available
	Number of Companies	9,600+	9,600+
	Number of Data Fields	1,000	30+
	Number of Years of Data	8	1
	Ratios	✖	✖
	Financials	✖	✖ (fee)
	SEC Filings	✖	✖
	EPS Estimates/Ratings	✖	✖ (First Call, Zacks–fee)
	Industry Comparisons	✖	✖ (fee)
	Insider Activity	✖	
	Screening (Number of Data Fields)	✖ (50+)	
Technical Analysis	Pricing	free	free (with limits)
	Securities Covered	stocks, indexes, funds	stocks, funds, indexes, futures
	Charts	✖	✖
	Technical Indicators		✖ (fee)
	Historical Prices	✖ (5 years)	✖ (1988+)
Mutual Fund	Pricing (Source)	part of normal charges (Morning-star, Value Line)	free (Lipper, Morningstar)
	Number of Funds Followed	6,000+	7,500+
	Number of Data Fields	80	100+
	Screening (Number of Data Fields)	✖ (20)	✖ (110)
	Ranking (Number of Data Fields)	✖ (6)	✖ (110)

Financial Information Service		S&P Personal Wealth	SmartMoney.com
Company		Standard & Poor's	SmartMoney Magazine
Telephone		(800) 823-3209	
Web Address		www.personalwealth.com	www.smartmoney.com
Monthly Fee for Basic Access (Additional Hours)			
Monthly Fee for Unlimited Access		$9.95/mo. or $99.95/yr.	free
Portfolio Monitoring	Pricing	part of normal charges	free
	Current Quotes (Securities)	stocks, funds, futures, indexes, options	stocks, funds, indexes, options
	Automatic Portfolio Updates	✖	✖
	Real-Time Quotes	✖	✖
	Maximum Portfolios / Securities	unlimited/50	20/30
	Alerts (News, Price, Rating, Vol)		✖ (News)
	E-Mail (Mrk Summary, Portfolio)	✖ (Market)	✖ (Market)
	News Search (Primary News Wires)	✖ (S&P, Business Week)	✖ (Dow Jones, Business Wire, PR News, SmartMoney)
	Message Areas		✖
	Software Library		
Fundamental Analysis	Special Products (Additional Costs)	regular reports part of basic, 10 premium reports per month	free
	Number of Companies	9,000	9,600+
	Number of Data Fields	400+	300+
	Number of Years of Data	6	5
	Ratios	✖	✖
	Financials	✖	✖
	SEC Filings	✖	
	EPS Estimates/Ratings	✖	✖
	Industry Comparisons	✖	✖
	Insider Activity		✖
	Screening (Number of Data Fields)	✖ (28)	
Technical Analysis	Pricing	part of normal charges (BigCharts)	free
	Securities Covered	stocks, indexes, funds	stocks, indexes, funds
	Charts	✖ (1985+)	✖ (6 years)
	Technical Indicators	✖	✖
	Historical Prices		
Mutual Fund	Pricing (Source)	part of normal charges (Micropal)	free (Lipper)
	Number of Funds Followed	10,000+	6,000+
	Number of Data Fields	110	52
	Screening (Number of Data Fields)	✖ (34)	✖ (26)
	Ranking (Number of Data Fields)	✖ (5)	✖ (13)

Financial Information Service		Stockpoint	Thomson Investors Network
Company		Stockpoint, Inc.	Thomson Financial Services, Inc.
Telephone		(415) 394-6800	(301) 545-4999
Web Address		www.stockpoint.com	www.thomsoninvest.net
Monthly Fee for Basic Access (Additional Hours)			
Monthly Fee for Unlimited Access		free	$34.95/yr.
Portfolio Monitoring	Pricing	free	free
	Current Quotes (Securities)	stocks, funds, indexes, options	stocks, funds
	Automatic Portfolio Updates		✖
	Real-Time Quotes	✖	✖
	Maximum Portfolios / Securities	unlimited	1/10 or 25/25
	Alerts (News, Price, Rating, Vol)		✖ (News, Price, Rating, Vol)
	E-Mail (Mrk Summary, Portfolio)	✖ (Market, Portfolio)	✖ (Portfolio)
	News Search (Primary News Wires)	✖ (AP, Comtex, Business Wire, PR News)	✖ (PR News, Business Wire, Comtex, UPI)
	Message Areas		✖
	Software Library		
Fundamental Analysis	Special Products (Additional Costs)	free	free
	Number of Companies	9,000+	7,300+
	Number of Data Fields	700+	500+
	Number of Years of Data	5	5
	Ratios	✖	✖
	Financials	✖	✖
	SEC Filings	✖	✖
	EPS Estimates/Ratings	✖ (Zacks)	✖
	Industry Comparisons		✖
	Insider Activity		✖
	Screening (Number of Data Fields)	✖ (31)	✖ (20)
Technical Analysis	Pricing	free	free
	Securities Covered	stocks, funds, indexes	stocks, funds
	Charts	✖ (5 years)	✖ (1 year)
	Technical Indicators	✖	
	Historical Prices		
Mutual Fund	Pricing (Source)	free (Value Line)	free (CDA)
	Number of Funds Followed	7,500+	9,000+
	Number of Data Fields	48	300+
	Screening (Number of Data Fields)	✖ (15)	✖ (35)
	Ranking (Number of Data Fields)	✖ (4)	

Financial Information Service		Wall Street City	Wall Street Journal Interactive Edition	Yahoo! Finance
Company		Telescan, Inc.	Dow Jones & Company	Yahoo! Inc.
Telephone		(800) 324-8246	(800) 369-2834	(408) 731-3300
Web Address		www.wallstreetcity.com	wsj.com	quote.yahoo.com
Monthly Fee for Basic Access (Additional Hours)				
Monthly Fee for Unlimited Access		Free–$149.95/month (range of free and fee plans available)	$59/yr. ($29 for Wall Street Journal, Barron's or SmartMoney subscribers)	free
Portfolio Monitoring	Pricing	part of normal charges	part of normal charges	free
	Current Quotes (Securities)	stocks, funds, indexes, futures	stocks, funds, index, options	stocks, funds, indexes
	Automatic Portfolio Updates			
	Real-Time Quotes		✖	
	Maximum Portfolios / Securities	1/150 (free), 7/150 (fee)	5/30	unlimited/200
	Alerts (News, Price, Rating, Vol)	✖ (News, Price Limits)	✖ (News)	✖ (Price)
	E-Mail (Mrk Summary, Portfolio)		✖ (Market)	
	News Search (Primary News Wires)	✖ (Reuters)	✖ (Dow Jones, Business Wire)	✖ (Briefing.com, Business Wire, CBS MarketWatch, Motley Fool, PR News, Reuters)
	Message Areas	✖	✖	✖
	Software Library			
Fundamental Analysis	Special Products (Additional Costs)	part of normal charges	part of normal charges	free
	Number of Companies	9,600+	9,600+	9,000+
	Number of Data Fields	200+	80+	100+
	Number of Years of Data	5	5	3
	Ratios	✖	✖	✖
	Financials	✖	✖	✖
	SEC Filings	✖	✖	✖
	EPS Estimates/Ratings	✖	✖	✖
	Industry Comparisons	✖		
	Insider Activity	✖		✖
	Screening (Number of Data Fields)	✖/40		✖/8
Technical Analysis	Pricing	part of normal charges	part of normal charges (BigCharts)	free
	Securities Covered	stocks, funds, indexes, futures	stocks, funds, index	stocks, funds, indexes
	Charts	✖	✖ (1985+)	✖ (1960+)
	Technical Indicators	✖	✖	
	Historical Prices	✖ (1973+)		✖
Mutual Fund	Pricing (Source)	part of normal charges (J&J Financial)	part of normal charges (Lipper)	free
	Number of Funds Followed	9,000+	6,000+	6,000+
	Number of Data Fields	82	66	125+
	Screening (Number of Data Fields)	✖ (82)		✖ (8)
	Ranking (Number of Data Fields)	✖ (82)		✖ (8)

Appendix

GUIDE TO INVESTMENT WEB SITES

Today, individuals in search of investment data and information need venture no further than their computer screens, where they can tap into the vast resources of the World Wide Web. From stock and market statistics to financial and retirement planning calculators, from charting services to on-line brokerage accounts—there is probably something helpful to you somewhere on the Web.

Finding it, though, is another matter. While many sites provide in-depth financial statistics, research, and other information, other sites are purely promotional, with little or no useful information; even worse, still other sites offer pure junk. In addition, some sites have free access to useful information, while other sites charge a fee. Sorting through various sites to weed out the junk and to determine their value can result in an enormous investment of your time.

This guide is designed to lower your investment costs and help you find the most useful investment-related Web sites more easily. The AAII editors have spent hours researching and rating various sites. The guide presents the top-rated sites for the most common investment needs as well as a directory that lists 465 sites of interest to individual investors. Included in the directory are details about the information and services each site offers to help you decide whether or not to pay a visit.

To facilitate use of the guide, AAII's Web site at www.aaii.com presents the complete list with hyperlinks directly to each site, as well as lists of the top-rated sites by subject.

What the Guide Includes

The Web guide is a complete alphabetical listing of all the Web sites we found that provide at least some investment information or interactions that would be useful to individual investors.

The list includes stock exchanges, data providers, mutual fund companies, brokerage firms, and government agencies, as well as sites devoted to options and futures, taxes, financial planning, portfolio tracking, foreign investing, and technical analysis. Broker sites are limited to discount brokers, and mutual fund sites are limited to no-load and low-load fund families. Investment sites that charge a fee for some or all content are included, but are identified as fee-based by the ratings columns. Many fee-based sites will provide a sample of its data or a demonstration of its service so that visitors to the site can see what is offered.

The guide is organized alphabetically by the name of the Web site (first column). To help you identify sites that suit your needs, we give details on the services and information available at each site, along with a short description of the main purpose of the site and what types of securities are covered. Keep in mind, however, that Web sites are prone to frequent changes and the details we provide may not match what you find by the time you reach a site listed here.

For further guidance, we also include ratings for each site. The ratings range from one ⊕ as lowest to five as highest; sites were judged based on content and thoroughness; sites that have fee-based content were judged against other sites' fee-based sections, and free content was judged relative to the free offerings of other similar sites.

Reading the List

The first column in our guide gives the **name** of the site. Many of these are the official sites of investment-related companies and agencies with which you are probably already familiar, such as Standard & Poor's, the New York Stock Exchange, and the SEC (U.S. Securities & Exchange Commission). Other sites belong to on-line providers and are less well-known to the general public. While familiarity with a site provider can serve as one guide to the dependability of the information provided, prudence and good judgment on your part should always prevail.

The second column provides the Web address for the site, also referred to as the **URL.** Addresses must be entered as shown to reach a site, but sites do change frequently, and if a site moves, you may have to perform an Internet search or call the organization to obtain a new URL.

The **primary focus** column gives you an idea of the general investment area to which the site is primarily devoted. Some sites defy classification by offering multiple services; in these cases, we assigned either the category 'comprehensive' or one category that best describes the major focus of the site. The checkmarks across the page fill in the details as to the range of content provided. For example, the Fidelity Investments site lists 'mutual funds' as the site's primary focus, but the site also provides information on a range of securities and offers on-line trading services, as well.

The **ratings** compare the site to other sites with a similar focus and cost policy—mutual fund company sites are rated against other mutual fund sites and stock data providers are compared to other stock data providers. Ratings range from a low of one ⊕ to a high of five. Highly-rated sites do not necessarily have numerous checkmarks across the list; a site may focus on only one particular area of investing but provide substantial information and services in that area. Sites may offer some content for free and charge for other content; we include ratings for both where appropriate.

The **securities covered** column shows you what investment vehicles the site provides information on. These can include stocks (**stk**), fixed-income (**fixed**), international (**int'l**), mutual funds (**fund**), closed-end funds (**closed**), options and futures (**opt/fut**), real estate (**RE**), annuities (**annty**), and insurance products (**insur**). Note that some sites do not provide information on specific securities, but do have useful investment-related information (for instance, educational sites); these sites would not have any markings in this column.

The **Functions Performed** section details investing-related actions that can be carried out at the site. **Financial planning** functions include such capabilities as retirement planning calculators and mortgage calculators; **portfolio tracking** functions allow you to build and follow the progress of a portfolio of securities on-line. **Screening** functions give you access to a database of securities that you can filter based on various criteria, such as stock size, earnings per share, or 12-month return. Screening functions offered by Web sites vary widely in their power and versatility. In some cases, a site may provide prescreened lists of stocks or funds that are updated frequently. **Charting** functions allow site visitors to build or view charts of security prices over various periods of time. Many Web sites provide access to charts for individual securities along with a stock quote retrieval service. **Brokerage** functions allow investors to trade securities on-line. Sites with **downloading** functions provide files that visitors can download to their own computer and view or use later. These can include text files such as IRS publications and software or spreadsheet files to install for use. **Message boards** are where visitors can exchange opinions by posting messages.

The **Information and Documents Provided** section describes what kind of investment information you will find at the site. **News** refers to daily updates on company or fund activity, usually in the form of press releases or news bureau bulletins. **Quotes** refers to current stock or fund price quotes accessed by ticker symbol and kept updated throughout the day when the markets are open, normally with a 15-minute delay. News and quotes are common features of many investing sites and are usually provided by a few main services such as Reuters for news and Quote.Com for quotes.

Mutual fund data refers to dividends and capital gains, returns, and expense figures. **Stock data and ratios** can include financial statement data such as cash flow and earnings per share as well as financial ratios such as price-earnings ratios. The range and depth of stock and fund data offered can vary between sites, so you will need to examine each to see if it provides the information you need. **Estimates/research** can include projected earnings estimates or recommendations based on analyst study of a company. **Technical indicators** such as relative strength measures and momentum indicators look at security price movement. The **Company/fund filings** column is checked if the site provides or allows you to order company or fund prospectuses or annual reports on-line. Sites may provide **industry data** to give you information on particular segments of the market. When data is provided on a market—for example, the S&P 500— or the economy—such as interest rates—the column **market/economic data** is checked.

Financial planning encompasses information on budgeting, retirement planning, and estate planning. **Taxes** includes tax forms and tips on handling your taxes. **Educational** refers to information made available that can help you learn more about specific investing topics.

Links give you the ability to access other Web sites through the current site. Most sites provide these pathways to related information, which you access by simply clicking on the name of the link (usually underlined or shown in a different color). For example, a site that lists companies with dividend reinvestment plans may include links to each company's home page or to the SEC database of company reports so that you can quickly obtain more information about the firm. Other sites may contain an area with a list of interesting investing Web sites that you can click on to access.

To visit the sites listed in the guide, you need a computer with a modem, an Internet service provider, and a Web browser.

Once connected to the Internet, simply type the Web URL into the address window at your service provider's home page and press enter. This takes you to the home page of the site. The baud rate (speed) at which your modem connected to the Internet will determine how fast the home page is brought up onto your computer screen.

From here, you can explore the contents of the site. If you are unsure about who is responsible for the information presented at a particular site, check the bottom of the home page for a link to a company or person's name or look for an "About" icon. Not all sites will be clear as to where the information is coming from, however, so be wary and do not accept information as "fact" just because it has popped up on your computer screen.

When exploring a site, it's easy to get lost after clicking on several icons or links that take you to different pages on the site or take you to other sites. Web browsers provide "back" and "forward" buttons so that you can retrace your steps or return to a particular page. You can tell if a click of your mouse has taken you to a link outside of the site by checking the URL in the address window—it will either be a long extension of the original URL you entered or a completely different URL.

If you pan through the sands of the Internet, you really can find valuable nuggets of investment information. This Investment Web Guide will lead you to the best prospecting sites on the Internet, and as long as you view your prospects with a critical eye, you should be able to hit pay dirt.

Name of Site	URL	Primary Focus	Free Rating	Fee-Based Rating	Securities Covered
.xls	www.xls.com	stock data/analysis	na	⊕⊕⊕	stk, int'l
1040.Com	www.1040.com	tax information	⊕⊕⊕⊕	na	
401(k) Resource Center	www.401kresource.com	financial planning	⊕	na	
401Kafe	www.401kafe.com	financial planning	⊕⊕⊕	na	
401k Forum	www.401kforum.com	financial planning	⊕	na	
A.B. Watley	www.abwatley.com	on-line trading	⊕⊕⊕	⊕⊕⊕	stk, fixed, fund, opt/fut, annty
AARP Investment Program	aarp.scudder.com	mutual funds	⊕⊕⊕⊕	na	fund
ABN AMRO Funds	www.abnamrofunds-usa.com	mutual funds	⊕⊕	na	fund
ADR.com	www.adr.com	ADRs	⊕⊕⊕⊕⊕	na	stk, int'l
AFTrader	www.aftrader.com	on-line trading	⊕⊕	⊕⊕⊕	stk, fund, opt/fut
AOL Personal Finance	quicken.aol.com	comprehensive	⊕⊕⊕⊕⊕	na	stk, fixed, int'l, fund, annty, insur
ASK Research Stock Charting & Analysis	www.askresearch.com	technical analysis	⊕⊕⊕	na	stk, int'l, fund, opt/fut
AccuTrade	www.accutrade.com	on-line trading	na	⊕⊕⊕⊕	stk, fixed, fund, opt/fut
Acorn Funds	www.wanger.com	mutual funds	⊕⊕	na	fund
Adams Owens Kirwan (attorney)	www.estate-planning.net	estate planning	⊕⊕	na	
Alert-IPO!	www.ostman.com/alert-ipo	IPOs	na	⊕⊕⊕	stk
Alliance for Investor Education	www.investoreducation.org/	investment Web links	⊕	na	stk, fixed, fund, opt/fut
Amcore Funds	www.amcore.com	mutual funds	⊕⊕⊕	na	fund
American Association of Individual Investors	www.aaii.com	educational			stk, fixed, int'l, fund, closed, annty, insur
American Century Funds	www.americancentury.com	mutual funds	⊕⊕⊕⊕⊕	na	stk, fund, opt/fut
American Express Financial Services	americanexpress.com	on-line trading	na	⊕⊕⊕	stk, fund, annty, insur
American Institute of CPAs	www.aicpa.org	regulations	⊕	na	
Ameritrade	www.ameritrade.com	on-line trading	na	⊕⊕⊕	stk, fixed, fund, opt/fut
Andrew Peck Associates Inc.	www.andrewpeck.com	on-line trading	na	⊕	stk, fixed, opt/fut
Annual Report Gallery	www.reportgallery.com	company reports	⊕⊕	na	
Aquinas Funds	www.aquinasfunds.com	mutual funds	⊕	na	fund
Armchair Millionaire	www.armchairmillionaire.com	financial planning	⊕⊕	na	
Australian Securities & Investments Commission	www.asic.gov.au	foreign investing	⊕⊕	na	stk, int'l
Australian Stock Exchange	www.asx.com.au	foreign investing	⊕⊕⊕	na	stk, int'l, opt/fut
Babson Funds	www.jbfunds.com	mutual funds	⊕⊕⊕	na	fund

426

Functions Performed | Information and Documents Provided

Financial Planning	Portfolio Tracking	Screening	Charting	Brokerage	Downloading	Message Boards	News	Quotes	Mutual Fund Data	Stock Data & Ratios	Estimates/Research	Technical Indicators	Company/Fund Filings	Industry Data	Market/Economic Data	Financial Planning	Taxes	Education	Links	Name of Site
		✗			✗		✗	✗		✗	✗			✗	✗				✗	.xls
							✗										✗		✗	1040.Com
✗					✗											✗				401(k) Resource Center
																✗		✗		401Kafe
																✗				401k Forum
	✗	✗	✗	✗			✗	✗	✗	✗	✗		✗	✗	✗					A.B. Watley
					✗		✗	✗	✗				✗			✗	✗	✗	✗	AARP Investment Program
							✗	✗	✗				✗					✗		ABN AMRO Funds
		✗	✗				✗	✗		✗	✗		✗	✗	✗			✗	✗	ADR.com
			✗	✗			✗	✗		✗	✗	✗	✗		✗			✗	✗	AFTrader
✗	✗	✗	✗			✗	✗	✗	✗	✗	✗				✗	✗	✗	✗	✗	AOL Personal Finance
	✗		✗				✗	✗				✗			✗				✗	ASK Research Stock Charting & Analysis
✗	✗	✗		✗			✗	✗	✗	✗	✗		✗	✗	✗	✗				AccuTrade
								✗	✗				✗						✗	Acorn Funds
																				Adams Owens Kirwan (attorney)
										✗									✗	Alert-IPO!
																		✗	✗	Alliance for Investor Education
✗							✗	✗	✗				✗			✗		✗	✗	Amcore Funds
	✗	✗			✗	✗		✗	✗	✗	✗					✗	✗	✗		American Association of Individual Investors
✗	✗	✗		✗			✗	✗	✗	✗	✗		✗		✗	✗	✗	✗	✗	American Century Funds
✗				✗			✗	✗		✗	✗		✗	✗	✗	✗		✗	✗	American Express Financial Services
																		✗	✗	American Institute of CPAs
	✗		✗				✗	✗		✗	✗		✗		✗			✗	✗	Ameritrade
			✗																	Andrew Peck Associates Inc.
																			✗	Annual Report Gallery
														✗					✗	Aquinas Funds
✗						✗										✗	✗	✗	✗	Armchair Millionaire
					✗		✗											✗	✗	Australian Securities & Investments Commission
					✗		✗	✗							✗			✗	✗	Australian Stock Exchange
✗				✗	✗			✗	✗				✗			✗	✗	✗		Babson Funds

Name of Site	URL	Primary Focus	Free Rating	Fee-Based Rating	Securities Covered
Bank Rate Monitor	www.bankrate.com	personal finance	⊕⊕⊕⊕⊕	na	fixed
Baron Funds	www.baronfunds.com	mutual funds	⊕⊕	na	fund
Barra	www.barra.com	stock data/analysis	⊕	na	
Barron's (Wall Street Journal Interactive Edition)	www.barrons.com	finance news/analysis	na	⊕⊕⊕⊕⊕	stk, fixed, int'l, fund
Barry Murphy & Co.	www.barrymurphy.com	on-line trading	na	⊕	stk, fixed, fund, opt/fut
Berger Funds	www.bergerfunds.com	mutual funds	⊕⊕⊕⊕	na	stk, fund
BestCalls.com	www.bestcalls.com	webcasts	⊕⊕⊕⊕⊕	na	stk
Bidwell & Co.	www.bidwell.com	on-line trading	na	⊕⊕	stk, fund, opt/fut,
BigCharts	www.bigcharts.com	stock charts & analysis	⊕⊕⊕⊕⊕	na	stk, int'l, fund
Bloomberg Financial	www.bloomberg.com	finance news/analysis	⊕⊕⊕⊕⊕	⊕⊕⊕	stk, fixed, int'l, fund, opt/fut
Bonds Online	bondsonline.com	bonds	⊕⊕⊕⊕	na	fixed
Bradynet, Inc.	www.bradynet.com	bonds	⊕⊕⊕	⊕⊕⊕	fixed, int'l
Bramwell Funds	www.bramwell.com	mutual funds	⊕⊕	na	fund
Bridge Information Systems	www.bridge.com	stock quotes	⊕⊕⊕	⊕⊕⊕	stk, int'l, fund, opt/fut,
Briefing.com	www.briefing.com	finance news/analysis	⊕⊕⊕	⊕⊕⊕⊕	stk, fixed, int'l, fund, opt/fut
Broadcast.com	www.broadcast.com	webcasts	⊕⊕⊕⊕	na	stk
Brown & Co.	www.brownco.com	on-line trading	na	⊕	stk, opt/fut
BuckInvestor.com	www.investyoung.com	personal finance	⊕⊕	na	
Bull & Bear Securities Inc.	www.bullbear.com	on-line trading	⊕⊕	⊕⊕⊕	stk, fixed, fund, opt/fut
Bull Session	www.bullsession.com	stock quotes	na	⊕⊕⊕	stk, opt/fut,
Burke, Christensen & Lewis	www.bclnet.com	on-line trading	na	⊕⊕⊕⊕	stk, fixed, fund, opt/fut
Bush Burns Securities	www.bushburns.com	on-line trading	na	⊕	stk, fixed, fund, opt/fut, annty
Business Week	www.businessweek.com	finance news/analysis	⊕⊕⊕	⊕⊕⊕⊕	stk, fixed, int'l, fund, closed, opt/fut
CANSLIM.net	www.canslim.net	stock advisory service	⊕⊕⊕	na	stk
CBS MarketWatch	cbs.marketwatch.com	comprehensive	⊕⊕⊕⊕⊕	na	stk, fixed, int'l, fund, opt/fut, RE, insur
CGM Fund	cgmfunds.com	mutual funds	⊕	na	fund
CIA World Factbook	www.odci.gov/cia/publications/factbook/index.html	foreign investing	⊕⊕⊕⊕	na	int'l
CIGNA	www.cigna.com	financial planning	⊕⊕	na	
CNN Financial Network	www.cnnfn.com	comprehensive	⊕⊕⊕	na	stk, fixed, int'l, fund

Functions Performed   Information and Documents Provided

Financial Planning	Portfolio Tracking	Screening	Charting	Brokerage	Downloading	Message Boards	News	Quotes	Mutual Fund Data	Stock Data & Ratios	Estimates/Research	Technical Indicators	Company/Fund Filings	Industry Data	Market/Economic Data	Financial Planning	Taxes	Education	Links	Name of Site
✗							✗		✗									✗	✗	Bank Rate Monitor
			✗					✗	✗				✗							Baron Funds
			✗		✗										✗					Barra
✗	✗		✗				✗	✗	✗	✗	✗	✗	✗	✗	✗	✗		✗	✗	Barron's (Wall Street Journal Interactive Edition)
				✗				✗												Barry Murphy & Co.
✗				✗			✗	✗	✗				✗		✗	✗	✗	✗	✗	Berger Funds
							✗												✗	BestCalls.com
				✗				✗	✗	✗	✗		✗		✗	✗		✗	✗	Bidwell & Co.
		✗	✗				✗	✗	✗	✗	✗	✗		✗	✗				✗	BigCharts
✗	✗		✗				✗	✗	✗	✗	✗		✗	✗	✗		✗		✗	Bloomberg Financial
				✗			✗	✗							✗			✗	✗	Bonds Online
			✗				✗	✗			✗	✗								Bradynet, Inc.
								✗	✗				✗						✗	Bramwell Funds
	✗		✗		✗		✗	✗	✗	✗		✗			✗					Bridge Information Systems
	✗		✗				✗	✗			✗			✗	✗					Briefing.com
							✗												✗	Broadcast.com
			✗																✗	Brown & Co.
																		✗	✗	BuckInvestor.com
	✗		✗	✗			✗	✗			✗	✗			✗			✗	✗	Bull & Bear Securities Inc.
	✗		✗				✗	✗		✗										Bull Session
	✗	✗	✗	✗			✗	✗	✗	✗	✗		✗	✗	✗			✗		Burke, Christensen & Lewis
				✗				✗											✗	Bush Burns Securities
	✗						✗	✗						✗	✗			✗	✗	Business Week
						✗			✗									✗	✗	CANSLIM.net
	✗		✗			✗	✗	✗	✗	✗	✗	✗		✗	✗	✗		✗	✗	CBS MarketWatch
												✗								CGM Fund
															✗					CIA World Factbook
✗																✗		✗		CIGNA
✗	✗						✗	✗		✗					✗	✗		✗	✗	CNN Financial Network

Name of Site	URL	Primary Focus	Free Rating	Fee-Based Rating	Securities Covered
Cabot Market Letter	www.cabot.net	stock advisory service	●	na	stk
Cal Law's IPO Watch	www.callaw.com/ipo	IPOs	●●	na	stk
Calif. Investment Trust Funds	www.caltrust.com	mutual funds	●	na	fund
Calvert Group	www.calvertgroup.com	mutual funds	●●●	na	fund
Central Europe Online	www.invest.centraleurope.com	foreign investing	●●●●	na	stk, int'l
Certified Financial Planner Board of Standards	www.cfp-board.org	investment associations	●●	na	
Charles Schwab & Co.	www.schwab.com	on-line trading	●●●	●●●●●	stk, fixed, int'l, fund, opt/fut
Chicago Board Options Exchange (CBOE)	www.cboe.com	options/futures	●●●●●	na	opt/fut
Chicago Board of Trade (CBOT)	www.cbot.com	options/futures	●●●●●	na	opt/fut
Chicago Mercantile Exchange	www.cme.com	options/futures	●●●	●●●	opt/fut
Chicago Stock Exchange	chicagostockex.com	stock exchange	●●●	na	stk, int'l, fund, opt/fut
ClearStation	www.clearstation.com	stock charts & analysis	●●●●	na	stk, int'l, fund
Clipper Funds	www.clipperfund.com	mutual funds	●	na	fund
Co-op America	www.coopamerica.org	social concerns	●●●	na	fund
Coffee, Sugar & Cocoa Exchange	www.csce.com	options/futures	●●●●	na	opt/fut
Cohen & Steers Funds	www.cohenandsteers.com	mutual funds	●●	na	fund, closed,
College Savings Bank	www.collegesavings.com	financial planning	●	na	fixed
College for Financial Planning	www.fp.edu	financial planning	●	na	
Columbia Funds	www.columbiafunds.com	mutual funds	●●●	na	fund
Commodity Futures Trading Commission	www.cftc.gov	options/futures	●●●	na	opt/fut
Commodity Systems Inc.	www.csidata.com	options/futures	●●	●●●	stk, fund, opt/fut
Company Sleuth	www.companysleuth.com	investment Web links	●●●●	na	stk
CompuTEL Securities	www.computel.com	on-line trading	●●●	●●●	stk, fixed, fundopt/fut
Consumer Information Center	www.pueblo.gsa.gov/	personal finance	●●●	na	
ConvertBond.com	www.convertbond.com	bonds	na	●●●	fixed
Crabbe Huson Funds	www.contrarian.com	mutual funds	●●●	na	fund
CyberInvest.com	www.cyberinvest.com	investment Web links	●●●●	na	stk, fixed, int'l, fund
DLJdirect Financial Network	www.dljdirect.com	on-line trading	●●●	●●●●	stk, fixed, fund, opt/fut
DRIP Central	www.dripcentral.com	direct stock purchase	●●●	na	stk
DRIP Investor	dripinvestor.com	direct stock purchase	●●	na	stk
DTN.IQ	www.dtniq.com	stock quotes	●●	na	stk, fund
Daily Stocks	www.dailystocks.com	investment Web links	●●●	na	stk, fixed, fund, opt/fut
Darwin	darwin.ameritrade.com	options/futures	●●	na	opt/fut

Functions Performed / Information and Documents Provided

Financial Planning	Portfolio Tracking	Screening	Charting	Brokerage	Downloading	Message Boards	News	Quotes	Mutual Fund Data	Stock Data & Ratios	Estimates/Research	Technical Indicators	Company/Fund Filings	Industry Data	Market/Economic Data	Financial Planning	Taxes	Education	Links	Name of Site
											✖	✖							✖	Cabot Market Letter
										✖									✖	Cal Law's IPO Watch
									✖				✖							Calif. Investment Trust Funds
✖								✖	✖				✖			✖	✖	✖	✖	Calvert Group
						✖	✖	✖							✖			✖	✖	Central Europe Online
																✖		✖		Certified Financial Planner Board of Standards
✖	✖	✖	✖	✖			✖	✖	✖	✖	✖	✖	✖	✖	✖	✖	✖	✖	✖	Charles Schwab & Co.
		✖			✖		✖	✖							✖			✖	✖	Chicago Board Options Exchange (CBOE)
		✖			✖		✖	✖										✖	✖	Chicago Board of Trade (CBOT)
		✖					✖	✖										✖	✖	Chicago Mercantile Exchange
		✖					✖	✖		✖		✖			✖				✖	Chicago Stock Exchange
	✖		✖			✖	✖	✖		✖	✖	✖			✖			✖	✖	ClearStation
									✖				✖							Clipper Funds
							✖									✖		✖	✖	Co-op America
			✖		✖		✖	✖				✖			✖			✖	✖	Coffee, Sugar & Cocoa Exchange
									✖	✖			✖							Cohen & Steers Funds
✖																		✖	✖	College Savings Bank
																✖		✖	✖	College for Financial Planning
✖							✖	✖	✖				✖			✖		✖		Columbia Funds
							✖											✖	✖	Commodity Futures Trading Commission
					✖			✖						✖	✖					Commodity Systems Inc.
		✖				✖	✖	✖		✖	✖								✖	Company Sleuth
	✖		✖	✖			✖	✖		✖	✖	✖	✖	✖	✖				✖	CompuTEL Securities
																		✖	✖	Consumer Information Center
	✖		✖				✖	✖		✖	✖				✖					ConvertBond.com
✖							✖	✖	✖				✖			✖		✖		Crabbe Huson Funds
							✖									✖		✖	✖	CyberInvest.com
	✖	✖	✖	✖			✖	✖	✖	✖	✖		✖	✖	✖			✖	✖	DLJdirect Financial Network
					✖													✖	✖	DRIP Central
					✖													✖	✖	DRIP Investor
								✖											✖	DTN.IQ
		✖																	✖	Daily Stocks
			✖															✖		Darwin

Name of Site	URL	Primary Focus	Free Rating	Fee-Based Rating	Securities Covered
Data Broadcasting Corporation	www.dbc.com	stock/fund data	⊕⊕	na	stk, fund
Datek Online	www.datek.com	on-line trading	⊕⊕	⊕⊕⊕	stk, fund
Day Traders On-line	www.daytraders.com	trading strategies	na	⊕⊕⊕	stk
Decision Point	www.decisionpoint.com	technical analysis	⊕⊕	na	stk, int'l, fund, opt/fut
Deja.com	www.deja.com	message boards	⊕⊕⊕	na	stk, fixed, fund, opt/fut, insur
Delafield Fund	www.delafieldfund.com	mutual funds	⊕	na	fund
Deloitte & Touche	www.dtonline.com	tax information	⊕⊕⊕	na	
Delphi Investors Forum	www.delphi.com/invest	message boards	⊕⊕	na	stk, fixed, fund
DeltaTrader	www.preftech.com	on-line trading	na	⊕⊕	stk, fixed, fund, opt/fut
Depository Receipt Services	www.bankofny.com/adr	ADRs	⊕⊕⊕⊕	na	int'l
Dick Davis Online Financial Newsletter	www.dickdavis.com	stock advisory service	⊕⊕	na	stk, fund
Disclosure-Investor.com	www.disclosure-investor.com	stock data/analysis	⊕⊕⊕	⊕⊕⊕	stk, int'l
Discover Brokerage Direct	www.discoverbrokerage.com	on-line trading	⊕⊕⊕⊕	⊕⊕⊕⊕⊕	stk, fixed, fund, opt/fut
Dismal Scientist	www.dismal.com	economic data	⊕⊕⊕⊕⊕	na	
Dodge & Cox Funds	www.dodgeandcox.com	mutual funds	⊕⊕	na	fund
Doh! Stock Picks	www.doh.com	stock advisory service	⊕⊕⊕	na	stk
Domini Funds	www.domini.com	mutual funds	⊕⊕⊕	na	fund
Dorsey, Wright & Associates	www.dorseywright.com	technical analysis	na	⊕⊕⊕⊕	stk, fund, opt/fut
DoubleHappy	www.doublehappy.com	investment Web links	⊕⊕	na	stk, fixed, opt/fut
Dow Jones Markets	www.djmarkets.com	stock data/analysis	⊕⊕⊕	na	stk, fixed, opt/fut
Downstate Discount	www.downstate.com	on-line trading	na	⊕	stk, fixed, fund, opt/fut
Dreyfus Brokerage Services	www.edreyfus.com	on-line trading	na	⊕⊕	stk, fixed, fund
Dreyfus Funds	www.dreyfus.com	mutual funds	⊕⊕⊕	na	fixed, fund, annty
Duff & Phelps Credit Rating Co.	www.dcrco.com	bond ratings	⊕⊕⊕⊕	na	fixed
Dupree Funds	www.dupree-funds.com	mutual funds	⊕⊕	na	fund
E*Trade Securities	www.etrade.com	on-line trading	⊕⊕⊕	⊕⊕⊕⊕	stk, fixed, fund, opt/fut
EC Investor	www.ecinvestor.com	advisory service	⊕⊕⊕	na	stk
EDGAR Online	www.edgar-online.com	company reports	⊕⊕⊕	⊕⊕⊕	
Eclispe Funds	www.eclipsefund.com	mutual funds	⊕⊕	na	fund
Economist	www.economist.com	finance news/analysis	na	⊕⊕⊕	
Emerging Markets Companies	www.emgmkts.com	foreign investing	⊕⊕⊕⊕	na	stk, fixed, int'l, opt/fut
Empire Financial Group	www.lowfees.com	on-line trading	na	⊕⊕	stk, fixed, fund, opt/fut
Equis International	www.equis.com	technical analysis	⊕⊕⊕⊕⊕	na	stk, int'l, fund

Functions Performed / Information and Documents Provided

Financial Planning	Portfolio Tracking	Screening	Charting	Brokerage	Downloading	Message Boards	News	Quotes	Mutual Fund Data	Stock Data & Ratios	Estimates/Research	Technical Indicators	Company/Fund Filings	Industry Data	Market/Economic Data	Financial Planning	Taxes	Education	Links	Name of Site
			✘		✘			✘					✘						✘	Data Broadcasting Corporation
				✘			✘	✘	✘	✘			✘	✘	✘			✘	✘	Datek Online
											✘	✘							✘	Day Traders On-line
			✘		✘							✘						✘	✘	Decision Point
						✘														Deja.com
									✘				✘							Delafield Fund
							✘								✘	✘				Deloitte & Touche
						✘													✘	Delphi Investors Forum
			✘				✘	✘			✘								✘	DeltaTrader
					✘		✘			✘	✘			✘	✘			✘	✘	Depositary Receipt Services
											✘								✘	Dick Davis Online Financial Newsletter
	✘	✘					✘			✘	✘								✘	Disclosure-Investor.com
✘	✘	✘	✘	✘			✘	✘	✘	✘	✘	✘	✘		✘	✘			✘	Discover Brokerage Direct
						✘								✘	✘					Dismal Scientist
									✘				✘		✘					Dodge & Cox Funds
										✘									✘	Doh! Stock Picks
									✘				✘		✘					Domini Funds
	✘	✘	✘								✘	✘			✘			✘	✘	Dorsey, Wright & Associates
																			✘	DoubleHappy
✘							✘	✘						✘	✘				✘	Dow Jones Markets
					✘														✘	Downstate Discount
				✘	✘		✘	✘		✘					✘				✘	Dreyfus Brokerage Services
				✘			✘	✘	✘				✘			✘			✘	Dreyfus Funds
											✘									Duff & Phelps Credit Rating Co.
									✘	✘			✘					✘		Dupree Funds
✘	✘	✘	✘				✘	✘	✘	✘	✘	✘	✘		✘	✘	✘	✘	✘	E*Trade Securities
										✘	✘			✘					✘	EC Investor
					✘					✘									✘	EDGAR Online
									✘				✘							Eclispe Funds
							✘								✘					Economist
							✘	✘			✘				✘			✘	✘	Emerging Markets Companies
			✘					✘											✘	Empire Financial Group
			✘		✘		✘	✘		✘	✘	✘						✘	✘	Equis International

Name of Site	URL	Primary Focus	Free Rating	Fee-Based Rating	Securities Covered
Equity Analytics	www.e-analytics.com	IPOs	◉◉◉◉	na	stk, fixed, opt/fut, insur
EquityTrader	www.equitytrader.com	stock charts & analysis	◉◉◉	na	stk
Ernst & Young Tax & Financial Planning Corner	www.wiley.com/ey	tax information	◉◉	na	
Estate Planning Concepts	www.estateplanningconcepts.com	estate planning	◉◉	na	
Estate Planning Learning Center	www.estateplanning.com	estate planning	◉◉	na	
FAM Funds	www.famfunds.com	mutual funds	◉◉	na	fund
Fairmont Fund	www.fairmontfund.com	mutual funds	◉◉	na	fund
FedStats	www.fedstats.gov	economic data	◉◉◉◉	na	
Federal Deposit Insurance Corp.	www.fdic.gov	regulations	◉◉	na	
Federal Reserve Bank of Atlanta	www.frbatlanta.org	economic data	◉◉◉	na	
Federal Reserve Bank of Boston	www.bos.frb.org	economic data	◉◉◉	na	fixed
Federal Reserve Bank of Chicago	www.frbchi.org	economic data	◉◉◉	na	fixed
Federal Reserve Bank of Cleveland	www.clev.frb.org	economic data	◉◉◉	na	
Federal Reserve Bank of Dallas	www.dallasfed.org	economic data	◉◉◉	na	
Federal Reserve Bank of Kansas City	www.frbkc.org	economic data	◉◉◉	na	
Federal Reserve Bank of Minneapolis	woodrow.mpls.frb.fed.us	economic data	◉◉◉	na	fixed
Federal Reserve Bank of New York	www.ny.frb.org	economic data	◉◉◉	na	fixed
Federal Reserve Bank of Philadelphia	www.phil.frb.org	economic data	◉◉◉	na	fixed
Federal Reserve Bank of Richmond	www.rich.frb.org	economic data	◉◉◉	na	fixed
Federal Reserve Bank of San Francisco	www.frbsf.org	economic data	◉◉◉	na	fixed
Federal Reserve Bank of St. Louis	www.stls.frb.org	economic data	◉◉◉	na	
Federal Trade Commission	www.ftc.gov	regulations	◉	na	
Fidelity Investments	www.fidelity.com	mutual funds	◉◉◉◉◉	◉◉◉◉	stk, fixed, int'l, fund, annty, insur
FileYourTaxes.com	www.fileyourtaxes.com	tax information	na	◉◉◉	
FinAid	www.finaid.com	personal finance	◉◉◉	na	
Financenter.com	www.financenter.com	personal finance	◉◉◉◉	na	stk, fixed, fund
Financial Engines	www.financialengines.com	personal finance	◉◉◉◉◉	◉◉◉◉	
Financial Planning Magazine Online Edition	www.fponline.com	financial planning	na	◉◉	stk, annty
Financial Times	www.ft.com	finance news/analysis	◉◉◉	na	stk, int'l, fund, opt/fut
FinancialWeb	www.financialweb.com	comprehensive	◉◉◉◉	na	stk, int'l, fund, opt/fut
Fination.com	www.fination.com	stock advisory service	◉◉◉	na	
First Call Corporation	www.firstcall.com	stock data/analysis	na	◉◉◉	stk, fixed, int'l

Functions Performed / Information and Documents Provided

Financial Planning	Portfolio Tracking	Screening	Charting	Brokerage	Downloading	Message Boards	News	Quotes	Mutual Fund Data	Stock Data & Ratios	Estimates/Research	Technical Indicators	Company/Fund Filings	Industry Data	Market/Economic Data	Financial Planning	Taxes	Education	Links	Name of Site
					✖		✖			✖	✖				✖	✖		✖	✖	Equity Analytics
		✖	✖			✖					✖	✖								EquityTrader
																✖	✖			Ernst & Young Tax & Financial Planning Corner
																				Estate Planning Concepts
																				Estate Planning Learning Center
							✖	✖	✖				✖		✖					FAM Funds
								✖	✖				✖							Fairmont Fund
															✖					FedStats
							✖											✖	✖	Federal Deposit Insurance Corp.
							✖								✖			✖	✖	Federal Reserve Bank of Atlanta
							✖								✖			✖	✖	Federal Reserve Bank of Boston
							✖				✖				✖			✖	✖	Federal Reserve Bank of Chicago
							✖				✖				✖			✖	✖	Federal Reserve Bank of Cleveland
							✖				✖				✖			✖	✖	Federal Reserve Bank of Dallas
							✖				✖				✖			✖	✖	Federal Reserve Bank of Kansas City
							✖				✖				✖		✖	✖	✖	Federal Reserve Bank of Minneapolis
							✖				✖				✖			✖	✖	Federal Reserve Bank of New York
							✖				✖				✖			✖	✖	Federal Reserve Bank of Philadelphia
					✖		✖				✖				✖			✖	✖	Federal Reserve Bank of Richmond
							✖				✖				✖			✖	✖	Federal Reserve Bank of San Francisco
							✖				✖				✖			✖	✖	Federal Reserve Bank of St. Louis
																		✖	✖	Federal Trade Commission
✖	✖	✖	✖	✖	✖		✖	✖		✖			✖		✖	✖	✖	✖	✖	Fidelity Investments
																	✖			FileYourTaxes.com
✖																✖		✖	✖	FinAid
✖																✖				Financenter.com
✖	✖															✖				Financial Engines
						✖	✖											✖	✖	Financial Planning Magazine Online Edition
	✖						✖						✖	✖	✖				✖	Financial Times
		✖	✖	✖			✖		✖	✖	✖		✖	✖	✖				✖	FinancialWeb
																				Fination.com
							✖			✖	✖								✖	First Call Corporation

Name of Site	URL	Primary Focus	Free Rating	Fee-Based Rating	Securities Covered
Firstrade.com—First Flushing Securities	www.firstrade.com	on-line trading	⊕⊕	⊕⊕⊕	stk, fund, opt/fut
Fleet	www.fleet.com	financial planning	⊕	na	
Flex Funds	www.flexfunds.com	mutual funds	⊕	na	fund
ForbesNET	www.forbesnet.com	on-line trading	⊕⊕	⊕⊕⊕	stk, fixed, fund, opt/fut
Fortune magazine	www.pathfinder.com/fortune	finance news/analysis	⊕⊕⊕	na	stk, fund
Founders Funds	www.founders.com	mutual funds	⊕⊕⊕⊕	na	fund,
France-Bourse de Paris	www.bourse-de-paris.fr	foreign investing	⊕⊕⊕	na	stk, int'l
France-Commission Des Operations De Bourse	www.cob.fr	foreign investing	⊕	na	int'l
Franklin-Templeton Funds	www.franklin-templeton.com	mutual funds	⊕⊕⊕⊕	na	fund
Free Real Time.com	www.freerealtime.com	stock quotes	⊕⊕⊕	na	stk
Freedom Investments	www.freedominvestments.com	on-line trading	na	⊕	stk, opt/fut
Freeman Welwood & Co.	www.freemanwelwood.com	on-line trading	⊕⊕⊕	⊕⊕⊕	stk, fund, opt/fut
Fremont Funds	www.fremontfunds.com	mutual funds	⊕⊕	na	fund
FundAlarm	www.fundalarm.com	mutual funds	⊕⊕⊕⊕	na	fund
Futures Industry Association	www.fiafii.org	options/futures	⊕⊕⊕⊕	na	opt/fut
Futures Trading Group	www.futurestrading.com	options/futures	⊕⊕	na	opt/fut
FuturesWeb.com	www.futuresweb.com	options/futures	⊕⊕	na	opt/fut
GFN Investment	www.gfn.com	on-line trading	⊕⊕⊕	⊕⊕⊕	stk, fund, opt/fut
Gabelli Funds	www.gabelli.com	mutual funds	⊕⊕⊕	na	fund, closed
Galaxy Funds	www.galaxyfunds.com	mutual funds	⊕⊕⊕	na	fund
Global Financial Data	www.globalfindata.com	foreign investing	⊕⊕⊕	⊕⊕⊕	stk, int'l
Global Investor	www.global-investor.com	foreign investing	⊕⊕⊕	na	stk, int'l
Globe Information Services	www.globeandmail.ca	foreign investing	⊕⊕⊕⊕	na	stk, int'l, fund
Gomez Personal Finance	www.gomez.com	personal finance	⊕⊕	na	
Good Money	www.goodmoney.com	social concerns	⊕⊕⊕⊕	na	stk, fund
Gray, Gray & Gray	www.graymail.com	tax information	⊕	na	stk
Green Jungle	www.greenjungle.com	mutual funds	⊕⊕⊕⊕	na	fund
GreenMoney On-Line Guide	www.greenmoney.com	social concerns	⊕⊕	na	
H&R Block	www.hrblock.com	tax information	⊕⊕⊕	na	
Heartland Funds	www.heartlandfund.com	mutual funds	⊕⊕	na	fund
Homestead Funds	www.nreca.org/homestead	mutual funds	⊕⊕	na	fund
Hoover's Online	www.hoovers.com	stock data/analysis	⊕⊕⊕⊕	⊕⊕⊕⊕	stk
IAA Trust Funds	www.iaatrust.com	mutual funds	⊕⊕	na	fund

Functions Performed / Information and Documents Provided

Financial Planning	Portfolio Tracking	Screening	Charting	Brokerage	Downloading	Message Boards	News	Quotes	Mutual Fund Data	Stock Data & Ratios	Estimates/Research	Technical Indicators	Company/Fund Filings	Industry Data	Market/Economic Data	Financial Planning	Taxes	Education	Links	Name of Site
			✖	✖			✖	✖		✖	✖		✖		✖			✖	✖	Firstrade.com—First Flushing Securities
✖																✖				Fleet
							✖		✖											Flex Funds
			✖	✖			✖	✖			✖		✖		✖			✖	✖	ForbesNET
✖							✖	✖							✖			✖	✖	Fortune magazine
✖				✖				✖	✖				✖			✖	✖	✖		Founders Funds
							✖	✖		✖									✖	France-Bourse de Paris
							✖												✖	France-Commission Des Operations De Bourse
✖						✖		✖	✖				✖			✖	✖	✖		Franklin-Templeton Funds
						✖	✖	✖			✖				✖				✖	Free Real Time.com
			✖		✖			✖											✖	Freedom Investments
	✖		✖	✖			✖	✖	✖	✖	✖		✖	✖	✖					Freeman Welwood & Co.
				✖			✖	✖	✖				✖							Fremont Funds
						✖	✖		✖									✖	✖	FundAlarm
							✖											✖	✖	Futures Industry Association
																		✖	✖	Futures Trading Group
			✖			✖					✖								✖	FuturesWeb.com
			✖	✖			✖	✖		✖			✖		✖	✖		✖	✖	GFN Investment
✖							✖		✖				✖			✖	✖	✖	✖	Gabelli Funds
✖									✖						✖	✖		✖		Galaxy Funds
					✖					✖	✖				✖				✖	Global Financial Data
						✖	✖	✖							✖				✖	Global Investor
	✖	✖	✖				✖	✖	✖	✖			✖		✖			✖		Globe Information Services
✖																✖				Gomez Personal Finance
							✖								✖			✖	✖	Good Money
																		✖	✖	Gray, Gray & Gray
							✖						✖			✖	✖	✖	✖	Green Jungle
																		✖	✖	GreenMoney On-Line Guide
																	✖			H&R Block
							✖	✖					✖					✖	✖	Heartland Funds
								✖	✖				✖						✖	Homestead Funds
		✖	✖				✖	✖		✖				✖					✖	Hoover's Online
✖							✖	✖	✖							✖				IAA Trust Funds

Name of Site	URL	Primary Focus	Free Rating	Fee-Based Rating	Securities Covered
IBC Financial Data, Inc.	www.ibcdata.com	mutual funds	●●●	na	closed
ICI Mutual Fund Connection	www.ici.org	mutual funds	●●●●	na	fund, closed
INVESCO	www.invesco.com	mutual funds	●●●●	na	fund
IPO Data Systems	www.ipodata.com	IPOs	●●●	●●●	stk
IPO Intelligence Online	www.ipo-fund.com	IPOs	●●●	●●●	stk, fund
IPO Maven	www.ipomaven.com	IPOs	●●●●●	na	stk
IPO Monitor	www.ipomonitor.com	IPOs	na	●●●	stk
IQC.com	www.iqc.com	technical analysis	●●●	na	stk, int'l, opt/fut
Ibbotson Associates	www.ibbotson.com	market data (historical)	●	na	
Individual Investor Online	www.iionline.com	stock/fund data/analysis	●●●	na	stk, fund
InfoBeat—Finance	www.infobeat.com	e-mail service	●●	na	stk, fund
InfoFund	www.infofund.com	portfolio tracking	●●●	na	fund
InsWeb	www.insweb.com	life insurance	●●●	na	insur
Institute of Finance and Banking at the University of Göttingen	www.wiso.gwdg.de/ifbg/ifbghome.html	foreign investing	●●●●	na	stk, int'l, fund, opt/fut
Insurance News Network	www.insure.com	life insurance	●●●●●	na	annty, insur
InterQuote	www.interquote.com	stock quotes	na	●●●	stk, fixed, fund, opt/fut
Internal Revenue Service	www.irs.ustreas.gov	tax information	●●●●	na	
International Assoc. for Financial Planning	www.iafp.org	investment associations	●	na	
Internet Closed-End Fund Investor	www.icefi.com	closed-end funds	●●●	●●●●	closed
InternetTrading.com	www.internettrading.com	on-line trading	na	●	stk, fixed, fund, opt/fut
InvestEXpress On-Line	www.investexpress.com	on-line trading	●	●●	stk, fixed, fund, opt/fut
InvestIN Securities Corporation	investin.com	on-line trading	na	●	stk, fund, opt/fut
Investing in Bonds.com	www.investinginbonds.com	bonds	●●	na	fixed
Investment FAQ	www.invest-faq.com	personal finance	●●●	na	stk, fixed, fund, closed, opt/fut, RE, annty
Investment Research Institute	www.options-iri.com	options/futures	●●●	●●●	stk, opt/fut
INVESTools	www.investools.com	comprehensive	na	●●●●	stk, int'l, fund, closed
Investor Home	www.investorhome.com	investment Web links	●●●	na	stk, fixed, int'l, fund, RE
Investor Square	www.investorsquare.com	stock/fund data/analysis	●●●	na	stk, int'l, fund, closed
Investor's Business Daily Web Edition	www.investors.com	finance news/analysis	●●	na	stk, fixed, fund, opt/fut
Investor-Advice	www.investoradvice.com	stock advisory service	●●●	na	stk
InvestorGuide	www.investorguide.com	investment Web links	●●●●	na	stk, fixed, int'l, fund, closed, opt/fut, insur

Financial Planning	Portfolio Tracking	Screening	Charting	Brokerage	Downloading	Message Boards	News	Quotes	Mutual Fund Data	Stock Data & Ratios	Estimates/Research	Technical Indicators	Company/Fund Filings	Industry Data	Market/Economic Data	Financial Planning	Taxes	Education	Links	Name of Site
							✗		✗									✗	✗	IBC Financial Data, Inc.
							✗		✗		✗				✗	✗	✗	✗	✗	ICI Mutual Fund Connection
✗		✗		✗	✗		✗	✗	✗			✗			✗	✗	✗	✗	✗	INVESCO
						✗	✗	✗		✗									✗	IPO Data Systems
						✗	✗			✗	✗							✗		IPO Intelligence Online
									✗					✗					✗	IPO Maven
							✗			✗	✗									IPO Monitor
		✗	✗		✗	✗	✗	✗		✗	✗	✗		✗	✗			✗	✗	IQC.com
✗																				Ibbotson Associates
	✗		✗			✗	✗	✗		✗								✗		Individual Investor Online
	✗						✗													InfoBeat—Finance
	✗								✗										✗	InfoFund
																✗		✗		InsWeb
															✗			✗	✗	Institute of Finance and Banking at the University of Göttingen
							✗				✗							✗	✗	Insurance News Network
	✗		✗		✗			✗				✗			✗				✗	InterQuote
					✗		✗										✗	✗	✗	Internal Revenue Service
																✗		✗		International Assoc. for Financial Planning
			✗			✗	✗	✗	✗									✗	✗	Internet Closed-End Fund Investor
				✗															✗	InternetTrading.com
				✗			✗	✗											✗	InvestEXpress On-Line
				✗				✗							✗			✗	✗	InvestIN Securities Corporation
																		✗	✗	Investing in Bonds.com
																✗		✗	✗	Investment FAQ
							✗	✗										✗		Investment Research Institute
	✗	✗	✗				✗	✗	✗	✗	✗	✗							✗	Investools
																		✗	✗	Investor Home
	✗		✗				✗	✗	✗	✗		✗			✗	✗				Investor Square
							✗								✗			✗		Investor's Business Daily Web Edition
											✗	✗							✗	Investor-Advice
	✗		✗			✗												✗	✗	InvestorGuide

Name of Site	URL	Primary Focus	Free Rating	Fee-Based Rating	Securities Covered
InvestorLinks	www.investorlinks.com	investment Web links	⊕⊕⊕	na	stk, fixed, int'l, fund, opt/fut
InvestorWords	www.investorwords.com	educational	⊕⊕⊕	na	
Investorama	www.investorama.com	investment Web links	⊕⊕⊕⊕⊕	na	stk, int'l, fund, opt/fut, RE, annty, insur
Investors Alley.com	www.investorsalley.com	finance news/analysis	⊕⊕	na	stk, fixed, int'l, fund
Investorville	www.investorville.com	message boards	⊕⊕⊕	na	stk, int'l, fund
Investrade	www.investrade.com	on-line trading	⊕⊕	⊕⊕	stk, fund, opt/fut,
J.B. Oxford & Company	www.jboxford.com	on-line trading	⊕⊕	⊕⊕⊕	stk, fixed, fund, opt/fut, insur
Jack White & Company On-Line	www.jackwhiteco.com	on-line trading	⊕⊕	⊕⊕⊕	stk, fixed, fund, opt/fut, annty
Janus Funds	www.janus.com	mutual funds	⊕⊕⊕	na	fund
Kansas City Board of Trade	www.kcbt.com	stock exchange	⊕⊕⊕	na	stk, opt/fut,
Kaufmann	www.kaufmann.com	mutual funds	⊕⊕	na	fund
Key Partners Quote Service	www.bloodhound.com	life insurance	⊕	na	insur
Keynote Systems	www.keynote.com	advisory service	⊕⊕	na	
Kiplinger Online	www.kiplinger.com	finance news/analysis	⊕⊕⊕	na	stk, fixed, int'l, fund, closed
Kiplinger TaxCut Online	www.taxcut.com	tax information	⊕⊕⊕⊕⊕	na	
League of American Investors	www.investorsleague.com	portfolio tracking	⊕⊕	na	stk
Legg Mason	www.leggmason.com	mutual funds	⊕⊕⊕	na	fund
Levitt & Levitt Trutrade	www.trutrade.com	on-line trading	⊕⊕	⊕⊕⊕	stk, fixed, fund, opt/fut
Lexington Funds	www.lexingtonfunds.com	mutual funds	⊕⊕⊕	na	fund
Life Insurance Analysis Center	www.underwriter.com	life insurance	⊕	na	insur
LifeNet	www.lifenet.com	life insurance	⊕⊕⊕	na	insur
Lindner Funds	www.lindnerfunds.com	mutual funds	⊕⊕⊕	na	fund
LoanWeb.com	www.loanweb.com	personal finance	⊕⊕⊕	na	
Loomis Sayles Funds	www.loomissayles.com	mutual funds	⊕⊕	na	fund
LowRisk.com	www.lowrisk.com	stock advisory service	⊕⊕	na	
MSN MoneyCentral Investor	moneycentral.msn.com	comprehensive	⊕⊕⊕⊕⊕	na	stk, fixed, fund, RE, annty, insur
Mark Bernkopf's Central Banking Resource Center	www.patriot.net/users/bernkopf	foreign investing	⊕⊕⊕	na	fixed, int'l
Market Guide	www.marketguide.com	stock data/analysis	⊕⊕⊕⊕	na	stk
MarketEdge	www.stkwtch.com	stock charts & analysis	na	⊕⊕⊕	stk

Functions Performed | Information and Documents Provided

Financial Planning	Portfolio Tracking	Screening	Charting	Brokerage	Downloading	Message Boards	News	Quotes	Mutual Fund Data	Stock Data & Ratios	Estimates/Research	Technical Indicators	Company/Fund Filings	Industry Data	Market/Economic Data	Financial Planning	Taxes	Education	Links	Name of Site
	✖		✖			✖	✖	✖											✖	InvestorLinks
																		✖		InvestorWords
	✖	✖	✖		✖		✖	✖										✖	✖	Investorama
							✖	✖	✖	✖	✖		✖		✖			✖		Investors Alley.com
	✖		✖			✖		✖											✖	Investorville
	✖		✖	✖			✖	✖											✖	Investrade
	✖		✖	✖			✖	✖	✖	✖	✖	✖	✖						✖	J.B. Oxford & Company
	✖		✖	✖			✖	✖	✖	✖			✖	✖	✖				✖	Jack White & Company On-Line
✖			✖				✖	✖					✖			✖	✖			Janus Funds
		✖					✖	✖		✖		✖			✖				✖	Kansas City Board of Trade
									✖				✖							Kaufmann
✖																				Key Partners Quote Service
											✖								✖	Keynote Systems
✖	✖						✖	✖							✖	✖	✖	✖	✖	Kiplinger Online
					✖												✖			Kiplinger TaxCut Online
	✖																	✖	✖	League of American Investors
✖			✖				✖	✖	✖				✖		✖	✖				Legg Mason
				✖	✖		✖	✖		✖	✖		✖		✖			✖	✖	Levitt & Levitt Trutrade
			✖				✖	✖					✖			✖		✖	✖	Lexington Funds
✖																				Life Insurance Analysis Center
✖																✖	✖	✖	✖	LifeNet
			✖					✖	✖			✖	✖					✖		Lindner Funds
✖								✖											✖	LoanWeb.com
							✖	✖	✖				✖					✖	✖	Loomis Sayles Funds
															✖				✖	LowRisk.com
✖	✖	✖	✖			✖	✖	✖	✖	✖	✖	✖	✖	✖	✖	✖	✖	✖	✖	MSN MoneyCentral Investor
							✖								✖				✖	Mark Bernkopf's Central Banking Resource Center
		✖	✖				✖	✖		✖	✖	✖		✖	✖				✖	Market Guide
		✖								✖	✖	✖		✖	✖					MarketEdge

Name of Site	URL	Primary Focus	Free Rating	Fee-Based Rating	Securities Covered
Markman Funds	www.markman.com/funds.html	mutual funds	⊕⊕	na	fund
Marshall Funds	www.marshallfunds.com	mutual funds	⊕⊕⊕⊕	na	fund
Max Ule	www.maxule.com	on-line trading	na	⊕	stk, fixed, fund, opt/fut
Maxus Funds	www.maxusfunds.com	mutual funds	⊕⊕⊕	na	fund
Media General Financial Services	www.mgfs.com	stock data/analysis	⊕⊕⊕	na	stk
Merrill Lynch Online	www.merrill-lynch.ml.com	financial planning	⊕⊕	⊕⊕⊕	
MidAmerica Commodity Exchange	www.midam.com	options/futures	⊕⊕⊕	na	opt/fut
Midas Funds (Bull & Bear Funds)	www.midasfunds.com	mutual funds	⊕⊕	na	fund, closed
Moby Data	www.mobydata.com	market data (historical)	na	⊕⊕	
Moloney Securities Company	www.stocktrader.com	on-line trading	⊕	⊕⊕	stk, fixed, fund
Monetta Funds	www.monetta.com	mutual funds	⊕⊕⊕	na	fund
Money Manager Review	www.slip.net/~mmreview	advisory service	⊕⊕	na	
Money.com	www.pathfinder.com/money	personal finance	⊕⊕⊕	na	stk, fund, RE, insur
MoneyScope	www.moneyscope.com	stock quotes	⊕⊕⊕⊕	na	stk, fund
Moneypaper	www.moneypaper.com	direct stock purchase	⊕⊕⊕	na	stk
Monster Tax Center	tax.monster.com	tax information	⊕	na	
Montgomery Funds	www.montgomeryfunds.com	mutual funds	⊕⊕⊕⊕⊕	na	fund
Moody's Investors Service	www.moodys.com	bond ratings	⊕⊕	na	stk, fixed, fund
Morgan Stanley Capital International (MSCI)	www.msci.com	foreign investing	⊕⊕⊕⊕	na	stk, int'l
Morningstar Net	www.morningstar.net	comprehensive	⊕⊕⊕⊕	⊕⊕⊕⊕⊕	stk, fixed, fund
Mosaic Funds	www.mosaicfunds.com	mutual funds	⊕⊕	na	fund
Motley Fool	www.fool.com	stock data/analysis	⊕⊕⊕⊕⊕	na	stk, int'l, fund, insur
Mr. Stock Online Trading	www.mrstock.com	on-line trading	⊕	⊕⊕⊕	stk, fund, opt/fut
Muhlenkamp Funds	www.muhlenkamp.com	mutual funds	⊕	na	fund
MunisOnline	www.munisonline.com	bonds	⊕	na	fixed
Muriel Siebert & Co.	www.msiebert.com	on-line trading	⊕⊕	⊕⊕⊕	stk, fixed, fund, opt/fut
MurphyMorris, Inc.	www.murphymorris.com	stock charts & analysis	na	⊕⊕⊕	stk
Mutual Discovery	www.mutualdiscovery.com	trading strategies	na	⊕⊕	
Mutual Fund Investor's Center	www.mfea.com	mutual funds	⊕⊕⊕⊕⊕	na	fund
Mutual Fund Investors Resource Center	www.fundmaster.com	mutual funds	⊕⊕	na	fund
Mutual Funds Interactive	www.fundsinteractive.com	mutual funds	⊕⊕⊕⊕	na	stk, fixed, int'l, fund, closed, opt/fut
Mutual Funds Magazine Online	www.mfmag.com	mutual funds	⊕⊕⊕⊕	⊕⊕⊕⊕	fund, closed
Mydiscountbroker.com	www.mydiscountbroker.com	on-line trading	⊕⊕⊕	⊕⊕⊕⊕⊕	stk, fund, opt/fut

Functions Performed | Information and Documents Provided

Financial Planning	Portfolio Tracking	Screening	Charting	Brokerage	Downloading	Message Boards	News	Quotes	Mutual Fund Data	Stock Data & Ratios	Estimates/Research	Technical Indicators	Company/Fund Filings	Industry Data	Market/Economic Data	Financial Planning	Taxes	Education	Links	Name of Site
								✗	✗				✗						✗	Markman Funds
✗				✗			✗	✗	✗				✗		✗	✗				Marshall Funds
			✗																✗	Max Ule
								✗	✗				✗		✗	✗			✗	Maxus Funds
							✗		✗					✗	✗				✗	Media General Financial Services
✗	✗			✗			✗	✗		✗	✗		✗		✗	✗				Merrill Lynch Online
			✗	✗				✗				✗						✗	✗	MidAmerica Commodity Exchange
				✗				✗					✗						✗	Midas Funds (Bull & Bear Funds)
					✗									✗	✗				✗	Moby Data
			✗	✗				✗		✗	✗	✗							✗	Moloney Securities Company
								✗	✗				✗		✗			✗		Monetta Funds
											✗									Money Manager Review
✗	✗						✗	✗	✗	✗	✗			✗	✗				✗	Money.com
	✗	✗					✗	✗	✗	✗					✗				✗	MoneyScope
											✗							✗	✗	Moneypaper
																	✗			Monster Tax Center
✗			✗	✗			✗	✗	✗				✗		✗	✗	✗	✗	✗	Montgomery Funds
							✗			✗				✗	✗				✗	Moody's Investors Service
														✗	✗					Morgan Stanley Capital International (MSCI)
✗	✗	✗	✗			✗	✗	✗	✗	✗	✗						✗	✗	✗	Morningstar Net
								✗					✗				✗	✗	✗	Mosaic Funds
	✗	✗			✗	✗	✗		✗	✗	✗				✗	✗	✗	✗	✗	Motley Fool
	✗		✗	✗			✗	✗		✗	✗		✗		✗			✗	✗	Mr. Stock Online Trading
									✗				✗							Muhlenkamp Funds
								✗					✗							MunisOnline
	✗		✗	✗			✗	✗		✗	✗		✗		✗					Muriel Siebert & Co.
										✗		✗								MurphyMorris, Inc.
											✗									Mutual Discovery
✗	✗	✗					✗	✗	✗				✗		✗	✗	✗	✗	✗	Mutual Fund Investor's Center
✗													✗					✗		Mutual Fund Investors Resource Center
	✗		✗			✗	✗	✗	✗	✗	✗			✗	✗			✗	✗	Mutual Funds Interactive
	✗	✗	✗			✗		✗					✗					✗	✗	Mutual Funds Magazine Online
	✗	✗	✗	✗			✗	✗	✗	✗	✗	✗	✗	✗	✗	✗		✗	✗	Mydiscountbroker.com

Name of Site	URL	Primary Focus	Free Rating	Fee-Based Rating	Securities Covered
myTrack	www.mytrack.com	stock quotes	●●●	na	stk, int'l, opt/fut
NAREIT Online	www.nareit.com	REITs	●●●	na	RE
NASD Regulation Inc.	www.nasdr.com	regulations	●●●	na	fixed
Nasdaq-Amex	www.nasdaq-amex.com	stock exchange	●●●●●	na	stk, fund, opt/fut
National Assoc. of Personal Financial Advisors	www.napfa.org	investment associations	●●●	na	
National Assoc. of Investors Corp. (NAIC)	www.better-investing.org	educational	●	na	stk
National Discount Brokers	www.ndb.com	on-line trading	●●●●●	●●●●●	stk, fund, opt/fut
National Fraud Information Center	www.fraud.org	fraud	●	na	
National Futures Association	www.nfa.futures.org	options/futures	●●●	na	opt/fut
National Network of Estate Planning Attorneys	www.netplanning.com	financial planning	●●	na	
Navellier Funds	www.navellier.com	mutual funds	●●●	na	stk, fund
Nelson Investment Management Network	www.nelnet.com	advisory service	●●●	na	
Net Investor	www.netinvestor.com	on-line trading	●●	●●●	stk, fixed, fund
Net Stock Direct	www.netstockdirect.com	direct stock purchase	●●●●●	na	stk, int'l, fund
Net Tax 9X	www.nettax.com	tax information	●●●	na	
Neuberger & Berman	www.nbfunds.com	mutual funds	●●●●	na	fund
New York Cotton Exchange	www.nyce.com	options/futures	●●●	na	opt/fut
New York Mercantile Exchange	www.nymex.com	options/futures	●●●	na	opt/fut
New York Stock Exchange	www.nyse.com	stock exchange	●●	na	stk
Newport Discount Brokerage	www.newport-discount.com	on-line trading	●●	●●●	stk, fixed, fund, opt/fut
News.com Investor	www.news.com/investor	stock data/analysis	●●●	na	stk, int'l, fund
Nikkei Net Interactive	www.nni.nikkei.co.jp/	foreign investing	na	●●●●	stk, int'l
Nirvana Systems	www.nirv.com	trading strategies	●●●	●	
No-Load Stocks Info	www.becoming.net/noload	direct stock purchase	●	na	stk
Nolo Press Selp-Help Law Center	www.nolo.com	estate planning	●●	na	
Nomura Securities Fin'l Research Center	www.nomura.co.jp/QR	foreign investing	●●	na	int'l
North American Quotations	www.naq.com	stock quotes	●●	na	stk, int'l, opt/fut
North American Securities Administration Assoc.	www.nasaa.org	regulations	●●	na	fixed
Norwest Brokerage Direct	www.norwest.com	on-line trading	na	●	stk, fixed, fund, opt/fut
Nottingham Funds	www.fundsrus.com	mutual funds	●●	na	fund
O'Shaughnessy Funds	www.oshaughnessyfunds.com	mutual funds	●●●	na	fund

Functions Performed   Information and Documents Provided

Financial Planning	Portfolio Tracking	Screening	Charting	Brokerage	Downloading	Message Boards	News	Quotes	Mutual Fund Data	Stock Data & Ratios	Estimates/Research	Technical Indicators	Company/Fund Filings	Industry Data	Market/Economic Data	Financial Planning	Taxes	Education	Links	Name of Site
	X		X		X	X	X	X		X		X			X				X	myTrack
					X		X							X	X			X	X	NAREIT Online
X							X									X		X	X	NASD Regulation Inc.
	X	X	X				X	X	X	X	X		X		X			X	X	Nasdaq-Amex
																X			X	National Assoc. of Personal Financial Advisors
																		X		National Assoc. of Investors Corp. (NAIC)
X	X	X	X	X			X	X	X	X	X	X	X	X	X	X	X	X	X	National Discount Brokers
																		X	X	National Fraud Information Center
							X											X	X	National Futures Association
																X			X	National Network of Estate Planning Attorneys
							X	X	X				X					X		Navellier Funds
										X						X				Nelson Investment Management Network
	X		X	X			X	X	X	X	X		X		X				X	Net Investor
		X	X					X	X										X	Net Stock Direct
X																	X		X	Net Tax 9X
X					X			X	X				X			X	X	X	X	Neuberger & Berman
			X	X			X	X							X			X	X	New York Cotton Exchange
			X				X	X										X	X	New York Mercantile Exchange
			X				X	X							X			X	X	New York Stock Exchange
			X	X			X	X			X		X		X			X	X	Newport Discount Brokerage
			X				X	X	X					X					X	News.com Investor
			X				X	X		X	X			X	X				X	Nikkei Net Interactive
																			X	Nirvana Systems
																			X	No-Load Stocks Info
																			X	Nolo Press Selp-Help Law Center
			X												X				X	Nomura Securities Fin'l Research Center
								X											X	North American Quotations
																		X	X	North American Securities Administration Assoc.
				X				X												Norwest Brokerage Direct
								X	X				X							Nottingham Funds
							X	X	X				X					X	X	O'Shaughnessy Funds

Name of Site	URL	Primary Focus	Free Rating	Fee-Based Rating	Securities Covered
OTC Financial Network	www.otcfn.com	small stock profiles	●●	na	stk
Oakmark Funds	www.oakmark.com	mutual funds	●●	na	fund
Oberweis Funds	www.oberweisfunds.com	mutual funds	●	na	fund
Options Industry Council	www.optionscentral.com	options/futures	●●●●	na	opt/fut
PBHG Funds	www.pbhgfunds.com	mutual funds	●●●	na	fund
PC Quote Online	www.pcquote.com	stock quotes	●●●●●	na	stk, int'l, fund, opt/fut
PR Newswire	prnewswire.com	finance news/analysis	●●●	na	stk, int'l
PRS Online	www.countrydata.com	foreign investing	na	●●●	
Papp Funds	www.roypapp.com	mutual funds	●●	na	fund
Pax World Fund Family	www.paxfund.com	mutual funds	●●	na	fund
Payden & Rygel Funds	www.payden.com	mutual funds	●●●	na	fund
Peremel & Co.	www.peremel.com	on-line trading	●	●●●	stk, fixed, fund, opt/fut, annty
Philadelphia Stock Exchange	www.phlx.com	stock exchange	●●●	na	stk, opt/fut
PitMaster	www.thepitmaster.com	options/futures	●●●	na	opt/fut
Power Investing w/DRIPS Newsletter	www.powerinvestdrips.com	direct stock purchase	●●	●●●	stk
PowerOptions	www.poweropt.com	options/futures	na	●●●●	opt/fut
Prophet	www.prophetfinance.com	stock charts & analysis	●●●	●●●	stk, int'l, fund, opt/fut
Prudential	www.prudential.com	financial planning	●●	●●●	insur
Public Register's Annual Report Service (PRARS)	www.prars.com	company reports	●	na	
Quick & Reilly, Inc.	www.quick-reilly.com	on-line trading	na	●●●	stk, fixed, fund, opt/fut, annty
QuickQuote	www.quickquote.com	life insurance	●●●	na	annty, insur
Quicken Insure Market	www.insuremarket.com	life insurance	●●●	na	insur
Quicken.com	www.quicken.com	comprehensive	●●●●●	na	stk, fixed, int'l, fund, closed, insur
Quote.com	www.quote.com	comprehensive	●●●●	●●●●●	stk, fixed, int'l, fund, opt/fut, insur
QuoteShopper	www.quoteshopper.com	life insurance	●●●	na	annty, insur
Quotesmith Corp.	www.quotesmith.com	life insurance	●●●●	na	annty, insur
Raging Bull	www.ragingbull.com	message boards	●●●●	na	stk, int'l, fund
Rate Net	www.rate.net	bonds	●●●	na	fixed
RealEstate.com	www.realestate.com	real estate	●●●	na	RE

Functions Performed   **Information and Documents Provided**

Financial Planning	Portfolio Tracking	Screening	Charting	Brokerage	Downloading	Message Boards	News	Quotes	Mutual Fund Data	Stock Data & Ratios	Estimates/Research	Technical Indicators	Company/Fund Filings	Industry Data	Market/Economic Data	Financial Planning	Taxes	Education	Links	Name of Site
			✗							✗									✗	OTC Financial Network
				✗				✗	✗				✗							Oakmark Funds
									✗				✗							Oberweis Funds
					✗		✗	✗										✗	✗	Options Industry Council
			✗				✗	✗	✗				✗							PBHG Funds
		✗	✗				✗	✗	✗	✗	✗	✗			✗				✗	PC Quote Online
							✗	✗		✗			✗	✗	✗				✗	PR Newswire
					✗		✗			✗					✗			✗		PRS Online
							✗	✗	✗				✗							Papp Funds
								✗	✗				✗						✗	Pax World Fund Family
			✗				✗	✗					✗		✗			✗		Payden & Rygel Funds
✗		✗	✗	✗			✗	✗	✗	✗	✗		✗		✗	✗			✗	Peremel & Co
			✗				✗	✗							✗			✗	✗	Philadelphia Stock Exchange
			✗		✗		✗	✗										✗	✗	PitMaster
											✗								✗	Power Investing w/DRIPS Newsletter
	✗	✗						✗										✗	✗	PowerOptions
			✗		✗	✗		✗		✗		✗			✗				✗	Prophet
✗	✗			✗			✗	✗		✗			✗		✗	✗				Prudential
																			✗	Public Register's Annual Report Service (PRARS)
		✗	✗				✗	✗		✗	✗	✗			✗					Quick & Reilly, Inc.
✗																		✗	✗	QuickQuote
✗																✗		✗	✗	Quicken Insure Market
																			✗	No-Load Stocks Info
✗	✗	✗	✗			✗	✗	✗	✗	✗	✗		✗	✗	✗	✗	✗	✗	✗	Quicken.com
	✗	✗	✗		✗		✗	✗	✗	✗	✗	✗		✗	✗	✗		✗	✗	Quote.com
✗																✗		✗	✗	QuoteShopper
✗											✗							✗		Quotesmith Corp.
			✗			✗	✗	✗		✗	✗								✗	Raging Bull
								✗		✗									✗	Rate Net
✗								✗							✗					RealEstate.com

Name of Site	URL	Primary Focus	Free Rating	Fee-Based Rating	Securities Covered
Reality Online Inc.	www.moneynet.com	finance news/analysis	⊕⊕⊕	na	stk, fund, opt/fut
RealtyStocks & Funds	www.realtystocks.com	REITs	⊕⊕⊕⊕	⊕⊕⊕⊕	fund, RE
Regal Discount	www.eregal.com	on-line trading	na	⊕⊕	stk, fund, opt/fut
Reuters	www.reuters.com	finance news/analysis	⊕⊕	na	stk, fixed, int'l, opt/fut
RightQuote	www.rightquote.com	life insurance	⊕⊕	na	annty, insur
Robertson Stephens Funds	www.rsim.com	mutual funds	⊕⊕⊕	na	fund
Roulston Funds	www.fairport.com	mutual funds	⊕	na	fund
Royce Funds	www.roycefunds.com	mutual funds	⊕⊕⊕	na	fund, closed
S&P Personal Wealth	www.personalwealth.com	comprehensive	na	⊕⊕⊕⊕⊕	stk, fixed, int'l, fund, opt/fut
SEC Law.com	www.seclaw.com	regulations	⊕⊕	na	
SIT Funds	www.sitfunds.com	mutual funds	⊕⊕	na	fund
SSgA Funds	www.ssgafunds.com	mutual funds	⊕	na	fund
Safeco Funds	www.safecofunds.com	mutual funds	⊕⊕⊕⊕	na	fund
ScoTTrade Scottsdale Securities	www.scottrade.com	on-line trading	na	⊕⊕	stk, fixed, opt/fut
Scout Funds	www.umb.com	mutual funds	⊕⊕	na	fund
Scudder Funds	www.scudder.com	mutual funds	⊕⊕⊕⊕	na	fund, annty
Seaport Securities Corp.	www.sea-port.com	on-line trading	⊕⊕	⊕⊕⊕	stk, fixed, fund, opt/fut
SecureTax	www.securetax.com	tax information	⊕	⊕⊕⊕	
Securities Fraud & Investor Protection	www.securitieslaw.com	fraud	⊕⊕⊕	na	
Selected Funds	www.selectedfunds.com	mutual funds	⊕⊕	na	fund
Sentry Funds	www.sentry.com	mutual funds	⊕	na	fund
Sherry Bruce State Discount	www.state-discount.com	on-line trading	⊕⊕	⊕⊕⊕	stk, fixed, fund, opt/fut
Silicon Investor	www.techstocks.com	message boards	na	⊕⊕⊕	stk
SmartMoney Interactive	www.smartmoney.com	comprehensive	⊕⊕⊕⊕⊕	na	stk, fixed, fund
Smith Breeden Funds	www.smithbreeden.com	mutual funds	⊕⊕	na	fund
Social Investment Forum	www.socialinvest.org	social concerns	⊕⊕⊕⊕	na	fund, annty
Social Security Online	www.ssa.gov	regulations	⊕⊕⊕⊕	na	
Society of Financial Service Professionals	www.financialpro.org	investment associations	⊕	na	
Sound Shore Fund	www.soundshorefund.com	mutual funds	⊕⊕	na	fund
Stat-USA	www.stat-usa.gov	economic data	na	⊕⊕	
SteinRoe Funds	www.steinroe.com	mutual funds	⊕⊕⊕⊕	na	fund
Stock Data Corp.	www.stockdata.com	stock/fund data/analysis	na	⊕⊕⊕	stk, int'l, fund
Stock Power	www.stockpower.com	direct stock purchase	⊕⊕	na	
Stock Smart	www.stocksmart.com	portfolio tracking	⊕⊕⊕	⊕⊕⊕	stk, int'l, fund, closed, opt/fut

Functions Performed / Information and Documents Provided

Financial Planning	Portfolio Tracking	Screening	Charting	Brokerage	Downloading	Message Boards	News	Quotes	Mutual Fund Data	Stock Data & Ratios	Estimates/Research	Technical Indicators	Company/Fund Filings	Industry Data	Market/Economic Data	Financial Planning	Taxes	Education	Links	Name of Site
	✖	✖	✖				✖	✖	✖				✖		✖				✖	Reality Online Inc.
			✖				✖		✖	✖				✖	✖			✖	✖	RealtyStocks & Funds
				✖			✖	✖										✖	✖	Regal Discount
							✖	✖							✖				✖	Reuters
✖																		✖		RightQuote
							✖	✖	✖				✖							Robertson Stephens Funds
								✖					✖							Roulston Funds
				✖				✖	✖				✖						✖	Royce Funds
✖	✖	✖	✖				✖	✖	✖	✖	✖		✖	✖	✖	✖		✖	✖	S&P Personal Wealth
																		✖	✖	SEC Law.com
								✖					✖			✖				SIT Funds
								✖					✖							SSgA Funds
✖			✖				✖	✖	✖				✖				✖		✖	Safeco Funds
			✖				✖	✖		✖	✖		✖						✖	ScoTTrade Scottsdale Securities
✖							✖		✖				✖							Scout Funds
✖	✖		✖				✖	✖	✖				✖		✖	✖	✖	✖	✖	Scudder Funds
		✖	✖				✖	✖			✖		✖		✖			✖	✖	Seaport Securities Corp.
					✖												✖			SecureTax
																		✖		Securities Fraud & Investor Protection
								✖	✖				✖					✖		Selected Funds
								✖					✖							Sentry Funds
			✖	✖			✖	✖		✖			✖		✖			✖	✖	Sherry Bruce State Discount
				✖		✖		✖											✖	Silicon Investor
✖	✖	✖	✖				✖	✖	✖	✖	✖					✖	✖			SmartMoney Interactive
								✖					✖						✖	Smith Breeden Funds
							✖		✖						✖			✖	✖	Social Investment Forum
																✖	✖		✖	Social Security Online
																✖			✖	Society of Financial Service Professionals
								✖					✖						✖	Sound Shore Fund
															✖					Stat-USA
✖	✖			✖			✖	✖	✖				✖		✖	✖	✖	✖		SteinRoe Funds
					✖			✖		✖					✖					Stock Data Corp.
									✖										✖	Stock Power
	✖		✖				✖	✖	✖	✖	✖		✖	✖	✖				✖	Stock Smart

Name of Site	URL	Primary Focus	Free Rating	Fee-Based Rating	Securities Covered
Stock Smart Pro	www.stocksmartpro.com	stock/fund data/analysis	na	●●●	stk, fixed, fund, closed, opt/fut
StockMaster	www.stockmaster.com	stock/fund data/analysis	●●●	na	stk, fund, closed
StockSite	www.stocksite.com	stock data/analysis	●●●●	na	stk, fixed, int'l, fund
StockWinners.com	www.stockwinners.com	stock data/analysis	na	●●●	stk, opt/fut
StockWizard	www.stockwizard.com	investment Web links	●●	na	stk, fixed, int'l, fund, opt/fut
Stockguide	www.stockguide.com	small stock profiles	●●●	na	stk
Stockpoint	www.stockpoint.com	comprehensive	●●●●	na	stk, fund, opt/fut
Stockz.com	www.stockz.com	stock data/analysis	●●●	●●●	stk, opt/fut
StreetEYE	www.efrontier.com	investment Web links	●●●	na	
Strong Funds	www.strong-funds.com	mutual funds	●●●●●	na	stk, fund
Summit Discount Brokerage	www.summitdiscount.com	on-line trading	na	●	stk, fund, opt/fut
SureTrade.com	www.suretrade.com	on-line trading	na	●●●	stk, fixed, fund, opt/fut
Sydney Futures Exchange	www.sfe.com.au	foreign investing	●●●	na	int'l, opt/fut
Syndicate	www.moneypages.com	investment Web links	●●●	na	stk, fixed, int'l, fund
T. Rowe Price	www.troweprice.com	mutual funds	●●●●	na	stk, fund, closed
TAguru.com	www.taguru.com	technical analysis	●●●	na	stk, int'l, opt/fut
Tax Analysts Online	www.tax.org	tax information	●	na	
Tax Foundation	www.taxfoundation.org	tax information	●	na	
Tax Help Online	www.taxhelponline.com	tax information	●	na	
Tax Library	www.taxlibrary.com	tax information	na	●●●	stk
Tax Logic	www.taxlogic.com	tax information	●	●●	
Tax Prophet	www.taxprophet.com	tax information	●●●	na	
Tax Tips and Facts	www.rak-1.com	tax information	●	na	
TaxWeb	www.taxweb.com	tax information	●	na	
Taxfreebond.com	www.taxfreebond.com	bonds	●●	●●●	fixed
Taxing Times	www.maxwell.com/tax	tax information	●●	na	
Taxwizard	www.taxwizard.com	tax information	na	●●	
Technical Analysis Charting	www.alphachart.com	technical analysis	●●	na	stk
TheStreet.com	www.thestreet.com	stock/fund data/analysis	●●●	●●●●	stk, fixed, int'l, fund, opt/fut, insur
Third Avenue Value Fund	www.mjwhitman.com	mutual funds	●●	na	fund
Thomson Investors Network	www.thomsoninvest.net	comprehensive	●●●●	●●●●	stk, fixed, int'l, fund, closed
Thomson Real Time Quotes	www.thomsonrtq.com	stock quotes	●●●	na	stk, opt/fut

Functions Performed | Information and Documents Provided

Financial Planning	Portfolio Tracking	Screening	Charting	Brokerage	Downloading	Message Boards	News	Quotes	Mutual Fund Data	Stock Data & Ratios	Estimates/Research	Technical Indicators	Company/Fund Filings	Industry Data	Market/Economic Data	Financial Planning	Taxes	Education	Links	Name of Site
	✗	✗	✗				✗	✗	✗	✗		✗		✗	✗				✗	Stock Smart Pro
	✗		✗			✗	✗	✗		✗					✗				✗	StockMaster
	✗		✗		✗	✗	✗	✗		✗	✗			✗	✗			✗	✗	StockSite
			✗				✗	✗		✗	✗	✗						✗	✗	StockWinners.com
					✗			✗											✗	StockWizard
			✗				✗	✗		✗									✗	Stockguide
	✗	✗	✗				✗	✗	✗	✗	✗			✗					✗	Stockpoint
	✗	✗	✗			✗	✗	✗		✗	✗	✗							✗	Stockz.com
																			✗	StreetEYE
✗	✗		✗	✗			✗	✗	✗					✗		✗	✗	✗	✗	Strong Funds
				✗																Summit Discount Brokerage
			✗	✗			✗	✗	✗	✗	✗	✗	✗		✗				✗	SureTrade.com
					✗		✗	✗							✗			✗	✗	Sydney Futures Exchange
						✗												✗	✗	Syndicate
✗	✗		✗	✗	✗		✗	✗	✗	✗	✗		✗		✗	✗	✗	✗		T. Rowe Price
		✗	✗					✗		✗	✗	✗			✗			✗	✗	TAguru.com
																	✗		✗	Tax Analysts Online
																	✗	✗		Tax Foundation
																	✗			Tax Help Online
																	✗		✗	Tax Library
																	✗			Tax Logic
																	✗	✗	✗	Tax Prophet
																	✗	✗		Tax Tips and Facts
																	✗	✗		TaxWeb
✗			✗				✗								✗		✗	✗		Taxfreebond.com
																	✗		✗	Taxing Times
																	✗		✗	Taxwizard
		✗										✗							✗	Technical Analysis Charting
✗	✗		✗			✗	✗	✗	✗	✗	✗	✗			✗		✗	✗	✗	TheStreet.com
								✗	✗				✗							Third Avenue Value Fund
✗	✗	✗	✗				✗	✗	✗	✗	✗		✗		✗	✗		✗	✗	Thomson Investors Network
							✗	✗		✗	✗		✗						✗	Thomson Real Time Quotes

Name of Site	URL	Primary Focus	Free Rating	Fee-Based Rating	Securities Covered
Timely.com	www.timely.com	technical analysis	⊕⊕⊕	na	stk, int'l, fund
Trade-Well Discount Investing	www.trade-well.com	on-line trading	na	⊕	stk, fixed, fund, opt/fut
TradeStar	www.4tradestar.com	on-line trading	⊕⊕	⊕⊕	stk, fixed, fund, opt/fut, annty
Tradehard.com	www.tradehard.com	trading strategies	⊕⊕⊕⊕	⊕⊕⊕⊕⊕	stk, opt/fut
Trading Direct	www.tradingdirect.com	on-line trading	⊕⊕⊕	⊕⊕⊕⊕	stk, fixed, fund, opt/fut, annty
Tradingtactics.com	www.tradingtactics.com	trading strategies	⊕⊕⊕	na	stk
Treasury Direct/U.S. Bureau of the Public Debt	www.publicdebt.treas.gov	bonds	⊕⊕⊕⊕	na	fixed
Trusts, Wills & Estates	www.wsfpc.com	estate planning	⊕⊕	na	
Tucker Anthony	www.tucker-anthony.com	financial planning	⊕⊕	na	stk
TurboTax Online	www.turbotax.com	tax information	⊕⊕⊕	⊕⊕⊕⊕	
U.S. Securities & Exchange Commission (SEC)	www.sec.gov	regulations	⊕⊕⊕⊕⊕	na	stk, fund
USATaxNet	www.usataxnet.com	personal finance	⊕	na	
United Services Funds	www.us-global.com	mutual funds	⊕⊕⊕	na	fund
Value Line Investment Research & Asset Mgmt	www.valueline.com	stock/fund data/analysis	⊕⊕⊕	na	stk, fund, opt/fut
Van Wagoner Funds	www.vanwagoner.com	mutual funds	⊕⊕⊕	na	fund
Vancouver Stock Exchange	www.vse.com	foreign investing	⊕⊕⊕	na	stk, int'l
Vanguard	www.vanguard.com	mutual funds	⊕⊕⊕⊕⊕	na	fund, annty
Vcall	www.vcall.com	webcasts	⊕⊕⊕⊕	na	stk
Vision Securities	www.visiontrade.com	on-line trading	⊕⊕	⊕⊕⊕	stk, fund, opt/fut
Vontobel Funds	www.vontobelfunds.com	mutual funds	⊕⊕	na	fund
WEBS	www.websontheweb.com	index fund products	⊕⊕	na	fund
WIT Capital	www.witcapital.com	on-line trading	na	⊕⊕⊕	stk, fixed, fund
WWQuote	www.wwquote.com	stock quotes	na	⊕⊕⊕	stk, int'l, opt/fut
Wachovia Investments	www.wachovia.com	on-line trading	na	⊕	stk, fund, opt/fut
Wall St. Directory	www.wsdinc.com	investment Web links	⊕⊕	na	stk
Wall Street Access	www.wsaccess.com	on-line trading	⊕⊕	⊕⊕⊕	stk, opt/fut
Wall Street City	www.wallstreetcity.com	comprehensive	⊕⊕⊕⊕⊕	⊕⊕⊕⊕	stk, fixed, int'l, fund, insur
Wall Street Discount	www.wsdc.com	on-line trading	⊕⊕	⊕⊕	stk, fixed, opt/fu
Wall Street Electronica	www.wallstreete.com	on-line trading	⊕⊕⊕	⊕⊕⊕	stk, fixed, fund, opt/fut

Functions Performed — Information and Documents Provided

Financial Planning	Portfolio Tracking	Screening	Charting	Brokerage	Downloading	Message Boards	News	Quotes	Mutual Fund Data	Stock Data & Ratios	Estimates/Research	Technical Indicators	Company/Fund Filings	Industry Data	Market/Economic Data	Financial Planning	Taxes	Education	Links	Name of Site
			X					X				X		X	X				X	Timely.com
				X															X	Trade-Well Discount Investing
			X	X			X	X			X	X			X			X	X	TradeStar
	X	X					X	X		X	X	X		X	X			X	X	Tradehard.com
	X	X	X	X			X	X	X	X	X	X	X		X			X		Trading Direct
	X				X	X	X					X						X	X	Tradingtactics.com
				X				X									X	X		Treasury Direct/U.S. Bureau of the Public Debt
																				Trusts, Wills & Estates
X	X		X				X	X							X	X		X		Tucker Anthony
																	X			TurboTax Online
					X		X						X					X	X	U.S. Securities & Exchange Commission (SEC)
X																			X	USATaxNet
X			X					X	X						X	X		X		United Services Funds
					X			X							X			X		Value Line Investment Research & Asset Mgmt
								X	X						X					Van Wagoner Funds
			X		X		X	X							X				X	Vancouver Stock Exchange
X	X		X	X	X		X	X	X	X	X		X		X	X	X	X	X	Vanguard
							X												X	Vcall
			X	X			X	X			X				X			X	X	Vision Securities
									X	X					X					Vontobel Funds
								X	X						X					WEBS
			X	X			X	X		X	X	X	X		X				X	WIT Capital
	X	X			X	X	X	X	X						X				X	WWQuote
				X																Wachovia Investments
																			X	Wall St. Directory
			X	X			X	X		X	X	X	X		X			X	X	Wall Street Access
X	X	X	X		X	X	X	X	X	X	X	X		X		X		X	X	Wall Street City
	X		X	X			X	X		X					X					Wall Street Discount
	X		X	X			X	X	X	X	X		X	X	X					Wall Street Electronica

Name of Site	URL	Primary Focus	Free Rating	Fee-Based Rating	Securities Covered
Wall Street Equity, Inc.	www.wsei.com	on-line trading	na	⊕	stk
Wall Street Journal Interactive Edition	interactive.wsj.com	finance news/analysis	na	⊕⊕⊕⊕⊕	stk, fixed, int'l, fund
Wall Street Research Net	www.wsrn.com	investment Web links	⊕⊕⊕⊕	⊕⊕⊕	stk, fund
Wall Street on Demand	www.wallst.com	stock data/analysis	na	⊕⊕⊕	stk, int'l, fund
Wall-Street.com	www.wall-street.com	investment Web links	⊕⊕⊕	na	stk, int'l, fund
Warburg Pincus Funds	www.warburg.com	mutual funds	⊕⊕⊕	na	stk, fund, annty
Wasatch Funds	www.wasatchfunds.com	mutual funds	⊕⊕	na	fund
Waterhouse Securities	www.waterhouse.com	on-line trading	⊕⊕⊕⊕	⊕⊕⊕⊕	stk, fund, opt/fut
Wayne Hummer Funds	www.whummer.com	mutual funds	⊕⊕⊕	na	fund
Web Center for Futures and Options	www.ino.com	options/futures	⊕⊕⊕	⊕⊕⊕	stk, opt/fut
Web Street Securities	www.webstreetsecurities.com	on-line trading	⊕⊕	⊕⊕⊕	stk, fixed, fund, opt/fut
Weiss, Peck & Greer Funds	www.wpginvest.com	mutual funds	⊕	na	fund
Wells Fargo WellsTrade	wellsfargo.com/wellstrade	on-line trading	na	⊕⊕⊕	stk, fund, opt/fut, annty, insur
White Oak Funds	www.oakassociates.com	mutual funds	⊕⊕⊕	na	fund
William Blair Funds	www.wmblair.com	mutual funds	⊕⊕	na	fund
Worden Brothers Online	www.tc2000.com	stock/fund data/analysis	⊕⊕	na	stk, fund
WorldWide Index Funds	www.worldwideindexfunds.com	mutual funds	⊕⊕⊕	na	fund
Worldlyinvestor.com	www.worldlyinvestor.com	foreign investing	⊕⊕⊕⊕	na	stk, int'l, fund
Yacktman Funds	www.yacktman.com	mutual funds	⊕⊕	na	fund
Yahoo! Finance	quote.yahoo.com	comprehensive	⊕⊕⊕⊕	na	stk, fixed, int'l, fund, opt/fut
Yahoo! Loan Center	loan.yahoo.com	personal finance	⊕⊕⊕	na	RE
York Securities	www.yorktrade.com	on-line trading	⊕⊕	⊕⊕	stk, fixed, fund, opt/fut
Young Investor	www.younginvestor.com	educational	⊕	na	stk
Your Discount Broker	www.ydb.com	on-line trading	⊕⊕	⊕⊕⊕	stk, fund, opt/fut
ZDNet Interactive Investor	www.zdii.com	finance news/analysis	⊕⊕⊕	na	stk, fund
Zacks Investment Research	www.zacks.com	stock data/analysis	⊕⊕⊕	⊕⊕⊕⊕	stk, int'l, fund
Ziegler Thrift Trading	www.investroute.com	on-line trading	⊕⊕	⊕⊕⊕	stk, fund, opt/fut, annty

Functions Performed / Information and Documents Provided

Financial Planning	Portfolio Tracking	Screening	Charting	Brokerage	Downloading	Message Boards	News	Quotes	Mutual Fund Data	Stock Data & Ratios	Estimates/Research	Technical Indicators	Company/Fund Filings	Industry Data	Market/Economic Data	Financial Planning	Taxes	Education	Links	Name of Site
				✖				✖												Wall Street Equity, Inc.
✖	✖		✖				✖	✖	✖	✖	✖	✖	✖	✖	✖	✖		✖	✖	Wall Street Journal Interactive Edition
		✖			✖	✖			✖										✖	Wall Street Research Net
	✖		✖	✖			✖	✖	✖	✖	✖			✖	✖					Wall Street on Demand
																			✖	Wall-Street.com
							✖	✖	✖	✖			✖		✖					Warburg Pincus Funds
							✖	✖	✖				✖							Wasatch Funds
	✖	✖	✖	✖			✖	✖	✖	✖	✖	✖	✖		✖		✖	✖		Waterhouse Securities
✖							✖	✖	✖				✖			✖		✖		Wayne Hummer Funds
		✖			✖	✖	✖	✖											✖	Web Center for Futures and Options
	✖		✖	✖			✖	✖					✖		✖				✖	Web Street Securities
							✖		✖											Weiss, Peck & Greer Funds
		✖	✖	✖			✖	✖		✖					✖	✖				Wells Fargo WellsTrade
		✖					✖	✖	✖				✖						✖	White Oak Funds
								✖	✖				✖							William Blair Funds
			✖					✖		✖	✖			✖				✖		Worden Brothers Online
								✖	✖				✖		✖			✖		WorldWide Index Funds
	✖	✖				✖	✖	✖						✖	✖			✖		Worldlyinvestor.com
								✖	✖				✖						✖	Yacktman Funds
	✖	✖				✖	✖	✖		✖	✖			✖	✖			✖	✖	Yahoo! Finance
								✖										✖	✖	Yahoo! Loan Center
			✖				✖	✖		✖	✖				✖					York Securities
					✖													✖		Young Investor
	✖		✖	✖			✖	✖					✖		✖					Your Discount Broker
✖	✖	✖					✖	✖		✖					✖				✖	ZDNet Interactive Investor
✖	✖	✖	✖			✖	✖	✖		✖	✖							✖	✖	Zacks Investment Research
			✖	✖			✖	✖		✖	✖		✖		✖			✖		Ziegler Thrift Trading

INDEX